A Framework for Political Analysis

EUGENE J. KOLB

Alma College

Prentice-Hall, Inc. Englewood Cliffs, New Jersey 07632

Library of Congress Cataloging in Publication Data

Kolb, Eugene J
  A framework for political analysis.

  Bibliography: p.
  Includes index.
  1. Political science. 2. Power (Social sciences)
I. Title.
JA71.K65   320   77-24045
ISBN 0-13-330217-2

© *1978 by* PRENTICE-HALL, INC., *Englewood Cliffs, N.J. 07632*

PRINTED IN THE UNITED STATES OF AMERICA

10 9 8 7 6 5 4 3 2 1

PRENTICE-HALL INTERNATIONAL, INC., *London*
PRENTICE-HALL OF AUSTRALIA PTY. LIMITED, *Sydney*
PRENTICE-HALL OF CANADA, LTD., *Toronto*
PRENTICE-HALL OF INDIA PRIVATE LIMITED, *New Delhi*
PRENTICE-HALL OF JAPAN, INC., *Tokyo*
PRENTICE-HALL OF SOUTHEAST ASIA PTE. LTD., *Singapore*
WHITEHALL BOOKS LIMITED, *Wellington, New Zealand*

Contents

iii

3 THE ASSESSMENT AND EVALUATION OF POLITICAL SYSTEMS 64

part II
environmental factors and
their political consequences 87

4 THE POLITICAL CULTURE AND SOCIALIZATION PROCESS 89

5 THE SOCIO-ECONOMIC AND GEOGRAPHIC SETTING 109

6 THE POLITICAL CONSEQUENCES OF ENVIRONMENTAL FACTORS 119

part III
linkage-communication
structures and processes 151

part IV
government
decision-making systems 219

Preface

This book is intended as a comprehensive primer of political analysis, designed for use either as an introduction to political science or for introductory and upper-level analysis or comparison of political systems. It is designed to provide a basic understanding of politics, government, and political power. However, it goes beyond description and explanation by providing basic guidelines and tools needed for systematic and disciplined political analysis and for reasonably informed and meaningful thinking about both empirical and normative aspects of politics and political problems. It sets forth what students should focus on, and what major questions they should ask, when analyzing any political system, when comparing political systems, and when thinking about political problems of the present and the foreseeable future. The book also avoids narrow parochialism and an overly abstract approach and attempts to enrich analysis and understanding by a transnational approach. Basic concepts, principles, and propositions are grounded in reality by way of numerous examples drawn not only from the American but from all kinds of political systems around the world. Hence, the book can serve as a viable core for the organization of additional teaching materials, lectures, and discussions, and can be used in conjunction with other books for the analysis of specific political systems.

The overall strategy for political inquiry set forth entails a synthesis of major concepts, propositions, principles, and generalizations drawn from some older but more predominantly from major contemporary empirical theories and approaches. The synthesis is cast within the general framework of systems theory and involves substantial use of the structural-functional approach. Despite the drawbacks and problems inherent in both, systems theory provides a most useful ordering device for introducing students to politics, and the structural-functional approach enriches understanding of the roles of political institutions and processes. Systems theory is also a useful organizing device for integrating enduring older and newer approaches, and for synthesizing varied contemporary approaches and theories. Hence, within such a framework the book weaves together major concepts, principles, and generalizations into an orderly, logically consistent, meaningful, and coherent pattern.

This effort to develop such a synthesis as a teaching instrument grew out of the frustrations resulting from attempts to teach both introductory and upper-level courses in the context of contemporary theories. Specialization in a discipline is obviously essential for progress, yet poses painful problems for teachers and students. Students in particular tend to flounder in a sea of specialized theories and varied approaches, and to be confused by contradictions which seem to abound among contending theories. Yet to a substantial extent the varied theories and approaches entail only differences of emphasis, and specialized concepts and theories are but different aspects of the entire field of politics. To a great extent they do fit together; on the whole they are more complementary than contradictory. Continuing efforts towards some kind of a synthesis may eventually lead to some kind of agreement on what the core elements of the discipline really are, and may eventually produce sets of basic principles of the kind developed by other disciplines.

Part I of the book establishes a foundation for political understanding and analysis. It introduces some basic concepts and propositions about politics, government, and political conflict; discusses the nature and role of power; and explores the major questions which should be asked in connection with the assessment and evaluation of political systems. Parts II through V follow the systems approach by discussing in turn the nature, political importance, and relationships of environmental factors, linkage and communication systems, decision-making processes, and policy output patterns. Introductory paragraphs to each Part provide a preview of what is to come, and discuss the major questions which should be asked with respect to each component. Introductory paragraphs to each chapter follow the same pattern. Valid and useful synthesis particularly requires logical and consistent organization. Hence, throughout the book emphasis is placed on the logic of interrelationships: on relationships between various concepts, propositions, principles, and theories; and on interrelationships between components and sub-components of political systems. The concept of power, as developed in Chapter 2, is applied throughout. The book also emphasizes the theme of change, and the relationship among changes in the four components of a system. The final chapter constitutes somewhat of a summary of the entire book by focusing on the potential consequences of change for political stability, effectiveness, and democracy.

A broad synthesis inherently comprises the contributions of numerous social scientists. The book is the product of many years of reading and thinking about politics. Hence it is impossible to acknowledge all intellectual debts, and to acknowledge all known ones would require extensive and complex footnoting. A few basic debts I can easily acknowledge—to Gabriel Almond, Samuel Beer, Robert Dahl, Karl Deutsch, David Easton, Samuel Huntington, V. O. Key, Seymour Martin Lipset, and David Truman. I must also add Dean Pruitt, whose seminal suggestion for a theory of compliance with respect to international politics I have elaborated on and applied to domestic politics. But this brief list unhappily overlooks numerous others who have made political science the vibrant discipline that it is.

Introduction

This book is about politics and power. It is designed to give the reader some understanding of the basic nature of politics and government and of the role of power in political processes. It is also intended as an introduction to political analysis: it explains what one should focus on to understand a political system, and what major questions ought to be asked to understand a system's strengths and weaknesses. This text sets forth an overall strategy for political analysis by synthesizing some major contemporary theories about politics.

One of the unfortunate features of our time is that too many people shy away from even attempting to understand politics, much less partic- ipating in political processes. They either find politics and power abhor- rent, too complex, or too remote from their more immediate concerns. Yet, neither politics nor power merit their poor reputation, and politics is so closely related to our daily lives that we ignore it at our peril. Today the need for understanding politics and government is acute; the modern state, due to a variety of reasons explained throughout this book, under- takes a wide range of complex tasks and functions.

The modern state has resulted in the politicization of much of human life. Today the long arm of the government reaches out to affect almost all aspects of our lives, from the cradle to the grave. Governmental action affects our methods of birth; the kind of health care we get before, during, and after birth; and the extent to which we enjoy security in the cradle. Acquiring an education, securing and maintaining employment, earning an income that allows for a decent standard of living—all of these factors are partly dependent on our individual efforts, but all are ultimately dependent on the state of the economy, which is increasingly affected by governmental action. A nation's energy supply is increasingly related to governmental policies, which means that politics has an impact on our ability to drive cars for even the essential commutation to school or jobs, and it partly determines if we will have enough fuel to light and heat our homes and schools, or to power our industrial machinery. Politics affects how and where we live, work, and the general quality of our life-styles. Individual self-help seems less and less adequate for such things as affordable health care, adequate housing, and security in old age; hence, we turn to government for action in these and other spheres. The long arm of government even reaches out to affect how and where we shall be buried. Given this politicization of human life, it behooves us to be concerned with politics and government.

The need for understanding politics is also underscored by people's increasing disenchantment with politics and their declining trust in government. Authoritarian systems all over the world suffer from such malaise, and democracy in particular has come under furious attack in those countries in which it has managed to survive. Such distrust and disenchantment are also symptoms of the politicization of daily life. We look to government for so much, but then become frustrated because we cannot seem to control it, and disenchanted because it seems to fail us.

The end result is a pervasive feeling of dual powerlessness: people believe that they are unable to control their governments, and governments find it increasingly difficult to deal with problems entrusted to them by the people. Such feelings are particularly pervasive in democracies. More and more people seem convinced that democracy is a sham, with powerful interests really governing and politicians who are only interested in money or power. They conclude, therefore, that it doesn't really matter who wins the elections. Similar discontent with the failure of governments to be responsive to public needs prevails in most non-democratic societies. Governments everywhere are judged as having grown too big and fat, as extracting too much money from taxpayers, as being staffed with incompetent people, and as encroaching more and more on our personal lives. Yet governmental action seems to aggravate rather than ease the problems of soaring crime rates, economic downturns, declining standards of living, and urban decay. The fairness of governments is also increasingly questioned: it is perceived as rewarding the rich and the powerful, the shiftless and the lazy, or both at the expense of common folk.

The feeling of dual powerlessness also accentuates the need for an understanding of politics and government. First, because we need to know whether such feelings are in fact justified. Are governments really controlled by powerful interests, immune to public influence, incompetent and wasteful of taxpayers' money? Close scrutiny of how governments function, and an understanding of why they function the way that they do, is essential before we draw such conclusions. And, if the accusations are true, we need to do more than just complain; we need to diagnose the nature of our political ailments and determine their basic causes. Is the powerlessness of people due to impervious political institutions, the corruption of politicians, the power of special interests? Or might it be the reluctance of people to use what methods are available to them to influence governments? Is the weakness of government due to the nature of the system, the incompetence of public officials, the corruption of powerful politicians and lobbyists? Or might it be due to the power of ill-informed public opinion, or the difficulty and complexity of problems that governments are called upon to resolve? And once the diagnosis is made, we need to concern ourselves with proper remedies —politicial reforms that are based on informed diagnosis and hence are likely to cure rather than kill the patient. All of this requires the basic understanding of politics, power, and government, and those who spurn such understanding shirk their responsibilities not only to their fellow human beings, but also to themselves.

But what *does* an understanding of politics entail? What kinds of knowledge do we need to cultivate so that we can make sense of bewildering variety of political information that constantly clamors for our attention? What do we need to focus on? Are there any guidelines, any basic principles of politics, any analytical tools which would enable us to sort out important information, relate some information to other facts and data, and interpret and draw valid conclusions from such information about political events and developments? What kinds of questions should we ask to acquire the information needed for political understanding; to assess and determine the roots of strengths and weaknesses of a political system; and to assess what kinds of approaches, and in which spheres of politics, might enhance strengths and reduce weaknesses? These questions relate to the second and third objectives of this book: to provide a framework or overall strategy for political analysis by way of a synthesis of major contemporary theories.

This text describes the spheres of key concern that one must focus on in order to understand politics and government. It introduces and connects key concepts, propositions, and guidelines, which should enable a reader to make sense of a great diversity of political information, to sort out the more significant from less important events and developments, and to gain a better understanding of political phenomena. The book provides an analytical tool, a method of thinking about politics in a reasonably systematic and meaningful way. It consists of a series of inter-related questions which the reader should ask when analyzing any particular political system, when comparing political systems, and when thinking about political problems of the past, present, and probable future. It provides a fruitful way to determine the nature and sources of the strengths and weaknesses of political systems, and to assess possible reforms designed to make systems more responsive to the public will and more effective in coping with the complex problems of modern societies.

But before we plunge ahead, we must initially take note of a theme emphasized throughout this book—that the road to political reform is not an easy one. First, politics remains the "art of the possible." Many "ideal" remedies, ideal because they seem to offer solutions to most if not all of our problems, often turn out to be quack remedies because they cannot be translated into action. In the real world, too many constraints—in the nature of human beings, power, institutions, and many other things—effectively limit what actually can be done. Second, the political problems faced by the modern world, and the varied problems we expect governments to resolve, are complex problems that defy easy resolution. As the late H. L. Mencken once wrote, "for every political problem there is an answer which is simple, neat, and wrong." And finally, politics illustrates a basic truth inherent in a witticism commonly attributed to the late W. C. Fields: "There ain't no such thing as a free lunch." In politics nothing is free; there is a price tag attached to every action. Everything involves a value tradeoff, and every proposal must be assessed in terms of its cost-benefit ratio. Just as human beings cannot hope to attain all of the values and goals that they aspire to because one goal invariably entails the sacrifice of some other values, so political reforms designed to bring certain benefits invariably entail some costs. This pertains particularly to remedies designed to cope with dual powerlessness, and is illustrated by the old maxim that the price of democracy is high. More democracy—more popular control over government—may well entail high costs in governmental effectiveness, while more effectiveness may require less governmental responsiveness to the public will. In an imperfect world we should strive for perfection, but we must not despair and become disillusioned when all we achieve are relative and imperfect improvements.

Politics, Power, and Political Systems

Fundamental to an understanding of politics and government is an understanding of what governments actually do, the nature of governmental power and authority, the relationship between government and politics, and what generates political conflicts and governmental action. Part I provides such a foundation by introducing some basic concepts intended to give us at least a preliminary understanding of these topics. Chapter 1 develops the theme that governmental action essentially involves the authoritative creation and allocation of certain values presumably in the public interest, that such action invariably arouses conflict, and that governmental authority is accepted under certain conditions. It stresses that politics involves all the processes whereby a society and various groups use the government to attain certain goals and values for the society and for individual groups, and also explains the methods used for the resolution of conflicts over what values should be created and how they should be allocated. By explaining the concept of a "political system," the chapter initially explores the basic features of a society that must be analyzed in order to understand its politics (themes pursued in Parts II through V). Chapter 2 elaborates on these initial themes by exploring the nature of power and its roles in political processes. Chapter 3, which discusses the assessment and evaluation of political systems, introduces the most fundamental factual and value questions we should ask when we analyze or compare political systems.

The Nature
and Functions
of Goverment
and Politics

1

One way to begin our exploration might be with a set of definitions. Unfortunately, the words politics and government are everyday terms that have acquired a variety of ambiguous meanings and connotations; dozens of definitions abound in the literature of political science. Besides, brief and precise definitions of complex phenomena often produce confusion, rather than clarification and understanding. Hence, we shall explore instead a series of empirical propositions about politics and government that should serve as a foundation for an understanding of these phenomena of human activity. But what follows in this chapter is merely a preliminary explanation; many of these propositions will be explored in greater detail in later chapters.

GOVERNMENT: WHAT IT IS AND WHAT IT DOES

What government is and does would not appear to require much explanation: it obviously consists of certain kinds of institutions making and enforcing laws. But this explanation raises more questions than it answers. What is a law, and what does a law do? What actually is involved in the enforcement of laws? Why is there so much controversy over the nature and content of law and over the lawmaking functions of various institutions? Why does politics involve so much conflict, and what is or should be the role of government with respect to conflicts over law? Several initial propositions should help us to answer these questions. First, governmental actions involve the creation and allocation of values, which invariably arouse conflict over what values should be created and who should benefit therefrom. Second, we generally agree that values ought to be created and allocated in the public interest, but conflict arises over what the public interest might be and how it should be determined. Third, governments have legal authority to determine what is in the public interest and to make and enforce laws in its name, but actual compliance with governmental authority and laws depends on the legitimacy of a government and its actions. Fourth, although government consists of a set of structures or institutions, governmental processes involve human activity and behavior.

Governmental actions create and allocate values. A fundamental concept of politics to be understood is that any government action—laws passed by legislatures, rules made and applied by administrators, decisions made by judges—have the intent or the effect of creating and allocating values. Government officials intend by their actions to create, promote, or maximize certain values either for themselves or for the society, and to distribute such values among the varied groups of people that make up the society.

By a "value" we mean an object of human desire, something humans pursue, and with varying degrees of intensity strive to attain. Some we can label ego-centered acquisitive values: tangible or intangible objects of desire we strive to attain for ourselves. The list includes such goals as wealth, power, physical well-being, respect and affection, knowledge and skill, leisure time, freedom, and physical and economic security. Others we frequently label moral values, such as justice and respect for the rights and welfare of others. Moral values may also be acquisitive values in that we seek to acquire them, not for ourselves alone, but also for others and for the society as a whole. Moral values also have an effect on our acquisitive values: the intensity with which we pursue wealth, power, wisdom, or other goals is influenced by our individual moral values, or by the standards of conduct which prevail in the society. Since values are many in number and in conflict, most individuals are guided in their conduct by some kind of priority ordering; for instance, they may prefer wealth over leisure and affection, or security over freedom. Values sought for the self might also be given precedence over moral values: power and wealth may be preferred to justice or freedom for others.

Domestic order and security is one value that all governments try to create. They do so by actions designed to protect people against other people and by imposing certain obligations on the members of a society. Laws that define killing and theft as criminal actions are intended to provide people with security of life and property. Actions that impose restraints, such as a requirement for peaceful rather than violent settlement of disputes, tend to promote domestic tranquillity. Security against external enemies is another value governments seek to maximize, and they do so by laws designed to enhance defense capabilities, by varied foreign policy actions, or by laws imposing an obligation of military service.

But actions designed to create or promote such values also involve the allocation of values among the diverse groups composing the society, and generally entail the unequal (although not necessarily unjust) distribution of values. Certain groups may benefit, or benefit more than others; other groups may not benefit at all, or may be deprived of values. Society may benefit from the imprisonment of a criminal, but the latter is deprived of his freedom. Laws that prohibit mass demonstrations in the name of public order may deprive some people of effective means for expressing their grievances. Conscription may promote the security of a society, but the draftee is deprived of his freedom of choice. Tax laws designed to raise money for police and military forces may impose a heavier burden on some income groups than on others. Defense expenditures may require reductions in other governmental programs, such as education or health services, which may hurt some groups more than others.

Most modern governments also try to promote the values of economic prosperity, stability, and growth, and such actions again tend to result in an uneven allocation of values. Taxes may be reduced to cope with a recession by giving individuals and business enterprises more money to spend and invest; but the specific provisions of a tax law will invariably benefit some income groups and types of business more than others. Unemployment benefits may be fair and benefit the entire society by promoting economic growth, but at the expense of the employed taxpayer. Business and labor may be required to limit wage and price increases to protect the society against inflation; but such a restriction impairs the freedom of business and labor, or may be disadvantageous to underpaid workers or to business enterprises operating on a very thin profit margin. High taxes on gasoline or restrictions on its use may promote economic prosperity by ensuring an adequate supply of energy, but such actions may hurt rural dwellers and suburbanites more than city dwellers.

Equality and justice are values that some governments seek to promote, but again with unequal (although not necessarily unjust) value allocations. Racial minorities may benefit from laws against discrimination, and the society as a whole may ultimately benefit when such laws promote social peace, equal opportunity, and legal and social justice. But the freedom of those prone to discriminate may be impaired, along with their income and status. Tax measures and welfare programs designed to promote equality by reducing disparities of income may be just and benefit low-income groups, but at monetary cost to middle-to-upper income groups. Social security may ultimately benefit an entire society, but the more immediate benefits accrue to the elderly, and the immediate costs to younger generations.

Such creation and allocation of values is inherent in all governmental actions. Environmental protection laws promote many values, but they also may impose high monetary costs on certain industries. Health programs may enhance the physical well-being of a society; educational policies the knowledge, skill, and prosperity of a nation; laws against deceptive advertising the values of truth and justice. But all entail costs to some elements of society. Even governmental actions designed to promote the value of human freedom may result in uneven allocation patterns. Political freedom may mean much to those with good incomes and job security, but little to those virtually enslaved by poverty and inequality. The securing of such rights and liberties may also require access to the judicial system, and hence may not really benefit those who cannot afford attorney fees.

Governmental action not only entails uneven allocation of values among groups, but also uneven maximization patterns among values. Just as individuals must make choices among many and frequently conflicting values, so governments must make choices. The pursuit of economic prosperity through governmental intervention in the economy entails some impairment of the freedom of business people, laborers, or farmers, for example, to do as they please. Energy policies require choices between immediate economic growth, long-term growth, and acceptable levels of environmental damage. Education programs may promote skill, wisdom, and knowledge, but at the expense of immediate wealth. Governmental promotion of equality, no matter how just, invariably entails some costs in terms of the freedom of people to do as they please.

The creation, promotion, and allocation of values—whether by individuals, groups in society, or government—always entails frequently difficult problems of choice. It involves trade offs, or cost-benefit assessment and evaluation, in that the maximization of one or a set of values invariably requires some costs in terms of minimization or deprivation of other values. As W. C. Fields put it: "There ain't no such thing as a free lunch."

Political Scientist Harold Lasswell has put it in a more sober vein: "Politics involves Who Gets What, When, and How."[1] We shall return to this problem of value in subsequent chapters.

Governmental action involves means-ends conflicts over the public interest. Most people generally believe that governments ought to promote the public interest, and governments invariably justify their actions as being in the public interest. This concept of the public interest entails the idea that governmental actions ought to create and promote values that are for the good of the general public, and that are made with the welfare of most of society in mind. Also, benefits and costs ought to be distributed in a just manner, commensurate with the public and not merely with some private interests. But two aspects of the public interest invariably arouse controversy. One relates to means: how or by what means a government should determine what is in the public interest. The second relates to the ends of government: what value creation and allocation activities of government really are in the public interest.

Government is most commonly thought of as a means, as a set of institutions or a process for getting certain things done, and as a method of establishing rules of conduct for people in the society. This is one aspect, and it raises several important factual and normative questions about government, which will be pursued throughout this book. Empirical aspects focus on factual questions about government as a means to promote the public interest: how does a government function as a means? What institutions are involved and what roles do they play? How do the rules and decisions actually get made, and why do they get made the way that they do? What are the actual value creation and allocation patterns of a government, and to what extent do they appear to be commensurate with the public interest? Such questions invariably arouse controversy.

Even more conflict is generated by normative questions about government as a means: Who should define the public interest, or by what processes should it be defined? What kind of government is better in terms of creating and allocating values in a manner commensurate with the public, rather than merely private interests? How should a society structure its government so as to create and distribute values in a just manner and to promote the general welfare of all? These questions invariably provoke controversy over the nature, structures, and processes of government and their relationship to the determination of the public interest.

But governments must also be analyzed and evaluated in terms of ends. Rules are made with certain purposes, certain goals that rule-makers hope to attain, certain values they aspire to promote, and certain value-

[1]Harold Lasswell, *Politics, Who Gets What, When, How* (New York: Meridian, 1958).

distribution patterns they seek to establish. This aspect invariably arouses controversy over what value creation and allocation patterns are in the public interest. It entails the age-old conflict over what the ends of government ought to be, what the legitimate tasks and functions of government are, and in what spheres a government ought to be used as means to ends. Throughout most of the world there continues to be general agreement that governments ought to promote two fundamental values: domestic order and security against external enemies. But beyond that, controversy prevails over whether using government as a means to other ends is truly in the public interest; whether or not governmental authority ought to be used to promote economic prosperity, equality, social security, better health care, and other human values. Conflict persists over priority-ordering among values to be promoted by government: freedom versus equality, or economic growth versus environmental protection. Also, conflict over what specific value allocation patterns are truly in the public interest is endemic in all societies. Hence, in analyzing and comparing political systems, we must consider not only factual and value questions about the nature and processes of government, but we must also consider the ends of government—what values they actually do or should seek to promote, and what value distribution patterns they actually seem to or should be attempting to establish.

Governments make, administer, and enforce legally-binding authoritative policies and rules in the public sphere. A key attribute of government is its authority; specifically, its right to make rules which are legally binding on its citizens. A *government policy* is an authoritative plan of action for the promotion and allocation of selected values, which is deemed by governmental authority to be in the common interest of the people. A policy consists of some general or specific goal, which policy-makers hope to attain; it may also include the general course of action to be followed and the specific means by which the goal is to be pursued. For such pursuit, governments enact laws and make other kinds of authoritative decisions, which in effect are rules that are legally binding on society and government. These binding rules prescribe the rights and obligations of members of the society: the rights and obligations of individuals and groups toward one another, and the rights and obligations of citizens and government towards each other. To promote the values of economic prosperity and domestic order, for example, a government may legally establish labor's right to strike, but require peaceful collective bargaining between labor and management, and termination of a strike under certain conditions involving the public interest.

All organized human activity embraces policy- and rule-making in some kind of authoritative fashion to promote the common interests of the members of an organization. Colleges, sororities, corporations, labor unions, scout troops, and football teams all have some kind of regularly established procedures for determining what goals ought to be pursued for the membership's common interest, what general courses of action ought to be undertaken in the pursuit of common values, and what rules of conduct apply to the membership. Such institutional processes often bear a striking resemblance to "governmental politics," and the rules carry the stamp of authority insofar as the membership is concerned.

But what distinguishes the "private" from the "public sphere" and "common group" from "common public interests" in goal selection, policy formulation, and rule-making is that governments function with respect to society as a whole, and that its rules are legally binding on all people within the government's legal jurisdiction (which in the modern state includes all individuals within its territory). "Private" governments —the directors of a corporation, the leadership of a fraternity, the coach and captain of a football team—only have jurisdiction over the members of their organization, and from a legal standpoint membership in the organization is voluntary.

Effective governmental authority is related to its legitimacy. Authority is a legal concept. It means that a government has the legal right to determine what value creation and allocation patterns are in the public interest; the legal right to make decisions, which people are legally required to obey; and the legal right to use coercion to enforce its laws.

Authority is extremely important for goal attainment. Governmental policies are not likely to be effective if the rules established to implement the policy are not obeyed, and the stamp of authority behind law, combined with a government's authority to enforce law, does tend to produce compliance. But a mere glance around the world indicates that authority by itself is not enough, that legal authority does not necessarily mean effective authority. In some societies most people comply voluntarily and almost automatically with virtually all laws, and force must be used against only a small percentage of the population. Yet police states appear to be able to obtain compliance only through extensive and repressive use of force and terror. Still other governments rely heavily on coercion, but often unsuccessfully as they encounter frequent waves of riots, demonstrations, and other forms of illegal violence. Patterns of compliance with specific laws, and among different sectors of society, also vary. Tax evasion is widespread in Italy, Spain, and Latin America, but is fairly limited in the United States and Britain. In the United States, *most* people voluntarily comply with *most* laws *most* of the time. But there is also substantial disobedience among some groups in American society, and substantial disobedience with respect to some laws: teachers strike even though it may be illegal; property owners and real estate agents illegally discriminate on the basis of color; substantial numbers of people illegally smoke marijuana. While the relative effectiveness of a government's coercive apparatus plays some role with respect to these varying patterns of obedience to authority, something more fundamental is involved—perceptions of legitimacy.

While authority is a legal concept, legitimacy is a psychological concept. Its primary ingredients are ideas, attitudes, subjective perceptions, and evaluations about the nature and role of authority. Legitimacy involves mental convictions that a particular government is the right or most appropriate kind for that society, that it is structured in the right sort of way, staffed by the right kinds of people, makes decisions in the right way, and enacts and enforces the right kinds of laws. It includes the beliefs that obedience is not merely a legal, but also a moral obligation, and that it is not just legally right, but it is also morally right, to comply with the authoritative decisions of government. While its most important aspects pertain to the *type* of government, legitimacy is also important with respect to specific leaders and specific laws. The decisions of a specific leader who is considered legitimate, and a law that is perceived as legitimate, are much more likely to be complied with, while laws that are considered illegitimate require much more coercion.

Precisely because legitimacy is significant, governments try to justify their authority on the basis of certain principles. These vary from society to society—traditions concerning succession to leadership; religious ideas, such as the divine right of kings to rule; ideology as in communist states; constitutional authority; and the right to rule due to elections, as in democracies. In essence, governments try to ensure that their decisions are accepted and heeded not solely out of fear, but on the basis of a belief that it is morally right to do so. It is a basic lesson of history that governments cannot hope to enjoy long-term durability and effectiveness by relying on coercion. What is needed is voluntary compliance founded on perceptions of legitimacy.

The varied aspects and sources of legitimacy are discussed in Part II. At this point it suffices to emphasize that legitimacy is linked with cultural norms and values, which prevail in the society, and also with the extent to which people perceive the actions of government as promoting those values and goals that they particularly desire. When a people evaluate a government as legitimate, they are prone to accept (although not always with enthusiasm) the exercise of governmental authority without direct coercion or obvious inducements. When specific laws are perceived as legitimate, widespread voluntary compliance tends to follow. When a society as a whole, or specific groups within it, perceive a government or specific laws as illegitimate, then governments are forced to either rely on coercion or to "buy" compliance by offering or promising various kinds of rewards; but neither one of these methods is a sound basis for durable and effective government.

A government is a set of interrelated and interacting human structures, institutions, and processes. This proposition seems fairly obvious, for we are familiar with the complex of legislative, executive, bureaucratic, and judicial institutions that govern modern states, and with simpler structures (village councils, tribal chiefs) that rule small-scale societies. Two aspects, however, merit emphasis.

First we must consider the often overlooked but obvious fact that politics and government involve human beings and human behavior, and that governmental institutions are only organized groups of human beings. Due to their nature, functions, legal authority, and institutional goals, institutions as such have a major impact on policy formulation, value creation, and allocation patterns, as well as influencing the behavior of the humans who make up their membership. In analyzing politics it is important to determine the power of various institutions; the respective legal rights and obligations of executives, legislatures, and other structures; and the precise roles which specific institutions play in decision-making. It is also important to assess the impact of institutions on their members: how the institutional goals and rules, which prevail within the Senate, for example, affect the behavior of individual senators, as well as affecting the role the Senate plays in policy-making; or, how the nature, functions, power, and goals of a bureaucracy influence the behavior of individual bureaucrats. But institutions are nonetheless collectivities of human beings, and political behavior is but one aspect of human behavior. How a senator acts in the political process is conditioned by his membership in the Senate, by his role and power as a senator, and by his obligation to consider the public interest. But his actions are also conditioned by his individual beliefs, values, and interests as a human being; and the actions of any legislative body result from the collective behavior of the individuals who make up its membership. Hence, political analysis must include a focus on human behavior in terms of the group, and sometimes even individual behavior.

A second aspect is that a government involves processes and organized activities. Analysis of institutions—their historic development, structure and organization, and legal authority—is important. And equally important is a focus on processes and interrelationships. To understand and to analyze governments we need to determine by what kinds of processes the various institutions and officials arrive at their authoritative decisions. To determine and understand these processes we must go beyond legal rules and formal procedures and analyze the realities of such processes: what actually takes place within legislative or executive institutions; how the various institutions interact, relate, and influence each other; and how various smaller groups within institutions interact, relate, and influence each other. It is a fact of life that the behavior of humans is only partly conditioned by formal rules and procedures.

POLITICS: WHAT IT IS AND WHAT IT INVOLVES

In essence, government is human beings involved in structures and processes, which make binding authoritative decisions that have the intent or effect of creating and allocating values supposedly in the public interest. Politics, in turn, refers to the entire complex of processes by which goals and means are selected, policies are made, and patterns of value creation and allocation are determined. More specifically, politics involves demand inputs from government officials or groups in society— demands that the government make certain decisions so as to promote certain values or to distribute them in a certain way. Such demand inputs are effective, and will produce some favorable reaction from government, to the extent that they are backed by power. Support inputs may also be effective in influencing governmental action, to the extent that governments need or seek support. Demand inputs produce cooperation when groups have similar ideas or interests. But they produce political conflict when groups levy competing demands based on conflicting interests and ideas. Hence, *the primary task of government is the resolution of conflicts among competing demands.* We shall explain and amplify this general statement with a series of more specific empirical propositions about politics.

Politics involves governmental-environmental interaction. Although public policies and laws are the end products of governmental processes, more fundamentally they result from interaction between governments and their domestic and international environmental settings. What happens in any political arena is the result of the interaction of the ideas and interests of those who govern with the ideas and interests of the governed, and often also with ideas and interests prevailing in other societies. To put it another way; government officials "make" laws, but the making of laws is conditioned and sometimes even determined by various groups in society, by the society as a whole, and by governments abroad. Why this is so, and how such external factors influence governmental decision-making, is briefly explored below but more fully explained throughout this framework.

Which factor is most important depends very much on the nature of the political system, the kind of policy involved, and the specific issue at stake. In highly authoritarian systems, the ideas and interests of the rulers tend to be more dominant, but even the most powerful dictators are seldom, if ever, immune to external pressures from home or abroad. In democratic systems powerful interests and ideas in the society tend to prevail, but government officials have the final word. On some issues authoritarian or democratic government officials may have relative autonomy to do as they choose; on other issues, external pressures may virtually dictate a policy. Some spheres of policy may be relatively immune to influences from abroad; others—foreign or economic policy—may be heavily influenced by other governments and their societies. In any case, policy-making is the end product of governmental-environmental interaction. And to again emphasize the often overlooked obvious; it involves both institutional and human interactions.

Political processes begin with demand inputs. The political process with regard to any issue, policy, law, or other kind of governmental action begins with a "Demand Input." Some individual, group, lower or upper level of government, or foreign government puts a demand into the governmental machinery that the government take some kind of action with respect to some need or problem. The demand may be very general in nature, urging any kind of governmental action to curb inflation or unemployment, to resolve educational problems, or to improve race relations. Or it may be very specific: a proposal for a tax increase on gasoline, national health insurance, specific measures for school desegregation. In any case, the wheels of government grind into action when stimulated by demand inputs.

Implicitly involved in such demands are expectations with respect to values. Proposals will usually be justified on the basis of the public interest, and hence will assert that governmental action will create or allocate some value to most if not all of society. But the demanding groups also anticipate some benefits. The anticipated benefit may be direct and material: property owners demanding a reduction of taxes. It may be indirect: varied groups in society demanding governmental action to improve the economy, public safety, energy conservation, from which they hope to benefit. Or it may be anticipated benefits in terms of moral values: antidiscrimination actions to promote equality, limiting police power to promote civil liberties. The expectation of value maximization is the fundamental wellspring of demands, even though the final consequence of political action may be quite contrary to the expectations of the demanding groups.

The governmental process begins as some government official levies a demand: a legislator introduces a bill proposed as a law; an executive proposes a policy or introduces a legislative program; a bureaucrat proposes an administrative regulation. But this is not necessarily indicative of the real origins of the demand. In some instances the demand may originate within the government itself. A legislator or executive may personally experience or become aware of some problem and demand governmental action. Judges may demand action to remedy overcrowded dockets or underfunded court systems. A bureaucracy may demand broader authority to cope with problems in its sphere. But more often the demand originates from some source within the domestic, and sometimes the international, environment. Some group in society will demand some kind of general or specific action, will communicate its demand to some elected official or bureaucrat, and the government official exercises governmental initiative in response to such external demands. Or public officials, through the various means whereby general public opinion is communicated, become aware of more generalized demands on the part of many in society and introduce proposals in response to such widespread demands. This pattern of governmental initiative as response to environmental demands is generally characteristic of both authoritarian and democratic systems even though authoritarian governments tend to be much more selective in their responsiveness. Policy proposals debated in the cabinet of the King of Saudi Arabia tend to be responses to demands made by business, industry, and finance as are those in American and British cabinets, although labor unions are not likely to get the kind of hearing in the former as they do in the latter.

Interaction between ideas and interests determines the nature, content, and objectives of demands. The values which groups or government officials hope to maximize result from the interaction of the ideas and interests of the demanding groups. It is the interaction of ideas with interests which determines individual and group goals, as well as the means and intensity of seeking goal attainment. This requires some explanation of what is meant by ideas and interests.

Interests are related to what we previously referred to as ego-centered acquisitive values, prized objects which individuals and groups desire for themselves. Interest-based demands are levied in the expectation of group rewards, in the hope that political action will accrue to the advantage of the group. Most common in industrial societies are material interest demands arising from the group's socio-economic role or status: demands based on the interests that business, labor, farmer, and varied income groups have in acquiring wealth, material security, physical well-being, and power. But these and other groups also seek to acquire non-material values for themselves: respect, freedom, justice, and either privilege or equality. Different kinds of groups may have interests in acquiring values not directly related to material values. Muslims in India levy interest-based demands for the protection of their religion or for equality of opportunity. Minority tribes in African states, minority nationalities in the Soviet Union, French-speaking people in Canada levy similar kinds of interest-based demands for cultural autonomy, equality, or enhanced status.

Ideas are more related to what were previously referred to as moral values—beliefs concerning the rights and duties of individuals and groups and standards of conduct. Unlike ego-centered acquisitive values which stem from both the cultural and socio-economic environment, ideas are more rooted in the former—from the basic beliefs, moral values, and norms which prevail either throughout the society, or within a subculture (see Chapter 4). They involve not just goals or expectations of material or non-material reward for the demanding groups themselves, but also beliefs and opinions as to what is good for all of society, or for other groups. Most often they involve the values and standards of justice and equality, and also other values—but defined in terms of broader benefits than just to the demanding group. Idea-based demands manifest, at least superficially, a degree of selflessness or altruism. A group which in the name of justice demands a tax cut which would immediately benefit only other groups could be considered as levying an idea-based demand. So could demands made by majorities to benefit religious, racial, cultural, or linguistic minorities.

Many political demands appear to be clearly interest-based. Demands by the petroleum industry for tax preferences, by property owners for lower real estate taxes, by teachers for the right to strike, all clearly are based on expectations of direct rewards. Others appear to be idea-based, in that expectations of immediate or direct reward play minimal or no roles with respect to the demand: environmentalists demanding regulation of strip mining, social reformers demanding penal reform. But in reality, most demands result from the interaction of ideas and interests. Several factors account for this.

Ideas acquired by individuals and groups from either the prevailing cultural setting or from specific socialization processes influence priority ordering of values, and thus may determine which prime interests or values will be pursued with intensity. Some individuals and some societies give priority to wealth and pursue material interests most vigorously. Others give precedence to leisure, security, affection, or wisdom, and hence define interest quite differently. Some groups may vigorously demand improved educational programs, social security benefits, expansion of museums and parks, even though they recognize that major tax increases are involved. In some societies economic expansion is vigorously opposed by many groups, simply because they treasure some traditional values much more than they do material goods. Many environmentalists recognize the potential for a lower standard of living for themselves and others which may be implicit in their demands, but they may also be quite willing to forego this due to their interest in other values.

Some individuals treasure individual freedom, and hence will vigorously oppose any governmental action which infringes on this value even though they recognize the possible adverse consequences for such other values as economic growth, security, stability, or equality.

Ideas condition individual and group definitions of justice and equality, of rights and obligations, and of standards of conduct. Some groups tend to define these in very narrow ego-centered terms, and hence will vigorously support demands based on immediate material or nonmaterial interests of the group, with little consideration of consequences for others or for the entire society. Others are more prone to make sacrifices for others or for the public interest. The latter might demand a national health insurance program even though they recognize it means higher taxes and benefits primarily for others; the former would vigorously oppose unless direct benefits are expected.

Ideas also affect perceptions of relationships between group interests and the public interest. Some individuals may fail to see any such connection with regard to specific issues; they may vigorously oppose costly educational, mass transportation, or environmental protection programs simply because they fail to recognize that the overall benefits to society inherent in such programs may eventually benefit themselves. Others, by virtue of the ideas they have acquired, may be more prone to see the relationship between the public and private interests: taxpayers willing to accept tax increases, businesspeople accepting restrictions on their freedom in the interests of labor stability or economic growth, elderly people demanding costly educational programs.

But interests also tend to condition ideas, and particularly individual and group definitions of rights, obligations, standards of conduct, and such values as justice and freedom. All humans are prone to rationalize and justify the pursuit of ego-centered acquisitive values in the name of human rights, justice, equality, or the public interest. Educators will invoke such values as they demand improved educational programs, and although they may be right, self-interest is clearly also involved. Businesspeople will justify higher profit-making opportunities in the name of society's economic growth, laborers higher wages in the name of economic growth via expanded buying power, farmers governmental subsidies for the sake of expanded food production. And those with secure wealth or income will treasure political freedom, with little concern for governmental programs designed to promote the economic freedom of those who have no real political freedom because they are mired in poverty.

Effective demand inputs are most relevant in politics. We have so far emphasized that the political process with regard to any issue begins with demand inputs, originating sometimes with government officials but more
often with environmental groups, based on the interplay between ideas
and interests. And as will be explained later, the process continues as
additional demands, counter-demands, and modified demands are levied
on government officials with regard to the same, similar, or related issues.
But this general proposition must be modified by emphasizing the rele-
vance of *effective* demands—demands which are effective in that they have
some impact on political processes because they are backed or energized
by power.

In a market-place economy where the ratio of supply to demand plays
a significant role, price levels and supply are significantly affected by
effective demands. If there is a heavy, effective demand for shoes but only
a limited supply, the price of shoes will climb, but eventually the supply
of shoes will increase because of the demand—because the consequent
potential for selling more shoes will prompt shoe manufacturers to produce more shoes. But what counts is effective demands—demands
backed by purchasing power. The price of shoes is not likely to climb, nor
are shoe manufacturers likely to increase production, if those who demand shoes do not have the money to pay for shoes. What counts in
economics is buying power, money backing up or energizing demand
with currency.

As will be discussed in Chapter 2, power is the currency in the political
market place; demands must be backed or energized by power in order
to have impact on political processes. Demands will not set the wheels of
government in motion unless they are backed by some form and degree
of power. Demands levied during the course of the subsequent political
process must similarly be backed by power. Governments are not likely
to respond to demands with value allocation action unless power is involved. But further explanation of this proposition must be delayed until
we have explored the concept of power.

One further qualification must be added at this point, again with later
elaboration. Ineffective demands—not backed by power—frequently
have long-range political consequences. Groups in society may have high
priority interests so that they consider themselves as being in dire need
of value satisfaction—hungry people, landless peasants, oppressed minorities. They may not have the power to back up their demands and
governments will consequently fail to respond to their needs. Such
groups generally tend to be entirely shut out of political processes. But
given an interplay between intense ideas and interests, such groups will
invariably seek some form or degree of power to make their demands
effective. As they continue to press their demands without adequate

response from the political system, unrest and instability invariably result. And as they acquire some forms and degree of power—as they organize and acquire pitchforks, clubs, or firearms—the consequence may be violence, insurrection, and revolution.

Support inputs are also of major political significance. So far we have only explained the role of Demand Inputs. But another type of input which emanates from either the environment or from within the government itself is equally important—the input of support.

Support entails both actions and attitudes, behavior and states of mind, which tend to buttress, sustain, or maintain a political system, a particular government, a policy, or a particular course of political action. Most visibly, a politician needs majority support in order to get elected; an executive in a democratic system needs legislative support in order to govern effectively. But the concept has much broader and deeper aspects.

An aspect we have already discussed and will probe more deeply in Part II is the concept of Legitimacy. People will support a political system (although not necessarily the individuals who govern at the moment, nor their specific actions) to the extent that they consider it legitimate. In the short run, and in certain situations, some governments can maintain themselves and enforce their decisions by using coercion. But for long-term stability and real effectiveness, governments need some degree of support from at least some elements in society.

Political processes also involve the search for and cultivation of support by governments, by individual branches and agencies within governments, and by individuals within governments. Governments try to legitimize themselves, and this involves a search for support. They endeavor to make their policies effective in the sense of gaining compliance, and this entails developing support for these policies. As executives compete with legislatures, legislators with other legislators, and bureaucrats with other bureaucrats or with legislatures, they try to develop support for themselves and for their policy positions. And as governments try to resist some powerful pressures from society, they try to develop support. Finally, support inputs like demand inputs are based on the interaction between ideas and interests; people will support a government, an official, or a demand or course of action to the extent that they are congruent with their ideas and interests.

In essence then, political processes involve the interplay of interest-and-idea based effective demand and support inputs, which emanate from both governments and environmental groups. This leads us to the next proposition.

Politics involves both cooperation and conflict. Since the dawn of history, humans have organized in groups for two basic purposes: for cooperative endeavor because cooperation was found to be essential (to satisfy some basic needs or in quest of common purposes); and for conflict as competition developed because humans pursue not just common but also divergent goals. Hence politics, since it entails the use of political means to attain both common and divergent goals, also involves both cooperation and conflict.

In many societies there frequently exists a wide and strong consensus, based either on widely shared ideas or similar interests or both, which produces a kind of spontaneous, unorganized cooperation leading to fairly common support for fairly common demands. Quite frequently this manifests itself in the form of a prevailing political culture which tends to produce a particular type of political system. When many or most people in a society, for example, believe in what we might call democratic principles, patterns of cooperation develop which tend to produce democratic systems. Or when many people share a common religion—Muslim, Hindu, or others—and believe that there ought to be close links between government and religion, then patterns of cooperation may produce a theocratic state. Similar widespread shared beliefs concerning equality or social justice, or very common economic interests, may produce cooperation which shapes the scope and general policy direction of government —major efforts to redistribute wealth throughout the society, major governmental intervention in economics. Many times such spontaneous cooperation becomes organized cooperation as governments resist widely supported demands; humans then organize into interest groups, political parties, mass movements, and sometimes revolutionary movements.

A less permanent consensus sometimes develops when many groups perceive major threats to some common interests, and somewhat spontaneously begin to levy and support common or similar demands: "do something" about inflation, unemployment, gasoline shortages, rising crime rates. Such patterns of cooperation may be society-wide, or they may involve specific sectors of society: more-or-less spontaneous cooperation among various farm groups supporting demands for governmental subsidies; Orthodox Jews demanding a theocratic Israel; Dravidian-speaking people in India demanding that their language replace Hindi as the official language; automobile manufacturers cooperating with unions to support demands for governmental assistance to the auto industry.

More frequently however, and particularly when more specific ideas or interests are involved, patterns of cooperation tend to be or become organized. Interest groups, political parties, and other kinds of voluntary associations develop to provide cooperative support for more-or-less common demands based on common, similar, identical, or shared ideas and interests. Leaders of these groups then frequently attempt to broaden the base of cooperative political endeavor by coalition-building, enlisting the support of other groups by various political tactics. But then, as some groups in society cooperate either spontaneously, or through organization and coalition-building, competing groups tend to engage in similar political activity: labor organizes against business, Muslims versus Hindus, the Ibo tribe against the Hausa in Nigeria. Patterns of conflict then develop.

In older and more stable political systems, consensus and consequent patterns of cooperation are most significant with respect to the general context of politics—the basic type and nature of government, the general scope of governmental activities, the spheres of human activity in which it intervenes and plays roles, the general types of policies it produces. But even in these systems conflict is much more the substance of politics over specific issues and the processing of demand inputs. Even when a broad and deep consensus prevails with regard to the basic nature of government, conflicts tend to develop over specific structural arrangements and over specific power relationships. When consensus prevails over the general scope of government and over the general direction of governmental policy, conflicts erupt over such issues as to precisely when and how far the government should intervene in economic affairs, or to what extent it should pursue the value of social justice by using taxation and other methods to redistribute income.

Similarly, even when widespread common or similar ideas or interests generate demands for the government to "do something," conflict will erupt over specifically what should be done. A program to curb inflation might require tax increases and budget cuts, and would immediately arouse conflict over whether tax increases are warranted, whose taxes should be increased, which kinds of governmental programs should be cut due to budgetary retrenchment. A common demand for a government program to conserve existing and to develop new sources of energy will arouse conflict over specifics of gasoline rationing or taxation, strip mining of coal, tax incentives to various kinds of energy producers, and the specifics of programs to develop new sources of energy.

Conflict is even more the substance of politics in the newer and less stable political systems. As we shall see in Part II, conflict there involves not merely competition over the specifics of policy, but over the fundamentals of politics and the basic nature and scope of authority. In these societies a major characteristic is the absence of any broad consensus with regard to anything—the nature of government, who should rule, the scope of rule, and the manner of rule.

Conflicts are inevitable in any society, due simply to the diversity of ideas and interests which characterize the people of even the smallest and most homogeneous societies. People will differ because they have different ideas as to what is just, rational, or in the public interest; they differ because they have different material or non-material interests; they differ because they assign different priorities to different goals. Most basically they will compete because governments create and allocate values, and because value allocation patterns invariably are uneven. But the fact that conflict patterns are most significant features of all political systems does not mean that all political processes are the same, for as will be explained in Part II, differences in the range, number, complexity, types, and intensity of conflict patterns are very significant. Nonetheless, in any type of society conflicts of some type are inevitable and cannot be eliminated so long as humans remain diverse in their ideas and interests. (What a boring world this would be if we all thought the same way!) And while it may be the task of a government to foster and expand conditions and patterns of cooperation, even this basic task essentially involves effective conflict resolution.

In summary then, politics is the label we apply to all of the processes whereby a society and various groups within it use the government to attain certain goals and values for the society and for individual groups. The political process is set and kept in motion by a continuing flow of interest-and-idea based demand and support inputs, some from within the government itself, but more frequently in some form or manner from the domestic and international environment within which the government functions. Sometimes these demands arise out of consensus and lead to cooperative action, but more frequently they arise out of disagreement and result in conflict. Governments tend to respond to such demands to the extent that they are backed or energized by some form or degree of power. As the consequence of these effective demand and support inputs governmental processes are set in motion which eventually produce the authoritative decisions, which have the effect of creating, promoting, and allocating values to, and throughout, the society.

GOVERNMENT AND THE RESOLUTION OF CONFLICTS

As discussed earlier, what functions governments should perform is a highly controversial value question, and controversy even surrounds the question of what functions some governments actually do perform. But one empirical proposition about the actual functions of government can be stated with a high degree of certainty. Governmental and political institutions, as they formulate authoritative public policies and make decisions, engage in the resolution of conflicts.

The word politics has acquired a somewhat disreputable connotation because it connotes conflict, while human values normally sanctify cooperation. But as pointed out in the preceding section, conflict is the warp and woof not merely of politics, but of human life and endeavor, and as politicians and government officials engage in conflict, they do so in a very real sense as representatives of conflicting groups of people, and also as conflict resolvers. While politics may to some extent add a dimension of conflict to other social conflicts—conflict for partisan advantage or power—politics entails more the management and less the creation of conflict.

PATTERNS OF CONFLICT RESOLUTION

Governments attempt to alleviate or resolve conflicts and make decisions with regard to conflicting demands in a variety of distinctive ways, but the distinctive approaches generally fall into one or more of four patterns.

Patterns of indifference have been most common throughout history, are still characteristic of contemporary authoritarian systems, and are by no means absent in democratic systems. They do not really constitute efforts to resolve, but rather to ignore conflicts, in that the demands of one group locked in conflict with others are ignored because the demanding group lacks the power necessary to influence the government (or the competing groups have the power to cause the government to ignore the demand). Examples abound in all societies. For generations the American government (as well as others) ignored the demands of Blacks, Indians, and other minority groups in their conflicts with other social groups over equality, civil rights, and other values, and refused to intervene on behalf of minorities. More recently the Nigerian government ignored the conflict between the Hausa and Ibo tribes, the Pakistani government ignored the demands of Bengalis, the North Irish and British governments those of the Catholics. The pattern of indifference is often resorted to on the basis of expediency, but can be dangerous as ignored groups resort to violence to make their demands heard. Hence violence in American society, the civil wars in Nigeria and Pakistan, and the terrorism in North Ireland.

Another all-too-common pattern is that of repression, the use of coercion to suppress or inhibit the capability of one or more groups to wage a conflict. Again examples abound: decades in western societies when governmental decisions favored business and when labor-management conflicts were resolved through policemen's clubs, the successful Nigerian repression of the Ibo insurrection, the unsuccessful efforts of Pakistan to deal with the Bengalis, the repression of all opposition elements in totalitarian systems. The pattern is very common in authoritarian systems, but has by no means vanished from democratic societies. Yet it is a very risky approach to conflicts. It requires overwhelming force, and the vanquished very often do not accept defeat but merely wait to rise again another day.

A third pattern, relatively rare at least in the modern world, is that of decision-making by command. Some individual or small group, possessing both the requisite power and the determination to make the decision, does so either with or without hearing the relative merits of each side. The parties involved accept the decision, be it a compromise or total victory for one side, because of the overwhelming power of the decision-maker, or because they respect authority and possibly the judgement. The decisions of a judge, of a bureaucrat with quasi-judicial authority, or of an arbitrator to some extent reflect this pattern. Superficially the decisions of a Hitler or Stalin, or of a Congress deciding by majority vote, would appear to fit this pattern. But all of these are more likely to reflect the fourth pattern of bargaining.

Most patterns of conflict resolution involve a bargaining process. This much more common pattern involves either direct or indirect interaction between or among the contending parties, with the government playing varied roles. It entails efforts to at least partially accommodate and satisfy some of the demands levied by the competing groups, or the substitution of other benefits for those demanded by one or more groups. The final outcome might be a compromise, or total victory for one party, and possibly also the subsequent use of repression or command. In many instances some degree of bargaining precedes the use of other approaches.

The process involves sometimes a very simple and quick, but more often a very complex and lengthy continual interchange of demands, counter-demands or objections, offers of benefits (or threats of punishment or deprivation) and counter-offers, each rationalized, explained, and justified on the basis of merit, rationality, justice, or mutual benefit. In a simple case a property owners' association might demand and present justification for a 10% tax cut; budget-conscious groups might oppose for a variety of reasons, present their arguments, but make concessions and offer a 3% cut; and after more exchanges agreement might settle on a 5% cut. But few conflicts are that simple or so easily resolved. Most involve a bewildering variety of demands from many sources, complex concessions to many parties, numerous efforts at varied compromise formulas, log-rolling where one side supports another in exchange for support on another controversial matter, substitutions or side payments whereby some benefit not demanded may be offered in exchange for dropping a demand, and similar kinds of actions. But throughout the process there is a constant search for alternatives and for mutually beneficial outcomes, so that each side will get something and no side goes away empty-handed or completely defeated. Further, the "final" outcome may be only temporary, as losing parties seek to reopen the conflict and bargaining process at a later date or in other forums.

This pattern is most visible in democratic societies. This is the way policies and legislative programs make their way through executive establishments, bills through legislatures, and administrative regulations through bureaucracies. It is even the way many judicial decisions evolve. Bargaining is complex and extensive in these systems not merely because of the great diversity of interests and ideas, but also because (for a variety of reasons to be discussed throughout this framework), policy making processes are open to a variety of demands and influences and governments are virtually forced to be responsive to a variety of conflicting demands.

This pattern is also characteristic of most authoritarian systems, but is less visible simply because veils of secrecy are deliberately drawn around decision-making processes. An absolutist king bargains with ministers even though the latter may have only advisory roles; the ministers and their advisors bargain with each other; and the ministers and their advisors often bargain as surrogate representatives of varied elements of society—the landed aristocracy, the religious hierarchy, the commercial class, the army, the bureaucracy. The pattern is quite complex in industrial authoritarian systems. Decision-making in the Soviet Union might appear to be by command of the Politburo. The final decision is indeed a command, but most often it is a command based on compromise, after intense, prolonged, and complex bargaining involving varied elements and bureaucrats of the Communist Party, the governmental hierarchy, the economic apparatus, the military, and the police apparatus.

PATTERNS OF BARGAINING: PLURALISM, COMPETITION, AND REPRESENTATION

While bargaining is characteristic of most political systems most of the time, distinct differences in patterns of bargaining arise from the configuration of power within the system, at any given time, and with respect to the specific conflict issue. Although the subject of power is explored in Chapter 2, at this point mention must be made of four power factors which seem to condition specific bargaining patterns.

1. The pattern depends on the power of government over society. A very restricted type of bargaining is characteristic of highly authoritarian systems in which only a few groups in society have the power needed to influence government and to participate in decision-making.

2. The pattern depends on the distribution of power within government. Bargaining tends to be restricted in a system dominated by an absolutist king or dictator, but very extensive and complex when power is widely dispersed as in democratic systems.

3. The pattern depends on the power of varied groups in society. A restricted pattern develops when only one or a few groups (such as a landed

aristocracy) have power; a complex pattern when many types of groups (landowners, landless peasants, businesspeople, organized labor) have some power.

4. The pattern depends on the need of specific governments and systems for support. Some governments may be dependent on only a few groups, such as the landowners, clergy, and army, and hence can restrict admission to bargaining to such groups. Others may need a much broader base of support, and hence must admit many more to decision-making processes.

The interaction of these four aspects of power configurations produces different bargaining patterns along three dimensions—pluralism, competition, and representation. Pluralism is characteristic of some systems and conflict situations: many groups are involved, differing in their ideas and interests, but all having some form or degree of power they can bring to bear during the bargaining. The degree of pluralism—the number of groups with power and the diversity of their objectives—conditions the degree of competition in bargaining, and hence the extent and variety of concessions which have to be made for an eventual decision or outcome. Degrees of representation also vary: those participating in the bargaining may be representing the ideas and interests of only a few groups in society, or may be representative of a broad range of ideas and interests prevailing throughout the society. Hence bargaining processes differ in their degree of pluralism, competition, and representation.

In the more authoritarian systems bargaining and decision-making may entail little pluralism, competition, or representation: a king who listens to and bargains with only a few chief ministers, who agree more often than they disagree, and pay little heed to varied groups in society. In such instances the final decision may be a real command decision, and conflict resolution patterns of indifference and repression may be quite common. In the more complex industrial authoritarian systems bargaining is substantially more complex. In the Soviet Union, for example, a command decision to shift some investment capital from heavy industry to agriculture could be imposed by the few in the Politburo; in reality, such a demand would involve intense and prolonged bargaining among many bureaucrats involved in all sectors of the Soviet economy; substantial competition among the interests of agriculture, steel, machine building, the party, the military, and many others; and even some elements of surrogate representation as the bureaucrats directly involved in the negotiations represent to some degree the interests of various groups in the society—farmers, consumers, and others. Superficially, the process bears little resemblance to democratic processes: no really elected representatives are involved, action in formal legislative forums entails rubber stamp action, and the Politburo has the final word and is in a position to impose a command decision. But the process, nonetheless, entails prolonged and extensive bargaining, with the outcome highly likely to be a compromise. And in most democratic systems, of course, there is substantially more pluralism, competition, and representation in policy-making processes.

Bargaining entails governmental-environmental interaction. The governmental phase of the bargaining process which produces the eventual authoritative decision involves bargaining among elected or appointed government officials and takes place in governmental forums. But the process involves continuing governmental-environmental interaction between the ideas and interests of government officials and those of various social groups which have stakes in the issue. Various interest groups will bargain with various officials, various officials will bargain with each other, and various interest groups will bargain with each other. Bargaining within a congressional committee, within a king's palace, or within the chamber of the Politburo may indeed be bargaining within a closed "smoke filled room," but the doors are seldom really closed to "outside" ideas and interests. What counts is how many are in fact admitted, how much competition results from the diversity of ideas and interests among those admitted, and how representative they are of the varied ideas and interests which prevail throughout the society.

Roles of Governments in Bargaining

Although perhaps all bargaining involves some degree of governmental-environmental interaction, the specific roles of governments and government officials vary from system to system, official to official, and issue to issue.

It is sometimes argued that governments ought to be above social conflicts, that they ought to act as impartial mediators or referees and apply fixed rules, give objective consideration to the views of all sides, and then resolve conflicts by decisions based on such standards as law, justice, rationality, or the public interest. This is the role which some government officials try to play with regard to some conflicts, and despite some superficial appearances to the contrary, most officials in many if not most systems try to be impartial, rational, just, and public-minded in their decision-making—as they define these terms. They do try to create and allocate values which in the long-run will benefit most people most of the time—as they see things. But humans have argued since the beginning of time over precisely how to define justice, rationality, and the public interest; and in any specific situation involving any specific issue, humans will disagree as to just precisely what course of action is just, rational, and in the public interest. As Austin Ranney has put it, "The process of government should not be thought of as a process which should find perfect solutions to national problems and thereby still all disagreement and conflict. It should be thought of, rather, as a process by which a nation decides which proposals of its various groups shall, for the time being, be adopted as governmental policy and which proposals shall be rejected."[2] And in making their decisions the groups of decision-makers will differ as much as the groups in society who originate the proposals for governmental policy.

The humans who make up the collectivity we call government tend to be participants more often than neutral mediators for a number of reasons. For one, they may also have stakes in the conflict, and on some issues they may favor one side not because of the merits of the case but because the victory of that side may be politically advantageous in the sense of weakening the opposition, or ensuring re-election, or otherwise augmenting their political power. More common is the "political expediency" involved in favoring the more popular side, even though it may have less merit; but one wonders whether expediency is the right word for this since for the democratic creed it is ultimately the people who are supposed to determine public policy. But much more common is the partisanship which develops as the result of their own ideas and interests which, as humans, they are bound to share with some groups in society. Whether elected or appointed, due to their background, education, and other factors which produce their own value preferences, they are bound to lean in favor on one side or another, and to act as elected or surrogate representatives of one side or another. Various legislators are bound to be more business, labor, or farmer oriented than others. And no matter how firmly the door to decision-making rooms may be closed, throughout the entire governmental bargaining process government officials invariably are subjected to a barrage of influence from groups in society, and for reasons which will be explained later, they will be highly susceptible to such influence most of the time. Hence governmental participation in conflicts and bargaining is much more characteristic than is impartial mediation.

Despite this general tendency towards participatory rather than mediatory roles, governments, nonetheless, play extremely significant conflict resolution roles. For one, many groups involved in the conflict may perceive the government's role as being one of mediation, and the mere perception of this has major psychological consequences for peaceful and effective resolution. For another, at least some officials may actually play such roles, again of significance in terms of what happens within governmental forums. Also, governments as a whole and specific officials may play leadership roles; governments do not merely react to external pres-

[2]Austin Ranney, *The Governing of Men,* rev. ed., (N.Y.: Holt, Rinehart and Winston, 1966) p. 19.

sures, but also act to influence the thought and behavior of their societies and the groups involved in conflict. Most important, by imposing the authority of government on a conflict situation they help to keep the conflict peaceful, promote at least temporary or partial settlements, and ensure that the parties will abide by the terms of the settlement and accept, at least temporarily, the outcome as a binding decision. When workers and factory owners, and racial or religious minorities and majorities, evaluate government as legitimate and its actions as relatively fair, they will abide by governmental decisions rather than take up arms against each other.

Power is the chief currency in conflict resolution processes. As money is the currency of economics, so power is the currency of politics. All conflict resolution processes involve the use and application of varying degrees and forms of power by the contending parties, and the configuration of power (distribution patterns among the conflicting groups) in any given conflict determines the final outcome and decision. But the reader who might judge these statements as a cynical or simplistic view of politics is urged to withhold judgment until he reads the discussion of power in Chapter 2. At this point we will simply define power as "influence over the thought and behavior of others."

It is power, thus defined, which determines whether or not a specific conflict will become a political conflict. Governmental action with respect to conflicts begins as the result of effective demand inputs either from within the government or from the environmental setting—demands backed by some degree and form of power, and hence effective in eliciting some degree of governmental attention and response. Governments will intervene in conflicts only if some or all of the groups involved have some means—peaceful or violent—to convince government officials that some kind of intervention is desirable or necessary. Minority groups in conflict with majorities, or women in conflict with male chauvinists, will cause governments to intervene on their behalf to the extent that they have power to energize their demands.

Power is the currency which is constantly used, applied, and exchanged during conflict resolution processes. A pattern of governmental indifference merely reflects the relative weakness of power of the parties which seek governmental involvement. A pattern of repression reflects either governmental responsiveness to the more powerful groups, or the relative powerlessness of the repressed groups. Patterns of command decision-making reflect overwhelming concentrations of power in and within governments. When bargaining ensues, the scope and degree of bargaining reflects the configuration of power in that situation; extensive bargaining ensues when many groups with power are involved, restricted when only a few have power.

In the bargaining process, all groups and officials involved apply some form and degree of power, for it is the configuration of power in a specific conflict situation which determines the final outcome. This involves the power of the contending social groups as well as of the government officials who participate on their behalf. If government officials who attempt to play the role of neutral mediators have more power than the participants, then the government's role will tend to be that of the neutral mediator. If not, then the government's role will be that of active participant (although in many instances the government's role may be both).

If all of the parties involved have and apply substantial power during bargaining, then the final outcome and decision will be somewhat of a compromise which at least partially and temporarily satisfies the interests and ideas of most participants. If the conflict is characterized by an equilibrium of power, then stalemate, inaction, and no decision are probable consequences unless some real middle ground can be reached. If one side has overwhelming power its interests and ideas will be accommodated at the expense of the opposition. But due to the unequal distribution of power which usually prevails, even compromise outcomes will tend to be tilted and to confer somewhat more values on those who have the power edge in a given conflict situation at a given time.

THE CONCEPT OF POLITICAL SYSTEM

From all that has been said so far, it should be evident that meaningful political analysis must focus not just on governmental institutions and their actions, but also on factors which produce institutions and generate governmental actions—which produce conflicting demand and support inputs, energize them with power, affect bargaining or other conflict resolution processes, and have an impact on a government's legitimacy and its creation and allocation of values. By focusing on a society's overall "political system" we can isolate, identify, and analyze such forces and assess their impact. This entire book explains what the analysis of a political system entails, but some preliminary explanation provides a useful introduction.

A political system consists of all of the forces, processes, and institutions of a society which generate effective demand and support inputs and attendant political cooperation or conflict; and which are involved in the resolution of conflicts and the subsequent evolution of authoritative political decisions. To clarify the meaning of system some analogies with mechanical and organic systems may be helpful.

A system can be visualized as a complex machine or living organism into which several elements are injected (inputs such as gas and oil into an automobile, food, air, and water into a human body, demand and support into a political system); these elements are then processed by the system, and the processing results in the conversion of inputs into certain end products, outputs, and consequences (the automobile moves, the human body lives and moves, and the political system grinds out policies which create and allocate values). Some things we call systems may be parts of larger systems and hence should perhaps be termed sub-systems. The automobile is part of a transportation system, the circulatory system part of a living organism, the political system part of society which also has other systems such as economic, cultural, and religious. But scientists usually use the word system to refer to whatever their principle focus is, and sub-systems to refer to their system's component parts. Hence we use the term political system.

A system is a composite of sub-systems or component parts, which are generally recognizable as such and distinguishable from other components. Thus the human body as a system is a composite of such systems as the circulatory, respiratory, digestive; the automobile of steering, transmission, exhaust; and a political system a composite of the sub-systems described below. Sub-systems are also composites of related units: the blood, heart, and other units make up the circulatory system. Relative cohesion among the parts characterizes systems; the parts fit and stick together, and form a recognizable whole.

The four units we single out as the component elements of political systems are the environmental, linkage-communication, decision-making, and policy output components (briefly described below). Each one in turn is a complex of interrelated units or sub-systems.

Component elements of systems are functionally interrelated; they interact with one another to process and convert the inputs into outputs. The circulatory, respiratory, digestive, and other systems interact to maintain human life and produce human activity; steering, transmission, exhaust and other systems interact to move the automobile in some direction. Covariance is another characteristic of systems: as one unit changes, so do the other units which make up the system. A change in the circulatory system will produce changes in the digestive and other human systems. And as an event or chain of events begins in one unit, it has effects on other units and ends in another, with consequences for the overall system: the ignition system is put into action by turning the key, the motor and exhaust systems hopefully begin to function, and as we set the transmission into operation and disengage the braking system, the automobile moves.

THE FOUR COMPONENT ELEMENTS OF A POLITICAL SYSTEM

Although some disagreement persists among political scientists as to precisely what parts of a political system should be considered as the major sub-systems or components, we will use a four-fold classification scheme which probably would encounter few major objections. Each element, however, is in turn a cluster of interrelated and interacting sub-units. Further, each component element interacts with the others, and has consequences for the others. Each component is further described in Parts II through V of this framework.

The environmental setting (both domestic and international), which is a composite of the political culture, the socio-economic-geographic setting, and the power configuration within the society. As is explained in Part II, the interaction of these three variables produces patterns of ideas and interests among the groups which compose the society, patterns of conflict and cooperation, and effective demand and support inputs in the pursuit of desired values. The interaction of these environmental factors has a significant impact on the nature and functioning of the linkage-communication, decision-making, and policy output components in terms of both their structure and functioning; and it also has major consequences for the structure and functioning of the political system as a whole. Significant cultural changes, for example, will produce changes in the party system, the decision-making structure, and the policies of government. But in turn there will be feedback on the environmental component from the other components and the system as a whole: consequences for the political culture, the socio-economic setting, the power configuration, and in turn on the patterns of ideas and interests and on effective demand and support inputs. Governmental policies, for example, may significantly raise the expectations of some minority groups, and may stimulate them to organize and press demands for material and other benefits.

The linkage-communication system or infrastructure This, as explained in Part III, includes the cluster of institutions, structures, and processes which link society with government, which provide two-way communication channels. It includes such structures as political parties and interest groups which process environmentally-based demand and support inputs and communicate or relay them to the decision-making system. But such structures may also serve as instruments of government, whereby the government can have an impact on the environmental setting and on demand and support inputs. Again patterns of interaction are involved: actions and changes within the linkage-communication system, for example a change in the party system, may have significant consequences for the structure and functioning of the other three components, and on the system as a whole.

The decision-making system (Part IV) consisting of the cluster of structures and processes which receive demand and support inputs as relayed through the linkage-communication system, and convert them into policy outputs which create, promote, and allocate values for all components and for the system as a whole. Interrelationship and interaction is again characteristic: structures and processes within the decision-making system interact and have consequences for each other, and the decision-making system is interrelated and interacts with the other components of the system.

Patterns of policy outputs (Part V), meaning the overall pattern of policy and specific patterns within such spheres as economic, cultural, and social policies. Complex patterns of interaction are again involved: the interaction of the first three components has major consequences for the kinds of policies that the system produces; the nature of policies made in one sphere—the economic for example—may have consequences for policies in other spheres; and policies, by creating and allocating values may have a significant impact on the environment, the linkage-communication system, and governmental decision-making structures and processes. The consequences on the environmental component should particularly be noted, for this illustrates the circular nature of political processes. Demand and support inputs tend to originate in the society, to be relayed through linkage-communication system, and to be converted into policies by the decision-making machinery. But then policies impact the society, and have significant impact on idea and interest and conflict and cooperation patterns and goals, with consequences for subsequent demand and support inputs into the system.

The Nature
and Role
of Political Power

2

Power, as briefly discussed in the preceding chapter, plays a crucial role in politics. It determines the effectiveness of demand inputs, the impact of bargaining and other conflict resolution processes, and a government's value creation and allocation patterns. Governmental effectiveness, in turn, is related to a government's power. Before we proceed to an examination of the varied components of political systems, then, we need to explore the nature and role of political power. In this chapter we define power as "influence over thought and behavior." As such, it is primarily a psychological phenomenon which is rooted in a complex pattern of interaction between four component elements. For example, the ability of a power-wielder (an individual or group) to influence a target depends on the power-wielder's resources of power, his or her credibility, the extent to which the target needs or places a high value on the power-wielder's resources, and the relationship of good will that prevails between the power-wielder and the target. We also explore the various ways in which power is used in politics, and various patterns in various societies, with respect to the location and distribution of power.

THE GENERAL ROLE OF POWER

All individuals, politicians, and government officials seek some form and degree of power, although some pursue it more intensely and consciously than others. Some seek it as a value or an end in itself; we are all familiar with "power-hungry" individuals and governments. But more often power is sought as a means, as an instrument with which we may pursue other values, just as most people seek money not for its own sake but to acquire food, clothing, and other desirable objects. In politics it must be pursued and used, just as money is needed to buy something in the economic marketplace. To get something in the political marketplace —to attain political office, to get a bill enacted into law, to have people obey the law—one needs to influence others and to have the requisite power over others so that one may be appointed or elected.

The word "power" has acquired some unfortunate connotations, and idealists in particular are prone to consider power and its use as immoral. All of us would probably prefer that reason and ethics govern and determine political outcomes. They often do, and it is simply the result of using certain resources of power in a generally persuasive way. Moral considerations, however, pertain not to the search for and use of power per se; they apply to pursued goals and the forms of power used in their pursuit. What counts is the morality or immorality of the ends sought by politicians and governments, and of varied means such as violence, bribery, or coercion. What matters is whether or not a moral goal can in fact be attained through the form or degree of power that is used; and whether, for example, domestic stability and peace can be reached through excessive coercion, or if human rights can be attained by violent means.

But regardless of these normative and utilitarian problems, politicians must seek and use power to be effective, and governments must have power to govern effectively. Hence political analysis must focus on power and on conflicts arising from competition over power, but must also focus on the forms and purposes for which power is sought and used. Four aspects of power are of concern in political analysis, and have constituted political problems since the beginning of time.

The Power of States over Other States

This aspect of power is of primary concern to the analyst of international politics. But it is also relevant to domestic politics because demand and support inputs into domestic processes frequently originate from or are affected by the international environment. For example, the power wielded by Arab states as the result of their possession of scarce oil resources has had major consequences for the domestic politics of oil-consuming states.

THE POWER OF GOVERNMENT OVER SOCIETY

An age-old problem of politics has been the organization of power for effective control of the governed so that authoritative decisions will be binding. Despite well-grounded fears of governmental power, government officials must, after all, have power commensurate with their responsibilities so that they can effectively function as instruments of society. Normative concerns relating to this aspect of power pertain not to the possession and use of governmental power per se, but to the extent of power, the means used, and the purposes of use.

THE POWER OF SOCIETY OVER GOVERNMENT

The necessity of governmental power raises another age-old problem: how to limit or control governmental power. Societies must have some degree of power over governments not merely to ensure degrees of human freedom, but also to ensure that governments do serve as instruments of society and make policies in the public interest.

POWER IN CONFLICT RESOLUTION AND DECISION-MAKING PROCESSES

Some political scientists define power in terms of participation in decision-making. But participation can be both direct and indirect. Government officials directly involved in congressional or bureaucratic bargaining certainly have some degree of power, but those who do not directly participate but have influence over participants (such as interest groups or lobbies) may have substantially more power than some of the actual participants. The analytical focus with respect to this aspect of power is the interplay of power brought to bear on general and specific conflict resolution processes—which government officials and which social groups bring to bear what forms and degrees of power for what purposes, and what the power configuration is which produces the policy outcome or decision which determines who gets what, when, and how. It involves analysis of the relative power of social groups over other social groups, their relative power over branches of officials of government, and the relative power of branches and officials with respect to each other.

DEFINITIONS, NATURE, AND PURPOSES OF POWER

Throughout this framework we use the term power in the context of the following definition: *Power is a composite of various elements which can be used to influence the thought and behavior of others.* We use this definition because it seems the most useful way of approaching both the complex nature and ultimate purposes of using power.

A case can be made for distinguishing among such terms as power, influence, authority, strength, and force, because governments and people do use different means. Power, as Karl Deutsch points out, connotes a degree of authority and compulsion, operates on the personality, and is difficult to reject; while influence tries to get inside the personality by appealing to thought and feelings and can be rejected more easily.[1] Similarly strength and force imply compulsion, authority as appeal to moral standards, and influence inducements. Each one of these words conjures up different mental images which may produce different reactive behavior. Authority has favorable connotations (although not to all people) and tends to evoke compliance; power, strength and force tend to provoke at least mental resistance. No one likes to be forced to do something, while many, if not most, people tend to respect authority, to heed the advice of authorities, and to comply with authoritative decisions. Influence often has unfavorable connotations, implying something a bit suspect or sleazy, getting someone to do something he shouldn't do, favoritism, or buying a public official.

Distinctions might also be merited because of the different moral implications of some of these terms, and because ethical considerations do enter into the use of power. Authority might imply the the legitimate and moral use of power for legitimate and moral ends, and force and strength the opposite. From both a legal and moral standpoint it is also important to distinguish between legitimate authority and use of force, and the misuse or usurpation of authority and an illegal or immoral use of force.

But given the present state of the social sciences, these distinctions only serve to confuse the nature of politics and government. The unhappy fact is that neither social scientists nor philosophers have agreed on definitions of such words as power, authority, or influence. Whatever particular word we use, the reference is to the use of some means to affect other people so that certain objectives can be attained; these words do not really permit us to distinguish among varied means. When a government invokes its authority, it operates on the personality with a degree of compulsion which may be difficult to reject, but it also tries to get inside the personality by the appeal of legitimacy to the thought of citizens. The

[1]Karl W. Deutsch, *Politics and Government* (Boston: Houghton Mifflin Co, 1970), pp. 23–25.

use of force involves an effort not merely to directly affect behavior, but to affect behavior via thought—fear. Governmental power over society does not rest solely on authority; many factors are often involved. Authority also has psychological connotations which go beyond legal authority—it can mean someone with credibility or superior knowledge who knows what he or she is talking about. And the words as used today do not permit us to distinguish between legal or moral uses of power.

Whatever term we use—power, authority, influence, force, strength— we are referring to a relationship between actors in which one tries to persuade, induce, or coerce others to do what they ordinarily would not do, to make things happen that otherwise would not happen, to change the probability of outcomes. Each term involves some means to attain some goals, although the means may be somewhat but perhaps not completely different. Governmental power refers to a government's effort or ability to obtain compliance, which basically means an effort or ability to influence at least the behavior, if not thought, of people. The major prop of governmental power might be its legal authority to make decisions and use coercion when necessary, but as will be explained below, effective governmental influence involves much more. The power of society over government refers to ability to at least partly control the processes of government, which entails influence over the thought and behavior of government officials within governmental structures. Power in bargaining processes refers to the efforts of direct and indirect participants to influence the thought and behavior of each other to affect the outcome.

What we are after in this framework is a basic understanding of the nature of politics and government. For this purpose the definition we use —power as the composite of various elements which can be used to influence the thought and behavior of others—followed by an exploration of the component elements of power and then of the varied ways in which these elements are and can be used to change the probability of outcomes, seems most useful.

THE COMPONENT ELEMENTS OR SOURCES OF POWER[2]

Power is rooted in the possession of certain tangible resources, such as wealth or weaponry. But intangible things also constitute resources, for the exercise of power involves psychological phenomena and, hence, is rooted in complex psychological sources. Most basically the use of power involves efforts to modify, change, or control human behavior by

---

[2]Much of what follows is based on the brief proposal for a "theory of compliance" by Dean G. Pruitt, "National Power and International Responsiveness," *Background* VII (1964), pp. 165–178; and on various works by Robert A. Dahl.

some kind of appeal to the target's values. It may be an appeal to ego-centered acquisitive values, an effort to convince the target that certain behavior will produce direct benefits or directly reduce deprivations. A bribe may be offered to someone who values money, a threat of imprisonment may influence the behavior of someone who values freedom. The use of power may involve an appeal to normative values—a persuasive argument to a legislator that a vote for a certain bill is a vote for justice and is the right thing to do. The use of power may involve an appeal to both kinds of values—enactment of a certain tax law will not only result in a more equitable sharing of the tax burden, but will also ensure re-election.

Efforts to influence behavior thus always involve efforts to influence the mind of the target. The human mind receives messages from the environment (the words, actions, arguments, promises, threats of various power-wielders), screens and evaluates such messages on the basis of its individual values, and then "decides," consciously or subconsciously, on a course of action. The "decision" and subsequent course of behavior may be on the basis of rational thought—a more-or-less rational calculation of the benefits and costs involved, such as the number of votes one is likely to win or lose by supporting the tax bill, or whether getting to some destination faster is worth the possible fine if one gets caught. The decision may also be on the basis of feelings or emotions about values —how strongly one feels about alleviating the tax burden on the poor, about acquiring money, about driving fast on a highway. Hence psychological forces are paramount in the exercise of power and significant resources include both tangible and intangible or psychological forces.

The psychological aspects of power are further accentuated by the fact that targets of influence are seldom static targets or empty blackboards. Humans have their own subjective value preferences, and their own standards of right and wrong. They are "moving targets" in that they have their own predispositions to behave one way or another on the basis of what is already written on the blackboards of their minds. Further, the relationship between power-wielder and target is not likely to be a one-way street: the target may also try to influence the power-wielder—as the legislator may try to persuade a constituent that what the latter proposes is wrong. Finally, the political setting is likely to be a complex one, as the target may be the object of influence emanating from a wide variety of power-wielders. But in all cases, as the consequence of a series of complex psychological phenomena involving rational and emotional appeals to values, the target eventually either persists in, modifies, or changes his behavior, depending on the configuration of internal and external influences at the given time in the given situation.

Power and its exercise appears to involve interaction among four component elements. The interaction among these four appears to be universal, characteristic of all societies both past and present. However, the specific nature and importance of each element, and the specifics of interaction vary from society to society, situation to situation, and individual to individual. First we briefly describe these four elements and then discuss their complex interaction in the following paragraphs:

1. The possession or control of certain tangible and intangible *resources of power* (sometimes referred to, particularly in international politics, as capabilities) which, when consciously or unconsciously wielded by the power-wielder, potentially have some impact on the target by affecting rational or emotional evaluations concerning value benefits or costs.

2. *The element of the target's needs or values.* Resources will influence a target and affect behavior only to the extent that the target calculates or evaluates the probable impact of the manipulated resources on value-determined needs. An offer of money as a benefit will influence behavior only if the target needs or places a high value on money, or a higher value on money than on the value he might be called upon to sacrifice by acceptance—such as self-respect, freedom of action, leisure time. A threat to inflict damage to a target's values—to undermine his prestige, jeopardize his security—will influence only to the extent that the target values prestige or security. In essence, the actual influence of resources depends on the target's rational or emotional cost-benefit assessment in terms of the target's value priorities.

3. *The element of credibility.* The effectiveness of resources also depends on perceptions and evaluations of credibility by the target. The target must believe, first of all, that the power-wielder actually has possession or control of the resources that are being manipulated—actually has the wealth, or the military power that is being manipulated. The target must also believe that the power-wielder will "deliver" the resources, will carry out the promise to bestow money or some other value, or the threat to inflict damage to the target's values.

4. *The element of good will and responsiveness.* In a sense, this could be considered a resource of power, is related to other resources to be discussed below, and also is related to the element of credibility. But this element nonetheless warrants separate consideration. Simply put, influence is enhanced to the extent that a relationship of good will exists between the power-wielder and the target. When a friendly relationship exists between two individuals, groups, governments, or between governments and people, then the two tend to be responsive to each other, to be amenable to influence from each other, to behave in accordance with reciprocal advice or counsel. Conversely, a power-wielder is likely to have difficulty influencing a target who views him with ill-will, regardless of the resources being wielded (unless major benefits or dire conse-

quences are involved). Credibility is involved in that proven credibility may engender good will relationships, and a good will relationship in turn may enhance perceptions of credibility. It is difficult to develop a friendship with a proven liar, and it is difficult to consider an established friend as a liar.

THE NATURE AND DYNAMICS OF POWER RESOURCES

In very general terms, it is possible to state and explain what the specific resources of power appear to be, how they are interrelated and interact with one another, and how these resources, individually or in clusters, interact with the elements of reciprocal need, credibility, and good will. Beyond that, however, specifics vary from society to society, situation to situation, and individuals to individuals. First of all, no individual resource appears to be more important than others; most often it appears to be the combination of resources which counts, together with the other elements of power. Secondly, no priority ordering among the resources appears to be possible, for precisely which resource may be more important than others again depends on the setting, the values of individuals and groups, and the specific situation. Thirdly, the specific importance of individual resources, and even the nature of some of the resources, depends on the socio-economic-cultural setting—the values or value priorities which prevail in specific societies. But through space and time, the possession or control of certain resources appears to provide at least a potential for influence; power-wielders who hope to exercise influence must possess one or more of the resources which can be used in a variety of ways to affect human thought and behavior. But in all cases the actual impact of resources on thought and behavior depends on needs and values of the target, the credibility of the power-wielder, and the kind of relationship that prevails between power-wielder and target.

Legal authority to make and enforce decisions which create and allocate values is a most important source of influence and the most important source of governmental power. Governments create and allocate various values which are ordinarily cherished by most people—domestic peace and order, stability, wealth, equality, and others—and thereby influence people to support governments and to obey laws. By unequal allocation of values they may also create variations in patterns of governmental influence—they may be more influential with favored groups than with those discriminated against. By the legal use of coercive instruments governments can also influence by threats or actions depriving individuals or groups of certain values—fines against violators of the law, deprivation of freedom by jail sentences, bodily harm against demonstrators. The general scope of a government's legal authority and the efficiency of its coercive apparatus may make some governments more influential than others.

Legal authority is also a power source for leaders of non-governmental organizations. The rules of an organization may bestow substantial authority on leadership to grant or withhold varied values from the membership, such as the authority of some labor union leaders to grant jobs. The rules may give the leadership substantial control over other resources—over the organization, its wealth, its information and communication channels. Such legal authority tends to enhance the power of leaderships not only over their groups and members, but also with respect to governments.

A target's needs and values, however, play a very significant role with respect to the actual influence of legal authority. The very existence of government is due to the need of a society for domestic peace. The expanded authority of governments—their roles in economic, social, cultural, and many other spheres—is related to perceived needs among people for governmental action in these spheres, anticipations that governmental authority can allocate economic and other values which are considered as needs. The greater complexity of needs in interdependent industrial societies, and the diminishing potential for satisfying such needs through self-help or voluntary cooperative action, has led to growing authority with respect to economic regulation, the provision of social services and health care, and to expanded influence over behavior in such spheres of human activity.

But definitions of needs, or priorities among cherished values, vary among individuals and groups of society, and, hence, partly account for variations in actual governmental influence. A hungry man may be prone to steal even though the long arm of the law may deprive him of his liberty. An oppressed minority may still cherish order and stability, but resort to violence because it places a higher value on equality and the economic and other benefits that accompany this value. A businessperson whose profit-making potential seems threatened by governmental action will perceive less need for governmental economic actions and may try to evade rather than be influenced in the way the government wants to influence that person. Some societies value freedom more than they do stability and order, and thus restrict or evade governmental authority.

Credibility is another important element for legal authority to actually influence thought and behavior—the people must believe that authority can and will deliver the values they desire, or inflict the punishment they wish to avoid. The probability of compliance with law depends primarily on perceptions of the legitimacy of the law-makers and of the law itself, but it also depends on probabilities of getting caught and punished for violations. Shoplifting, burglary, and tax evasion tend to become widespread if the credibility of the government's coercive ability is low; mass demonstrations and violence to attain priority goals may be tempting if mass action reduces the probability of individuals getting caught and punished; police officers may become a law unto themselves if the credibility of a government's ability to apply sanctions to them is low.

But more important may be mass and group perceptions concerning a government's intent and willingness to deliver and allocate values which respond to basic needs and resolve basic problems. Low credibility of governmental capabilities in such diverse fields as economic matters, health care, or public transportation tends to stiffen resistance to governmental authority in such spheres; perceptions of expanded capability will conversely tend to generate support for such governmental activities. As Watergate has demonstrated, the low credibility of executives may effectively destroy their real power, even though their legal authority may remain unaffected. Overall, governmental influence declines as credibility and trust decline, and the collapse or revolutionary overthrow of governments is frequently rooted in such factors. The collapse of South Vietnam is but one of many examples.

Good will plays a crucial role, for with respect to the resource of legal authority, it is an aspect of the cardinal element of legitimacy. When a government is evaluated as legitimate, the people will tend to view it with good will and to respond to its decisions with voluntary compliance. When not, governments are forced to rely on coercion, which in turn only breeds more ill will, and thereby further reduces the government's influence over thought and behavior. The same tendencies hold with respect to specific branches, officials, and laws. When a law is viewed with ill will by many, it will tend to be disobeyed; school teachers will strike and pot smokers will continue to smoke. When an executive is viewed with ill will, legislators and bureaucrats will defy him, and people will scorn his appeals for public support. But again, good will is not the only factor, for people may temporarily tolerate a government or leader which can deliver at least some basic values. People generally prefer order and stability to revolution, at least until they get thoroughly fed up with the government's allocation of values.

Position or office can bestow, or give the appearance of potentially bestowing or denying, a wide variety of values pursued by individuals, groups, or societies as a whole—justice, wealth, power, prestige, security, freedom, among others. In many cases this is simply because with position or office one may acquire the legal authority associated with it—the executive, the bureaucrat, the judge, the police officer, the labor union leader. But in many cases it provides access to and influence over those with legal authority. Individuals high in the hierarchy of the White House staff, assistants to senators and congressmen, advisors to policy-making bureaucrats, law clerks to Supreme Court judges, advisors to kings and emirs—all such individuals may be without any legal authority, but frequently enjoy tremendous influence by virtue of their advisory role, their general activities, and even just by controlling access to those with legal authority. The person who advises a President, or determines who sees the President, has a position with tremendous influence.

These resources may also endow with prestige, with legitimacy as a rule-maker, and with authority other than legal authority. Religious leaders in most Muslim societies, tribal chiefs in modern African states, family elders in modern China no longer have legal authority. But by virtue of their positions which once enjoyed legitimate legal authority, they frequently continue to have substantial influence over their sects, tribes, and clans. And these and similar types of individuals often enjoy substantial influence over government because governments need their support and their willingness to influence the behavior of religious groups, tribes, or clans.

A variety of other resources might also accrue to certain positions. It may provide an individual with control over numbers—many people. It might provide varying degrees of control over organizations. It might result in wealth or in the control of certain forms of economic power—a strategic position in a major corporation, trade association, or labor union. It might endow an individual with a reputation for a special skill or expertise—an agricultural official is likely to have some influence with respect to farm policy, a representative from the petroleum industry with respect to energy policy.

A prime example of power derived from position and office is the power of the American Presidency, whose real power hardly equals the few lines in the Constitution outlining his legal authority. The office requires him to function in at least six roles, each one of which not only gives him far more legal authority than stated in the Constitution, but also non-legal authority and other resources of influence. All of the potential for influence which grows out of the combined roles gives the position awesome potential power. As chief politician he functions as at least titular leader of his party, and as the primary source of efforts to build the coalitions and cooperation necessary for the formulation of public policies. As chief administrator he has extensive influence with respect to the specifics of legislation, control over the bureaucracy, and a major fund of patronage and favors he can dispense. As chief legislator he has the real power of legislative initiative, the power of the veto, and substantial influence while bills are being considered in the Congress. He is chief foreign-policy maker, Commander in Chief of the Armed Forces, and chief of state—the symbol of the nation. A similar interplay of roles is a major root of the real power of executives in other states and at state and local levels of government.

Prestige is frequently linked with the foregoing resources of power in that high position or substantial legal authority tends to cloak an individual with prestige. But it also operates independently as a resource simply because human beings tend to respect the opinions of those with prestige, to respect if not heed their supposedly superior views on what is just, rational, or in the public interest.

Prestige can flow from many sources. It may be rooted in the traditions or culture of a society: age confers prestige in some, religious status in others, military leadership in still others, wealth or business leadership in material-oriented countries. Prestige may flow from high credibility, or from a general reputation for skill, expertise, fairness, honesty, decency, and courage, or whatever values may be prized in a particular culture. It is frequently linked with a reputation for power, with the appearance of power, derived either from office, or from being close to the powerful, or from appearing to have a potential for high office. Prospective senators and presidents are very influential even prior to election day, as are prospective dictators before they launch a coup. But lame duck congressmen, second-term presidents, and dictators whose days appear to be numbered are frequently without any significant power despite their legal authority. For this reason most politicians are fearful of "losing face," of giving the appearance of being powerless, and, hence, quite frequently tend to be followers rather than leaders and to wait until strong support develops for a particular proposal. Leadership on behalf of noble but hopeless causes may endow some with the prestige attached to a hero-figure, but it may also generate a reputation of powerlessness.

A reputation of superior capability to meet needs, to accept the responsibility for tackling difficult problems, also endows individuals with prestige, and quite frequently results in the bestowal of other resources of power—legal authority, office, control of an organization, control of economic power. Election results are at least partly determined by public images of superior capability and willingness to accept responsibility; coups often elevate individuals with such prestige, even though the participants may later recognize the gap between their imagery and reality.

Wealth, or varied forms of economic power, can be used in a variety of ways to confer or deny needed or desired values on individual or group targets. It can be used to influence targets who have legal authority and need money—campaign contributions—or who for varied political reasons might need the support of powerful economic interests. It can be used to acquire other resources of power: positions with legal authority, control of organizations, control of communications media, the acquisition or control of information and skill, the manipulation of many people into an organization. The actions of powerful economic interests may have a direct impact on politicians and government officials (the potential of support for a campaign, or for a policy program), or they may have an indirect impact through their impact on the economic, political system or society as a whole (a strike in a key industry). Depending on the culture, wealth may also confer high prestige. The basic root of the power of wealth appears to be its ability to provide or deny others with means of livelihood.

In some cases it may be ownership of wealth which provides the re-source—of money, or land or business or other means which can gener-ate money. But in modern industrial societies it may be control rather than ownership which counts. Stockholders may own giant banks and corporations, but control and consequent political influence is vested in directors and management; members may own their labor unions, but control is vested in the leadership. Particularly significant is the degree of concentration of economic power, and its position in the overall econ-omy. Concentration of economic resources in giant banks, corporations and labor unions, are significant features not only of the economics but also the politics of our time. And very important in terms of not only economic but consequent political power is position in the economy. Labor unions which occupy strategic positions and thereby could disrupt the entire economy by their actions—railway workers, longshoremen, and even sanitation workers—have formidable economic and political power.

Governments have also acquired substantial economic power in recent decades. Their extensive taxing power has given them the means to proliferate programs which can bestow or deny values to varied groups in society, and has also given them value-allocation powers inherent in taxes themselves—to favor some groups, discriminate against others. Governments have gradually expanded their influence and control over the economic machinery of societies. The power of totalitarian govern-ments is in part based on their control over virtually all the means of production; and the power of other types of governments has also ex-panded due to control of varied economic levers, and in some cases of ownership of sectors of the economy.

Reciprocal need is a major factor with respect to the actual influence of wealth and economic power. A politician who has a safe seat in a legislature and hence has little need for campaign contributions, or one who has alternate sources of money, is less likely to be influenced by offers of money. Governments may need the support of some economic interests such as the landed aristocracy or giant corporations to attain or remain in power, but not the support of others such as a disorganized labor or peasant force. Governmental programs may require the support of certain economic interests for effective implementation through volun-tary cooperation, but not of others: a farm program will require the support of organized farmers, but not necessarily of bankers or industrialist. And the general need of any society for economic stability if not growth makes possible the political clout of business, financial, and labor concentrations of power in strategic positions in the economy.

Numbers may constitute another major resource depending on the nature of the society, the political system, and specific situations. Despite occasional protestations to the contrary, they play major roles in democratic societies, for the necessity to attain and retain power via elections forces politicians to cultivate the support of many people. The gradual expansion of the suffrage in western societies during the past 150 years has led to a significant increase in the power of societies over their governments, while the denial of free elections in other systems has limited the power of the many over the few who govern.

But even without elections, numbers frequently play significant political roles. The culture of a society may influence some rulers to govern for the benefit of the majority, as the general principle of majority rule also predisposes politicians to act in this manner. The general need of governments for support—either for retention of political power, or to ensure the effectiveness of their policies—forces a degree of responsiveness to the intense demands of the masses.

Also, many great changes have been created or brought about by the varied spontaneous, unorganized actions by many people. Changes in election participation and patterns of election preferences have had a significant impact in varied societies. The propensity of many people to organize has significant political consequences. The unwillingness of French people to join organizations has significantly weakened the power of the many in French politics. Mass attitudes concerning legitimacy, prestige, or wealth have had their political consequences. Changes in mass habits and preferences have had major consequences for governmental programs, such as preferences for transportation via automobiles, or for housing in suburbia. And many governments have collapsed because they lost the support of the many. It is extremely risky for any government to resist mass demands when people have serious needs and demand satisfaction by governmental action.

Organization and cohesion The influence of numbers is substantially enhanced when people organize and when organizations act in a cohesive manner. For what individuals cannot do alone they can do by cooperating with others. Labor, consumers, various minority groups have attained what influence they have as the result of organization; the weakness of their power in many societies is often due to lack of cohesive organization, or organization itself. Farmers in many societies and consumers in most tend to be weak because they are inherently difficult to organize. Even students, when organized, can be a formidable force. In 1973 organized students played a major role in toppling a military regime in Thailand; and in 1968 in almost toppling French President DeGaulle. It is the element of organization which accounts for the power of the most formidable elements in contemporary politics—interest groups.

Organization is a resource of power for a variety or reasons. It constitutes a pooling of the resources of numbers, wealth, and sometimes information and skill. It has psychological impact as many appear to act in unison. Organizational spokesmen have certain prestige and legitimacy in that they appear to speak for the interests of many people united by common interests. They also constitute a response to needs of governments, which frequently need the support of organized groups not only as props for governmental power, but also for the successful formulation and implementation of governmental programs. Bureaucrats often need the support of organized groups in their constant conflict with other bureaucrats, with legislatures, and with other organized groups.

But the power of organized groups is also dependent on their elements of credibility and good will. Groups which have low credibility as representatives of the public interest, and group leaders who have low credibility as spokesmen for their groups, tend to have less influence. This also is a reason why groups which are divided unto themselves may lack influence. Also important is the relationship between the group and its target. When a relationship of good will exists, when for example a labor organization attempts to influence a pro-labor senator, success is facilitated. And the element of group cohesion is extremely important. Organizations that lack cohesion constitute relatively ineffective pooling of the varied resources of their members; tend to lack the prestige and credibility of groups which by their cohesion do appear to represent some common interests; and also tend to lack credibility with regard to bestowal or denial of values. The leader of a badly divided organization is not in a position to promise delivery of the votes of his or her membership.

Organization is also a major resource of governments and executives. The organized coercive instruments and bureaucracies of governments, both generally controlled by executives, constitute formidable resources of power. Authoritarian governments recognize the power of organization, and hence only rarely tolerate independent organizations. And successful revolutionary movements depend on organization, initially in skill in underground organization, then in the development of cohesive and disciplined revolutionary organization.

Knowledge, information, skill, and expertise. These are separate yet related resources which can be used to influence thought and behavior.

Ultimately, successful influence is dependent on political skill, which requires the skillful mobilization and manipulation of resources so that they will actually influence targets, the use of appropriate tactics and strategies in the exercise of influence. Such skill also requires knowledge of and information about political institutions and processes, and about the individuals or groups whose manipulation is necessary for successful influence. The most successful lobbyist is the one who knows how to make the most of the meager resources he or she may have in opposition to those with similar or other resources; who knows the characteristics of his targets and how they can be exploited; and who knows where in the labyrinth of the political process to apply resources in order to attain the most favorable outcome. The most successful politician is the one who is most skilled in manipulating people so that they will support him and his policies, or who is skillful in building coalitions of diverse people so that proposals can be enacted into law. All this requires exploiting whatever resources he or she may have—prestige, position, or legal authority —to appeal to the needs and problems of people and to enhance credibility. The successful leader of an organization is one who is skilled in manipulating the resource of numbers into cohesive organizations.

Expertise, knowledge, information, and skill are important resources of influence over and within governments. The governments of complex technological societies cannot govern without experts; they need expert information in the various specialized fields of economics, politics, social affairs; they have become increasingly dependent on experts in such fields as finance, taxation, energy, industry, agriculture, education, military affairs, and many others. Hence governmental bureaucrats with such expertise, and interest groups and other outside groups which supply expertise and specialized information about a variety of spheres of human activity, have become increasingly influential and sometimes dominant in the making of governmental decisions. The same phenomenon has occurred within many national economies, where effective economic power has passed into the hands of the technostructure—the managerial-technical-professional elites who have the information, skill, and expertise necessary to keep business and the overall economic machinery running. This has occurred not only in democratic and capitalist, but also in totalitarian societies: the technostructure has become increasingly influental over the policy-making processes of the Soviet Politburo. Although governmental leaders may have the ultimate legal authority with respect to the making of decisions, they may ultimately become the prisoners of the experts whose advice is essential for the making of decisions.

Time, attention, and energy are related to a topic discussed below, the motivation to actually exercise influence. But they are resources in the sense that influence is often dependent on the time and energy that individuals and groups may have (or are willing to use) to devote attention to and influence political processes. In many cases this effectively reduces the influence of numbers and enhances that of experts and leaderships, for many people either do not have or are unwilling to use time for political education much less participation. Determination and will power are related assets: intense and determined activists, individually or in organized groups, can be very influential even though they may only represent minorities (the student movement during the 1960's). This factor helps explain why power tends to gravitate into the hands of those willing to accept responsibility; not only do they accrue prestige and credibility, but their willingness to devote time, attention, and energy to public matters leads people to entrust them with authority in policy-making.

Violent force is, in one respect, a technique for exercising influence over thought and behavior, but the capacity to mobilize and use such force, which basically entails the successful mobilization of other resources plus in some instances weaponry, can be considered a resource. Its efficacy is rooted in the potential or actual infliction of damage to cherished values. Governmental use of force may deprive individuals and groups of freedom, property, or physical well-being and life. The use of force by groups in society may entail similar deprivations and threaten the stability and effectiveness of government by terrorism, mass demonstrations and riots, strikes which may cripple an economy, and insurrections.

The influence of violence depends on the force which can be mobilized and used, such as numbers of people and their organizational cohesion, skill in their effective manipulation, the use of wealth or other means to acquire weaponry, means of transportation and communication. Violent force may also enhance the influence of groups by its impact on the credibility of such groups, for violence displays how intensely groups are pressing their demands. When students seize administration buildings, labor engages in sit-in strikes, and minority groups demonstrate or riot, it indicates to many that the demands of these groups can no longer be safely ignored. And when governments threaten to or use force against other governments, credibility may be enhanced.

However, the use of violent force as the use of other power resources always entails cost-benefit assessments on the part of targets. Individuals, communities, and societies may capitulate to those wielding force if the threats to life, limb, homes, shops, factories, or means of earning a livelihood are clearly visible. Governments may capitulate or at least bend if public order is seriously threatened, social or economic stability endangered, or the political power of the leadership appears to be in serious jeopardy. But people and governments frequently calculate that other values and goals might be jeopardized by capitulating to force—social order and stability because yielding to force might encourage violence on the part of others; freedom because yielding might result in oppression;

power because yielding results in a loss of power. And targets of violent force—governments, groups in society, individuals—might also calculate that their prestige and credibility are at stake, and, hence, their power. Consequently, violent force, while sometimes successful given the skillful use in an appropriate conflict setting, often begets counter-violence. In many instances it can be counter-productive, it may influence targets in a direction opposite to that desired by the wielders of force.

POTENTIAL VERSUS ACTUAL POWER

In summary, then, the ability to influence depends on the possession of one or more of the resources of power which can be credibly manipulated to appeal to perceived value-needs of targets of influence, within limitations resulting from relations of good or ill will. But all this only makes for potential power, that the power-wielder can exert a degree of influence if he chooses to. The transformation of potential into actual power, the decision to actually use capabilities to influence thought and behavior, is a matter of choice for the power-wielder. Three major considerations appear to affect such choice.

The prime factor appears to be a conscious or unconscious cost-benefit evaluation, for while the use of power may result in the maximization of certain goals or values, it invariably entails some value costs. In a very general sense this means that some individuals (including some government officials) who place a very high value on power itself, on political activity, or on public service as they define it, will be quite prone to use whatever resources they may have most of the time and with respect to many issues. Others prefer to use their money, time, energy, position, or prestige in pursuit of other values such as wealth, leisure activities, knowledge, or acquiring non-political skills. Many millionaires shrink from any sort of political activity, while some people below the poverty line become activists.

More important, however, may be the cost-benefit assessment in terms of specific issues or conflicts—the particular stakes involved which affect the values of potential power-wielders. In such instances the calculation takes the form of assessing the value of what could be gained in the particular effort, as opposed to what it might cost. If the stakes are high in terms of particular interests or ideas, potential power will be translated into actual power. Labor leaders will become activated if the right to strike seems at stake; business people if profit potentials are seriously threatened; environmentalists if strong moves develop to terminate all pollution controls; pacifists if foreign policy seriously threatens war. Or, on a positive note, varied economic groups could be expected to participate actively on tax or major economic issues; educators on educational matters; the medical profession on health care conflicts; some religious groups on behalf of aid to denominational schools.

But costs will also be considered, since most groups prefer to conserve scarce resources and not spend them on peripheral issues. Business groups are not likely to devote time, attention, money, or other resources on conflicts involving religious issues, not only because no business values are at stake, but also because it might entail a loss of prestige, credibility, or good will with the religious and other groups directly involved in the conflicts. Labor leaders are not likely to become involved for similar reasons, and because the effort to influence might result not only in loss of organizational cohesion but perhaps their leadership positions. Politicians might be reluctant to be drawn into particular issues because it might cost them the support of some groups, or because they might wind up on the losing side and thereby lose their reputation for power.

A second factor which enters into the calculation as to whether to use resources involves possibilities of attaining goals by non-political means. Farmers entered American politics only when it came evident that only political action with respect to transportation rates and other matters would bring them a fair return on their produce; environmental groups when voluntary action by industries failed to stem pollution; religious or minority groups when it appeared that governmental protection was essential.

Assessment of the probability of success appears to be a third factor. Unless the stakes are extremely high, individuals and groups will use their power resources only when they anticipate some degree of success. If the power configuration in a particular conflict situation seems stacked against them, they may not even begin to exert influence, or may give up rather early in the conflict. Similarly, groups will not even try to influence particular government branches or officials totally immune to their influence.

THE RELATIVITY OF POWER

Since power results from the interaction of four very complex variables, no individual, group, or government can have a fixed or absolute amount of power. While some may generally have more power than others, influence is always relative to the specific target, the situation, and varies over time.

Power is relative to the specific target because of the elements of need, credibility, and good will, as well as the nature of some of the resources of power. Campaign contributions may be very influential with politicians who face hot contests for re-election, but they are likely to be less so with those who have tenure or occupy safe seats. A government energy agency which lacks its own data and expertise may become heavily dependent on the petroleum industry due to the latter's expertise, but the latter is not likely to be very influential with bureaucrats who have their own, or who have alternate sources of information and expertise. Liberals tend to enjoy substantial prestige and credibility with other liberals, but are far less influential with conservatives because there is less congruence of values between liberals and conservatives. Some officials, government agencies, or governments may need the support of some organizations —labor, religious types, tribal associations; others may not, or may have alternate sources of organizational support—rival labor or tribal organizations, business groups, farmers. Variations in need for support also affects variations in power over governments. Democratic governments tend to be more susceptible to external influences because of society's legal authority in the form of elections. Such susceptibility is further enhanced to the extent that pluralism and competition are characteristic of policy-making processes: when substantial competition occurs between branches of government, various bureaucracies, or other elements of government, those involved in the competition need varying degrees of support from groups in society. The development of bureaucratic competition within the Soviet Union, for example, has substantially enhanced the influence of various groups far removed from the pinnacle of power.

Power is relative to specific situations for similar reasons, and particularly because the impact of various resources and the configurations of competing power tend to vary from situation to situation. The petroleum industry is likely to be very influential in the formulation of energy policy because it will be highly motivated, will have information and expertise, may enjoy prestige and credibility with policy-makers involved in that sphere of policy, will be able to bring to bear a coalition of allied business and some labor interests, and may face but weak competition from such groups as conservationists, liberals, and others. But that same industry may be far less influential when it faces stiffer competition over tax issues or labor matters, and would have very little influence in such spheres as health or education policy even if it chose to exercise influence.

The power of individuals, groups, and governments also varies over time. Resources tend to fluctuate as the cohesion or funds of organizations change, and influence tends to match fluctuations in prestige and credibility. Labor tends to become less influential as economic downturns splinter its ranks and deplete its treasuries; the petroleum industry as high profits become public knowledge; governments as evidence of corruption or incompetence accumulates. Changes in public mood or opinion may produce changing relations between some groups and the government as such mood changes produce changes in the norms and goals of policy makers: such changes during the past decade seem to have produced declining influence on the part of business groups and increasing influence on the part of environmental and consumer groups.

PATTERNS OF POWER DISTRIBUTION

Even though power is relative, certain types of power distribution patterns are characteristic of various societies and political systems simply because in any setting, certain individuals and groups generally tend to have more power than others. Because of the specialization of functions which exists in every society, the different advantages that accrue to different specializations, inherited differences, and variations in biological and social inheritances, an uneven distribution of power exists in every political system. Such uneven distribution, however, takes on some distinct and significant patterns. Although the differences involved may often appear to be only differences in degree, meaningful qualitative differences result. The distribution pattern will always have a significant impact on the bargaining process described in Chapter 1.

CUMULATIVE CONCENTRATION VERSUS NON-CUMULATIVE DISPERSION

In some societies the distribution pattern is one of cumulative concentration, in that virtually all the resources of power have accumulated into the hands of a few groups, with few or none in the hands of most of society. A traditional agrarian society is a classic case: power is concentrated in such groups as the government, the landed aristocracy, and perhaps the military and the clergy. The rest of society—peasants, the small commercial class—has but the resource of numbers. In other societies the uneven distribution pattern is one of non-cumulative dispersion: some individuals and groups are still more powerful than others, but resources are so widely dispersed among many so as to preclude cumulative concentration in the hands of a few. Modern democratic societies are examples. Many societies fall somewhere on a spectrum between these two opposing poles.

ELITES: OLIGARCHY VERSUS POLYARCHY

Elite is a rather loose, but, nonetheless, useful term. By an elite we do not mean intellectual or similar kinds of superiority, we refer to superiority in power. Elites are groups which have substantially more power than others in society (and precisely what is meant by "substantially more" is impossible to assert with any degree of precision). When we refer to elites we mean those groups who have substantially more influence over authoritative decision-making than other people. Some kind of elite structure is characteristic of any society due to uneven distribution of power, and the elite structure may include a variety of elites on the basis of the primary roles they play in the society—political, economic, military, religious, and other elites. By these we mean the people who have more power than others within their respective spheres—the economic, religious, and other leaders. By the political elite we mean the political leadership. But the other elites may also play significant roles in political decision-making by transforming their potential into actual power. Elite structures on the basis of various criteria can be crudely grouped in a hierarchical arrangement of mid and marginal elites, with various graduations in between.

All political systems may be labeled as "elitist" in that elites either make the decisions or have more influence than others over them. But two kinds of elite patterns are politically significant, although again as with dispersion patterns, systems actually belong somewhere on the spectrum between two poles.

A pattern of oligarchy is an elite structure composed of only one or a very few elites functioning with respect to governmental policy. These few elites also tend to have either common or at least similar ideas and interests, and to represent only a few sectors or a small segment of society. Hence in oligarchic settings one finds but limited pluralism, competition, and representation in bargaining and decision-making.

A pattern of polyarchy is an elite structure composed of many elites. Such a pluralistic structure invariably entails a diversity of elites—a variety of economic, religious, and other kinds—and a consequent diversity of ideas and interests. A polyarchic structure generally tends to be at least somewhat representative of many segments and strata of society, of the diversity of ideas and interests that prevail in society. Hence in polyarchic settings policy-making tends to be pluralistic, competitive, and representative (as in modern democracies).

THE POLITICALLY RELEVANT AND THE APOLITICAL STRATA

Below the elite structure is the rest of society, which may be crudely grouped in two categories.

The politically relevant strata consists of those people who have some interest in and concern about politics and government. They at least have some awareness, no matter how dim, that government has some impact on their wallets and other interests, and some expectations that government action ought to allocate benefits to their values. They have often extremely limited but some information about the actual impact of governmental policies on their interests, and have some resources and, under some instances, are prone to use them to act on behalf of their interests. They include those groups likely to vote in elections, likely to strike on behalf of their interests, who may try to influence the political orientation of their peers, who might demonstrate or take up pitchforks if intense demands are not satisfied. This strata generally has but little direct influence over the actual process of policy-making and over the specific content of policy. But it is politically relevant because governments must take it into account for both political stability and effectiveness—because governments need the support of this strata for staying in power and for implementation of policies.

The apolitical strata consists of those who have absolutely no interest in and concern about politics, who frequently are totally unaware of the consequences of governmental action even with respect to their priority interests, and who seldom can be provoked into even the mildest form of political participation. They include the citizens who never turn out on election day; the illiterate masses in many cities of Africa and Asia; and the illiterate and apathetic peasants in the hills, mountains, and remote areas of Africa, Asia, and Latin America.

THREE STRATEGIES FOR EXERCISING POWER

Power-wielders generally have the option of using three basic strategies to modify, change, or control human thought and behavior by some kind of appeal to the target's values (although in many instances all three are combined). All three strategies are used by governments to secure compliance (which is why the distinction between authority, power, influence, strength, and force is so blurred). All are also used by politicians as they strive to build the coalitions needed to win elections, by would-be dictators to develop the support needed to launch a coup or revolution, and by direct and indirect participants in bargaining processes. And all are used, consciously or not, by groups in society and by society as a whole in order to exert group or general public influence over government.

Simple persuasion This is the most common strategy, and simply involves efforts to persuade a target that what the power-wielder proposes is good, just, rational, and in the public interest. However, it frequently overlaps with other strategies since persuasion may include efforts to convince a target that the proposed course of action will benefit or at least not hurt the target. But in any case, simple persuasion involves the manipulation of whatever resources the power-wielder may have, but particularly prestige, credibility, skill, information, and expertise.

A relationship of good will is important for effective persuasion, for the power-wielder must convince the target that there is congruence between the target's values and what the power-wielder proposes; the power-wielder must demonstrate that the recommended course of action is rational, just, and moral from the perspective of the target's ideological or value inclinations. A labor lobbyist, for instance, may have difficulty convincing a strongly business-oriented government official that increasing business taxes to increase unemployment benefits is really good for business and the economy. Credibility, skill, and perceived expertise are essential, for when arguments are presented, the facts and figures do not speak for themselves; what counts is whether targets believe the interpretation of facts and figures as presented by power-wielders who claim to have accurate information and expertise. The element of need is also important, for the effort to persuade will succeed only to the extent that the target needs information and advice, and is uncertain as to which alternative courses of action appear to be best or more rational. A legislator who is uncertain about the impact of a strip-mining bill on coal production is amenable to persuasion; one who is convinced that such a bill is absolutely essential for environmental protection is not likely to be influenced by coal mining interests.

This strategy is most common in bargaining processes. The parties directly and indirectly involved constantly exchange proposals and counter-proposals accompanied by efforts to persuade others. The efficacy of such persuasion depends on reciprocal needs, credibility, information, skill, and expertise. Some may be convinced from the very beginning that they know what the right course of action is, may not perceive a need for more information or argument, and will be quite immune to simple persuasion. Others may be uncertain, or prone towards a compromise, and may be swayed by arguments presented by those whose prestige and credibility are high, or who seem to have the accurate data and the expertise to interpret such data. Organizational cohesion may also be important, for organizations known to be divided with respect to an issue tend to be less influential than those who speak with one voice.

The strategy of simple persuasion is also the most common one used by governments which enjoy legitimacy and relations of good will with their societies—securing voluntary compliance with governmental actions by convincing people that such actions are just, rational, and in the public interest.

Inducements, the offer or grant of benefits Simple persuasion is frequently accompanied by inducement, involving the tacit, implicit, or explicit promise, offer, or actual delivery of some reward congruent with the values and goals of the target of influence. With regard to politicians it may involve campaign contributions, the promise of organizational support during an election, a promise to support him with respect to another bill he has a prime interest in, a promise to favor his constituency in some sort of way. With regard to bureaucrats it may be a promise of support in his conflicts with other bureaucrats, or support for a higher position. With regard to other groups, similar resources may be manipulated in an effort to build a strong coalition.

The promise or offer may be made quite explicitly, but quite often is tacit or implicit—hinted at rather than stated explicitly—for no target likes to be accused of taking a "bribe," no matter how legal or moral the offer of a reward might be. Simple persuasion may also entail inducements in terms of assessment of the consequences of action by a target of influence or a participant in bargaining. In certain situations, for example, a constituency may not need to explicitly try to influence its representative, for politicians are quite likely to assess the consequences of a particular action, such as a vote on a bill, in terms of their chances for re-election. Similar considerations influence the actions of executives, bureaucrats, and organizational leaders.

Governments also use inducements to provide voluntary compliance. Prisoners are promised parole if they behave in jail. Societies are promised peace, security, and prosperity if they support incumbents and comply with the law. Defeated groups may be promised benefits at a later date in return for their support. But in all instances, it is not merely resources which count, but also credibility and the intensity of needs or priority of values.

Coercion, the threat or infliction of damage also frequently accompanies both simple persuasion as well as the manipulation of inducements. It involves a threat, or the actual infliction of damage, to some values desired by the target—his or her pocketbook, position, authority, prestige, power, or freedom.

Threats to values are the basis of a government's coercive power, such as its legal authority to impose fines or to imprison. But the actual influence of such coercion again depends on credibility—the probability of getting caught and actually being punished; the effectiveness of organizations of coercion; and what might be considered as prestige or the relationship of good will—for lack of legitimacy may lead to such massive and widespread evasion of law so that the probability of getting caught and punished declines.

Threats may be involved and may accompany persuasion (as well as inducements) in bargaining processes: threats to withhold campaign contributions or organizational support; to demote bureaucrats; to oppose competitors on other issues if they fail to cooperate on the specific issue under consideration. And coercion is, of course, the prime strategy of violent force.

The efficacy of coercion is very much linked with the elements of credibility and need. Warnings and bluffs may be very effective, but if bluffs are called and the power-wielder fails to carry through, the efficacy of future threats is reduced and overall influence declines. With regard to needs, the threat to one value always entails questions as to what value may be threatened if the target of influence does comply, and the value the target is being asked to yield may be prized more than another value. A threat to withhold organizational support during an election campaign may be effective, but not if the target places a high value on prestige or independence, or on the support of competing organizations. A threat to strike and thus cripple the economy may be effective, but not if the government places a higher value on support from business, or on its ability to control the labor movement. A hungry man may value physical well-being more than freedom, and thus defy laws against stealing.

THE EXERCISE OF POWER: GOVERNMENT VERSUS SOCIETY

As stated earlier in this chapter, the balance of power between government and society is a perennial problem. Governments need power to effectively perform their functions and to secure compliance. But societies also need power, in a negative sense to restrict the power of government, and in a positive sense to ensure that government will be in the public interest. The balance of power between the two ultimately depends on the balance and interaction of resources, needs, credibility, and good will. And as will be pointed out in later chapters, governments seem to be gaining resources and thereby expanding their power, but may be losing capability to respond to expectations, and thereby losing credibility and good will.

The effective exercise of governmental power depends on the persuasive and coercive manipulation of governmental resources to respond to needs, and the consequent generation of credibility and good will. Governmental resources include its legal authority, its prestige and reputation for information, expertise, and skill to meet problems, the wealth and economic power it controls to dispense material and non-material values, and the organizational apparatus of the bureaucracy and enforcement machinery. By using these resources governments can respond to the needs of society; for domestic peace and order, for defense against external enemies, and whatever other functions appear to be necessary given the simplicity or complexity of the society. But the exercise of power to ensure influence over thought and behavior of society must be such as to enhance governmental credibility and trust in government—expectations that the government can be trusted with whatever functions it has, that its efforts to meet society's needs are likely to be at least partly successful. Governments must also maximize relationships of good will with society—a composite of legitimacy, credibility, and trust; for failure to do so may jeopardize influence over thought and behavior, and thereby the essential ingredient of widespread voluntary compliance.

The effective and durable exercise of governmental power thus requires a skillful and judicious mixture of simple persuasion, inducements, and coercion, all designed to convince people that they are benefiting and will continue to benefit from governmental action—convince them with respect to both ego-centered acquisitive values and normative values. Simple persuasion by such means as propaganda, speeches, a controlled education process are helpful, but will not do by themselves. Inducements, in the form of evidence that government actions are indeed satisfying the values and at least partly matching the expectations of the society and of the diverse groups that compose it, are essential. This is not to assert that governments must "buy" support; it simply means that they must function in such a manner that society is aware that the government is serving as a needed instrument of society. And occasional coercion is also essential; to control deviant behavior which can otherwise become infectious, to protect people and their property, and to ensure domestic peace and order.

The effective exercise of power by society requires a similar manipulation of the four components of power. Societies also have resources, although in many cases the balance is heavily tipped in favor of governments. They may have legal authority—in such forms as elections to change governments, elected representatives with direct roles and legal authority in decision-making, and constitutional limits on the power of governments. Certain groups and elites in society may have substantial prestige, leading to influence over both other groups and governments. The power of many governments is substantially limited by the prestige of such people as religious, nationality, minority, ethnic, and racial leaders. Individuals and groups in society may have substantial wealth and economic power. The power of numbers in society may be enhanced by the development of cohesive organization. And throughout the society there may be a pool of skill, information, and expertise which a government must tap in order to formulate and implement rational and effective policies.

Even the most authoritarian governments have some needs, which groups in society and societies as a whole can capitalize on. For stability and effectiveness they need legitimacy, support, and voluntary compliance. They need the support of the individuals and organizations with prestige and wealth. They need inputs of information and expertise. And governments also need domestic peace and social stability, for no functions can be effectively performed in settings of massive disobedience, chronic violence, or insurrection.

The exercise of society's power also requires a skillful and judicious mixture of simple persuasion, inducements, and coercion by the elites in society, to convince government officials that they and the government will benefit by responding to the varied demand inputs from society. Again, simple persuasion is helpful, but generally must be accompanied by inducements which appeal to the values of governments and their officials. Elites must demonstrate their credibility in the eyes of government, and also the credibility of the public will. And occasionally coercion also becomes necessary, as governments fail to respond to the vital pressing needs of either the entire society or of groups within it.

POWER AND THE ROLES OF POLITICIANS

The preceding discussion of the nature and role of power raises some fundamental questions about the role of politicians—empirical questions as to why and how politicians respond to power and why their decision-making depends on the configuration of power present in a conflict, and normative questions as to why and to what extent they should respond to influences from varied sources. These questions are implicit in the unfavorable connotations that the word politician has acquired in the American vocabulary—an individual primarily concerned with self-interest defined either in terms of power or money, who manipulates people for the pursuit of self-interest, and who is less concerned than he ought to be with the promotion of the public interest. To what extent are such characterizations valid?

POLITICIANS AND SELF-INTEREST

Politicians are human beings, and as such, base their actions at least partly on self-interest. Students normally do what they think they need to do to pass courses, workers what they think needs to be done to obtain job security and a satisfactory income, people in business are there to make profits, and politicians are interested in their political careers.

Whether elected or appointed, they must respond to power—to those individuals and groups in the government and in society whose support they need to maintain or enhance their careers. Some degree of "political expediency"—doing what seems best to maximize one's career—is a requisite of the profession. Failure to do so means a high probability of being replaced by someone who has been more politically expedient— who has generated more support among the powerful. Politicians in authoritarian societies and appointed bureaucrats in democratic societies need the support of certain elites; without their support they can neither remain in office nor govern effectively. Elected officials must develop the mass support needed to win elections, and this means responding to the power of some elites and of a significant proportion of the electorate. Responding to the effective demand inputs of the electorate—doing what the voters want done—is, after all, not incompatible with democracy.

POLITICIANS AND POLITICAL LEADERSHIP

The question of political leadership is a highly controversial one, as reflected by American uncertainty as to whether government ought to exercise leadership—do what needs to be done—or "followership"— respond to the will of the voters. The question is bound to be controversial for it entails normative considerations concerning the nature of the public interest, who ought to define it, or how it ought to be defined. But whatever the answer, it entails responsiveness to power.

The authoritarian answer emphasizes leadership. It stresses that the public is seldom aware of its true interests and generally is concerned only with varied short-term special interests, and that the general interest of all is not just the sum of the particular interests which prevail in society. The public interest ought, therefore, to be defined by some all-wise and public-spirited leader—a philosopher-king or benevolent despot who knows what is truly in the public interest and has the requisite power to govern accordingly. This answer has some seductive appeal, for many times public opinion is not the best way to determine what is in the public interest. People invariably demand lower taxes and more and better governmental services, and seldom recognize that short-term sacrifices may be necessary to attain long-term goals. But too often philosopher-kings have turned out to be Adolf Hitlers and Joseph Stalins. And too often it eventually develops that such authoritarian leaders define the public interest by responding to the power of certain elites in society who equate their interests with the public interest.

Hence a degree of followership, of responding to varied definitions of the public interest emanating from varied groups in society, seems warranted. But leadership is also required, which entails the education of the public with regard to immediate and future problems, and which on occasion requires defying the public will. A lesson of history is that governments which attempt to buy support by promising all kinds of rewards—bread and circuses—invariably fall as they cannot deliver the promised values. The ensuing pain and damage is suffered not only by the ousted leadership, but by society. If humans are to engage in purposeful action to attain rational and moral goals, they have to be organized and someone has to point the way. All this requires initiative and leadership.

The fundamental issues of politics involve conflicting human value preferences and disagreements over definitions of values and of standards of conduct. This places politicians into leadership roles with respect to conflict resolution. In this process decisions have to be made, values have to be selected and priority ordered, appropriate standards of conduct have to be defined and applied to specific situations and conflicts, and determinations have to be made as to what is truly in the public interest. But while politicians must, and generally do, play leadership roles while participating in such decision-making, from both an empirical and normative standpoint they must also be responsive to outside influences.

POLITICIANS AND THE PUBLIC INTEREST

Altruism is not a rare commodity in the political marketplace. Most politicians do endeavor to make decisions on the basis of justice, morality, rationality, the public interest, and similar criteria. But these are abstract standards, extremely complex and difficult to apply in a truly "objective" manner in specific conflict situations. Who is likely to benefit more, and how much more, and who is likely to pay more, and how much more, from a specific and complex tax program, energy policy, health care proposal, educational policy? And will the overall program in terms of the value creation and allocation consequences be just and equitable, rational and moral, in the short-term public interest, the long-term general interest, or merely good for some private interests? Human beings, given different backgrounds, experiences, roles in society, interests, and value systems will disagree over these and related questions. Given such conflicts of ideas and interests over specific policy issues, politicians tend to be highly uncertain as to what constitutes the right or rational thing to do. Only the most arrogant and imperious—and most dangerous—politicians spurn outside advice and counsel on such questions, and refuse to respond to outside influences.

POLITICIANS AND COALITION BUILDING

Effective leadership requires support, which entails responding to power to the degree required for the necessary degree of support. This requires the building of coalitions and the development of degrees of consensus. In democratic systems it requires the building of a coalition to win an election; it subsequently requires building coalitions and developing consensus behind specific policies and legislative proposals so that they will be enacted into law. In both democratic and authoritarian systems it requires development of a sufficient consensus in favor of specific policies and laws so as to ensure effective implementation—the assent of the affected elites, and at least the grudging acquiescence of affected masses. This requires transforming patterns of conflict into patterns of cooperation—pragmatic efforts to accomodate diverse and conflicting ideas and interests, bending some absolute principles to attain degrees of harmony and trust, and somehow emerging with a compromise which at least approximates the public interest. The absolutists who refuse to sacrifice sacrosanct principles, who arrogantly insist that their definition of the public interest is morally and rationally right, may be right. But as politicians, if they cannot build consensus and a winning coalition, they will be failures.

POLITICIANS AS GENERALISTS

Politicians play specialized roles with regard to the resolution of conflicts and the building of consensus-based coalitions. But in such specialized roles they function as generalists. The interests, ideas, and perspectives of experts usually develop out of their specialized fields. Economists, tax specialists, educators, businessmen, labor leaders, environmentalists, and other types are generally preoccupied with their primary spheres of endeavor, are equipped to make rational recommendations on the basis and because of their narrow expertise, but may not be aware of the consequences of their recommendations for other spheres and may be prone to define the public interest in terms of their speciality. It is the function of the generalist to integrate and harmonize the interests and ideas of experts so as to maximize the interests and ideas of the whole enterprise. Top level management of an industrial enterprise must harmonize material procurement, varied aspects of production, and distribution and sales; a military general must integrate the various service, procurement, and combat services which make up an army. The politician must integrate and harmonize all the varied aspects of governmental or public activity.

Political systems need generalists—individuals who have broad and general perspectives of society and of the varied aspects of human aspirations and endeavor. Politicians, within such a general perspective, must harmonize and integrate the diverse perspectives and recommendations of diverse experts, must harmonize economic policies as recommended by various specialists in finance, manufacturing, energy, agriculture, commerce, and harmonize these with activities in the fields of education, health, welfare, environmental protection, and many others. They must integrate these so that the interest of the whole, of the entire society, is truly served. Representatives must represent their entire constituency, which means harmonizing the diverse interests of diverse business, agricultural, transportation, educational, and other interests present within it. National executives must integrate such diverse interests on the national plane and also harmonize the interests of the varied regions which make up the nation. All this again entails at least partial accommodation of diverse and conflicting interests, and responding to varied influences as one strives to ascertain what is truly in the public interest.

The Assessment and Evaluation of Political Systems

3

We have introduced some basic concepts and propositions about government, politics, and power that furnish a foundation for political analysis. But the key to meaningful analysis is asking the right kinds of questions about political phenomena, such as questions that help us to understand systems, their origins and nature, their particular strengths and weaknesses, and questions that might help us to improve systems. This involves more than just gathering and examining empirical data. It entails the assessment and evaluation of facts and values on the basis of certain important criteria. In this chapter we discuss the processes of assessment and evaluation, and we discuss five key questions that should be asked about political systems and that apply major criteria.

1. What type of political system is a particular system? In what important ways do systems differ? What factors tend to produce different kinds of systems? What are the particular strengths and weaknesses of different types of systems?

2. What appear to be the goals and objectives of systems and their ruling elites? How all-embracing are such objectives? What are the origins and implications of such objectives?

3. What appears to be the relative stability of a system? What factors tend to breed stability or instability, and what are the consequences of instability?

4. What are the capabilities and performance characteristics of a system? To what extent does it appear to function as an instrument of society? What factors tend to enhance or reduce effective performance?

5. What appears to be the system's level of ability to adapt to change? What factors enhance or diminish adaptability to changing environmental needs and problems?

THE THREE APPROACHES OF POLITICAL SCIENCE

Before we explain these five questions in somewhat greater detail, we need to discuss briefly the processes of assessment and evaluation, and the separation of facts from values that is inherent in these processes. Basically, the three major approaches and problem areas of political science are involved.

The empirical descriptive-explanatory approach and problem area is primarily concerned with factual data that describes and explains political phenomena. It emphasizes the analysis and appraisal of empirical data, the sorting out of more from less significant data, the establishment of important relationships among facts, and the drawing of conclusions based on certain criteria pertaining to significance. The general objective is to develop empirically-based propositions and generalizations (empirical theory) about universal political realities, much as astronomers develop theories about the behavior of solar systems, planets, and other bodies that make up the physical universe. Factual description of the real nature, structure, and functioning of political systems, coupled with explanation of the reasons for such structures and functioning, is the primary focus. Empirical assessment is inherent in this approach in that it entails the formulation of factually-based judgments and appraisals about the nature and significance of political systems and phenomena.

Some of the major questions asked in connection with this approach have initially been explored in the preceding chapters; these and others will be explored further in later chapters. What do political systems actually do, how do political processes function in certain societies, how do decisions get made, and why do processes function the way that they do? Why, and under what circumstances, do certain patterns of conflict and cooperation develop, and what are the political consequences of such patterns? What is the nature of political power, what is the actual distribution of power within a system, and what appear to be the consequences of different patterns of power distribution? What are the significant features and consequences of environmental settings, linkage-communication systems, decision-making processes, and policy output patterns? Empirical assessment involves the development of empirically-based generalizations about our five major areas of concern: the nature of systems, their objectives, their stability and performance characteristics, and their adaptability to change. It entails factual generalizations about the actual value creation and allocation patterns of systems. But, as will be discussed later, the actual extent to which such factual analysis can be separated from value considerations is a matter of some controversy.

The normative approach and problem area While the empirical approach is primarily concerned with realities, or "things as they are," the normative approach is primarily concerned with "things as they ought to be," which are the preferred or desirable political norms and values as applied to means and ends. It involves the definition and application of moral values —the rights and duties of humans, proper standards of conduct, justice, priority ordering among human values—in relation to political structures, processes, goals, and value allocation patterns. Although realities and empirical data are by no means ignored, normative theory endeavors to develop value-based rather than empirically-based generalizations and propositions as to how systems ought to be structured, how they ought to function, how policies ought to be formulated, who ought to have power, what goals ought to be pursued by political means, and how values ought to be allocated.

Evaluation entails making value judgments based on values we deem to be of high priority. It entails assessment of factual data, but includes judgments about the merits and demerits of systems based not merely on the facts themselves, but on human value preferences and moral standards. The overall effort is to go beyond description and explanation and to prescribe an ideal political order and its specifics. Analysis is undertaken with ethical concerns about proper and legitimate means to pursue proper and legitimate ends. The central concern is the development of universal and specific generalizations (normative theory) about political structures, processes, behavior, and goals, which appear to be desirable on the basis of preferred norms and values. The normative approach to our five key questions asks what type of political system a society ought to have, what goals it ought to pursue, whether stability is desirable in certain circumstances, what a system's performance characteristics ought to be, and what kinds of change may be desirable.

The prescriptive approach and problem area is primarily concerned with political reform and prescriptions for the improvement of systems. It combines both the empirical and normative approaches to the extent that it is concerned with closing the gap between what *is* and what *ought to be.* Proposals for reform are invariably based on normative considerations or value preferences with respect to the structure and performance of systems, political goals, and value distribution patterns. But they are also based on the assessment and evaluation of factual data, which lead to conclusions about the inadequacies or demerits of a system. Empirical data is also essential in determining why systems are not performing as desired, what constraints on change may exist within the system or society (or within human nature), what specific means seem most likely to produce the ends we desire, and what the consequences of proposed reform measures might be.

The five key questions we pose are also relevant to the prescriptive approach. Assessment of the various types of systems and objectives of political elites provides data about the alternative ways governments can be structured and processes can be organized so as to attain preferred goals. Empirical data about stability gives us clues as to how to attain stability, the consequences of stability or instability, and its relationship to effectiveness. Assessment of the performance characteristics of different systems can educate us about how to use political means to maximize some values, the probable costs in terms of other values, and the probable consequences of certain power distribution patterns. The focus on political change can provide needed facts about the nature of changes taking place, the choices available to societies, the possible means of controlling change, and the probable or possible consequences for human values of change.

EVALUATION AND THE PERMANENT ISSUES OF POLITICS[1]

Ever since humans began to associate with one another and to develop primitive forms of government, certain basic political issues have involved controversy. These issues remain permanent issues because they involve conflicts over basic values. Since the beginning of time, humans have argued as to whether values are absolute and universal, whether they are simply matters of preference, or whether one man's values are as good as another's. They have disagreed over the origin of values and over how one can ascertain what a proper value is—whether values are learned through divine revelation, logical reason, intuition, or analysis of factual data. Humans conflict over the definition of values—what constitutes justice, freedom, equality, the rights and obligations of man; over priority ordering among values—whether freedom comes before equality, order before justice; and over what values should be pursued individually or collectively. The conflict over what is truly in the public interest dates since the beginning of man. These basic issues will remain permanent ones because they entail different human preferences, different value-based solutions to fundamental questions and problems of government. None of these questions can be fully answered on the basis of empirical data.

[1]For an excellent discussion of these issues see Leslie Lipson, *The Great Issues of Politics,* 4th ed. (Englewood Cliffs, N.J.: Prentice-Hall, Inc., 1970).

68

Who should rule, who has the right to govern, who is best qualified to rule, is perhaps the most fundamental question which through time has evoked a variety of responses. It is linked with the question of equality, and with different versions of what equality entails. One school of thought argues for rule by the people: that humans are basically equal, that commoners are qualified to govern themselves and must at least have equal opportunity to participate in processes of government. Another school argues for rule by elites: that humans are inherently unequal, that only those specially qualified should rule, and that people should be viewed as subjects of the state to be ruled over, not as participants in decision-making. But elitists invariably quarrel among themselves as to which kinds of elites are best qualified to rule, and whether the right to rule is derived from a mandate from some deity, or the basis of ideological principles, from racial or biological superiority, or from superior wisdom. And there are a variety of alternative answers to this problem which combine elements of elitism with rule by the people. No definitive answer to the basic problem can be established only on the basis of empirical evidence. All answers entail human preferences based on different values, assumptions, and biases.

How rule should be performed is a related question, which entails questions relating to the proper organization of government—whether authority should be concentrated or dispersed. Elitists generally argue for concentration of power—since a divinely-anointed king or some kind of elite has the right to rule, authority must be concentrated in the hands of those qualified. Populists who favor people power opt for dispersed power, as Americans who insist on separation of power between the states and the federal government and checks and balances resulting from dispersion of power among the three branches of government. Still others favor some kind of balance, as the British who favor some dispersion but prefer to concentrate authority at the national level and in the hands of Parliament and its ministers.

The answers to these questions also depend on value preferences and priorities. Those most concerned with domestic stability and order tend to opt for concentrated power; those who emphasize freedom accept that a degree of instability and low effectiveness is the price that may have to be paid, and hence prefer decentralization of power. Similar questions pertain to other values; some prefer concentrated power because they perceive governmental intervention as necessary to economic stability and growth, or to promote equality by concentrated governmental efforts to relieve poverty and promote social justice.

Another basic question concerns the legitimate scope of governmental activity; how broad its authority over society ought to be, where the line lies between private and public endeavor, in what spheres and to what extent the government ought to intervene and play roles, and what the patterns of value allocation ought to be. The American tradition has been to venerate individual freedom, self-help, and voluntary cooperation, and hence has emphasized a limited role for government. Yet some Americans and some other societies emphasize equality, and hence support governmental efforts to promote this value by efforts to redistribute wealth and income, and actions to eliminate discrimination. Still others vigorously champion the idea of very active governmental intervention in and even control of the economic system as the way to material plenty and equality. The American tradition has been for separation of church and state; but in the past, and in some societies today, the tradition has been for very close links and for governmental action to promote particular religious creed—as some Hindus, Zionists, and Muslims today press for theocratic states in India, Israel, and Islamic States.

These and similar fundamental issues are beyond the purview of empirical political science, of the descriptive-explanatory approach which is primarily concerned with factual data. One can, in a very real sense, speak about the immunity of values to scientific analysis, for one cannot establish the validity or priority of values only by examining empirical data and drawing generalizations from such data. One cannot solely on the basis of facts assert who is most qualified to rule, how a government ought to be structured, what goals ought to be pursued through political processes, what values ought to be created by government, and what a government's value allocation pattern ought to be. Hence in this sense, facts and values are separate and distinct.

But facts and values are also related, in that a concern with values must include a concern with facts. Facts are relevant with respect to human preferences in three distinct ways. First, facts can be helpful in clarifying the varied meanings or ramifications of complex values, and with explaining the real alternatives from which humans can choose. Second, facts are necessary for the selection of the right means to attain preferred ends. Third, they can help us to assess the possible or probable consequences of human choices: the kinds of ends likely to result from selected means, and also the probable consequences of the selection of certain ends. Factual assessment of political systems along five dimensions—types of systems, scope and objectives, stability, performance characteristics, and adaptability to change—can tell us much about the real choices we have in the modern world with respect to structuring political systems and pursuing various goals by political means. These five dimensions can help us to determine what kinds of political systems are most likely to maximize the values we accord high priority to. And factual assessment can help us to make an educated guess at least about the probable consequences of our choices concerning the basic questions of who should rule, how rule should be performed, and what goals we want to pursue through political action.

The construction of a typology involves determining significant shared and distinguishing characteristics among systems—the ways in which some systems appear to be similar in nature, the significant ways some systems differ from others. Typologies of systems are very useful analytical tools. They help us focus on the important characteristics of systems, such as the location of power and the real nature of decision-making. They are useful for establishing relationships among the various components of systems—such as the kinds of environmental settings which seem to produce specific kinds of systems, or the policy output patterns peculiar to certain kinds of systems. They are very useful with respect to assessment of relative stability, performance characteristics, and adaptability of various kinds of systems. Typologies are also important with respect to evaluation, in that their use may provide information about the capability of different types of systems to maximize or minimize certain values.

Systems have many characteristics, hence, it is possible to construct elaborate typologies based on a variety of criteria. Rather elaborate typologies are warranted by the fact that in the modern world some 150 national-level systems exist, plus a tremendous number and variety at subordinate levels. Complex typologies are also needed to avoid simplistic conclusions about the characteristics and performance of systems. But for our purposes we can use what is essentially a simplistic typology of three: democratic, authoritarian, and totalitarian systems. In using this typology we focus on the key criteria of power: the degree of concentration or dispersion within government, and the power of government over society.

Assessment of systems to ascertain what type they are entails factual analysis; it does not involve making value judgments about superiority or inferiority. But values do intrude to some extent in the constructing of models and in defining the basic attributes of each type.

Any typology requires the construction of descriptive models (not normative models as to what is desirable). A model is an intellectual construction of a "perfect" case, a system which incorporates all of the characteristics of a particular type; thus "model" totalitarian system does not mean an ideal totalitarianism in the sense of the best kind, but simply a model in the sense that it possesses all the characteristics which the analyst associates with that type of system. Descriptive models are thus divorced from reality, not photographic descriptions of actual systems in the real world, because specific systems seldom if ever perfectly match the description of the model—the mental construction of the analyst.

We will not only avoid an elaborate typology but also the construction of models of democracy, authoritarianism, and totalitarianism. For the fulfillment of our basic purpose does not require the complexities involved in either intellectual exercise. But it is important to note that no existing system is a case of the perfect type, and that with respect to the crude yardstick of concentration and dispersion of power, it is more often a case of differences of degree. Thus some democracies are characterized by substantial dispersion of power, others less so; some authoritarian systems seem almost dictatorial, while others seem somewhat pluralistic in their power configurations. But it is also evident that at certain points the overall cumulative weight of differences of degree is so great that significant differences in degree do constitute differences in kind. Hence it is valid to assess specific real systems as democratic, authoritarian, or totalitarian. But assessment should also be thought of as placement of specific systems somewhere along a spectrum between extreme dispersion and extreme concentration of power—between a nonexistent democracy in which power is diffused to every one, and a non-existent totalitarianism where one individual has absolute power over both government and society.

Hence, even with respect to this simple typology, rigorous empirical analysis of systems is essential to determine which category a particular system fits into, and where along the spectrum it should be placed. Objectivity and a value-free approach are desirable, but a degree of subjectivity is almost certain to intrude, particularly as models are constructed describing the specific characteristics of systems. Also, analysis is required not merely of governmental structures and processes, but also of the distribution of power in the society and the linkage-communication system.

DEMOCRATIC SYSTEMS

The literature of political science is rich with variant definitions of democracy and with debate over the basic characteristics of this type of system. Most of the contemporary debate, however, has been a normative one, over what democracies ought to be. Some would restrict the label to what is frequently called Populist Democracy—systems in which there is very broad and perhaps even an equal distribution of power, so that the people really rule. They dismiss contemporary Representative Democracies (in which the people rule only indirectly in that they select their representatives to govern) as frauds because, they charge, elites rather than masses invariably rule. Others insist that Representative and even Elitist Democracies qualify for the label. But on the basis of our crude but useful yardstick—broad dispersion of power throughout the entire political system, and the decision-making processes, and substantial limits to the power of government over society—it is evident that there are substantial and most often clear-cut differences between democratic and other types of systems. Of the 150-odd systems in the contemporary world, perhaps 20 to 25 qualify for the label of democracy, although these 20-25 vary with regard to dispersion of power, power of governments, and institutional arrangements.

More specifically, referring to patterns of power distribution described in Chapter 2, these systems are characterized by polyarchy, broad and non-cumulative dispersion of power, and large politically relevant strata, so that policy-making is very pluralistic, competitive, and representative. As in any system, elites do make the decisions, but are many and varied in their interests and ideas, intensely competitive, and generally representative of many-to-most of the varied segments and strata that make up the society. Such pluralism is manifested by a multiplicity of governmental structures and of organized political groups in society, all involved in highly competitive bargaining processes which produce compromise outcomes rather than policies by command or dictation.

Other characteristics of democracy both reflect and reinforce such pluralism, competition, and representation. Constitutions disperse legal authority within government, limit the legal authority of government, provide for civil rights and liberties of citizens, and establish the legal-political equality of citizens. Basic laws and procedures provide for more-or-less equitable representation, for free elections so that people may choose their representatives and perhaps even the general course or direction of public policies, and for decision-making by qualified majority rule—some protection for minority rights and interests. A variety of means and channels usually exist to provide varied groups in society access to decision-making processes, to ensure varying degrees of popular consultation during these processes, and to provide substantial responsiveness to the public will.

AUTHORITARIAN SYSTEMS

Substantial diversity characterizes the 100-plus contemporary systems which merit the label of authoritarian systems. Some have the trappings of democracy—elections, parliaments, political parties—but hardly the substance. Some are absolute monarchies; some are ruled by military dictators or juntas, or by civilians who took off their uniforms after seizing power; some are ruled by dictators elevated to power by revolutions, mafia-style politics, or even elections. They differ in terms of the number who have ultimate legal authority, in degrees of concentration of power, in efforts to extend government control over society, and in the socio-economic composition of the elites who either hold or control governmental power. But they all have two things in common; substantial concentration of power within government and in the society, and few if any legal restraints on the power of government over society.

More specifically, power configurations tend to be oligarchic and to be characterized by cumulative concentration of resources. Large, politically relevant strata may exist in that many people may have political interests and expectations, but tend to have few if any means to influence the political elites. Policy-making patterns tend to be significantly less pluralistic—although in contemporary systems it is seldom a case of one or even very few elites; less competetive—although again, much competition may not be open and visible, and less representative—although some elites involved in policy-making may at times act as surrogate representatives of some sectors of society. In general, bargaining tends to be significantly less open and extensive than one finds in democratic systems; and patterns of command decision, indifference, or repression may be fairly common with respect to conflict resolution processes.

Other characteristics again both reflect and reinforce such concentration of power. There may be occasional elections, but thoroughly controlled so as to guarantee results. Legislative bodies may exist, but are composed of individuals appointed by executives or elected via rigged elections, and will have very limited if any legal authority. Political parties may be tolerated, but if so a single party controlled by the government dominates the party system. The judicial system is controlled by the executive; civil liberties are either non-existent or only casually treated; a powerful bureaucracy, police, and military apparatus are available for coercive control of society, and power is frequently personalized in some individual. In general, a sharp gap between the rulers and the ruled is clearly evident.

Totalitarian Systems

Some diversity also characterizes the 15–20 systems which merit this label. These systems are special variants of authoritarian systems, they have all the basic characteristics of authoritarian types. What distinguishes these systems from others, however, is the word "total." They attempt, in varying degrees and with varying degrees of success, total control of the total society—to ultimately control all aspects of human activity, in all of the economic, social, cultural, religious, and other spheres of human endeavor, and sometimes even try to control internal relationships within families. When totalitarian regimes seize power, they first attempt to atomize society so that nothing stands between the government and lonely individuals—to destroy all organizations and institutions which stand between the government and society and which might constitute means whereby individuals could resist the power of the state. After this, new organizations are developed, controlled by the political elites, to regiment and control all the various segments of society. Most communist and some fascist systems fall into this category.

Again, visible manifestations reflect and reinforce such efforts at total control. An official ideology is manipulated, generally all-embracing in its doctrines, which provides a mystique for rule, legitimizes the system, its rulers, and its policies, and is manipulated in an effort to develop ideological uniformity among all people—to influence their thought, and thereby ensure behavior as desired by the rulers. An authoritarian government-controlled single party is organized, but with membership restricted to selected elites, and designed as a tool to regiment and control people. Other mass organizations—open to mass membership are organized, but again for purposes of regimentation and control. A comprehensive police system exists and uses organized terror for effective control of society. The government has a monopoly of control over mass media. A centralized and hierarchically organized bureaucracy attempts to control not only the entire economic system, but also other spheres of human endeavor.

THE SCOPE AND OBJECTIVES OF POLITICAL ELITES

For purposes of assessment and evaluation it is important to analyze not merely the means of government—the type of system—but also the ends, the objectives political elites set for themselves, and the scope of governmental endeavor. Goals have normative implications, and need to be evaluated on the basis of preferred norms and values. They are also related to other assessment criteria—their relationship to type of system, stability, performance characteristics, and adaptability to change. We need to determine whether there is any relationship between types of systems and the kinds of goals pursued, and whether a particular type is commensurate with the goals the elites claim to aspire to. Is an authoritarian or totalitarian system, for example, compatible with the avowed aspirations of the political elites which control them—ultimate freedom, democracy, and equality? We need to analyze what kinds of conditions or factors seem to produce certain kinds of goals, what relationships there may be between certain kinds of goals and political stability, effectiveness, and adaptation, and the possible consequences of goals and of governmental actions taken in their pursuit. Above all we need to assess and evaluate goals in terms of the means-ends relationship: can the objectives set by political elites be attained through the means selected, and what kinds of outcomes seem to be inherent in the means chosen by elites.

The assessment of objectives presents some special analytical difficulties. For one, regimes usually pursue a wide variety of objectives, not always compatible with each other, and hence again political realities would seem to require complex classification schemes. A distinction between political goals—whether the elites intend to maintain or radically change the political system and the distribution of power—and socioeconomic goals—what their objectives appear to be with respect to society—seems particularly important. Objectives are often also highly dynamic, subject to frequent and sometimes drastic change as either elites or circumstances change. Some regimes appear to have relatively clear-cut objectives and govern accordingly; others appear to have none at all, save the retention of political power; and in some cases substantial intra-elite conflict with respect to goals prevails. A distinction must also be made between rhetoric and reality, in that some elites proclaim certain aspirations—socialism, development, equality, democracy—but pursue policies which appear to be totally incommensurate with their publicly-avowed objectives.

Despite these problems and complexities, a relatively simple classification has some utility for assessment and evaluative purposes:

1. Tradition, or Status-Quo Oriented Systems or Governments. These are systems or governments whose prime objective is to maintain and bolster the traditional system and society—to maintain things as they are in political, social, economic, and cultural spheres, and particularly with respect to the configuration of political power. Sometimes changes are pursued in one sphere, particularly in the economic sector such as economic growth or industrialization; but are accompanied by efforts to hold back change in other spheres. But in all cases where some degree of change is accepted as desirable or inevitable, the objective is a slow and controlled pace of change.

2. Change-Oriented Systems or Governments. In these, there is a commitment to substantial change in any one of the spheres, or to a transformation of the entire society and all of its ideas and activities—to substantial changes in political, economic, social, and cultural spheres. But a distinction must be made between two distinct types of change-oriented systems of governments (the distinction made here, despite the use of labels which have value connotations, does not assert the superiority of one or the other type).

a. Reactionary regimes or systems, where the objective is to return the society, or some aspect of that society, back to an earlier condition: to a previously-existing type of political or economic system, to a traditional culture or way of life, or to a previously-existing distribution of power which favored certain elites or groups which currently have less power then before.

   b. Progressive systems or governments, with an overall objective to transform the society into some kind of new society, or to change the culture, way of
life, social structure, economic system, or political system in a new direction.
Some such change-oriented governments are frequently labeled as reformist
types: they shade off from status-quo types in that they seek gradual, relatively
slow, and controlled changes. Others are appropriately labeled radical types, in
that they seek very rapid, forced-draft changes in one or more spheres, or the total
transformation of the entire society.

   Closely related to objectives are characteristics of systems and governments with respect to the scope of their endeavors and objectives. A
simple threefold typology distinguishing between *limited, interventionist,
and totalitarian* systems, has some utility, but is limited because of the rich
variety that exists in the modern world. Distinction among types is also
hampered by the loose way in which various labels are commonly used
today.

   In a few corners of the modern world some relatively limited systems
of government that undertake only a limited range of tasks and functions
and endeavor to promote only a few values for the society, still exist.
These are the governments that perform tasks related to basic governmental functions: the maintenance of domestic peace and defense against
external enemies. Other functions are performed only in a limited way:
education, road construction, some public works, coining of money, or
other limited actions to stimulate trade and commerce. In such systems
most activity takes place outside the political sphere and is left to individual self-help or voluntary cooperation among groups in society.

   The contemporary trend is in the direction of the interventionist state.
This involves increasing governmental intervention in more spheres of
human activity and intensifying governmental efforts to create and promote more types of tangible and intangible values. The trend is towards
more politicization of human life, and less individual self-help and private
voluntary cooperation. Sometimes the term "Positive-Welfare State" is
used, sometimes merely the label "Welfare State," and sometimes the
terms "Socialist Democracy" or "Socialist State." Whatever the label,
most modern governments endeavor or pretend to play a positive rather
than a negative role in human affairs with the avowed purpose of promoting the general welfare of the entire society. Most pronounced is governmental intervention in economic affairs: concerted efforts to regulate or
even manage the economic system in order to promote economic stability, growth, and prosperity. Also pronounced are so-called welfare activities: while individual standards of living are still left to individual
self-help, governments attempt to provide for the security and well-being
of all citizens and to ensure that basic needs of all people are met by a
variety of social security measures, governmental health care programs,
public housing facilities, welfare payments, and subsidized services for

the poor. The pursuit of "social justice" is an avowed objective of many such governments, which they pursue through various tax programs, welfare measures, and free or subsidized services designed to reduce disparities of wealth and income.

One important characteristic, however, distinguishes the interventionist system from the totalitarian system: in the former, some kind of a line, whether fuzzy or clear-cut, exists between the public and the private sphere. The line is often most pronounced with respect to the economy. In an interventionist state, particularly a limited one such as the United States, most of the means of production (factories, banks, farms, stores) continue to be privately owned and operated, while governmental action may substantially limit the freedom of owners, workers, farmers, and even consumers; but private ownership is still a key characteristic. In some, however, the line may be a bit blurred because of the existence of a "nationalized sector" or a "mixed economy." Some basic industries may be government owned and operated, while others may be in private hands. Thus, in Britain, coal, steel, transportation, and other means of production have been nationalized, but the bulk of the economy is still in private hands. Overall, in an interventionist state, despite the occasional massive governmental intervention, the scope of government is still limited in contrast to a totalitarian system.

Totalitarian systems are those in which government endeavors to establish and maintain almost total control over the entire society by regulating the economic, social, and cultural life of the society to the point where no visible line exists between the public and private spheres. Communist systems (for a variety of ideological reasons, which need not concern us here) proclaim themselves to be "socialist systems which are building communism"; but they are quite different from the socialist-democracy type of interventionist state in that they at best merely tolerate some private spheres of human activity not subject to control by the state. In the economic sphere, for example, some private enterprise may be tolerated, such as small farms, shops, and industries. Some degree of religious or cultural freedom may also exist. But in all cases the private sphere is merely tolerated, either for economic or political reasons, and is always subject to governmental intervention. Hence, a major characteristic of a totalitarian system is unlimited scope of governmental action.

THE RELATIVE STABILITY OF SYSTEMS AND GOVERNMENTS

From a normative standpoint, political stability may not be much of a virtue, either because some regimes try to maintain stability by repressive means, or because the objectives they pursue seem totally incompatible with cherished values. But stability is an important assessment criterion for it is closely related to system performance, in that unstable systems and governments simply cannot govern effectively, cannot adequately perform any of the functions they choose to perform. Hence, it is important to assess a particular system's stability, and also to analyze what factors, both in general and with respect to particular systems, tend to promote stability or instability. What is the relationship between stability, legitimacy, effective performance, type of system, regime objectives, or adaptation to change? What are the consequences of prolonged instability? What are the consequences of changes within the component parts of political systems for stability? Under what conditions might a successful revolution be desirable because it promises stability?

The assessment of relative stability poses special analytical problems, partly because a distinction must be made between surface and real stability. Many systems and governments seem to be quite stable, until a series of explosions reveal that they really have been living a very precarious existence. Others may experience periodic outbreaks of violence, yet demonstrate surprising tolerance for disorder and be quite stable. Nor is stability to be equated with the absence of change, for failure to change in response to new needs may bring about instability. And the stability of any system or government is also constantly subject to change, as systems and governments either adapt or fail to adapt to changing environmental conditions. A distinction must also be made between system and governmental stability, with the former considerably more important.

By systemic stability we mean the high probability of the long-term durability of a system with respect to its most basic structures and features; the basic political structures and processes, basic methods and scope of conflict resolution, the fundamental configuration of power within the system, basic methods and styles of government, and long-term basic objectives. It does not mean the absence of change, but rather gradual and evolutionary change, gradual adaptation of the system to the changing domestic and international environment. In a negative sense, systemic stability means the absence of frequent radical constitutional changes or breakdowns, the relative absence of revolutionary threats or of fundamental upheavals, and the absence of chronic large-scale violence within the society. Relative systemic stability seems most essential for system and governmental effectiveness.

By governmental stability we mean the high probability of the long-term durability of personnel and major policy orientations. We mean prospects that not necessarily the same individuals but the same types of individuals and elites will probably continue to govern the system for some years or decades to come, that they will continue to pursue the same general objectives and use the same kinds of methods to attain them, and that they will gradually adapt their policies to changing conditions in the environmental setting. We mean continuity in the sense that changes in personnel—whether by elections or coups or even violent revolutions—will not produce any significant changes in the types who govern or the policies pursued. In the negative sense, governmental stability means the absence or low probability of pendulum-like swings in policy or goals, but merely the probability of somewhat different policy orientations, but not radical changes, as personnel change. This type of stability may not be as important as systemic, but nonetheless can be important, for frequent radical changes in personnel and policy, even though they may not have any impact on the system, may substantially reduce political effectiveness.

THE PERFORMANCE OF POLITICAL SYSTEMS

The analysis of the relative performance of political systems is closely related to evaluative criteria—performance to maximize preferred values in accordance with preferred normative standards and rules of political behavior. Performance is linked with all of the permanent issues of politics, with the issues of who should rule, how rule should be exercised, and the legitimate scope of governmental endeavor. Hence the base for evaluating performance ought to be consideration of the legitimate scope of government, what tasks a government ought to engage in, what services it should provide, what the public interest really is, what values governments ought to create, and what their patterns of value allocation ought to be. Governmental performance can then be assessed on the basis of this value-based criteria. But it is precisely in this sphere of performance that facts and values are very closely linked, and that more-or-less objective assessment is essential for meaningful evaluation. And both assessment and evaluation can proceed from one common starting point—performance as instruments of society.

POLITICAL SYSTEMS AS INSTRUMENTS OF SOCIETY

The statement that it is the function of a political system to serve as an instrument of society would appear to be more of a normative than a descriptive statement. It asserts what governments ought to do, and is not in accord with what many systems actually do. Many systems clearly function as instruments of governments or of the elites who control governments. And in the past it has often been argued that governments function as instruments of some deity, not of the people. Yet generally, in both past and present, humanity has tended to accept the principle of political systems as instruments of society. Kings who justified their rule on the principle of divine right, dictators who justified theirs on the basis of ideological principles and special skills, acknowledged that their function was to rule for the good of the people, or claimed that they incarnated the general will or the interests of the people.

What little we know about the origins of government in the dim and distant past attests to the validity of the principle. Governments basically came to exist because they provided a society with a capacity for unified purposive action, means for the attainment of certain goals. They developed because of their capacity to perform certain essential tasks and to provide certain services which are difficult-to-impossible to perform and provide through individual self-help or voluntary cooperative action. They are a response to human needs, and they are of great utility if and when their authority is coupled with legitimacy, and hence becomes effective authority with respect to performance of necessary functions.

But beyond this basic principle, the issue of what types of functions governments ought to perform becomes mired in controversy. A global consensus of sorts has emerged with respect to only functions relating to ensuring security by maximizing domestic peace and defense against external enemies. But even this consensus is marred by controversy over the meanings of these terms, over methods, and over acceptable costs. Such controversy is inevitable, simple because whatever governments do, controversial values and value allocation patterns are involved. People might agree on what values governments should promote, but then will disagree over value priorities or specifics. The French Revolution of 1789 enshrined three major goals in the French pantheon of values: Liberty, Equality, and Fraternity. Ever since then the French have argued over which one takes precedence.

But one can separate the value-laden question of what functions a government ought to perform from the factual question of how well they perform with respect to whatever functions they do perform. It is possible to make a more-or-less objective assessment of the performance characteristics of specific systems or of types of systems with respect to specific types or kinds of functions and value creation and allocation. One can ascertain on an empirical basis how well a system performs the law-and-order function, or promotes economic prosperity and growth, without assuming that these are functions that ought to be performed. One can also objectively assess what the costs of performance are—what values are being sacrificed in order to maximize those preferred by governments. Empirical data can help to determine what relationship there might be between types of systems, their objectives, and their structures with performance levels in general or in specific spheres. Such data is essential for evaluating performance—the actual performance as compared with preferred, the actual costs as compared with the preferred. Assessment provides the empirical foundation needed for making valid normative evaluations.

In part, assessment of specific systems involves analysis of policy output patterns (discussed in Part V of this framework). The analysis of the scope, content, objectives, and consequences of policies makes possible the assessment and evaluation with regard to such crucial questions as whether governments serve all of society or only some special elites; what values they maximize and how they are allocated; how well the conflict resolution function is performed; to what extent governments are effectively dealing with the critical needs and problems of society; and in what spheres they appear to be most or least effective. But all this entails analysis of the performance characteristics which seem inherent within particular systems and types of systems, which such performance characteristics a compound of three specific criteria: capabilities, effectiveness, and efficiency.

Relative capabilities are related to the power of a government over society—the extent to which the thought and behavior of people can be influenced in the direction desired by government for attainment of goals. Hence it is dependent on governmental resources, credibility, perceptions of need by the varied groups in society, and the general relationship of good will and responsiveness. But five different kinds of capabilities are involved, and due to the interaction of all component elements of power, the capability of governments may be quite high in one respect, quite low in another. Hence, assessment of the relationship of a type of system with its particular capabilities is significant.

1. Extractive capability—the ability of a system to draw human and material resources—human talent, support, money—from the environment so that it may perform varied tasks. The analytical task is to examine the factors which tend to produce high or low extractive capabilities, the possible costs entailed in terms of other capabilities, and the relationship between types of systems and their extractive capability. Authoritarian systems, for example, tend to have high extractive capabilities with respect to material resources, but less with regard to human resources, and also seem to be weak with respect to other capabilities.

2. Regulative capability—to control individual and group behavior in the society, regulate the activities of the society. Similar analytical questions have to be asked, particularly with regard to the real and effective regulative capabilities of totalitarian systems which rely heavily on coercion.

3. Distributive capability—to create, allocate, and distribute material and non-material values throughout the society. A system's distributive capability may be dependent on extractive and regulative capabilities, but having the latter two does not ensure equitable or effective distribution. Perceptions of either equitable or effective distribution throughout the society may be essential for stability and successful performance of functions.

4. Responsive Capability—the ability of a system to meet demand inputs with policy outputs, to respond to the varied interest-idea based demands which emanate from varied groups throughout the society. As with distributive capabilities, normative evaluations may be involved; but responsive capability again is related to overall performance levels in terms of stimulation of support needed for effective performance.

5. Symbolic capability, again closely related to needed legitimacy and support, relates to the system's ability to tap and exploit popular beliefs, attitudes, or even myths by the creation and manipulation of power and popular symbols and slogans, so as to maintain or develop needed legitimacy and support for effective performance of functions.

Relative effectiveness relates to a system's overall ability to produce results, to create and allocate values. Like capability, relative effectiveness could be assessed on the basis of actual performance, on whether or not a system seems to have been effective with respect to doing what it intended to do, to attain whatever goals were selected by political elites. But the question of potential effectiveness is also important, which basically entails making an unlikely outcome more likely to happen. Systems may be quite effective in limiting their function to domestic peace in peaceful societies, but could be quite ineffective if they undertook a more ambitious program of activity. Effectiveness results from the interaction of all of the elements of governmental power, and of the five specific types of capability. But three kinds of abilities are essential for overall effectiveness with regard to any sphere of policy; and some systems may have high ability in one respect, low in others.

1. The ability to make timely (although not overly hasty) policies and decisions, when they are needed in spheres in which they are needed. Systems of concentrated power usually enjoy this ability but may be weak in others; while democratic systems tend to be low in this quality save in crisis situations, but higher in other aspects of effectiveness. Futuristic orientations are also involved —the ability to make policies before crises develop (an energy policy before an energy shortage cripples the economy).

2. The ability to make effective policies which have a positive impact as intended—which are likely to at least alleviate if not completely resolve the problem to which the policy is addressed. A hastily-enacted energy policy which temporarily eases a gasoline shortage but fails to deal with the fundamental problem of scarce energy resources is not symptomatic of effective government.

3. The ability to effectively implement policies, to translate paper into action programs is essential. It is one thing to be able to make timely and effective policies, but overall effectiveness depends on the extent to which they can be implemented. This depends very much upon the effectiveness of the bureaucracy, perhaps of the coercive apparatus, but more often on voluntary compliance—the extent to which affected groups in society are influenced in their behavior by the government's laws.

Relative efficiency relates to the ratio between the values created or maximized by governmental action and the costs incurred in terms of values minimized or lost. Business or economic efficiency is but one, and perhaps the lesser aspect of efficiency: is governmental performance worth the cost, is the taxpayer getting his money's worth, are varied governmental programs too costly; could the same programs be undertaken at a lower cost by voluntary cooperation? But much more significant are questions relating to non-monetary costs. It is probably impossible to pursue or maximize any one or a set of values without paying a price in terms of minimizing or losing other values. The maximization of freedom entails costs in terms of order, equality, and perhaps in today's world economic plenty. A system which attempts to maximize wealth through rapid economic development invariably impairs other values such as liberty, social justice, human rights, overall quality of life, and may even jeopardize future wealth through early depletion of natural resources. Hence, efficiency—reducing such costs to an acceptable level—is another major measure of the performance of systems as instruments of society.

RELATIVE ADAPTABILITY TO CHANGE

Change is a fact of life, and the modern world differs from earlier worlds only in that change seems to be much more rapid and complex. Change is occurring in all societies, again with differences in pace, nature, and direction. Hence, change has to be accepted as a fact, not as a value. Value preferences surround questions concerning the pace, nature, and direction of change, but also, they must be based on empirical data. And if one accepts the proposition that societies need governments of at least minimal stability and effective performance, then one must accept the need for political adaptation to change.

Substantial uncertainty prevails about the ultimate sources of change, but whatever the origins, major changes appear to involve interaction between technological, economic, demographic, sociological, cultural, and political changes. The stimuli for political change tend to come from one of three, or from the interaction of three sources; the political elites, groups in the domestic environment, and other political systems in the international environment. These seem to produce changing patterns of ideas and interests, conflict and cooperation, and demand and support inputs. Crucial questions then develop as to what extent the existing political forms, processes, and elites can effectively cope with such changing patterns, can adapt to cope with them, or can act to bring about, regard, accelerate, or modify environmental changes.

Hence, as we now go about the examination of the component parts of political systems we must avoid just taking "snapshots in time." The analysis must always include a focus on the nature of changes taking place, the apparent sources of change, the pace and direction of change, and the potential consequences for the society and system. The examination of environmental settings must include a focus on cultural and socio-economic changes to determine their nature and possible significance, as well as changes in the distribution of political power in society. The analysis of linkage-communication systems must ascertain what changes are taking place in that component, what the consequences of such changes are for both society and government, and whether these changes represent effective adaptation to changes in other spheres. Similar considerations must govern the analysis of decision-making systems and policy output patterns.

The assessment of the probability of a system's capability to adapt to change is perhaps the most difficult and imprecise of assessment tasks. One can get clues about adaptability from the past history of the system, the constraints on change which may result from status quo or slow change orientations of the political elites, from changes actually taking place within the political structure, from the changing nature of policy outputs and value allocation patterns, and from changes in support, trust, and perceptions of credibility and legitimacy developing in the society. But difficult or not, this kind of assessment is a critical intellectual exercise, particularly for political elites.

The analysis of change invariably also entails evaluation. Facts about change may require a reordering of value priorities or a rethinking of our preferences with regard to the basic issues of authority and scope. The ends we aspire to may have to be reshuffled because some goals may now seriously jeopardize others—in a complex interdependent world, an obsession with freedom may entail too high a cost in terms of security, order, or economic prosperity. Changes in priorities may be necessitated by social upheavals—as race riots may force societies to focus more on equality and minority rights. Changes in the international environment may require similar new thinking—as increasing poverty and misery coupled with rising expectations make the world a revolutionary one. Changes of varied kinds may force a thorough reconsideration of our traditional approaches to the power and role of governments.

Both assessment and evaluation require consideration as to the most appropriate way of effecting necessary political change. The question of evolution or revolution is in part a normative and value-laden question: are the norms and values of a given system so abhorrent that revolution is justified, or is violence in any form so abhorrent that it is at all times to be avoided? But it is also a question of more-or-less objective assessment of facts: given the circumstances, is evolution or revolution more likely to produce a political system capable of effectively performing as an instrument of society? But either way—radical revolution or gradual evolution—adaptation to change is a necessity. For political systems and societies which fail to adapt to a changing environment will invariably suffer the fate of the dinosaur.

Environmental Factors and their Political Consequences

part II

The search for answers to the key questions discussed in the preceding chapter about the nature of political systems and their goals, stability, performance, and adaptability to change, requires us to examine the social environment in which governments function. To briefly restate what was discussed in Chapter 1, an understanding of politics requires analysis not merely of governmental institutions, but of political systems and of interaction among a system's four components: the environmental setting, linkage-communication system, decision-making system, and policy outputs. Conflicting or cooperative effective demand and support inputs from the social environment have an impact on and are relayed through the linkage-communication system. Such inputs influence both the nature and dynamics of governmental institutions and processes, as well as a government's policy outputs. The latter in turn has an impact on the environmental setting, and on demand and support inputs into the machinery of government.

The environmental setting is a complex of various components which can be separated for analytical purposes, but which constantly interact with one another. Chapter 4 discusses cultural factors and Chapter 5 focuses on the social, economic, and geographic factors. Substantial controversy prevails as to which factor is most fundamental. But whatever the ultimate root of political institutions and behavior, the evidence indicates constant interaction among cultural, socio-economic, and power factors. Chapter 6 discusses such interaction in terms of the consequences of the nature, objectives, stability, performance characteristics, and adaptability to change of political systems.

The Political Culture and Socialization Process

4

The political culture is a major wellspring of a society's political institutions and processes. It is a prime source of the acquisitive and moral values that influence human behavior, of the ideas and interests that generate demand and support inputs, and of the patterns of conflict and cooperation that prevail in a society. Cultural patterns affect decision-making directly: when decision-makers share ideas that generally prevail throughout the society, such basic beliefs will influence their thought and behavior. They influence decision-making indirectly in that beliefs affect the thought and behavior of groups which seek to influence government.

In this chapter we first discuss the general nature of political cultures and their roles: How and why do cultures affect political thought and behavior? We then describe various aspects and basic types of political cultures, and we discuss how basic beliefs and values are transmitted from generation to generation and are either reinforced, modified, or radically changed. The discussion is intended to provide background information with respect to three major questions, which should be asked during political analysis of a society's political culture:

1. What are the major beliefs, values, and attitudes that prevail within a society and which affect its political patterns? To what extent and why do elite beliefs, values, and attitudes differ from the prevailing culture? What are the political consequences of shared or differing ideas?

2. To what extent does the society consist of diverse and divisive sub-cultures, and what are the political consequences of such patterns?

3. To what extent, at what rate, and in what direction does the political culture appear to be changing? What are the sources and potential consequences of such cultural changes?

THE NATURE AND CONTENT OF A POLITICAL CULTURE

A culture encompasses the beliefs, values, behavioral norms, attitudes, images, and expressive symbols which together help produce the distinct complex of tradition or way of life of a society. By a political culture we refer to those aspects of a culture which have some impact on political traditions, behavior, and institutions.

Most cultures that prevail in various contemporary societies are conglomerations of a variety of both old and new beliefs and values. The older ideas, usually the products of a gradual accumulation of various beliefs over many generations or centuries, tend to persist in the hearts and minds of people; but newer beliefs invariably creep in and either modify or coexist with older ideas and values. As a consequence, cultures often lack consistency and internal cohesion (as is the case with the conglomeration of ideas which most of us as individuals hold), but such ambiguity or internal contradiction does not reduce impact on behavior. No matter how confused we may be about basic values and beliefs, what and how we think still affects our conduct. Cultures also differ in their origins and nature. Some have religious roots and may or may not have been modified by the intrusion of newer secular ideas, such as in the case of contemporary Buddhist and Islamic societies, and in some Roman Catholic countries. Others are basically secular in origin but with some religious overtones: the persisting Confucianism in much of Asia, the ambiguous "American Way of Life" which prevails in the United States and which seems to be spreading in western Europe. In some states an explicit all-embracing ideology consisting of an integrated set of doctrines functions as the dominant cultural pattern, such as the Marxist-Leninist creed in Communist countries. In some instances this ideology is quite consistent with more traditional beliefs; in other cases the coexistence of the old and the new produces either uncertainty or conflict. In western societies the dominant cultural pattern is generally a less explicit and often somewhat ambiguous set of doctrines: the modern ideologies of liberalism, conservatism, democracy, democratic socialism, and fascism. But whatever the origins and nature of a particular culture, it consists of a set of beliefs and values, which in general or sometimes specific terms offers some kind of explanation of the physical and social universe and of the meaning and purpose of life. This set of beliefs and values establishes a person's place and role in the world, in the society, and in the political order.

Cultures also differ with respect to their permeation throughout the society and the intensity of attachment of people to prevailing beliefs. In some countries a distinct cultural pattern or creed is dominant in that it prevails among most people and is either explicitly subscribed to, or unquestioningly accepted by, most members of the society. Despite the intrusion of some new ideas, which may be weakening established cultural patterns, this is still the case in such diverse countries as the United States, Britain, Japan, and to a lesser extent, even in China and the Soviet Union. In other countries no truly national culture exists; instead, a complex mosaic of many sub-cultures exists within the frontiers of the state. This is particularly the case with the newer states of Africa and Asia, in which a sometimes bewildering variety of different tribal, ethnic, racial, religious, or regional sub-cultures exists and create problems in terms of national unity. Significant sub-cultures also exist within many national societies in which some kind of a national culture does prevail: the beliefs and values that prevail among ghetto dwellers in American cities differ significantly from those that prevail within white middle-class suburbia. Elites and masses within the same society may also differ in their ideas: the elites in many African and Asian societies, committed to "modernizing" their societies and imbued with both old and new ideas, subscribe to beliefs and values which are quite different from those that are prevalent among the more traditional masses. And in some societies the prevailing cultural pattern may be fairly stable or changing very slowly; in others the culture is in a state of ferment and flux. But in all societies there is some complex of belief systems and value orientations, which influence political behavior, institutions, and processes.

THE ROLES OF POLITICAL CULTURES

In all societies the prevailing political culture, or the sub-cultures that are subscribed to by some distinctive groups, function in three interrelated roles. The interaction of these roles produces a high probability (but not certainty) that those individuals who adhere to the creed will behave politically in a certain manner. By way of these interacting roles, the culture ensures that certain kinds of political behavior will occur most frequently among the decision-makers, other elites, and ordinary mortals who subscribe to, believe in, and accept that culture.

1. A culture functions as a framework for perception and evaluation. In essence, a culture provides a "view of the world" for those who subscribe to it. Its images, basic beliefs, and values serve as the framework or set of optical lenses by which individuals perceive, interpret, and evaluate the physical and social universe, the realities and conditions that surround them, and the events and developments that occur in the universe. A culture defines what is a good society, what values ought to be preferred, what standards of conduct are appropriate, what the rights and responsibilities of individual members of the society are, and how members of the society ought to behave towards one another. The political aspects of a culture shape and mold the subscriber's view of political institutions, processes, and events. The political culture defines what is a good or preferred kind of system, what kinds of political goals and values ought to be pursued, what standards of political conduct are appropriate for government officials and citizens, what the rights and responsibilities of citizens are, what roles individuals ought to play in political processes, and what standards ought to be applied in judging political institutions and behavior as good, just, or rational.

More specifically, a political culture produces three kinds of political orientations that affect attitudes and behavior.

Cognitive orientations pertain to knowledge and awareness of political objects and events. A culture conditions the extent to which people have some awareness or knowledge of government, an interest in politics, or pay attention to and focus on political events. In most western nations the prevailing creed prescribes that people ought to have the degree of knowledge and interest in all levels of government that is commensurate with their rights and responsibilities as citizen-voters in democratic societies. But sub-cultures among the poor and some ethnic minorities breed very low cognitive orientations. The cultures that prevail in many decentralized agrarian societies in Africa and Asia also breed low knowledge and awareness levels. People may have some interest in and knowledge of village government, but become only dimly aware of the existence of a higher level when the tax collector, military recruiter, or occasional bureaucrat appears in the village. In modern industrial societies in which people are much more interdependent and linked by modern communications technology, knowledge levels of government may be relatively low, but awareness levels tend to be higher because of expectations of governmental benefits, and interest levels may be very high within upper-income group sub-cultures. Therefore, the perception of the political system and its processes, and the extent to which people tend to focus on political events, tend to be relatively high, with significant consequences for political institutions and behavior.

Affective orientations relate to an individual's feeling of attachment to, involvement in, or identification with the political community and system. For those who believe in it, the "American Way of Life" prescribes that United States citizens ought to identify themselves as patriotic Americans within the national community. Believers feel strongly attached to and prefer the American democratic and capitalist economic systems, and become at least minimally involved as voters. But within some American sub-cultures such affective orientations are lacking; people feel alienated rather than attached to the system, which they view as one that exploits or oppresses them. In other countries such negative affective orientations are even more intense. Minority nationality groups such as some Basques in Spain, French-speaking people in Canada, Ukrainians in the Soviet Union, Eritreans in Ethiopia, and Muslims in India, have little feeling of attachment to the national community and may want to form their own political unit. Radicals in these and other societies may feel attached to and identify with the national community, but not with the governing political system that they want to overthrow. In decentralized agrarian societies in which parochial outlooks dominate, people feel attached to and identify with the local village or regional society and government, but have neither knowledge of nor affective orientations toward the national community and government.

Evaluative orientations, closely related to affective orientations, entail the moral or normative judgments made on the basis of individual or prevailing beliefs and values about the political community and system. Believers in a culture that emphasizes the values of equality, individual rights, and human freedom will tend to highly evaluate democratic systems, which maximize opportunities for participation, and which promote these and related values. Such a culture breeds very negative evaluations of authoritarian or totalitarian systems. By contrast, people who subscribe to an ideological creed which emphasizes the defects of capitalism and which asserts that equality and true democracy can only be attained through socialism, will tend to evaluate American-style democracy in negative terms. A devout Hindu who accepts his place in the rigid hierarchical social order sanctified by that creed will support and think highly of an authoritarian system based on the principle of inequality. A devout Muslim who believes in equality and who views the Indian political system as dominated by Hindus, will not find much to praise about government in India.

In essence, different cultures functioning as different frameworks for perception and evaluation tend to produce different answers to the permanent issues of politics discussed in Chapter 3: the questions of equality, freedom versus order, authority, and the scope of government. Democratic creeds lead to perceptions of government based on popular sovereignty and participation as essentially good, and to high evaluations of political goals that promote freedom, human dignity, and protection of individual rights against governmental encroachments. Within such cultures a broad spectrum of more specific ideologies may prevail, and may produce somewhat different perceptions and evaluations of the processes and value creation and allocation patterns of government. Conservatives will disagree with liberals over specific institutional arrangements and policies, but will tend to agree on the fundamentals of a democratic order. But specific sub-cultures based on either ideology, socio-economic criteria, or ethnic, racial, and religious factors, may perceive and evaluate the existing system and its outputs in highly negative terms.

In contrast, cultures that place less emphasis on these values and emphasize others, such as domestic order, conformity, and economic needs, may breed favorable perceptions and evaluations of authoritarian systems. Dedicated Marxist-Leninists perceive systems in which authority is concentrated in the hands of a Communist Party elite who controls people for the attainment of Marxist ideals as good and they evaluate democratic systems based on capitalism as unjust and inherently evil. But in any kind of society, as traditional or existing ideas begin to change under the impact of new beliefs and values, perceptions and evaluations of existing systems and policies may change, with significant consequences for the stability and effectiveness of governments.

2. A culture functions as a set of guidelines and predispositions to action.
Cultures seldom prescribe specific courses of action, which individuals ought to take in pursuit of valued goals; hence, they produce only probabilities, not certainties, about how adherents to a creed will actually behave. However, they do predispose people towards certain kinds or directions of action.

Some secular or religious creeds do so directly, by prescribing certain aspirations, goals, or values as priorities. The democratic tradition emphasizes the pursuit of freedom and individual dignity; the capitalist ethic encourages the pursuit of wealth by individual effort; and modern liberalism supports the promotion of social justice and equality. Socialist ideologies prescribe the eventual attainment of an egalitarian society by public ownership of the means of production, and emphasize that this requires the eventual peaceful or violent destruction of capitalism. Some creeds prescribe concerted efforts to spread the faith: to export democracy, to convince others of the merits of socialism, and to convert infidels to the Muslim faith. Some prescribe general courses of action in terms of human relationships, as Confucianism emphasizes the subordination of the individual and his interests to the family, and Communism encourages the subordination of the individual to the cause. These general kinds of prescriptions form the broader normative framework within which individuals take specific actions in specific situations, and thus influence the behavior of both elites and masses: the goals they pursue, the political roles they seek to play, and the standards they apply in evaluating their own and others' political actions.

But even without such direct calls to action, cultures predispose adherents towards certain kinds of actions due to their functions as frameworks for perception and evaluation. High cognitive and affective orientations breed tendencies toward active political involvement; beliefs about the inequality of man lead people to accept obedience to their superiors; conservatives will support conservative causes. When a particular kind of political order is perceived as good and just, it leads to actions aimed at protecting the specific order against one evaluated as bad and unjust; for example, the defense of democracy against communism, or of communism against capitalism. Fanatically-held beliefs of this sort are the kind that produce cold wars or hot holy wars within and between countries.

3. *A culture functions as a legitimization instrument.* As discussed in Chapter 1, governmental authority is very much dependent on its legitimacy. The latter in turn is very much dependent on cultural patterns within the society. People will tend to perceive a political unit, system, government, or policy as legitimate, and will tend to voluntarily comply with political decisions, to the extent that their beliefs and values produce favorable affective and evaluative orientations. American nationalism legitimizes the existence of the United States as a political unit, and other beliefs legitimize the specific system of government and policies that maximize American values, just as Marxism-Leninism legitimizes the Soviet system and its outputs. But certain sub-cultures—American ghettos, Ukrainians in the Soviet Union, Spanish radicals—may lead to perceptions of illegitimacy, and to passive or active resistance to the government and its laws.

Because legitimacy is so closely linked with culture, political elites endeavor to propagate or manipulate beliefs and values, and to manipulate various slogans and symbols designed to produce favorable affective orientations for their system and policies. The intent of democratic, communist, or any kind of political leadership is to convince people that their system is the right kind of system; namely, one that governs in the right sort of way, makes policies that are in the public interest, and that generates laws which people have not only the legal but also the moral obligation to obey. For again, authority is a legal principle, which may or may not produce compliance with the law; legitimacy is a psychological concept involving moral and normative judgments made on the basis of the beliefs and values of a people.

BASIC BELIEFS AND TYPES OF POLITICAL CULTURES[1]

The great diversity of beliefs and values which prevails in the modern world, precludes any simple and realistic typology of political cultures. But on the basis of answers that people tend to give to the basic authority

---

[1]This section is based to a substantial extent on Gabriel Almond and G. Bingham Powell, Jr., *Comparative Politics: A Developmental Approach* (Boston: Little, Brown, 1966); and on Samuel H. Beer's introduction to *Patterns of Government*, 2d ed. (New York: Random House, 1962).

questions, such as who legitimately has the right to rule, and how the process of rule should be performed, a useful and relatively simple distinction can be made between two types of cultural patterns: subject cultures, which tend to legitimize authoritarian systems, and participatory cultures, which legitimize democratic systems. These different cultures involve different beliefs with respect to four controversial normative issues, and hence shape the cognitive, affective, and evaluative orientations of elites and masses. They also involve different role conceptions: what roles elites and masses should play in political processes, and what the rights and responsibilities of citizens are.

As with types of political systems, in the real world individual cultures may contain elements of both types of authority conceptions; therefore, realistic assessment involves placing specific cultures somewhere on a spectrum between two opposing poles. But the distinction is a useful one in that it helps to explain the apparent stability and performance characteristics of systems, and leads us to focus on cultural changes which may have political consequences. The extent to which a particular system falls into either category depends on the types and number of people who view their proper political roles as being either participants in or subjects of the state.

Subject conceptions of authority are held by people who view their role in political processes as being that of subjects to be ruled over, not as participants in politics. They believe in subordination and submission to political authority to the point of unqualified and unquestioning obedience. Such people may be output-oriented in that they may expect some minimal benefits from government; for example, actions to protect their life and property, or perhaps some economic benefits. But they are not input-oriented: they do not conceive of having the right to influence governmental outputs, to participate in some form or manner, or to levy demand inputs. They may also be highly parochial in their outlook and their political roles, believing in limited participatory roles at the local community level, but having little interest in or awareness of government beyond that level. A subject culture may be said to prevail when the bulk of the people hold such subject conceptions, and when the elites believe such conceptions are appropriate and govern accordingly. Subject conceptions of authority thus legitimize rule by certain elites on the basis of some widely accepted criteria, and the concentration of authority in the hands of these elites who rule in a more or less authoritarian fashion.

Basic beliefs prevalent among people constitute the building blocks for a subject conception of authority. One such belief pertains to the relationship between human beings and their physical and social environment. The idea that a person can and should manipulate nature for human benefit is now widely accepted around the world. But older notions about submission to the environment, and passivity and resignation in the face of nature still persist, particularly with respect to the social and political environment. In many rural areas in Africa, Asia, and Latin America, and even in some sub-cultures in western industrial states, the emphasis is still on the necessity, if not the virtue, of accepting one's lot in life, to resign oneself to poverty, misery, exploitation, and even natural catastrophes as one's fate. This emphasis on submission rather than manipulation breeds low cognitive orientations about politics, and about ideas of obedience and submission to authority.

Beliefs about the inherent inequality of the human being, about the natural superiority of certain types of people because of their heredity, religious status, wealth, occupation, knowledge, education, or other criteria, also breed subject conceptions. When such beliefs prevail, a hierarchical social and political order based on submission and obedience to superior beings tends to be accepted as legitimate. The now fading Hindu culture, which sanctifies a rigid caste system, is one extreme example, although somewhat similar beliefs prevailed in Europe until a few centuries ago and legitimized rule by the monarch and the aristocracy. A modern version is propagated by Marxism-Leninism, which, although avowing the goal of an eventual egalitarian society, maintains that in the interim Communist elites are more qualified to rule because they alone can determine what is truly in the public interest.

Certain ideas about the nature of people and their rights also breed subject roles and conceptions. Some cultures emphasize the human's basic imperfections and irrational nature, his or her tendencies to encroach on the rights of others, and the consequent need to be controlled in order to protect society and maintain order. The consequence may be to accept authoritarian rule in the interests of social peace and stability. Closely related are beliefs concerning the relationship between the individual person and society. Some cultures emphasize the rights of society rather than individual rights, and stress either conformity or the subordination of individuals to collective social needs. This again is a major principle of Marxism-Leninism, Confucianism, and of some tribal societies in Africa and Asia. An authoritarian political order, based on the principles of hierarchy and the subordination of individuals as subjects to their superiors, tends to develop out of such ideas.

These beliefs, either individually or in combination, tend to produce conceptions that the proper role of the common person is that of a subject to be ruled over by whatever authority the culture endows with legitimacy. Such a culture does not necessarily imply a master-slave or blind command-obedience relationship. But it does produce a tendency to place far-reaching authority in the hands of rulers, although other beliefs or longstanding traditions may restrict political authority and the potential for arbitrary rule. The medieval principle of divine right of kings to rule also emphasized the monarch's responsibility to rule for the good of the people, much as the Muslim religion stresses authoritarian rule for the welfare of citizens. Traditions may require the ruler to arrive at decisions in a certain manner: they may require him to consult with persons deemed to be representatives of the people, to search out for a consensus, or to permit wider participation at the grass-roots level. But in these subject cultures the primary emphasis is on the sharp gap between the rulers and the ruled; the function of the rulers to govern, and the obligations of the subjects to obey.

Participatory conceptions of authority are held by people who view their proper political role as that of being a more or less active participant in political processes. Such people tend to be not merely output-, but also input-oriented: they expect the right and opportunity to levy demands on government, to be consulted and heeded in governmental decision-making, and to have some influence concerning what the government does. Beyond that, they may also expect the right and opportunity to participate in decision-making, either directly or through their selected representatives. Such conceptions invariably develop among elites, even though these elites may consider subject roles as appropriate for the masses; and elites will evaluate a system as legitimate to the extent that it permits some form or degree of participation, at the very least in the form of consultation in decision-making. When such participatory conceptions prevail among many people in a society, we refer to the prevailing culture as a participatory culture. Such cultures emphasize popular sovereignty and government by consent as basic principles, and legitimize systems based on these principles, which entails dispersion of power and opportunities for demand inputs and other forms of participation.

Beliefs about equality tend to breed such participatory conceptions. Elites may still believe in inequality and a natural hierarchy, but as they believe in relative equality among elites—as a new moneyed aristocracy or professional class considers itself equal to the titled and landed aristocracy—they tend to demand participation in government. And as ideas about equality develop among masses, participatory conceptions tend to expand throughout the society. Disagreements may prevail over the definition of equality, and people may in fact pay only lip service to the principle, but a belief in equality generally leads to demands for some voice in government.

Beliefs about the nature of people and their rights also have an impact. When a culture emphasizes that an individual, despite all imperfections, is inherently good, rational, and endowed with certain inalienable rights (such as the American creed, which stresses the right to life, liberty, property, and the pursuit of happiness), participatory conceptions tend to develop, simply because of perceived needs to protect such rights against arbitrary government by means of restraints on, or participation in, government. Similar conceptions about government are bred by cultures that emphasize the rights and dignity of the individual rather than the collective rights and needs of society. In such belief systems the individual is no longer a subordinate of society, conformity is less important, and the notion that the individual must subordinate himself and submit to authority is less emphasized by the political creed.

VARIATIONS AND CHANGES IN CULTURAL PATTERNS

As stated earlier, most contemporary political cultures are in a spectrum somewhere between subject and participatory conceptions of authority, simply because all societies consist of people with diverse beliefs and values. In western democratic societies most people hold to participatory conceptions and to beliefs that breed such political roles; yet in each, one finds some sub-cultures, particularly among lower socio-economic groups and some racial minorities, in which subject orientations still prevail. Variations in basic beliefs may also produce variations in participatory conceptions. At least until recently, for example, the British culture did not place as much emphasis on equality as did the American culture: while the American culture stresses the capability of the common person to rule, British people were prone to believe in the principle of rule by uncommon people. Hence, although both cultures breed participatory conceptions of authority, the British were inclined much more than Americans to defer to the discretionary judgment of an elitist leadership so long as it generally remained responsive to the public will. The French political culture is also a participatory culture, but French people tend to emphasize individualism to the point of egoism, with the consequence that two somewhat different conceptions of authority prevail. Some insist on maximizing participation through representation in parliament, so as to maximize opportunities for satisfying individual and local interests. Others insist that French individualism requires a more heavy-handed style of democratic rule in the form of a very strong executive. Similar variations in belief systems and authority conceptions, and some sub-cultures that emphasize participation, also exist in societies in which subject conceptions continue to be dominant.

The contemporary world is also undergoing substantial cultural change, with belief systems and role conceptions changing slowly and almost imperceptibly in some countries, while changing rapidly in others. The most pronounced changes are occurring in Asia, Africa, and Latin

America, where subject conceptions of authority still tend to be dominant but are either slowly or rapidly eroding. The traditional emphasis on passivity, fatalism, and resignation is fading, and beliefs about the rights and equality of the human being, and the priority of the individual over the society and state, are beginning to develop. As a consequence, the proportion of people who hold subject orientations is diminishing, participatory conceptions of authority are spreading, awareness of political processes along with expectations of benefits from government are expanding, and new evaluative orientations are undermining the legitimacy of heavy-handed authoritarian regimes. In most states, demands for participation in goverment are in most cases limited to new elites that have developed as the result of varied socio-economic and cultural changes, but in many input orientations have also developed among the masses. Meekness and docility are vanishing, and even subject-oriented people are now more prone to resort to violence when intense expectations are not met.

Similar trends are apparent in many totalitarian systems, even though traditional subject conceptions reinforce the authority principles of communist ideology. The new technical, professional, and managerial elites created by industrialization of these societies are certainly not demanding democracy, since the existing systems are the source of their incomes, privileges, and power. But they are developing participatory conceptions in terms of challenging the monopoly of Communist Party elites in decision-making. Masses are also acquiring some beliefs about equality and individual rights, and they are developing some input orientations, particularly in some East European states in which some participatory conceptions of authority prevailed prior to Communist takeovers. Even in some western democratic societies a new egalitarianism and individualism seems to be emerging, manifested by increasing disenchantment with elitist democracy and mounting demands for systems that enhance opportunities for popular participation—demands for Populist or Direct Democracy rather than merely Representative Democracy.

CONCEPTIONS OF SCOPE

Basic political beliefs, combined with socio-economic factors, also tend to produce different conceptions of scope among different people and different societies—different answers to the basic question of what the legitimate scope of government may be, what functions the state may or may not undertake, the extent to which the government may rightfully intervene in the various spheres of human endeavor, or where the line of demarcation is between the public and the private sectors. In the modern world the controversy swirls around governmental intervention in the economic system, in the social sphere to promote equality and social justice, and the government's role in promoting change.

In societies where prevailing belief systems emphasize individualism, self-help, the inherent rights of individuals, freedom, and the virtues of free enterprise capitalism, conceptions of scope tend to be limited and anti-interventionist. Although American conceptions of scope have been expanding, the traditional conception still dominates the thinking of many. When patterns of beliefs exist or begin to emerge (as they are in western democracies) emphasizing the inability of a capitalist system to regulate itself to promote prosperity and economic stability, and the need for public action to promote equality and to effect a fair distribution of wealth and income, much broader conceptions of scope develop. Whatever the nature of prevailing conceptions, they are important in that they help to condition the affective and evaluative orientations of peoples and elites.

The broadest conception of scope exists in totalitarian states, where at least the political elites accept the idea of total governmental involvement in all affairs to effect drastic changes in the society. Yet somewhat similar conceptions continue to prevail in some agrarian and tribal societies, where the village or tribal government controlled all spheres of human endeavor. In one respect such traditional attitudes have facilitated expansion of controls by new national governments (such as the Communist regime in China). But such attitudes also present problems for new national governments by raising the older question of the functional relationship between the central and local levels of government.

SUB-CULTURES AND CONSENSUS

So far we have been emphasizing prevailing cultural patterns within societies—cultural patterns which are dominant and prevail among most people. However, a degree of heterogeneity with respect to most fundamental beliefs and values is also characteristic of most societies, and many societies are heterogeneous to the extent that they are really complex mosaics of sub-cultures.

Sub-cultures exist when a particular set of political orientations, beliefs, values, and behavioral norms is fundamentally different in some respects and clearly distinguishable from others in the political system, when a prevailing cultural pattern is not shared by all. Sub-cultures involve different basic beliefs and conceptions of authority and scope, and usually result from membership in different ethnic, religious, or linguistic groups, from different geographic location, from different educational levels or socio-economic positions, or from adherence to different ideologies or attitudes towards change and modernization. Thus some Blacks in American society, the poor in most societies, radical and reactionary groups, tribal groups in Africa, religious groups in Asia, and many others constitute sub-cultures within the prevailing cultural pattern.

The political consequences of sub-cultures may be significant because beliefs and values, not being shared, may have a major impact on the range, complexity, and hostility of conflict patterns in the society. Most significantly, sub-cultures tend to create a sense of different rather than common identity, in that people may not identify as Americans, British, Pakistanis, or Nigerians, but as members of the ethnic, religious, or other group which possesses the distinctive sub-culture. While people in most societies tend to identify with several groups—Americans as New Yorkers, Catholics, workers—when a sub-culture creates a sense of identity it tends to be a dominant one and often conflicts with the national identity —a Black identifying as such rather than as an American, a Muslim identifying as such rather than as a citizen of India, an Ibo identifying as a member of his tribe rather than as a Nigerian. Members of sub-cultures thus tend to define the "society" as the sub-cultural group, with all others considered to be "outsiders" or "foreigners": other tribes in Africa, white society in the United States, Protestants in Northern Ireland, English-speaking people in Quebec. This again intensifies conflicts, makes it extremely difficult to organize an effective government at the national level, and mars the degree of cultural consensus necessary for political stability and effectiveness.

CONSENSUS

As stated earlier, diversity and conflicts are characteristics of any society, but societies differ significantly with respect to the nature, types, range and intensity of conflicts. Some societies are "consensual," in that despite the pervasiveness, complexity, and intensity of social conflict a degree of consensus on fundamentals prevails. It may be a substantive consensus, relatively broad agreement not on everything and not among everyone, but among most on the fundamental beliefs, values, behavioral norms, and goals of the society. It may be a procedural consensus, broad agreement on behavioral norms and particularly those relating to the resolution of conflicts, on how the government should govern, and how conflicts are to be resolved—above all, peacefully. In either case, there is a set of shared beliefs and values giving some sense of social solidarity, based on similar or common evaluations of what is good, moral, just, and legitimate.

A "dissensual" society lacks either or both of these dimensions of consensus. In some there may be relatively broad agreement on basic values and beliefs, yet intense disagreement on conceptions of authority and scope, or what the rules of conflict resolution ought to be. In many societies one finds agreement on virtually nothing—societies which are clusters of sub-cultures, with sharp cleavages among varied ethnic, racial, tribal, linguistic, religious, and other kinds of groups, and with distrust and hostility characteristic of group interactions. In these, conflict is not restricted to policy issues of the day, but involves fundamental matters of substance and procedure, with major adverse consequences for conflict resolution and political stability and effectiveness. In all cases, sub-cultures and the absence of consensus means that different groups will have different sets of ideas and values functioning as frameworks for perception and evaluation and as guidelines for action, and will have different conceptions of what is legitimate.

Consensus is particularly important with respect to conceptions of authority and scope. Political stability and effectiveness are enhanced when people have similar ideas as to what constitutes a legitimate form of government and a legitimate governmental undertaking. But when one major segment of society believes in an authoritarian style of rule (such as a strong executive) and others in a system of dispersed powers (parliamentary supremacy and a weak executive), or when people are sharply divided as to the line of demarcation between the public and private sectors, then resolution of specific conflicts over economic, social, or other types of issues becomes extremely difficult, and compromise may become impossible.

POLITICAL ATTITUDES

In addition to basic beliefs and conceptions of authority and scope, three types of political attitudes constitute important elements of political cultures.

TRUST VERSUS DISTRUST

The degree of trust which prevails within a society is usually although not always related to the coexistence of sub-cultures or the degree of consensus. But whatever its sources, the degree of trust has major consequences for the nature of conflicts and the task of conflict resolution.

Conflicts tend to be more muted and less hostile when a relative sense of trust prevails, when majorities trust minorities and vice versa, and when various minorities trust each other. In such settings groups seldom resort to violence and generally are willing to bargain and accept compromise. When distrust prevails, when greater hostility characterizes attitudes and relations among competing groups and classes, groups fail to be responsive to each other, offers of compromise tend to be spurned because motives and intentions are suspect, and violence is frequently resorted to. Distrust seems to be particularly characteristic of societies which emphasize individualism to the point of egoism (such as the French), in which violence among groups has been characteristic in the past (Muslims and Hindus in India, Turks and Greeks in Cyprus), or in which majorities have consistently exploited or oppressed minorities (Whites and Blacks in America, Protestants and Catholics in Northern Ireland).

Equally significant is a relationship of trust between people and government. To some extent such trust is directly related to prevailing conceptions of legitimacy, but even systems, governments, and high officials who are considered to be legitimate may be distrusted, with adverse consequences for political stability and effectiveness. When a people label a government as "they," voluntary compliance is difficult to attain.

PRAGMATISM VERSUS DOCTRINAIRISM

Distrust is also generated and conflict resolution made more difficult when dogmatism or doctrinairism is characteristic of the society or of specific groups. When people are firmly or fanatically attached to some closed ideology or some specific secular or religious principles which they consider as absolute truths, compromise is generally not acceptable because it involves yielding of sacrosanct principles. Bargaining may be impossible because opponents may be viewed as being absolutely wrong, and because politics is viewed as a discordant process involving a struggle for ultimate supremacy between right and wrong. When doctrinaire attitudes prevail, solutions to problems and conflicts are not sought on the basis of what will work, or what must be done to maximize cooperation in the search for solutions, but on the basis of doctrines—what the Bible, the Koran, the precepts of Marxism-Leninism assert to be the right solution.

Conflict resolution is facilitated and trust generated when societies and groups tend to be pragmatic in their approaches to problems and conflicts. In such settings peaceful and flexible bargaining and compromise are possible because <u>attachments to basic beliefs are less intense</u>, principles may be revered but <u>not as absolute truths</u>, a level of civility pervades conflicts, and politics is viewed as a harmonious process involving not a continuing struggle for mastery but a search for accommodation of legitimate interests. Compromise is accepted as legitimate either as a practical necessity, or because the competition's case is evaluated as having some validity. Solutions to problems, while they may be affected by basic beliefs, tend to be based on considerations of what will work. One demands governmental intervention in the economy because it seems necessary, not because Karl Marx said so.

ATTITUDES TOWARDS CHANGE

These attitudes may be very significant in that they may hinder or facilitate the adaptation of political systems to changing conditions—a very important problem in a world of pervasive and sometimes rapid change. Within any society some groups tend to be oriented towards the past, some towards the present, others towards the future. But what counts is whether prevailing or elite orientations are primarily concerned with the preservation of things as they are, or towards change.

In some societies the prevailing cultural pattern is tradition-oriented: the emphasis is on continuity, stability, and order, major changes in any sphere are viewed with suspicion, and only very slow and incremental changes may be acceptable. Such attitudes make it extremely difficult for change-oriented elites, such as many in African, Asian, and even western states, to attain their objectives. In other cultures adaptation is easier because change is accepted as inevitable if not desirable; innovation is preferred to tradition and stability; and pragmatic attitudes predispose people towards adaptation.

<u>Different attitudes towards change may constitute a major source of conflict within a society.</u> When modernizing elites committed to radical change seize political power they frequently come into conflict with other elites who have vested interests in the established order and with masses who venerate traditions. Changing socio-economic settings also produce conflicts over change as some groups benefit and others lose. Industrialization tends to produce conflict between landowning and business elites because the landed aristocracy tends to decline in power, status, and wealth. Further industrialization which produces major concentrations of economic power—big business and big labor—tends to deprive small businessmen and farmers of power and status and to squeeze them economically.

THE POLITICAL SOCIALIZATION PROCESS

The reasons why particular political cultures are peculiar to particular societies are not at all certain, but the roots of cultures are probably to be found in the peculiarities of the historic development of societies combined with geographic and economic factors. However, the immediate source of a culture or sub-culture is the political socialization process by which cultures are maintained, modified, or changed. By this term we refer to the life-long inculcation and absorption of beliefs, values, and behavioral norms which begins in the cradle and ends in the grave.

The process is carried on by various socialization agents common to most societies, but different in their specific nature and impact. The first, and generally most powerful agent, is the family circle, the nuclear family in some societies, the extended in others. Generally the most durable values, norms, and political orientations are acquired through exposure to attitudes and beliefs prevailing within the family—to include even political party preferences (since these are normally linked with more basic political values). The beliefs and values acquired from the family are subsequently either reinforced, modified, or in some cases, changed by subsequent socialization experiences. The educational system seems to be second in importance, not only in terms of the content of educational programs and the impact of teachers but sometimes more by the influence of student peer groups. Then follow influences resulting from employment experiences, subsequent peer group influences emanating from people one associates with through life, mass media, and experiences resulting from direct contact with the political system—satisfactions, dissatisfactions, and frustrations. Major traumatic events experienced by a society—war, revolution, depression—may have a significant impact insofar as they are relayed to individuals through the various socialization agents.

Considering the importance of a culture, political analysis must focus not only on the cultural and subcultural patterns prevailing in a society at a given time, but also on cultural changes which may be significant with respect to unfolding or potential political changes. One major approach to the study of change is analysis of the socialization process within a given system. Several major questions should be asked in connection with such an analysis.

1. Is the process generally homogeneous, consistent, and cumulative, so that the prevailing culture is reinforced and stabilized? When all socialization agents generally transmit the same kinds of prevailing beliefs and values then the culture is likely to remain relatively stable. And if the culture is generally supportive of the political system, then the system is likely to remain stable. For example, if family, educational, and other

exposures continue to emphasize subordination to society, deference, obedience to and trust in authority, then authoritarian systems are likely to remain stable and effective for the foreseeable future.

2. Is the process breeding a new set of beliefs and authority and scope conceptions needed by evolving political systems? Changing socio-economic and international settings may require substantial expansion of executive power and of the scope of government, yet if prevailing cultural patterns continue to emphasize dispersion of power and limited government, systems may be denied the firm cultural roots needed for stability and effectiveness.

3. Is the process discontinuous, inconsistent, non-cumulative, and thereby disruptive of the prevailing culture and sowing seeds of cultural and political change? Families and formal educational programs may continue to emphasize traditions, subordination to society and deference and obedience to authority, while peer group influences in school and beyond may be introducing new beliefs and values—the modernization of society, participation in political processes, new material and other kinds of expectations. In such socialization settings a normal generation gap may develop into a more significant cultural gap, a tradition-oriented society may be in process of transformation into a change-oriented one, and the cultural props supporting authoritarian systems may be undermined. Such discontinuous processes may also breed substantial cultural uncertainty and ambiguity which reduces stability and effectiveness. In some western societies, for instance, some socialization agents continue to stress the themes of free enterprise and limited government, while other influence and exposures tend to create opposing attitudes; this kind of cultural lag seriously inhibits the capability of governments to carry out economic functions demanded by many if not most in society. In the new states of Africa and Asia the clash between old and new beliefs and values has produced highly ambiguous attitudes and orientations, so that existing political systems do not have the firm cultural roots needed for stability and effectiveness. Discontinuity may also breed dissatisfaction and alienation. In some western societies, due to the transmission of new ideas by some socialization agents, governments are perceived by many as being unresponsive to the satisfaction of needs and to new participation expectations.

4. Is the process promoting or hindering integration, consensus, and trust within the political community? Particularly significant may be the nature and impact of national or community-wide socialization, and the process within subcultures. The latter tend to persist because these values and beliefs are inculcated by the earliest and most durable socialization agents—the family, peer group exposures during the formative years, and subsequent tendencies to associate with members of the same

subculture. Hence, political orientations to the subculture—the ethnic group, tribe, religious community, geographic region, linguistic group— tend to be most durable and frequently impose substantial barriers to national integration and to the degree of consensus and trust needed for domestic peace and for political stability and effectiveness. In some cases subcultural socialization processes may be weakening—as, for example, geographic and social mobility change patterns of association with members of a subculture. National socialization processes may also have a weakening effect leading to gradual assimilation of minority groups. In other instances, however, national processes may have the reverse impact: granting cultural autonomy to a subcultural group may serve to reinforce subcultural socialization processes, but failing to grant such autonomy may have a similar impact as consequent resentment and alienation weakens the impact of national processes. This dilemma is a major one confronting not only the new states of Africa and Asia, but also such older states as the Soviet Union, Canada, Belgium, and the United States.

The Socio-Economic and Geographic Setting

5

Like the cultural setting, the socio-economic environment impacts political decision-making both directly and indirectly. It directly influences the thought and behavior of decision-makers to the extent that these individuals are aware of problems and limitations imposed by economic conditions and social divisions and formulate economic and social policies. It also influences them directly because various government officials emanate from different socio-economic groups and strata and hence may be more attuned to the interests and ideas of their groups or strata of origin. The socio-economic setting also impacts decision-making indirectly in the form of influence generated by demand and support inputs based on socio-economic patterns of cooperation and conflict. The socio-economic setting also has an impact on cultural patterns, and in turn may be influenced by patterns of beliefs and values. Three major questions must be asked:

1. In what significant ways did or does the geographic setting impact a political system, either directly or through its impact on the culture or socio-economic setting? Are technological changes affecting the political impact of geographic factors?

2. What are the major characteristics of a society's economic system, and how do these affect the political system, again either directly or through impact on the culture or the social structure? What major economic changes are developing, with what actual or potential political consequences?

3. What are the major characteristics of a society's social structure, and what patterns of political conflict and cooperation result from this structure? What changes are taking place within this structure, and with respect to class or group attitudes?

THE GEOGRAPHIC SETTING

Due to the diversity of geographic settings of past and present political systems, technological changes which have impacted the importance of geographic factors, and the diverse political influence of cultural and socio-economic factors, few generalizations are possible with respect to the overall political consequences of geographic settings. But it can be asserted that geography is one of the major forces which has shaped the collective existence of the human race, and that any effort to understand the politics of any society requires some understanding of the geographic setting and its impact on both the cultural and socio-economic setting.

The Impact on the Political Culture

Geography can have cultural consequences in a variety of ways. Britain's insular setting for example, did much to isolate the British people from many of the cultural influences at work on the European continent and helped produce a relatively homogeneous culture. The geographic position of the United States, coupled with its vast land space and the open frontier did much to produce the peculiar characteristics of American culture. Modern technology has done much to change this impact of geography, helping to produce contemporary cultural changes in both Britain and the United States. By contrast, those areas which have been cross-roads for the migration of peoples and ideas—Central Europe, the Mediterranean basin, the Middle East—have had their cultures impacted by migrations. The cultures of South Asia have been affected by the cross-currents of Islamic, Chinese, and Indo-Aryan cultures due to waves of invasion and migration of people and ideas.

Location, size, and terrain features have interacted to produce a complex of sub-cultures rather than a national culture within many contemporary states. In the past, such geographic obstacles have inhibited communication and migration among peoples, so that parochialism and regionalism among isolated pockets of people developed with different languages, ways of life and different primary identifications. High mountain ranges, wide rivers, and impenetrable forests have in the past separated people as effectively as oceans, and such separation continues to constitute a major obstacle to national socialization processes even though these geographic barriers are no longer major obstacles to communication and other forms of transactions. A hostile climate, combined with terrain features which together produce scarcities and a severely challenging geographic environment, may have cultural and consequent political consequences.

THE IMPACT ON ECONOMICS

Some states, due to their large land space and abundant natural resources, have made a relatively easy transition from an agrarian to an industrial society, which in turn has helped to moderate conflict patterns in society. Other states trying to make this transition encounter substantial difficulty, with consequent social and political turmoil. The same factors make some economies—such as the American and the Soviet— relatively invulnerable to economic influences from abroad. Other economies—the British, Japanese—have few natural resources, inadequate land even for the food supply, and are vitally dependent on international trade to keep their economies going, with both cultural and political consequences. Overall, geographic factors including natural resources, climate, and population factors tend to set major constraints not only on economic but political processes.

THE ECONOMIC SETTING

The relationship between politics and economics is one of the classic basic issues of politics. However, it is not merely a normative but also a descriptive-explanatory issue, for controversy also exists as to the actual past and present relationship between the two spheres. Economic determinists insist that economics is the most important and perhaps the ultimate determinant of politics. Karl Marx, one of the more notable adherents of this school, argued that the economic modes of production produce social stratification patterns, that the class which controls economic power exploits and subjugates the working classes and controls political power in order to maintain its economic power and domination. Others have argued, at least in the past, that politics and economics are basically separate spheres.

The matter of the precise relationship between the two spheres continues to be a matter of controversy and may depend very much on the nature and type of society. But realistic assessment of empirical data suggests that economics again interacts with other factors, and as such has at least some, and in the modern world a very significant, impact on politics. Economic factors certainly condition such vital aspects of politics as prevailing cultural patterns, the distribution of power within the society, the class and group structure, patterns of conflict and cooperation, demand and support inputs, the structure, scope, and policies of government, and social and political change. In the contemporary world the impact of economics seems to be intensifying as "political economies," characterized by an increasingly blurred line between politics and economics, have become the rule rather than the exception; more and more what happens within the political market place is impacted by economics, and more and more of what occurs in the economic sphere is conditioned by politics.

But economics is also conditioned by other features of a society. The social structure may not be compatible with industrialization—as for example a society which is based on the extended family or clan system of organization. The culture of a society may impose substantial impediments to economic development—the persistence of traditions, attitudes of passivity and resignation, parochial perspectives. Economic group patterns may be cross-cut by cultural cleavages—as working class people identify primarily on the basis of religious or ideological principles rather than on economics. Substantial evidence indicates that modern capitalism could only develop as the culture of western society changed from the medieval to the protestant ethic.

Major features of an economy have indirect political consequences because they condition cultures, social structures, and power configurations. They have direct consequences as they breed or condition conflict and cooperation patterns, demand and support inputs, and policy output patterns. These major features appear to be the following.

THE DEGREE OF ECONOMIC DEVELOPMENT OR INDUSTRIALIZATION

A predominantly agrarian economy is frequently (but not always) associated with an authoritarian-subject culture, produces a relatively simple class structure of landowners, peasants, and a small middle class, and relatively simple conflict patterns. Industrial economies and agrarian societies which are moving in that direction are associated with entirely different cultural patterns, produce very complex social structures and very complex conflict and demand input patterns, while policy output patterns are composed to a great extent of policies in the economic sphere. Developing economies produce major cultural and social changes, very complex class structure and conflict patterns, a major political concern with economic development, and substantial social and political instability.

THE DEGREE OF POLITICIZATION OF THE ECONOMY

To some but only a limited extent, the degree of politicization is linked with the degree of economic development. However, some agrarian economies are also politicized in that government at the tribal or village level may in effect control economic activities, or in that higher level governments may be heavily involved due to efforts to develop the economy and move towards industrialization. Industrial and post-industrial societies show three basic patterns: a free enterprise capitalist system (rapidly becoming a vanishing pattern); politicized economies involving substantial governmental intervention and regulation including some ownership of some means of production; and totalitarian systems in which all of the major means of production and distribution are owned and controlled by the state.

THE VULNERABILITY OF AN ECONOMY TO EXTERNAL FORCES

Decentralized agrarian societies are generally relatively self-sufficient, while most industrial and post-industrial societies are becoming increasingly dependent on other states for raw materials or as markets. However, some are much more dependent than others. Britain and Japan, for example, have few of the raw materials and energy resources needed to keep their industries going, are even dependent on food imports, and badly need foreign markets to sell their goods so they can acquire the foreign exchange needed to pay for imports. The United States and the Soviet Union are still relatively self-sufficient—although increasingly less so. Developing states are also dependent on outside forces due to their needs for outside markets to sell their produce, and for foreign sources of capital and technology. The vulnerability of an economy to outside forces is one factor which tends to promote politicization of an economy as governments intervene in varied ways to secure foreign markets and needed raw material, capital, or technology imports.

THE PERSISTENT AND LONG-TERM PROBLEMS OF AN ECONOMY

These are usually associated with one of the three characteristics described above, but may warrant separate analysis in connection with the analysis of a political system. Chronic energy or capital shortages, persisting balance of payments problems, outmoded industrial technology, economic problems associated with rapid urbanization, chronic unemployment—these and similar kinds of long-term problems tend to produce substantial governmental intervention in economic affairs. Such intervention tends to occur either because of social conflicts over scarce material values, or because patterns of cooperation develop out of a consensus that governmental intervention is necessary to cope with problems of scarce values.

THE SOCIAL SETTING

In this sphere we are primarily concerned with the structure of society and the attitudes of varied segments and strata towards each other. By social structure we refer to the way and extent a society is vertically layered or stratified into various classes or castes, and the way a society is horizontally segmented or compartmented into various groups, with vertical classes and horizontal segments often cross-cutting each other. By attitudes we mean how the various strata and segments view their places and roles in society and the political system, the extent to which they are conscious of their status and role, and the degree of hostility or distrust which prevails. Social structure and attitudes are of political significance because political activity is usually group rather than individual activity. Conflict and cooperation are group patterns, demand and support inputs are generated by groups, power configurations reflect the relative power of groups, political bargaining involves group bargaining, and the human interactions which constitute politics are group interactions.

A group refers to an aggregate of people linked together by some awareness of one or more common or shared purposes based on similar ideas or interests. It involves a degree of interdependence, clearly or vaguely perceived, among its members due to shared or similar purposes. A group may or may not be formally organized but in either case, some kinds of group norms or formal rules often exist which help to knit the group together by prescribing norms or rules regulating the roles and behavior of members. Groups of various kinds horizontally segment a society, divide it into sometimes rigid, sometimes very loose and flexible compartments—although the compartmentation may be very loose and flexible as individuals share memberships by belonging to several groups. Groups which layer a society vertically are referred to as socio-economic classes, or as castes if the vertical division is very rigid.

Social Segmentation and Compartmentation

A diversity of ideas and interests exists within any society, so that a truly homogeneous society is at best a very rare thing. The analytical task is to determine what general kinds of ideas and interests characterize the horizontal group structure of a society, the extent to which such a group structure produces patterns of group conflict and cooperation, and the intensity of such cooperation or conflict. It is also important to assess the relative power of the groups with significant political roles, the extent to which group segmentation cross-cuts or is interrelated with social stratification, and the overall political consequences of such segmentation patterns.

Some groups have economic roots, with common or similar ideas and interests growing out of roles in the economic system. In modern industrial societies these are usually formally organized and commonly referred to as interest groups—the myriad of labor unions, business and trade associations, consumer groups, farm organizations which are all deeply involved in political processes. But some may not be formally organized, or in many societies and particularly in the new states of Africa and Asia the associations may include only a minority as formal members. Many workers are not members of labor unions, many farmers do not belong to any farm organization. Yet members of such economic groups generally have some awareness, dim or otherwise, of common or shared interests, and on occasion cooperate with one another in conflicts with other groups. Nonunion members frequently cooperate in strikes and demonstrations, consumers occasionally organize on a temporary basis to picket supermarkets and government offices, peasants occasionally rise up more or less spontaneously and dump excess produce across highways or seize pitchforks or firearms to launch insurrections.

Some groups have cultural or mixed socio-economic roots, again based on common, shared, or similar purposes, and again may or may not have formal organizations. Catholics, Muslims, Hindus, Buddhists generally tend to have group consciousness, with some belonging to formal organizations, others not, but the consciousness or membership producing on occasion degrees of cooperation and conflict with competing groups. Similar kinds of group identification and activity characterize the political life of many societies—racial and ethnic identifications in the United States, tribal identifications in Africa and Asia, linguistic groups in India, Switzerland, and Canada, ideological groups—Communists, Socialists, Liberals, Conservatives—in many states. Some groups have mixed roots —women demanding anti-sex discrimination action on both economic and ideological grounds, students spontaneously organizing to shut down college campuses or to demonstrate in the streets, political parties which may have both ideological and socio-economic foundations.

Sometimes the cultural purposes of groups interact with socio-economic purposes, a combination that frequently produces stormy politics and violence. The Catholic-Protestant conflict in Northern Ireland and the Muslim-Hindu conflict in India are in part religious in origin, but also involve socio-economic factors in that Catholics and Muslims have been socially and economically discriminated against in these respective areas. Tribal conflicts frequently erupt in Africa as one tribe attempts to establish or displace another in political or economic power. Racial and ethnic conflicts of mixed roots plague the United States and some other western societies. Minority linguistic-cultural groups are frequently discriminated against in such diverse places as India, Yugoslavia, the Soviet Union, and Canada, and frequently produce troublesome conflicts.

Shared group memberships and cross-cutting horizontal cleavages also exist in many societies, with varying political consequences. An auto worker as a worker comes into conflict with management, but he also shares with management interest in the well-being of the auto industry, which produces some cooperation. Shared group memberships thus frequently blunt or moderate conflict in a society. But cross-cutting cleavages may also complicate conflict patterns and reduce the effective power of some groups: labor and farmer organizations in France are divided into three major groups along religious and ideological lines, effectively reducing the power of these groups due to the absence of organizational cohesion.

CLASS AND CASTE STRATIFICATION

Inequality everywhere, coupled with at least degrees of discrimination against those less equal than others, is a fact of life, and hence some kind of vertical class division and conflict is characteristic of all societies. A socio-economic class or caste is also a group, but the element of formal organization is seldom present, and awareness of interdependence due to common or shared interests and purposes may be somewhat more dim in many instances. Class and caste are vertical divisions of society in that they involve status of groups, group and not individual prestige and rank based on a more or less recognized hierarchical organization of society. But societies differ in terms of the criteria which confer rank, the complexity of stratification patterns, disparities in wealth, status, and privilege among the classes, the potential for upward or downward mobility, and the extent and intensity of class conflict.

The traditional class structure of India (which still persists despite substantial cultural, socio-economic, and political change) is a very complex hierarchical ordering of several thousand castes into four social orders (plus a fifth, the Untouchables, who are below the others by being "outside" the structure). The basis of this structure is the Hindu religion, and membership in a caste is acquired by birth—no matter what one does or accomplishes in life, he remains within his caste of birth. Mobility was rare, and could only take the form of group mobility—a caste but not individuals could move slightly upward (or downward) in the hierarchic order. Disparities among adjacent castes were not very great, but tremendous between those near or at the top and those near the bottom. Caste conflict did not exist so long as this traditional order was accepted as preordained. It is now becoming intense in some areas of India as higher-caste landowners and lower-caste peasants increasingly resort to violence.

In other relatively simple and traditional agrarian societies of the past and present, a somewhat simpler class structure prevails. Membership in the aristocracy at the top is usually conferred by birth, but invariably is related to land ownership and also to political power: but membership can also be conferred by status-bearing occupation or role—the priestly or military classes—or by cultural factors such as status-bearing tribes or ethnic groups. The bulk of the population is constituted by the poor and relatively powerless peasantry, some of whom may own small plots of land, with others being landless. A small third class, with membership based on occupation as merchant, shopkeeper, or bureaucrat, also usually exists, with status sometimes below that of the peasantry, sometimes between the aristocracy and peasantry. These structures are also quite rigid, although upward mobility is sometimes possible by joining the priestly, military, or commercial occupations and sometimes even by somehow acquiring land. Disparities of wealth and privilege tend to be extreme, but class warfare was limited so long as passivity and fatalism were characteristic of cultural patterns.

Far more complex stratification and conflict patterns are characteristic of developing and industrial and post-industrial societies, although somewhat of a three-layered structure can be identified in most. Membership in the "upper class" is usually acquired through great wealth and high income, although the criteria of birth and occupation still persist. In developing societies the upper class is often clearly divided into the traditional landed and the new-moneyed commercial, financial, and industrial aristocracy. Membership in the "middle class" is determined by occupation and income, as is membership in the "lower class" on the basis of manual or unskilled labor and lower income. But within this three-layered structure, far greater complexity usually prevails in terms of gradations within the three main layers, as for example within the middle classes, and differences between skilled and unskilled workers. In addition, somewhat of a special class has emerged from the technostructure: a managerial, professional, and technical class which has significantly affected the politics not only of western but also of communist industrial systems. In some and particularly in developing societies a special class of "modernizing intellectuals," whose objective is rapid economic, social, and political change, can be distinguished, with important political roles. Disparities of wealth and privilege in the class structure of industrial societies vary, but greater fluidity and possibilities for mobility are common to most.

CLASS AND GROUP ATTITUDES

Class and group attitudes are very significant with respect to patterns of cooperation or conflict. Class consciousness is one such important attitude—the extent to which members of a particular income, occupational, or other kind of group are aware of being members of such a group or strata, of interdependence and common interests with other members of the group, and of conflicting interests with other groups or strata. In some societies (such as European), class consciousness is deeply ingrained. In others, such as the United States, most people tend to identify as members of the middle class—although class consciousness is expressed to a degree by voting alignments in that Democratic voting strength increases as one moves down the income and occupation ladder. In still other societies class consciousness is weakened because of primary identification with racial, ethnic, religious, or similar kinds of groups.

Perceptions of disparities and discrimination, and expectations with respect to upward mobility and an improved standard of living are also important attitudes. In traditional agrarian societies disparities were perceived but accepted as one's lot in life, but expectations are now rising with significant consequences for social conflict. The same phenomenon is developing in industrial societies where skilled and unskilled workers, various ethnic minorities, and others near the bottom of the hierarchy are demanding opportunities for upward mobility and expecting reduction of disparities and more material benefits from the society.

Suspicion and hostility among classes and other groups are also significant. In some societies, Britain and Germany for example, class consciousness is present, but, at least until recently, such consciousness was mixed with an element of deference to the upper classes. In others, intense hostility among classes is pervasive. Class-based political conflict involving intense class consciousness and hostility can be political dynamite, particularly when expectations increase while disparities are perceived as widening.

The Political Consequences of Environmental Factors

6

At various points in the preceding chapters we mentioned the political importance of individual environmental factors. In this chapter we systematically summarize the consequences of the interaction of these factors. We first discuss their impact on the location and distribution of power in the society; on the kinds of conflict and cooperation patterns which prevail; and the relationship between these factors and the maintenance or development of support inputs and legitimacy. We then continue with a discussion of broader consequences: the relationship between cultural, socio-economic, and power factors and the nature, scope and policy outputs, and the stability and effectiveness of political systems. We conclude with a brief discussion of the relationship between environmental and political change, and of the necessity of considering both facts and values with respect to political change.

THE CONSEQUENCES FOR POLITICAL POWER

Cultural and socio-economic factors affect the location and distribution of political power in a society in two major ways. First, they condition who or which groups have power, and the extent to which varied resources are indeed influential. Second, they shape the power distribution pattern within the society.

ENVIRONMENTAL FACTORS AND THE ELEMENTS OF POWER

Cultural and socio-economic factors affect the elements of power in a variety of ways. Prestige, for example, linked with credibility, is culturally-conditioned, with religion, lineage, tribal affiliation, seniority, or military leadership conferring status in different societies. While wealth tends to be a resource of power in most societies, the extent to which it confers prestige depends on the culture, and the degree to which it can be acquired depends on the socio-economic setting. The form of economic power also depends on the setting. Wealth by itself is a major resource in capitalist economies; it means less in socialist countries, where key position in the economic hierarchy is substantially more important.

Numbers is an important resource in settings which bestow legitimacy on popular demands, or settings which make possible mass actions—such as mass demonstrations in cities. But numbers mean less in authoritarian-subject cultures, or when widespread apathy, poverty, and illiteracy make it difficult to mobilize masses.

Organization is a most important power resource, but both the ability to organize and to maintain cohesion are dependent on environmental factors. Cultural settings such as the French, which emphasize individualism, are not conducive to the formation of cohesive organizations because individuals tend to avoid an associational life, and when they do join, find it difficult to act in a cohesive fashion. In societies where traditional identifications persist, people are reluctant to associate along economic or occupational lines, or do so on the basis of their primary group, so that one finds tribal-based labor unions in Africa, Muslim and Hindu chambers of commerce in India. The power of such groups is significantly reduced because of the absence of either organization or cohesion.

The influence of such resources as information, skill, and expertise seems directly related to the complexity of a society and its economy. Influence of organization tends also to be enhanced in complex societies because humans need to be organized to attain complex diverse goals. Thus a modern industrial society cannot function without the resources of the technostructure, and without the voluntary or involuntary cooperation of such diverse organizations as labor unions, trade and professional associations, and farm organizations for the implementation of economic policies.

In general, the influence of power-wielders is considerably dependent on the extent to which there is harmony between their goals and the cultural norms and socio-economic goals of the society. When traditional kinds of interest groups, for example, enjoy greater prestige and credibility in the society than do economic interest groups, the influence of the former will be substantially greater than that of the latter. Power-wielders who pursue goals at variance with those of most society, or who use methods which clash with accepted behavior norms, tend to have less influence. Even violent force tends to be less effective in societies where resort to violence is abhorred.

ENVIRONMENTAL FACTORS AND POWER DISTRIBUTION PATTERNS

In general but with some exceptions, more complex societies tend to have power distribution patterns of non-cumulative dispersion; societies with simpler cultural and socio-economic patterns tend towards patterns of cumulative concentration.

Agrarian societies tend to have an oligarchic elite structure consisting of land or herd owners and the upper elements of the religious order, the army and the bureaucracy. But as these economies become commercialized and then begin to industrialize, new elites with new commercial and industrial interests, with new and secular ideas, and with varying resources of wealth, skill, information, and even degrees of prestige and organization, begin to develop. This is one of the major sources of the instability of developing societies, for the older elites usually strive to perpetuate the old culture which propped up their power, to preserve their privileges, and to retain political power.

Substantially more pluralism and polyarchy is characteristic of all types of complex industrial and post-industrial societies. Some of the traditional elites may still retain some power, but the power configuration among the socio-economic elites also tends to be pluralistic. Businessmen, industrialists, bankers, and financiers may be united in conflicts against traditional elites but tend to be divided among themselves by different socio-economic and sometimes cultural interests. In addition the varied elements of the managerial, professional, and technical elites who may not have much wealth nor even the power to organize, may have substantial power due to their prestige, their control over key economic positions, and their needed resources of expertise and skill. Surrogates of the masses—labor and farmer leaders, organized or not—hold similar key positions and their support and services are needed. Complex societies also require complex channels of information and communication, so that elites who control such channels are added to the power structure. The net consequence is substantial pluralism, competition, and sometimes also degrees of representation.

Socio-economic development may have an impact on the respective size of the politically relevant and apolitical strata. In agrarian societies the masses seldom have any resources save numbers, and are too deeply mired in poverty to have any interest in politics save when oppression and exploitation become so great that they resort to mass action. But economic development brings about some dispersion of wealth and information and skills via literacy and education, and a greater awareness of interests and a consequent tendency to organize. Cognitive orientations may thus develop, expectations may rise, and some means may be available for the masses to levy effective demands. In turn, the elites may have greater need for the masses, either in terms of degrees of mass support for inter-elite conflicts, for stability and effectiveness of government, or for their special skills. The net effect again is to enhance pluralism and competition, and perhaps representation. However, this does not mean that socio-economic development will result in the evolution of democratic systems. The masses may still be lacking the cultural requisite—the participatory conception of authority and the basic beliefs—or the resources of power necessary to wrest political control from the more authoritarian minded elites.

CONFLICT AND COOPERATION PATTERNS

As a consequence of the interplay between cultural and socio-economic factors, in all societies there prevail cooperation and conflict patterns along three dimensions: between segments of the society (various kinds of organized or unorganized interest groups), strata of society (class lines), and patterns which involve both group and class alignments. Although the specifics of such interactions vary among societies, several kinds of distinct patterns tend to develop. Several major analytical questions must be asked to determine the major pattern characteristic of specific systems or types of systems.

PATTERNS OF COOPERATION

What major patterns of cooperation, if any, are characteristic of the system? To what extent does consensus produce cooperation on fundamental issues and on specific policy questions? Does there seem to be a proper balance between conflict and consensus so as to ensure social cohesion, despite cleavages in the society? What trends appear to be developing with respect to group or class cooperation, and with what potential consequences for stability?

Patterns of cooperation are characteristic of even the most conflict-ridden societies. The very formation of groups, whether it be for conflict or for other purposes, and the existence of class consciousness, involve degrees of cooperation and may promote degrees of integration of the society. Cooperation develops when segments or strata are aware of some degree of interdependence, when people realize that their fates are linked together to some extent, and anticipate that gains for either the entire society or for other segments or strata will also bring them some material or non-material values. Such patterns of cooperation based on recognition of common, similar, or converging interests have major consequences for the system, particularly to the extent they provide for a balance between cleavage and consensus, which seems essential for domestic stability and cohesion.

When a deep and strong consensus exists or develops concerning basic beliefs, values, and conceptions of authority and scope, which cuts across all group and class alignments, it tends to have major consequences for the basic nature of systems. If such a consensus settles on more-or-less democratic conceptions of authority, then democracies will be sustained, but authoritarian regimes will find it increasingly difficult to maintain themselves in power without gradually reforming themselves. The socioeconomic-geographic setting may produce fairly common economic problems and interests, in which case many groups and classes, recognizing their interdependence and expecting benefits from cooperative demands, may either consciously and in an organized way, or sometimes more or less spontanenously, cooperate in demanding a general policy orientation on the part of the system—expansion of scope by way of intervention in the economy, actions to cope with energy, unemployment, or other kinds of economic problems, actions to cope with law and order problems or with racial or religious strife. Either kind of consensus provides a framework which tends to balance conflict patterns and in which the resolution of specific policy conflicts is facilitated.

More limited and sometimes temporary patterns of cooperation result from similar factors of interdependence and expectations of positive rewards, but may have the consequence of intensifying conflicts. It may result in certain class alignments—middle and upper classes in Chile combining with the military to oust a left-wing government, lower and middle classes in Portugal cooperating with some military elements to topple a right-wing dictatorship. It may result in temporary or durable alignments of major groups—various labor unions behind demands for improved unemployment compensation, unions cooperating with consumers against governmental maintenance of farm prices, Ibos cooperating with Yorubas to weaken the Hausa tribe's domination of the Nigerian government. It may result in similar alignments cutting across group and class lines—auto workers cooperating with management to promote the interests of the auto industry, sometimes to the detriment of other industries, consumers, and taxpayers.

Of special importance in the analysis of such patterns of cooperation is the assessment of the extent to which the many special interests within the society overlap so that the idea of a common interest or good will have real meaning to most sectors and strata— so that they recognize their interdependence and expect a positive covariance of rewards with many issues. Overlapping special interests tend to produce a genuine sense of community of interests, and make possible the bargaining and compromise so essential for the peaceful resolution of conflicts and for the maximization of the public interest. When management, labor, farmers, and consumers all recognize that they have a common stake in the American economy, and majorities and varied minorities in equal opportunity and domestic peace and stability, a sense of community exists which facilitates resolution of conflicts over specifics. When privileged Protestants and underprivileged Catholics in Northern Ireland recognize that they have overlapping interests as producers, consumers, and human beings, and that they have a common interest in domestic peace and prosperity, then cooperation may begin to replace violent conflict. Modern nationalism, which is further discussed below, despite its divisive impact on humanity, has at least within national frontiers helped to promote cooperation and blunt the edge of group and class conflict.

PATTERNS OF CONFLICT

What kinds of conflict patterns prevail in the society? Is class conflict a major characteristic? If so, how intense is it? Do overlapping interests tend to weaken class alignments? What kinds of horizontal group conflicts prevail?

Patterns of conflict are characteristic of all societies, and are due simply to a natural diversity of ideas and interests. The more acute conflicts, particularly those involving violence, develop either because interdependence is not recognized, or because groups or classes fear major losses as the result of gains by opposing groups or classes.

Class conflicts of some type exist in most societies simply because of inequalities inherent in any society. The privileged classes, whatever the basis of their privilege, generally seek to maintain or enhance their advantages with varying degrees of intensity, while the less privileged seek to reduce disparities. Class conflicts of the type emphasized by Marxists, involving exploiting privileged landowners or capitalists and exploited peasants or workers, can be extremely dangerous and may breed violent revolutions. There have been elements of such conflicts in recent years in Chile, Portugal, France, Italy, and Vietnam.

More generally, class conflicts tend to be either muted or less violent, but also more complicated, for a number of reasons. For one, what counts with respect to the eruption of serious class conflict are attitudes, expectations, and perceptions, all bred by cultural and socio-economic factors.

The masses or a significant proportion of the less privileged may be fatalistic and passive and hence resigned to poverty, or even bondage (although such attitudes tend to change quite rapidly as societies evolve from traditional status). Disparities in status and wealth may not be perceived as being very great, or the attitudes of elites or other factors may produce some possibilities for upward mobility. Economic growth may also increase the overall size of the economic pie, so that even while disparities of wealth persist and the proportion of the pie available to the underprivileged remains the same, the size of the latter's slice nonetheless grows and, hence, the ardor for intense conflict may be minimal. Conversely, the less privileged may perceive the inequality as intense, the privileged classes may be obstinate in their attitudes, economic declines may increase the disparities and decrease possibilities for upward mobility, and ideological doctrines may lead to sharp social alignments along class lines. The emphasis on equality, for example, which began to get underway during the nineteenth century, first led to class consciousness and conflict, then to conflicts involving a variety of underprivileged minority groups, and now to the complex conflicts characteristic of former western colonies and even to conflicts between the rich and poor states of the world.

Overlapping interests and cross-cutting cleavages in society may also shatter class alignments or lead to more complex conflicts. Class consciousness may be weak, as in the United States, or superseded by regional, religious, tribal, or similar kinds of consciousness, so that individuals are more conscious of being Hindus or Ibos than they are of being workers or peasants. Clerical conflicts over the relationship between church and state may be more important and shatter class alignments, as they have in France and Italy. Or class alignments may be rivalled by others for political purposes, as workers and management combine in conflict against other economic groups, or as all strata within a particular geographic region, tribe, or linguistic group combine against other regions.

Group conflicts, among varied segments of a society, tend to be much more common, although they often involve some degree of class conflict in that the competing groups may be segments of different strata—auto workers versus management, skilled versus unskilled labor. They may be primarily cultural in nature—tribal conflicts, religious or ideological groups against each other, traditionalists versus secularists, linguistic groups against others. They may be primarily economic in nature—the conflicts which are most prevalent in modern industrial states. Or they may involve a combination of cultural, status, and economic issues, such as Hindus versus Muslims in India, Bengalis versus Pakistanis, and Blacks versus Whites in the United States and South Africa.

What is the range and complexity of conflict patterns? Is it a relatively simple and restricted range, mainly involving economic groups competing over economic issues of the day? Or is it a broad and complex pattern involving a variety of social, economic, and cultural groups competing over both immediate and fundamental issues? Even though conflict is prevalent in all societies, significant differences prevail with respect to such conflict patterns.

In some societies conflicts, even though they may be complex, are still *relatively simple* as contrasted with others. These are in relatively homogeneous, consensual, integrated societies, in which both a substantive and procedural consensus prevails, and in which conflicts only seldom erupt over fundamentals—over who should rule, the scope of governmental authority, or how conflicts should be resolved. In these, most conflicts involve competition among major economic groups over the specific allocation of material values—labor, business, finance, agriculture, consumers, and various segments and strata of such groups. The society is stratified, but possibilities for upward mobility exist, and the disparities are not perceived as very great. Some non-economic or cultural conflicts persist—among religious, ideological, ethnic, and similar kinds of groups —but only some of these cleavages involve substantial disparities and hostility. In such a society varying patterns of cooperation can be developed, of both the durable and short-term variety. A sense of community, common identity, and common interest integrates people of diverse ideas and interests. Most modern democratic industrial states fit this pattern to a greater or lesser degree, at least up to now.

By contrast, some societies are *fragmented,* often lacking both a substantive and procedural consensus, and also divided or fragmented along very complex lines involving socio-economic, cultural, and geographic issues. Most African, Asian, and many Latin American states fit this pattern, as well as some Europeans such as France, Italy, Yugoslavia. Conflicts prevail not only among major economic groups over material values, but also reflect the intense and hostile cleavages between tribal, ethnic, religious, and similar kinds of cultural and social groups. In these societies it is extremely difficult if not impossible to develop broad patterns of cooperation, as conflict more frequently involves not merely specific issues of the day, but fundamentals of the system and society. Intense and often violent conflict is a way of life because of the absence of a sense of community or common interest. Political stability and effectiveness are consequently absent, and the fragmented nature of the society invites either constant deadlock, or violence, chaos, and anarchy.

But even more debilitating with respect to political stability and effectiveness is a pattern of *compartmentation.* In some societies differences of ideas and interest do not splinter the people into numerous conflicting groups, but divide them into two or three extremely hostile groups.

Differences tend to be cumulative, in that the people in one geographic region differ radically from people in other regions over fundamental economic issues and also by way of culture, religion, ethnic derivation, language, and similar social and cultural factors. This kind of compartmentation breeds civil war, as in such diverse states as the United States, Northern Ireland, Yugoslavia, Cyprus, Nigeria, Pakistan. A milder but still dangerous form exists in some industrial states—Blacks versus Whites, urban dwellers versus suburbanites, Ukrainians versus Great Russians.

Patterns of conflict resolution are related to the range, complexity, and intensity of conflict patterns with a society. But some special environmental factors have a bearing on whether the pattern tends to be one of frequent or constant deadlock, violence, or peaceful accomodation. Most fundamental is the usual style of groups in conflict, and the climate for peaceful resolution which prevails throughout the society.

Most important again is the matter of a substantive consensus, broad agreement on the most basic beliefs and on conceptions of authority and scope. This limits the range of conflicts to the relatively easier types pertaining to policy issues of the day rather than to more intractable issues which involve fundamentals. It also tends to facilite resolution by enlarging the area of agreement on what would constitute a desirable solution—what is considered to be fair, moral, and in the public interest. A procedural consensus is also very helpful, particularly if it stresses pragmatic rather than doctrinaire approaches. A pervasive sense of trust is also very helpful, particularly as past experience with peaceful settlement and mutual attempts at accomodation promote such trust.

A socio-economic setting characterized by relatively few and less hostile cleavages and a consequent limited range of conflicts, in which there is more-or-less common recognition of common or similar socio-economic problems, has a similar beneficial impact; as does an economic setting of surplus rather than scarcity. Relative equality of coercive power is also helpful; although this factor may promote deadlock rather than resolution, it at least reduces the potential for violent resolution. Pluralistic conflict patterns rather than compartmentation patterns may also be helpful in avoiding violence and in promoting bargaining by the possibility of coalition building, although if hostilities accompany a fragmented conflict pattern, chaos is a likely outcome.

SUPPORT INPUTS AND LEGITIMACY

Chapter 1 discussed the nature and importance of support inputs and legitimacy, and Chapter 2 related these concepts to the power of governments over their societies. We now discuss the impact of interacting environmental factors on these qualities which are so essential for political stability and effectiveness.

DEGREES AND LEVELS OF SUPPORT AND LEGITIMACY

Precisely how much and whose support a particular political system may need for stability and effectiveness depends on a variety of situational factors peculiar to each individual system. But a few generalizations are possible. First, stability is necessary for but does not guarantee effective performance. In certain situations systems and governments may be able to maintain themselves in power (such as for example when the opposition is fragmented, or when people prefer any kind of government to chaos or revolution); but lacking support, will be unable to effectively perform whatever functions they select. Second, the degree of support must be commensurate with the scope and complexity of governmental endeavors and problems. Governments in relatively simple societies with functions related primarily to domestic security probably need less support than those attempting to manage complex industrial states. Generally, the greater the degree of detailed and technical control governments seek over the economic and other spheres of their society, the more they need consent and voluntary active participation by the various affected groups to ensure successful performance. Third, the less support available, the greater the need for a vast, expensive, efficient, and loyal coercive apparatus. But lack of support throughout society may ultimately affect the support and loyalty of police and military forces and the bureaucracy. Fourth, support must be related to the configuration of power in the society. Systems and governments need varying degrees of support among those in society with significant power and with expectations of government rewards. They need at least some elite support, and given substantial politically relevant strata, they need some mass support. Fifth, although all types of systems need legitimacy, democracies need more support than authoritarian systems.

The problem of the degree of support also involves levels of support. Three such levels may be distinguished, listed in order of decreasing importance. However, declining degrees of support for the lower levels may over time lead to erosion of support for the higher levels.

1. Support for the Political Unit or Community. For a given political unit or level of government—a tribe, county, city, state, or nation—to survive and govern effectively, it must be considered legitimate by those with power within that community, it must have actions and attitudes within the community which tend to sustain or preserve it. Lack of support will make the community prone to disintegration or the political unit

prone to absorption by other communities. Empires and nations disintegrate into smaller communities as they fail to maintain support from their populations and fail to integrate their societies. Small kinship groups or hamlets are prone to absorption by larger units if they fail to maintain support for their continued existence as political units. Although the legitimacy of the political community does not necessarily engender support for the existing political system or government, its illegitimacy will spill over into the lower levels: if the community does not enjoy support, its system and government are likely to be considered illegitimate.

2. Support for the Political System, for the "constitutional system," for the general nature and scope of government. Whether democratic, authoritarian, or totalitarian, any specific kind of system needs to be considered as legitimate by the more powerful elements in society. Systems lacking such support may, so long as support for the political community remains strong, enjoy some stability and effectiveness. However, failure to develop support for the system may, over time, erode support for the community. Opposition groups within the unit may, if they fail in their efforts to change the system, attempt to secede and form separate units, or may seek absorption by other units.

3. Support for the Government of the moment, for the specific party or political elites currently holding authority within the system, and for the specific laws of government. Some degree of support for this level is necessary for real stability and effectiveness, insofar as voluntary compliance with law tends to decline as governments or specific laws are considered illegitimate. Continuing long-term lack of support may also erode support for the system and community. Those with power in society, unable to change either the types of elites who govern or their laws, may try to change the system, or unable to do that, may try to secede from the community. When the Bengalis in South Asia could change neither continued rule by Pakistanis nor the system imposed by Pakistan, they fought a successful civil war to establish their independence.

THE DEVELOPMENT AND MAINTENANCE OF SUPPORT AND LEGITIMACY

Legitimacy is basically dependent on compatibility of values. The political unit, the system, the government and its policies must be compatible with the basic beliefs, values, and goals which prevail throughout the society. Such compatibility brings positive affective and evaluative orientations among those strata of society who are politically relevant because of their cognitive orientations. This also pertains to sub-cultures. Tribes, regions, religious, ethnic and other kinds of groups or social strata whose values are not in accord with those of the political unit, system, or government will not endow any of these levels with legitimacy. The support a system enjoys thus is directly related to the extent to which its values appear to fit the values of various segments and strata of society.

But as stated in Chapter 1, two kinds of values are involved: moral values—internalized standards of rights, obligations, justice, and proper norms of behavior—and acquisitive values, material and non-material goals pursued by individuals. Legitimacy and support are thus dependent on whether or not the nature of the system is in accord with prevailing basic beliefs and conceptions of authority; whether the unit, system or government came to power in accord with such values; whether it governs in accord with such values; and whether its overall performance is evaluated as satisfactory in the light of moral and acquisitive values. If these elements are present then political units, systems, and governments will be supported because denial of support and violation of laws would inflict damage to important values of individuals—psychological damage in terms of moral values, other kinds of damage in terms of acquisitive values. Thus legitimacy and support can be maintained or developed by two means: the *political socialization process* to maintain or develop support-ive culture, and *policy outputs* which create and allocate values matching the expectations of the various segments and strata of society. If socializa-tion processes within American Black communities emphasize the theme that American government is a white and racist government, and if policy outputs fail to match expectations of Black Americans, then the American system will be denied the support of many Black Americans.

To enjoy legitimacy, the political community, system, and government must have a supportive culture. All levels must develop or maintain positive evaluative orientations arising from the prevailing cultural pat-terns which function as frameworks of perception and evaluation. They will develop trust and enjoy support to the extent that each level matches prevailing beliefs about the nature of man and his rights, the relationship between the individual and society, and prevailing conceptions of author-ity and scope. The retention of support is thus dependent on the extent to which the socialization process is homogeneous, consistent, and cumu-lative so as to reinforce and stabilize the prevailing culture, or the extent to which it is modifying or changing the culture so as to reinforce and support a new or changing system. The winning of support by a new political unit or system is dependent on the extent to which the socializa-tion process transforms an older culture in a direction which will support the new unit or system.

The extent to which policy outputs match expectations is equally im-portant. Unsatisfactory performance is likely to produce disruptions in the socialization process, and to erode support because legitimacy is dependent not only on moral but also acquisitive values. Also, support-generating policies can compensate for a weak socialization process and can in time produce a supportive culture as people begin to see congruence of values between themselves and government. But three major qualifications are relevant. First, what counts are the value allocation expectations of those with cognitive orientations and some degree of power. Failure to resolve the basic needs or to respond to the ineffective demands of those who expect little or who have little or no power—an illiterate, passive, fatalistic, and submissive peasantry—does not endanger support (unless, of course, expectations and cognitive orientations are rising). Second, what counts are elite and mass perceptions and evaluations of policy outputs. Governments can, for example, at least for a time continue to generate support by creating the illusion of satisfactory outputs and by manipulating various symbols which generate or maintain affective orientations. Third, what counts is long-term satisfactory performance. Short-run failure to satisfy expectations does not necessarily endanger systems. They may continue to enjoy support and survive many economic downturns, defeats in war, and other kinds of crises either because of a strong supportive culture and a stabilizing socialization process, "reserve" support engendered by past performance, or anticipations of improved and future performance. But in the long run, failure to meet expectations leads to alienation, tends to undermine the culture, and erodes support for all three levels of government, systems, and political community. This is the crisis which confronts many democratic nations today as they seem unable to resolve chronic economic crises.

FOUR MAJOR CHALLENGES TO LEGITIMACY

A survey of history and of contemporary political systems suggests that all systems faced in the past or confront today four major problems of legitimacy, whose successful resolution seems essential for the survival of political units and systems and for continuing stability and effectiveness. Some states have vanished from the political map of the world because they failed to resolve them. Some contemporary nations have resolved some of them, and their continuing durability and effectiveness seems dependent on successful resolution of remaining challenges. The new states of Africa and Asia are struggling simultaneously with all four problems, and their very survival is at stake. Stability and effectiveness also seem directly related to the sequence and manner in which these challenges were confronted. The more stable and effective contemporary systems appear to be those which had to meet each challenge more or less one at a time, and which more or less satisfactorily resolved each problem as it arose—although resolution often took many generations and sometimes centuries. The more unstable and less effective systems seem to be those in which subsequent challenges arose before earlier challenges were satisfactorily resolved, or in which all four challenges arose almost simultaneously. In all cases these challenges arise as the result of the interaction of cultural, socio-economic, geographic, and political factors, with the consequent development of fundamental patterns of conflict and cooperation. And because of continuing change, particularly in the cultural and socio-economic spheres, some challenges which appear to have been satisfactorily resolved, may suddenly reappear.

The challenge of nation or community-building A major problem confronting a political system at any level—village, city, region, state, international—is developing a sense of community among the people subject to the system's jurisdiction. This is essential because it provides a sense of identification, loyalty, social solidarity, and affective orientations to the system. Such a sense of community integrates the diverse sectors and strata of society and produces the consensus and cooperation so vital to domestic peace and political effectiveness. Any society will have within it a number of factors which serve to integrate diverse segments and strata —class consciousness and membership in class-based political parties, religious identification, occupational or professional interest groups—so that a community of interest within these sectors and strata facilitates intra-group conflict resolution. The political problem is to develop such a sense of community and identification within the entire political unit.

The problem of the modern sovereign territorial state which claims exclusive legal authority over all people living within its territory is that of nation-building, of developing the concept of the legitimacy of the nation as the larger and central political system. This entails developing the nation-state, in which most people have such a sense of primary loyalty, commitment, and sense of common identity, so that a sense of community of interest pervades the entire state. This does not necessarily entail the development of a homogeneous society, or the erasure of sub-cultures, or the shedding of loyalties to sub-national units or communities. It does entail recognition of and loyalty to the nation as the primary community, and the consequent development of mutual trust, good will, and responsiveness among the various segments and strata of society. It does involve the development of a substantive and procedural consensus, and a socialization process which develops these and the consequent legitimacy of the nation as the central political unit. In the United States people still identify as and have some loyalty to regions (New Yorkers), occupation and class (auto worker), religion, and similar groups. But the primary identification and loyalty—particularly in relation to outsiders or "foreigners"—is that of being an American.

The problem persists to some degree in older nation-states: racial integration in the United States, Britain's occasional problems with Scots and Welsh, Canada and the French-speaking minority. Some older states are not yet really nation-states, such as the Soviet Union and Yugoslavia with their numerous national minorities. The major problem of nation-building is faced by the new states of Africa, Asia, and elsewhere, which are polyethnic rather than nation-states. These have only begun to transfer loyalties and commitments from kinship groups, tribes, villages, regions, religious communities to the new larger and central political system. Lacking a sense of national community of interest, patterns of cooperation tend to prevail only within those communities wherein there is a sense of social solidarity, while patterns of conflict persist among the sub-national communities and cultures.

The authority problem of state-building is closely related to and often parallels the challenge of nation-building, but it is a problem of a different order. It involves developing support for the political system, establishing the legitimacy of the national or central system, its institutions, and its manner of rule. It is in part a cultural problem—developing a consensus on conceptions of authority which will support the system. It is in part a structural and power problem: ensuring that the legal authority of the larger and central system (the national level) penetrates throughout the entire national community, integrates that community into a web of obedience to the central authority, and supersedes or takes precedence over the authority and power of subordinate political units. In medieval Europe it involved the problem of establishing the authority of the king over princes, barons, and fiefdoms, and still persists to some extent as some regions continue to be jealous of their prerogatives (Bavaria in Germany). In the United States it involved establishing and gaining acceptance for the balance of legal authority between the Federal government and the States, and still persists to some degree as occasional conflicts erupt over states' rights. Resolution of the problem is basically linked with that of nation-building; unintegrated minorities or nationalities are not likely to view authority of the central government as legitimate, they view it as rule by foreigners.

This authority problem arises whenever a new and larger political unit arises (the creation of the United States as a federation of states), or when major structural and procedural changes are effected within the existing system (more authoritarian or democratic patterns of rule). In either case two more impediments to establishing the legitimacy of the new authority usually arise and frequently make it difficult to obtain voluntary compliance (and sometimes even effective coercion).

The creation of a new or the restructuring of an old authority may threaten the status, privileges, and power of existing and traditional authorities. In Europe the establishment of the central monarchy threatened the power of the feudal nobility; the later establishment of more democratic institutions threatened the status and power of the monarchy, the aristocracy, and the established religious order. Thus the traditional elites, if they feel threatened, are likely to resist change. But also, considering the nature of power, the establishment of a new form of legal authority does not necessarily erode the influence of older elites. In the new states of Africa and Asia the power of the new authoritarian and democratic central governments and their bureaucracies to influence the thought and behavior of people is substantially less than their legal authority. Traditional leaders—landowners, tribal chiefs, religious leaders, village and kinship group elders, provincial authorities—not only tend to resist the new authority if such authority is evaluated as contrary to their interests, but also continue to have substantial influence over members of their tribes, religious communities, and similar legally-subordinate units.

The decisions of the new or restructured old authority may also threaten or conflict with traditional cultural patterns, customs, and ways of life. The communist leaders of China experienced substantial difficulty in establishing their authority because in many ways it conflicted with the Confucian pattern. The rulers of the new states are experiencing substantial difficulty because their approaches to government and economics conflict with some deep-seated customs pertaining to such things as decision-making by consensus, land use and tenure, religious principles and behavior norms. In essence, numerous environmental factors may interact to impede authority's ability to obtain compliance either voluntarily or through coercion.

While the authority problem does not necessarily entail the erosion of all support for sub-national or traditional authorities, it does require the development of thought and action patterns throughout the society whereby the authority of the state is harmonized with the authority of lesser or lower political units and authorities, and of convincing people that the new or restructured authority is theirs or at least rules for them and in their interests. It involves developing a degree of consensus on conceptions of authority and scope. When a society is divided or polarized around different authority conceptions, then the legitimacy of the system will constantly be questioned by those in opposition, and the opposition will be disloyal in the sense that it opposes not merely policies but the basic system. This problem of a consensus afflicts not only the new but also some older states. France and Italy are still plagued by fundamental conflicts over the relationship between church and state, and by conflicts between those who prefer a more authoritarian or democratic system.

The participation challenge is a legitimacy and support problem in that as various groups or elites seek access to or some degree of participation in political processes, failure to respond to such demands may threaten legitimacy and support not only for the system, but also for the community.

Various socio-economic or cultural changes frequently bring with them changes in power configurations, cognitive orientations, and expectation levels among varied groups and strata of society. In some instances new elites may develop who demand some degree of participation in decision-making, and on the basis of their power may be able to make such demands effective. This kind of challenge arose in Europe as the agrarian economy became commercialized and then industrialized, and as the merchant, banking, and industrial princes, and then the middle class, demanded degrees of participation. This problem has erupted in communist systems as the new elites in the technostructure challenge the monopoly of decision-making by party elites. It is a problem confronting the new states, still coping with the problem of nation and state building, as both traditional and new elites, who participated in the independence movements that led to the creation of new states, found their hopes for participation in the new system dashed.

In other instances participation demands may emanate from broader segments or strata of the society and may in effect entail the democratization of the system. This kind of pattern, mixed with elite demands for participation, brought about the gradual democratization of modern democratic systems. Middle classes and later workers demanded participation, and the right to vote was gradually expanded. Later women, 18-year olds, and various minority groups began to levy similar demands, with varying patterns of responsiveness from the political elites. The problem has by no means been completely resolved in the west, as many groups continue to be dissatisfied with the perceived effectiveness of the vote, or demand participatory rather than merely representative democracy. The decade of the 1960's has indicated the degree of alienation that can result from perceptions of inadequate participation.

The distribution challenge is one which confronts all contemporary political systems. It is related to the problem of legitimacy in that perceived unsatisfactory performance in this respect may breed alienation and threaten support for systems. Historically and in the contemporary world this challenge involves a rapid increase in the volume and intensity of sometimes elite and sometimes mass demands for the political creation and allocation of material and nonmaterial values.

The problem is a significant one for the older and stabler political systems which have more or less successfully resolved the first three challenges. It has arisen partly because of expanding conceptions of scope—because more and more people now consider it a governmental function to intervene in economic and other spheres and to generate economic and other values. Another root may be the relative affluence of post-industrial societies, for affluence appears to raise rather than reduce expectations. We are no longer content with a chicken in every pot and an automobile in every garage; we now want steak, CB radios, and snow-mobiles, and expect the government to ensure that we can afford them. A third root are the higher expectations and the more effective demands of underprivileged groups, coupled perhaps with greater concern with social justice on the part of some privileged groups. This has increased the volume and intensity of demands for governmental action to redis-tribute such values as income, wealth, opportunity, and status. In some democratic societies the net impact of demands resulting from all these sources may well be exceeding the capabilities of political and socio-economic systems to respond, so that some analysts are concerned that the basic foundations of democracy may be threatened. The challenge also confronts authoritarian and totalitarian societies, where first the old political and the new technostructure elite distribution demands, and then some mass demands, began to develop what communist elites dis-dainfully refer to as the "consumer goods mentality" or "goulash com-munism" which is producing some alienation.

But again the problem is most acute in the new states of Africa and Asia, where the first three problems still persist, and in some of the older but relatively poor states. Political independence, new exposures to the outside world, the communication revolution of the past two decades, the promises made by leaders in an effort to lead successful revolutions and then stay in power, and many other factors have produced the "revolu-tion of rising expectations." Many people in these societies are no longer passive, apathetic, and fatalistic, are beginning to develop the "wants disease," are increasingly alienated by glaring disparities between the rich and the poor, and are increasingly turning to political action for the resolution of pressing needs and problems. Yet few of these societies have the means to even partially satisfy these rising expectations. Failure to meet these demands makes it that much more difficult to resolve the challenges of nation and state building, and elite and some mass demands for participation.

THE IMPACT ON THE NATURE OF POLITICAL SYSTEMS

What happens within any political arena results from the interaction between environmental forces and the ideas and interests of those who govern. Consequently, ideas and interests which prevail throughout the society influence and condition, but do not determine, the basic nature, structure, scope, and dynamics of political processes. Throughout history powerful elites have been able to impose unwanted authoritarian systems on societies. The basic structure of the American system is more the product of the political elites who founded it in 1787, and of elites who subsequently modified the structure, than it is the product of the American people.

But in most settings, the attitudes and goals of those who govern, and the type of political system they construct, are influenced by environmental forces for several reasons. First, the political elites generally are products of their environments, and consequently tend to share ideas and interests which prevail throughout the society, or at least the ideas and interests which prevail within the segments and strata from which they originated. Second, political and other self interests, combined with the need for support and particularly the need to legitimize the system, prompt them to be somewhat responsive to the demands of the more powerful groups in society. Third, decision-makers tend to be guided primarily by their own interests and value systems in determining what is good, just, rational, or in the public interest. But in specific conflict situations these abstract standards are very difficult to apply, and substantial uncertainty may prevail with respect to what is even good for the elites' self-interest, much less the public interest. Hence, policy-makers tend to be susceptible to influence from at least the more powerful forces in society.

Hence, even when political systems are imposed on societies, their basic nature, structure, and dynamics reflect to a considerable extent the ideas and interests of the more powerful segments and strata of society.

AUTHORITARIAN AND TOTALITARIAN SYSTEMS

These types of systems generally are imposed from above, but even the most despotic kinds have been responses to certain environmental factors. Authoritarian-minded political elites are able to seize and maintain political power by controlling formidable instruments of coercion—police, military, street mobs—in settings where the society as a whole or specific opposition groups lack the power to prevent the seizure of power or to topple the regime. Hitler's seizure of power in Germany reflected the will of Hitler, and the system survived until 1945 by ruthless suppression of any potential opposition elements. Communist regimes invariably have been imposed by force rather than by the will of the people, consolidated their power by ruthless suppression of opposition elements, and rely to a substantial extent on coercion to maintain their authority. The regimes of the Shah of Iran, the King of Saudi Arabia, military regimes in Africa and Asia, all follow the same pattern.

But cultural factors play significant roles. Authoritarian regimes generally develop and prosper in societies where an authoritarian subject conception of authority dominates or prevails, where an authoritarian pattern of rule is considered legitimate either by most of society or by the more powerful segments and strata (as in Hitler's Germany and Stalin's Russia). This need for a supporting culture is recognized as authoritarian regimes seek to legitimize themselves by manipulating some ideology or varied expressive symbols which justify their rule. Instability and the chronic need to resort to oppressive force is characteristic of authoritarian systems governing societies where democratic ideas have made substantial inroads, and instability increases as democratic ideas widen their influence. This is a problem which confronts many authoritarian systems in the form of the participation challenge to their legitimacy.

Socio-economic factors in the environmental setting are also significant. Authoritarian regimes rise to power or maintain themselves by winning the support of powerful socio-economic and sometimes cultural groups and strata. Traditional monarchies were based on the support of the landed aristocracy and the church. The power of modern autocracies in some instances rests on the same base, in others on the support of the moneyed aristocracy, in some on a combination of both. Communist, fascist, and some other types of authoritarian regimes have been able to seize power, and initially to consolidate their power, by enlisting at least the initial support of broader strata of society—workers, peasants, elements of the middle class. Such support frequently evaporates after the regimes have established themselves, but then a new power base in the society is invariably needed and developed.

Authoritarian systems also develop out of an excess of conflict in a society, when socio-economic and cultural conflicts become so widespread, complex, or intense that little consensus or cooperation prevails within the society. It may be socio-economic conflict along class lines—peasants versus landowners, workers against other classes; it may be intense conflict along cultural lines—tribes against other tribes, ethnic groups, religious communities; or it may be a combination of both. Authoritarian regimes in Chile and elsewhere in Latin American have been bred by class conflicts. Brief experiments in democracy in the new states of Africa and Asia were abruptly terminated because of the complex and intense conflicts characteristic of their societies. Such conflict patterns tend to breed authoritarian regimes for three reasons. For one, the result invariably is a fragmented opposition. Those who oppose authoritarian systems, or the particular group which attempts to or seizes power, cannot unite in their opposition. Second, what counts in such situations is cohesive force, and revolutions or coups are successful to the extent that they possess such power in a fragmented setting. Third, in such circumstances people are prone to accept and to a degree legitimize an authoritarian regime as a necessary evil, as preferable to chaos, anarchy, or civil war. The short-lived parliamentary regime in Russia in 1917, Germany's democratic interlude in the 1920s, post-independence democratic regimes in Africa and Asia, were not really overthrown by communist, fascist, and authoritarian forces; they collapsed, and the revolutionary forces had the power to install themselves in government. France in 1958 reluctantly accepted the authoritarian style of DeGaulle, because the choice seemed to be DeGaulle or civil war. But in all these and most other cases authoritarian subject conceptions of authority were either prevalent throughout the society, or prevailed among significant groups and strata.

The power configuration throughout the society is a crucial variable. In the short run the power of those who control the institutions of government and its coercive instruments, as opposed to the power of those who contest such control, is most important. But in the long run the distribution of power in society is more significant. Authoritarian systems tend to develop in situations of oligarchy, cumulative concentration of the resources of power, and in societies where the bulk or a large proportion of the population is apolitical. Conversely, when substantial countervailing power is provided by a polyarchic elite structure, by a distribution pattern of noncumulative dispersion of resources, and by a substantial politically relevant strata, the system tends to be more democratic. Except, again, when such a power pattern is accompanied by intense and complex conflict pattern so as to deny opposition elements the important resource of cohesion. Also, authoritarian systems governing in polyarchic power settings tend to be considerably less stable and effective.

DEMOCRATIC SYSTEMS

While authoritarian systems are often the result of long continuity or sudden transition, democratic systems have been the products of evolutionary development. Democracy was not a very respectable word in 1789, and the current American system—as well as British, French, others—is a result of gradual development of over a century. In a later chapter in which we discuss theories concerning the requisites of democracy—the conditions which appear to be essential for democracy to develop and thrive—we will deal more fully with the environmental roots of democracy. But some generalizations need to be briefly stated at this point.

Democratic systems tend to develop when elites and politically relevant strata have or develop participatory conceptions of authority. The founding fathers of the American system, as well as British elites early in the 19th century, while generally distrustful of the masses and fearful of mob rule, did hold some of the ideas associated with democracy, and a participatory culture gradually developed and spread throughout the 19th century in the United States and in parts of Europe. There have been instances when certain elites, attached to the idea of democracy, attempted to develop more-or-less democratic systems in societies where subject cultures prevailed. But partly because of the lack of cultural congruence, these systems either failed to survive (China in 1911, Africa and Asia after 1945) or over time became more authoritarian than democratic (many Latin Americans).

The socio-economic setting, combined with the cultural setting, must also be conducive to the evolution of democracy. In brief, a balance between conflict and consensus seems to be required: a substantive and procedural consensus which breeds substantial cooperation, and a conflict pattern of limited range, complexity, and intensity so as not to disrupt the underlying consensus. Minimal cultural conflicts appear to be essential, because these often tend to be more intense than economic types and to be more disruptive of the needed consensus. Substantial economic prosperity also appears to be necessary, again to ensure that socio-economic conflicts will be of minimum intensity and will not mar the relative domestic peace essential for democracy.

Finally, the power configuration has to be one of polyarchy, noncumulative dispersion of resources, and must include a substantial politically relevant strata. In modern democracies such a power configuration did accompany the cultural and socio-economic developments of the nineteenth century, as middle classes and lower classes began to acquire some money, information, organizational power, the vote, and some other resources of power, and where similar developments gradually produced a highly polyarchic elite structure. Thus the American system of the 1970s is no longer dominated by the plantation aristocracy of the South and the merchant and banking princes of the Northeast, but by a power structure of bewildering complexity.

THE DYNAMICS OF SYSTEMS

The functioning of systems in conflict resolution and policy-making processes is similarly conditioned by cultural, socio-economic, and power influences from the environment.

Within authoritarian systems there may be a more limited pattern of pluralism, competition, and representation in bargaining, and a more frequent resort to conflict resolution processes of indifference, suppression, or command decision. But environmental conditions or changes may require substantially more extensive bargaining than superficial appearances would indicate. In the Soviet Union, for instance, the changed nature of the Soviet economy and society has produced substantial polyarchy in the overall elite structure, rising distribution demands not only from elites but also from peasants, workers, and the growing middle classes, and a growing awareness among the political elites that they must be more responsive to both participation and distribution demands. Substantial surrogate representation seems to be developing as the elites concerned with workers in industry and those with farmers to a degree at least represent the demands of these groups in bargaining processes. Similar developments are taking place in other authoritarian systems as the result of economic development and political modernization involving the replacement of traditional attitudes and structures. In Iran, for example, the landed aristocracy has only been partly replaced by the new-moneyed aristocracy and technostructure, middle classes have entered the politically relevant strata, and the political elite has been somewhat responsive to the demands of the peasants in its effort to build a political base against opposition from landlords. Such changes in political dynamics result primarily from the increasing complexity of modernizing societies, which requires the political elite to enlist a broader base of support for stability and effectiveness, tends to produce a polyarchic configuration of power, and introduces expectations to the formerly apathetic and docile masses.

But this entails paying a price, particularly in democratic systems where access channels to decision-making are open to many groups in society. As power configurations become more diffuse and complex, socio-economic needs and problems multiply, and expectations replace apathy, the bargaining among government officials, between them and numerous socio-economic groups, and among the latter, becomes extremely complex, slow, and tortuous. A settlement acceptable to all elites may involve accommodation of so many diverse ideas and interests that the resulting compromise may only be a patchwork approach rather than an effective solution to a problem. This is a familiar pattern in American politics, but it is also becoming more common in the Soviet Union, in Iran, and in other developing authoritarian societies.

The style and climate of bargaining is also influenced by environmental factors. Conflict resolution is facilitated when a procedural and substantive consensus and a pervasive sense of trust prevail, and when the bargainers approach a conflict with pragmatic rather than rigid dogmatic attitudes. But such a consensus and attitudes generally do not prevail in divided or fragmented societies where distrust and hostility are the norms. Such attitudes tend to be characteristic also of decision-makers in such systems, and the consequent verbal warfare and violence which is chronic in the parliaments of such systems have on numerous occasions provided authoritarian executives with the excuse for sending the representatives home and for assuming authoritarian power (as in the case of DeGaulle's France).

THE SCOPE, OBJECTIVES, AND POLICY OUTPUTS OF SYSTEMS

THE SCOPE OF SYSTEMS

As with respect to types of systems, so in authoritarian societies the degree to which the government intervenes in or controls the varied spheres of human endeavor is largely determined by the political elites. The decision to collectivize the Soviet economy and to establish total control over all of society was clearly Stalin's decision. Decisions to give priority to economic development, and to intervene in whatever spheres are necessary to pursue this goal, were made by authoritarian leaders of developing states. Hitler's decision to establish a corporate state in Germany was a decision made by the oligarchy which dominated Germany in the 1930s. Yet environmental factors played at least a permissive role. For one, the principle of free enterprise and limited government was not enshrined in the pantheon of values of these societies, and the idea of a broad range of activities on the part of lower levels of government—by the village in Russia, extended family or clan in China, the tribe in Africa —was a customary idea. The socio-economic situation also made varied elites and masses receptive to the idea of massive governmental intervention on behalf of economic goals, while other elites and masses actively demanded such governmental endeavors. And finally the generally oligarchic power structure in these societies at the given time enabled these political elites to make and enforce such decisions.

Environmental factors are more the root, and probably the primary root, of the expansion of scope of democratic and the more moderate authoritarian systems. The gradual evolution during the past several decades of the Interventionist State or Big Government is a universal phenomenon. The only thing that distinguishes the United States from other modern complex societies in this respect is that we are moving somewhat more slowly in this direction, although the pace is picking up. In the United States particularly we are prone to blame the growth of Big Government on the bureaucracy, which we sometimes visualize as a power-hungry octopus whose tentacles are constantly searching out for more tasks to perform but only to satisfy its hunger for power. There may be something to this, but it is a minor element. The real roots of the interventionist state are to be found in the interplay of environmental factors, which continues to produce a mounting volume of intense and effective demands for value creation and allocation—the distribution challenge.

THE CONVERSION OF IDEAS AND INTERESTS INTO POLITICAL DEMANDS

Most of us have some goals, based on our ideas and interests, which we try to attain by self-help or voluntary cooperation with others. If we want more income we look for a better job, or join a labor union to improve our bargaining position. If we want security we save money for a rainy day, or join with others in an insurance pool. If we want health care we again save money, or join a voluntary health care plan. If we want to bring prices down we stop buying certain goods, or perhaps even join a picket line around a supermarket. This is the traditional American dream—self-help and voluntary cooperation in the name of freedom and free enterprise. But it is a dream which is dying, and long since dead in many parts of the world, and two major environmental factors seem to be the cause of the mortal illness—rising expectations, and the increasing complexity of industrial and post-industrial societies.

There seem to be four conditions in which people stop seeking goals through self-help and voluntary cooperation and convert their varied demands into political demands—when they begin to look to the government for satisfaction of certain interests and for resolving needs and problems. All of these conditions are present in modern complex societies, and some are also evident even in the poorest societies. In essence, ideas and interests tend to be converted into political demands when the following four conditions are present:

1. When the group considers the fulfillment of a particular need, or the satisfaction of a particular interest as essential for well-being or survival. Needs are partly biologically conditioned—the basic necessities of life. But they are also culturally conditioned—what is deemed to be essential either in terms of prevailing life style or the life style of one's particular peer group. The American needs more than just a bowl of rice and piece of fish, and some Americans define steaks and motorboats as absolute needs. And needs are also conditioned by the socio-economic system. The automobile was once a luxury; today for many it is a necessity because it is the only means of getting to work. Hence, for a variety of reasons human expectations and political demands have increased. In industrial societies it is partly the result of rising affluence, which gener-

ates more wants than it satisfies, and partly the complexity of our societies. In the poor societies expectations also are rising for a variety of reasons, so that what Africans used to call the "wants disease" is also broadening the definition of need—for a bicycle, a tin roof, or many other things unheard of in years past. In essence, the broadened definition of need is prompting more people to look beyond self-help for the satisfaction of interests and wants.

2. When the potential for need fulfillment through self-help, voluntary cooperation, or action in the private sphere appears to be so low that governmental action in the public sphere appears to be essential. In a self-sufficient, agrarian society, most basic needs can be met by action in the private sphere. In a complex, interdependent, urbanized industrial society the private sphere has proven increasingly inadequate. Getting a job or improving one's standard of living is far less a matter of self-help. The elderly can no longer be taken care of by their children, the farmer is at the mercy of a complex and volatile market, the unemployed worker no longer has a plot of land to grow vegetables or raise a few chickens. Industrialization has also intensified the threat of major environmental damage, and voluntary cooperation has clearly failed to avert this danger. Hence, as needs are more broadly defined and as it becomes increasingly difficult to satisfy such needs outside the political arena, the demand level has multiplied and intensified.

3. When governmental action to respond to certain needs is considered to be within the legitimate sphere of governmental endeavor. Under the impact of the first two factors, conceptions of scope in many societies have gradually expanded so that what was once considered beyond the proper purview of the government is today considered the natural function of government. A century ago it would have been unheard of for the government to subsidize agriculture, to actively intervene in economic affairs, to provide a wide variety of social services. Today these and similar governmental activities are so widely accepted that a Republican president, acting under the pressure of demands from a wide variety of groups in American society, instituted wage and price controls.

4. When a group anticipates some degree of success in its demand for political action. Such anticipations tend to arise when the group perceives that it has acquired some degree and form of political power, or when it anticipates that success in the past can be repeated, or from a "demonstration effect"—perceptions of other groups succeeding in their political demands. The gradual industrialization and democratization of western societies has brought about substantial dispersion of the resources of power, so that more social sectors and strata have some means to make their demands effective. As business groups were quite successful in using the government throughout the 19th century, farmers entered the political market place, and then labor. And more recently other groups

have become much more active politically—Blacks, Indians, Spanish-speaking peoples, and even consumers and enviromentalists.

In essence, although there are variations among systems, the interplay of environmental factors which produces effective demands from varied social segments and strata plays a major role in conditioning the scope of political systems.

The objectives of governments tend similarly to be conditioned by environmental forces. In authoritarian systems they are, of course, set by the political elites, and in some instances such regime objectives may be rigidly adhered to. Stalin and Hitler set the course for their governments, and similar patterns tend to be followed by authoritarian regimes in their early phases. But over time and for a variety of reasons even authoritarian objectives tend to be at least modified by environmental factors. It may be because the political elites need to cultivate the support of powerful elements in society, a factor which has forced many reform-minded or change-oriented regimes to become status quo oriented or even reactionary. Sometimes mass pressures and the danger of insurrection force a reorientation of objectives, or they may produce a variety of economic and other influences from the international environment. In still other instances the environmental setting forces changes simply because regimes realize that their objectives are not attainable—a frequent phenomenon in the new states where drives for economic development and modernization are abandoned due to the lack of resources, the complexity of hostile conflict patterns in society, or international developments.

Policy output patterns are basically determined by the effectiveness of demand inputs into political systems. Consequently the patterns depend on the balance of power between the government and society, and the distribution of power among the society's groups and strata. This power pattern thus determines the spheres in which the government endeavors to make policies, as well as the general nature and direction of policies —whether it emphasizes economic or other policies, and whether its general orientation is liberal or conservative, change or status quo oriented. The equity of value creation and allocation patterns is also determined by the power configuration. But it is not power operating in a vacuum which constitutes the source of policy patterns. What also counts is the interplay between socio-economic and cultural interests and ideas: the economic and other self-interests of the more powerful elements in society and government, and also their norms, values, and attitudes. Equity and justice in value allocation are ultimately dependent on equity in the distribution of power, but they are also dependent on the degree to which elites subordinate all other interests to immediate self-interest, and how they tend to define such standards as justice, equity, and the public interest. In those societies where minority rights has real meaning, degrees of equity tend to prevail. In other societies, minorities invariably get short-changed.

THE IMPACT ON POLITICAL STABILITY AND EFFECTIVENESS

Later chapters will explore the various requisites for stability and effectiveness, what appear to be the essential conditions which make for long-term durability of systems and for effective performance of varied functions. At this point a summary of much of what has been stated before—the significance of socio-economic, cultural, and power factors with respect to these qualities—is useful.

Most basically, stability and effectiveness are dependent on support. Governments led by adroit despots who manipulate powerful coercive instruments can govern effectively if they restrict the functions of government to a few basic tasks—such as providing domestic peace. Given favorable conditions they may even enjoy longer-term durability and degrees of effectiveness while undertaking more complex functions. But generally, the need for support is directly related to the complexity of the tasks confronting particular governments. And support is dependent on two factors: a supportive culture and socialization process, and perceived satisfactory performance of functions.

The nature of the environmental setting also has more direct consequences for governmental stability and effectiveness. The range, complexity, and intensity of conflict patterns in the society may ease or make impossible the peaceful and effective resolution of conflicts, and some fragmented societies seem almost impossible to govern. Economic problems may be so acute because of the resource base, dependence on the international economy, and rising expectations so as to defy the abilities of even the most skillful governments to meet distribution demands. Or prevailing cultural patterns within the society—devotion to traditions and customs, the lingering dedication to free enterprise—may make it difficult for a government to effectively cope with major economic and related social problems.

The balance of power between government and society and the configuration of power in the society are crucial variables. When governments enjoy a substantial edge and the power configuration requires only restricted bargaining, then governments tend to be stable, can make timely decisions, and have at least a potential for making effective decisions—although the implementation of decisions is still partly at least dependent on environmental support. Dictators can impose domestic peace, can make trains run on time, but may be less effective with regard to policies which require voluntary cooperation for effective implementation. A power configuration which involves pluralistic, competitive, and representative bargaining poses serious problems. Wide dispersion of power throughout society forces governments to be responsive lest they lose the support needed for stability and effectiveness, yet extensive bargaining and accommodation to many diverse interests frequently entail excessive delays in the making of policies, and compromise outcomes which may satisfy many interests in the short-run, but be total failures with respect to critical problems. A pattern of "delayed and disjointed incrementalism" is common to most democracies: agonizing delays in the making of policies until problems become acute crises; policy changes made in small increments over years and sometimes decades so that problems continue to persist and are never resolved; and changes made in one policy sphere often incompatible and not harmonious with changes or lack of changes in other spheres, so that problems are compounded or new problems are created.

Finally, stability and effectiveness seem to be related to the sequence and manner in which systems face or faced the four basic environmental challenges. Considering contemporary environmental settings the distribution challenge is a most difficult one for those systems which have already resolved the earlier challenge in a more or less satisfactory manner. Systems which simultaneously face the participation challenge face more serious difficulties. But the probabilities are that the new states of the world face decades of instability and low effectiveness because of the persistence of the nation- and state-building challenges.

THE PROBLEM OF ENVIRONMENTAL CHANGE

The problem of political adaptation to change will also be more fully discussed in a later chapter. At this point it is simply emphasized that environmental change is of fundamental importance and will invariably produce changes in the political system. It is not a question of whether political changes will result. Questions relate to how soon environmental changes will produce political changes, whether the political changes will be evolutionary or revolutionary, and whether they will result in improved performance of systems as instruments of society.

The socio-economic setting may be changing under the impact of a variety of factors, may be resolving some old problems, but may also be creating hosts of new socio-economic problems. The contemporary world is being impacted by increasing technological changes, by demographic changes affecting both the size and composition of the population, by an increasing pace of social, geographic, and occupational mobility, and by major changes in the production of goods and services.

Such changes are bringing about a variety of changes in the environmental setting which have variant political implications. In some societies they are simplifying and easing, in others complicating and intensifying, conflict patterns and participation and distribution demands. Support inputs are also undergoing some profound transformations in various societies. Over time such socio-economic changes, while affected by cultural modifications, will also have an impact on the cultural foundations of existing systems.

Cultural changes are also pronounced in many societies. Due to a variety of reasons—socio-economic changes, the information and communication revolution, increasing influences from the international environment, expanding education and literacy—basic beliefs and prevailing conceptions of authority and scope are being modified and in some cases radically altered. In some societies a national sense of identity seems to be developing, with an attendant substantive and procedural consensus; in others the sense of community and consensus appears to be deteriorating as the existing belief systems, prevailing values, and traditional norms of behavior come under increasing attack from a variety of sources. A cultural lag is generally characteristic of most societies: cultures are changing, yet the persistence of traditional ideas acts to set constraints on political adaptation to change. People tend to cling to their traditional political beliefs, myths, and expressive symbols, even though they may be outmoded.

Power configurations are also undergoing transformation in the modern world. On the one hand a variety of processes have served to further distribute power in many societies, so that a variety of groups heretofore in the apolitical strata now have political expectations and have found means to make their demands effective. Hence, the disparities of wealth and power which the less equal have accepted for so many centuries are increasingly less acceptable. Yet at the same time new concentrations of power have developed, particularly in industrial societies—the economic giants in business, banking, and labor. This again poses significant problems—in authoritarian and totalitarian societies, how to maintain stability and effectiveness; in democratic societies, how to remain effective and democratic. These and many other environmental changes indicate a certainty of political change in the decades ahead, but great uncertainty as to the nature and direction of political change.

NORMATIVE IMPLICATIONS

Chapter 3 discussed the immunity of values to scientific analysis and the consequent impossibility of empirical political science to provide definitive and fact-based answers to the classic perennial issues of politics. But it was also emphasized that facts and values are related, and that factual assessment is essential with respect to value questions and evaluation in three specific ways: the clarification of values and available choices, the selection of appropriate means to attain preferred goals, and assessment of the probable consequences of selected means and ends. All of this holds with respect to the analysis, assessment, and evaluation of environmental settings. Empirical social science cannot offer definitive and fact-based answers as to what constitutes the good society, what kind of cultural setting is preferable, or what is the most desirable form of socio-economic organization. Nor can it offer answers as to a desirable rate or direction of change. But value-based answers which ignore or distort facts are more likely to kill than cure the patient—human society. Cures depend on fact-based diagnosis and on the art of the possible.

Diagnosis requires first the empirical analysis of what societies are really like, and the relationship between the environmental setting and the rest of the political system. Is the oppressive authoritarian nature of some systems, for example, due to the autocratic attitudes and rapaciousness of certain elites, or is it rooted in environmental factors? Are the weaknesses of the American system due to the nature of the constitution, the structure of the system, the incompetence of people who govern us, or due to American cultural patterns, the nature and power of public opinion, or the socio-economic structure? It then requires assessment of the real rather than ideal or illusory choices available to a society, what really can be done to maintain a system if that is desired, or to modify, change, or replace it if it seems incompatible with preferred values. Is the choice between Western-style liberal democracy and authoritarianism, for example, a real one for a society in which an authoritarian subject culture prevails, or in which a pattern of oligarchy exists, or in which conflict is so pervasive and intense that the necessary balance between cleavage and consensus seems unattainable? What are the real options open to Americans, who still treasure freedom, individualism, self-help, and limited government, but who increasingly cherish property and economic growth and in search of these values have created a complex and voracious industrial society increasingly dependent on governmental intervention? Given the nature, pace, and direction of cultural and socio-economic changes in any or all societies, and the domestic and international sources of such change, what real options are open with respect to restructuring of political systems? Answers to these and similar questions require rigorous empirical analysis, not guesswork or value-based preferences which ignore realities.

Facts and empirical analysis are also essential with respect to determining what available means are most likely to maximize the goals we prefer. For one, we have to respect the fact that some people may aspire to different goals. A bowl of rice, for example, may be more important to an Asian peasant than the right to vote. Then we have to ascertain what kind of political system and environmental setting is most likely to maximize rice or freedom, or both. If we prefer freedom, individualism, and human rights we have to use facts to determine what kind of political order is most likely to maximize these values, and what can and must be done to restructure the environmental setting as a means to produce a democratic political order. It we want to maximize domestic peace and cooperation, we need empirically to determine how a society can be integrated, how consensus can be developed, how a pervasive atmosphere of trust can be promoted. If we want to replace a system which seems capable only of delayed and disjointed incrementalism, we need facts to determine to what extent greater concentration of power is likely to promote political capability, effectiveness, and efficiency, and what can and should be done in terms of the environmental setting so that concentration of power within the decision-making system becomes possible.

Finally, facts and empirical analysis are essential for trying to determine what may be the consequences of our selected means and ends, for assessing the probable efficiency of our choices, for determining what value costs may be involved in our selections of values to be maximized. If we opt for greater concentration of power in the interests of domestic order, what are the possible consequences for human liberty, individualism, and equality? If we opt for a system which promises, on the basis of facts, to maximize rapid economic growth, what are the possible costs in terms of social justice and the promotion of harmony in an integrated society or the cost in terms of the material well-being of future generations? Or if we opt for so-called benevolent authoritarian system as the way to both peace and plenty and as an interim system between oppressive absolutism and democracy, what are the possible consequences of such a choice: does the empirical evidence suggest that such a system will really promote economic growth, social justice, equity of value allocations, and breed the kind of environmental setting needed for the eventual transition to democracy? Both facts and values must govern human choices.

Linkage-Communication Structures and Processes

part III

We now turn to the analysis of the second component of a political system, the linkage-communication system or infrastructure. Any kind of organized activity requires some kinds of structures and processes which link together the participants in such activity and which provide means for internal communication. A university, for example, functions more effectively when some kinds of structures link together and provide communication grids between students, faculty, and administrators. The same applies to scout troops, labor unions, or any other kind of organization. Within a political system, the linkage-communication system includes the cluster of institutions, structures, and processes which link society with government and provide multiple communication channels within the society, the government, and between the government and society. It is this system which makes possible interaction between environment and government, for the various environmental factors discussed in Part II influence policy-making primarily through linkage instruments. It is by means such as interest groups, political parties, election systems, news media, constituency representatives, and others that environmentally-based demand and support inputs are processed and transmitted to governmental decision-makers. The extent to which such inputs have an actual impact on governmental structures, processes, and policy outputs depends very much on the nature and effectiveness of the various components of the linkage-communication system.

In general, the size, complexity, and performance characteristics of the linkage-communication system should be commensurate with the size and complexity of the society, the governmental structure, and the scope and diversity of functions undertaken by the government. Because of their important roles, all political systems have some kind of infrastructure. However, they differ in the size and complexity of their linkage-communication systems. Systems governing small-scale societies have simple communication needs, hence village or tribal councils adequately serve the needs of village or tribal political system. But in large-scale complex societies, in which the government undertakes a variety of complex functions, more complex infrastructures have tended to develop because of the need for effective performance of a wide variety of linkage and communication functions. Political systems also differ with respect to the performance characteristics of their infrastructures. In some, the various linkage-communication functions are performed fairly well by a variety of relatively effective institutions. In others, such institutions are poorly developed and the necessary functions are inadequately performed, with adverse consequences for political stability and effectiveness.

As discussed in Chapter 3, political analysis entails both fact-based assessment and value-based evaluation of political systems. Such assessment and evaluation of linkage-communication systems is particularly important because the functioning and performance of any type of political system is very much dependent on the nature and performance of linkage systems. Democratic systems need well-developed infrastructures for it is only by such means that various groups in society can exercise influence over government. Nondemocratic systems also need adequate communication systems because, as will be discussed in Chapter 7, stability and effectiveness are very much dependent on effective performance of several linkage-communication functions. Consequently, political analysis must include consideration of the major characteristics of the infrastructure, and assessment and evaluation of such characteristics along the dimensions discussed in Chapter 3. Specifically, the following major questions should be asked:

1. What means exist within a political system for the performance of some or all linkage-communication functions? What are the major characteristics of the infrastructure, and what is the relationship between such characteristics and apparent performance of the varied linkage functions? Is the linkage system of adequate size and complexity, and are its performance characteristics such, that it adequately serves both the objective needs and value-based preferences and goals of the society and of individual groups and strata within the society?

2. To what extent, and how and why, do the infrastructure and its components contribute to political stability, and to the capabilities and performance of the political system as an effective, efficient, and equitable instrument of society?

3. To what extent does the linkage system serve most or all groups and strata of the society, and thus help to make the system a more-or-less democratic one in terms of maximizing public influence over policy-making?

4 To what extent does the linkage system facilitate political adaptation to change? What changes seem to be taking place within the infrastructure itself, which may have consequences for the nature of political system and for its stability and effectiveness? What changes may be necessary to enhance stability and effectiveness, or to make the system more democratic?

Chapter 7 discusses the general nature of the six major linkage and communication functions which must be effectively performed for stability and effectiveness, as well as the general means which exist in most political systems for such function performance. Chapters 8 and 9 discuss the major infrastructures which have developed in modern complex political systems—interest groups and political parties and election systems.

Linkage
Communication
Functions
and Instruments

7

For democracy, as well as for the stability and effectiveness of any type of political system, it is essential that adequate machinery exist for the effective performance of six specific linkage and communication functions. Effective performance also entails relatively equitable performance —the instruments should adequately serve most, if not all, groups and strata in society. It also entails relative autonomy—the instruments should function relatively independently of each other and relatively free of government control.

LINKAGE AND COMMUNICATION FUNCTIONS

Interest-idea articulation, or the effective communication of interest-idea based demand and support inputs from the society into the decision-making system, is a prime function. Some kind of machinery must exist which provides groups in society with means for the communication of their ideas, interests, needs, problems, and demands to the varied levels and agencies of government, and to other groups in the society. And governments need channels for communicating with the various groups constituting the society.

It is the very essence of democracy that the voice of the people be heard and responded to, and this, at the very minimum, requires that the people have some institutionalized means to communicate these demands in some manner likely to produce governmental responses. Democracy also entails equity or fairness, which requires that such articulation channels be available to most if not all groups of the society. Democracy is hardly possible if the means of communication serve only some elites, or upper socio-economic strata, or only some religious, tribal, or racial groups in a heterogeneous society. Relative autonomy is also essential, so that each group's particular channels are not dominated by those of other groups, and so that the entire institutional complex is controlled by the people rather than by the government.

Political effectiveness and adaption to changing enviromental conditions also require effective, equitable, and autonomous articulation channels. No government can function as an effective instrument of society without a continuing flow of information about those durable or changing needs and problems of society which require political action. Effective economic policies require timely, clear, accurate, and specific information from a variety of groups—bankers, industrialists, people in small business, farmers, consumers, skilled and unskilled workers, economists—about economic conditions, problems, and changes in all of the varied sectors of the economy, about the impact of current governmental policies, about economic prospects for the future, and about possible remedies for current problems. Even the basic function of government—the maintenance of domestic peace and tranquillity—requires such an information flow from diverse groups as to the roots or causes of racial or religious strife, social or economic discrimination, or other sources of domestic unrest, and about what needs to be done in order to alleviate such unrest. Effective government also involves not merely the formulation but also implementation of policies, and this requires information— articulation by varied groups as to what kinds of policies are acceptable and likely to enjoy the kind of support needed for voluntary compliance. An economic policy which may provoke a rash of strikes is not likely to be an effective policy.

Effective articulation machinery is also essential for the stability of any type of political system. As emphasized in earlier chapters, no system is likely to enjoy real stability without effective performance, which requires a continuing information flow between government and society. And more directly, governments need timely, accurate, and specific information about levels of support throughout the society, about the mood of general public, about existing or developing pockets of disaffection and alienation, about intense needs, problems, and demands which must be responded to lest support be jeopardized. For even the citizens of rigidly controlled totalitarian societies have resorted to violence when their grievances were not heard or ignored; and while a riot may function as an effective articulation instrument, frequent or constant violence is hardly conducive to stability.

Demand aggregation and conflict resolution is another major function which must be adequately performed for stability and effectiveness. By this term we mean the combination and consolidation of numerous, diverse, and competing demands, emanating from a multiplicity of diverse groups in society, into relatively fewer and simpler alternative policy and program proposals levied on governments.

Chapter 1 emphasized that politics involves both cooperation and conflict, and that a most basic task of government is the management or resolution of conflicts arising from competing demands. But the conflict resolution task cannot be left only to governments, for this would involve government in all aspects of human affairs, and would soon overload any kind of government to the point of political breakdown. Both stability and effectiveness are enhanced to the extent that non-governmental institutions and processes can assume at least part of the burden of demand aggregation and conflict resolution.

Farmers, for example, constitute a like-minded group who frequently cooperate to promote their common interest. But farmers also have diverse and competing interests. Corn farmers may clash with dairy or livestock interests who want cheap corn; the interests of small farmers are often different from those of large-scale farmers; midwest farmers often compete with far west agricultural interests; some farmers believe in free enterprise while others favor an interventionist state. No government can function effectively if it alone is burdened with the individual, raw, and unaggregated demands from all kinds of farmers from all regions of the country. What is needed is some kind of machinery which can process such a multiplicity of diverse farmer demands, develop compromises among them, and submit one or a few package proposals for a governmental agricultural policy which is acceptable to many or even most farmers. Similar diversities of ideas and interests prevail among different kinds of businesses, oil companies, workers, educators, students, consumers, and all the varied socio-economic and cultural groups which make up a heterogeneous society. Effective infrastructures which perform this demand aggregation and conflict resolution function within such occupational, socio-economic, or cultural groups (such as interest groups) hence enhance political stability and effectiveness.

In modern societies, conflicts are even more pronounced between groups whose interests are more diverse, and it is important to have machinery which can help resolve such conflicts. The development of an agricultural policy, for example, requires not merely the adjustment of conflict among farmers, but also the reconciliation of farm interests with those of city dwellers, consumers, workers, and businesspeople. The formulation of an economic policy requires similar adjustments among varied types of economic groups, and some preliminary aggregation of the ideas and interests of environmentalists, educators, and others. The development of governmental policies may involve different ideas or interests of varied religious, tribal, ethnic, racial, or similar kinds of non-economic groups. Again what is needed are institutions which can play effective roles in bargaining among such diverse groups; which can strike compromises among business, farmer, consumer, and worker interests, or among different religious, ethnic, or regional groups; and which can help to strike a balance between oft-clashing values such as economic growth, environmental protection, and individual freedom. Ultimately, the authoritative resolution of such conflicts often becomes the task of government. However, political stability and effectiveness are substantially enhanced when some non-governmental machinery exists which can take some of the load off government, preclude a government with being constantly confronted with a complex and bewildering mass of unaggregated demands, and which can perform some preliminary aggregation of complex demands and process them into fewer and relatively simplified alternative policy or program proposals. Such institutions can ease task of government by reducing the complexity of choices and decisions to be made and of conflicts to be resolved. They help to produce the degree of harmony, trust, and cooperation which facilitates further governmental conflict resolution. They tend to produce the broader cooperation and coalition of interests and power essential for eventual governmental action, and to develop the support needed for voluntary compliance with governmental decisions. But equity of demand aggregation and conflict resolution is also essential, for groups whose demands are ignored are unlikely to support either the process or the system. Effective political parties can play major roles with respect to this function.

Political recruitment, or the selection, recruitment, training, and promotion of human resources for varied roles, functions, and offices in government and politics, is a third important linkage-communication function.

Ultimately, political stability and effectiveness are dependent on the quality and skills of two types of human beings who hold political and governmental office. Political systems need specialist-experts, individuals who have some specialized knowledge and expertise in some particular field, and who perform specialized governmental functions related to their field of expertise—the economist, labor expert, health specialist, educational administrator, and many other types. They also need generalist-politician and managerial types, individuals who have broader interests and perspectives than narrow specialists, who have the capabilities

and skills needed to coordinate, integrate, and harmonize the recommendations and activities of varied experts, and who have the political talents
needed to develop coalitions and support for public policies. All kinds of
economic experts are needed for the development of a sound economic
policy, but managerial types are needed to ensure such experts work in
harmony on all facets of economic problems. And politician-generalist
types are needed to ensure harmony between economic and the other
goals of a society, and to ensure economic policies which the public or
major elites in the society will accept.

In all political systems, governments themselves play major roles with
respect to this recruitment function. All generally have some kind of civil
service system which selects, recruits, trains, and promotes specialist-
experts and managerial types for the governmental bureaucracy. A degree of government cooption for upper-level managerial and
politician-generalist positions also prevails in most systems—governmental officials at various levels select their subordinates, and also select
their fellow members for ruling bodies—as the Soviet Politburo selects
its own membership and the American President his own cabinet. Yet a
degree of participation in the recruitment process by autonomous linkage
and communication institutions is highly desirable not only for democracy, but also for stability and effectiveness.

For democracy, popular participation in the selection of key decision-
makers, and open opportunities for individuals from all sectors and strata
of society to attain political office, are essential. Such popular participation and opportunity becomes possible to the extent that an autonomous
linkage-communication system provides for effective and equitable political recruitment for both specialist and generalist types. Also, government-controlled recruitment systems tend to limit recruitment efforts to
a few groups or to a narrow elite, and to emphasize loyalty, obedience,
and conformity rather than talent, competence, honesty, and efficiency.
They thus often deny the political system the high quality of human
resources needed for stability and effectiveness. Although competitive
processes do not ensure the recruitment of talented and dedicated public
servants, competition provided by and effective linkage-communication
system seems preferable to government monopoly.

Political socialization, mobilization, integration and support building Earlier
chapters emphasized the importance of support for political stability and
effectiveness and the relationship between support and the socialization
process. Governments themselves, through their educational, informational, and propaganda activities seek to develop support for themselves,
to mobilize support behind their programs and policies, to integrate their
societies, and to promote supportive cultures. But again, stability and

effectiveness are enhanced to the extent that non-governmental institutions and processes are involved. Further, since these functions all involve the manipulation of ideas, for democracy it is essential that these functions not be monopolized by governments.

Such linkage-communication instruments as political parties, interest groups, and news media can do much to generate (or erode) support for the political community, system, and government of the moment, not only by their informational and socialization processes, but also by effective performance of other linkage functions. By similar means they play major socialization roles, can help maintain (or erode) a supportive political culture, can heal cleavages within and thus help to integrate a society, and can promote trust and confidence (or the reverse) between government and society. Political effectiveness also entails the effective implementation of governmental policies so that the aims of the governmental policy-makers may be attained. This requires that various groups in society be mobilized on behalf of governmental objectives, that they voluntarily comply with governmental demands and actively participate in tasks set for them by governmental programs. Such successful mobilization is very much dependent on the efforts of organizations and institutions which link the society with the government.

Public influence over government is almost synonymous with democracy, but degrees of same are also conducive to stability and effectiveness in any type of political system. And the extent to which the varied groups and strata of a society can influence governmental policy making depends directly on the autonomy, equity, and effectiveness of the system's infrastructure. Public influence requires voluntary organized action on the part of individuals, for but a few in any society can hope to have any significant impact by individual action. It is the infrastructure organizations which provide such means for effective citizen participation.

At the very least, democracy entails public choice via free elections of key government decision-makers, as well as some public voice in the selection of other officials. Hence, an equitable recruitment process open to public participation is essential. Democracy also requires some means whereby various publics can effectively relay their demands for governmental action with some expectations of governmental responsiveness. It also entails effective and equitable demand aggregation machinery, so that various groups can hope for fair treatment during conflict resolution processes. But all these functions require organization, and the organized participation of those who wish to influence public policy.

Degrees of public influence by means of linkage-communication processes also enhance the stability and effectiveness of nondemocratic systems. Both qualities require effective inputs about social, economic, cultural, and other needs and problems of the society, and adequate information about the actual impact of governmental policies. All this requires some degree of public influence to ensure that decision-makers do heed and pay attention to needs, problems, and the inadequacies of governmental actions. Political systems lacking minimal channels for public influence generally have but limited responsive capabilities, which adversely affects their ability to become aware of pressing problems, their ability to deal with them, and their ability to engender support and to mobilize people on behalf of governmental objectives. No government can hope to enjoy real stability and effectiveness if it effectively immunizes itself against all public influence by drawing an iron curtain around itself. The real weakness of totalitarian countries may be less the wall they erect against the inflow of ideas from the outside world, but more the barriers they construct between government and society.

The integration of governmental structures and processes Simple governmental structures in small-scale political systems do not need special institutions to integrate processes within the government itself. Face to face contacts, for example, suffice for harmonious, consistent, and effective decision-making in a system dominated by a king and his few ministers or when all decisions are made by a small tribal council or township meeting. But in large, complex, and elaborate governmental systems decision-making is apportioned among numerous officials grouped in several branches and agencies, the process of government is divided among many complex structures and agencies, and many competitive factions are involved in policy-making. In such systems a critical need exists for some institutions or processes which can link together the diverse attitudes, roles, policies, and activities of the varied branches, agencies, factions, and individuals so that harmonious and integrated actions develop with regard to timely and effective polices.

American democracy, for example, is based on the principles of separation of power and checks and balances. Legal authority is separated among the executive, legislative, and judicial branches, within these branches, and between the federal government and the states. The system was designed so that different branches and levels of government had the power to check and balance the power of other branches and levels. This produced a system of built-in institutional conflict between levels and branches of government, which aggravates the potential for conflict inherent in pluralistic America, and accentuates conflict in decision-making among numerous individuals and factions having different institutional, personal, regional, or constituency interests. This ensures a system of polyarchy and dispersion of power which precludes a dangerous concentration of power, provides for substantial pluralism, competition, and representation in decision-making, and ensures substantial responsiveness to the varied interests that make up America.

But timely and effective decision-making also requires some kind of a balance between conflict and consensus, a high degree of harmonious action among decision-makers, and substantial coordination and integration of the diverse actions and attitudes among these numerous decision-making individuals, agencies, and branches. In the American system timely and effective decisions can be arrived at only after a substantial consensus develops among the 535 members of the Congress, the two legislative houses, and between the executive and the Congress. Effective leadership within the government itself—as for example on the part of the President—can on occasion produce such harmony and consensus. But more frequently, some other kind of linkage is needed to produce the kind of cooperation needed for timely and effective policies. In modern complex systems, effective political parties can perform this integration function.

LINKAGE-COMMUNICATION STRUCTURES AND PROCESSES

A variety of means exist within various political systems for the performance of some or all of these foregoing six functions. But while all these structures and processes have some merits with respect to effective performance, some seem to be more effective than others, and still others appear to have at least the potential for the most effective performance of all functions.

Direction communication between individuals and governments is one means available in most systems for interest-idea articulation and even for some other functions. But except for very simple systems, and in more complex systems for a few individuals with substantial power, this method can hardly serve as a major component of linkage-communication.

Direct citizen participation is similarly limited to simple types of political systems. Although increasing demands have been raised in recent years for some form of "direct democracy," it would appear that participation can only be maximized by means of citizen involvement in some kind of organized activity, such as via political parties and interest groups, rather than directly in decision-making processes.

News media can and do perform some linkage-communication functions, particularly in those systems where a free press exists. The press, television, and other media do play roles with respect to interest-idea articulation, political socialization and mobilization, and exert some influence over governmental decision-making. But governments need much more complete and specific information than mass media are able or inclined to provide; the media's support-building role may be quite limited or even negative; and the degree to which the media actually articulate public opinion or influence government on behalf of the public is sometimes subject to question.

Public opinion polls constitute another means of linkage and communication, but only in a few societies where the means and techniques of polling have been well developed and in which social and economic factors facilitate polling. But even in these few, polls at best generally only articulate prevailing moods or broad public preferences rather than specific demands, and the extent to which they actually influence governments is also subject to question.

Government bureaucracies can and to some extent do perform articulation, aggregation, recruitment, and socialization-mobilization functions through their geographic network of offices, information services, civil service recruitment machinery, and conflict resolution processes. Indeed, some authoritarian governments which have banned political parties and interest groups rely mainly on their bureaucracies for linkage and communication. However, the effectiveness of their performance of these linkage (as distinguished from decision-making) functions tends to be hampered by their lack of autonomy: as governmental instrumentalities, they tend to speak for the government rather than for society. Further, particularly in large-scale societies, bureaucratic performance of all of these functions would require a massive governmental bureaucracy, and the involvement of government in all spheres and activities of society.

The representation of citizens in decision-making processes is the classic democratic approach to linkage and communication: public participation in decision-making via the election of individuals who represent the people in various branches of the government. This principle of participation via representation remains a major principle of democracy, and in small-scale systems can function well as the major means of linkage and communication. However, for large-scale complex systems, it has become increasingly inadequate for several reasons.

The principle on which it is usually based is that of geographic representation: the representative's constituency is a particular geographic area, and he is supposed to represent the interests and ideas of most or all people residing within that area. But if the area is large and heterogeneous, one individual cannot adequately represent and articulate even most of the complex ideas and interests of the diverse socio-economic, cultural, and other groups which make up that constituency. The problem becomes even more acute with respect to the chief executive—president, governor, prime minister—who in democratic theory is supposed to represent all the people. And even if a representative's function is deemed to be that of representing "majority views" or "dominant views," minorities also merit representation.

The specific role or function of the representative is also subject to some dispute, and role perceptions vary among representatives. Sometimes they are considered to be "instructed delegates"—individuals who are "instructed" by their constituents as to their political actions, and who should conform to and obey the demands of their constituents. But problems arise here with respect to the knowledge and wisdom of constituents and their awareness of what is truly in the public interest. Problems also arise as to how constituency sentiment can be accurately determined; whose views within the constituency truly reflect constituency opinion; and how to represent minority opinions. Another view is that representatives should function as "trustees" of their constituency; that they should be somewhat guided by constituency opinions, but in final decisions should make independent judgments based on their superior information, wisdom, and knowledge as to what is truly in the public interest. This raises problems about the representation of opinions which may not be in accord with the representative's. A third view has it that representatives should function as "honest brokers," that they should strive to mediate conflicts among diverse constituency interests, develop compromise positions, and represent the final compromise. This again raises problems with respect to representation of interests in the constituency bargaining process, and of interests which may be ignored in the final compromise outcome. Also, elected representatives are most susceptible to constituency influence and most likely to articulate general constituency interests prior to an election, and after election are more prone to act independently, or to articulate and represent some special or dominant interests. Hence again, some supplementary form of representation seems essential.

A third problem arises in connection with the previously-mentioned function of linkage within government. If the representative is to be a representative of his particular constituency, and to strongly promote its interests, what kind of process or structure can bridge the gap and resolve conflicts arising from the clash of constituency interests, so that the broader regional or national interest is truly served and not subordinated to the interests of very powerful constituencies, constituents, or representatives?

A fourth problem arises in connection with the fact that citizen representation is usually limited to representation in legislative bodies. Yet increasingly, in all types of modern political systems, substantial decision-making and other kinds of governmental authority is shifting into the hands of non-elected bureaucracies. This significant and continuing shift of power has created a need for institutions to articulate demands to bureaucrats, for instruments to maximize public influence over them, and for means to integrate bureaucratic with legislative actions and policies.

As a result of these inadequacies of geographic constituency representation, as well as the limitations of other linkage and communication instruments, two other major types of infrastructures have tended to develop, which in most contemporary political systems perform the principal linkage-communication functions: interest groups, and political parties. These two instruments, along with elections and election systems, warrant separate and more detailed analysis.

Interest Groups

8

An interest group is a collectivity of individuals who either formally organize or informally cooperate to protect or promote some common, similar, identical, or shared interest or goal. Sometimes the term "pressure group" is used because these groups appear to pressure governments. But the term interest group is preferable, because the basis of the organization or cooperation is the shared interest, because their political roles are frequently only intermittent, and because the word pressure is not accurately descriptive of their political tactics.

Interest groups are as old as politics itself, which has always involved some kind of group activity as individuals with similar interests cooperated to seize or maintain political power or to influence political decisions. What is new about contemporary politics is the tremendous proliferation of such groups, differences in styles of organization and political action, and the major roles they play as linkage-communication instruments in the determination of who gets what, when, and how.

In essence, the proliferation of interest groups and the expansion of their political roles is rooted in the needs of modern political systems. Groups in society need them because, as the scope of government expands, individuals must organize to influence government's creation and allocation of values. Systems need them for the performance of interest articulation and demand aggregation functions, and they can, to some extent, serve as instruments of public influence. Governments need interest groups to generate support for the system, for election support in democratic systems, and to develop support and consequent voluntary compliance with governmental policies. They are necessary in democratic systems, they can contribute to the stability and effectiveness of non-democratic types, and such groups can help all systems to adapt to changing conditions. The power of interest groups is rooted basically in their resources that are needed by government and society.

However, interest group systems differ very much with respect to their general nature, their power, and their actual political roles. To explore and explain these differences, we shall first discuss the varied types of groups that have evolved, the functions they have at least a potential for performing, the impact of environmental and political factors on the nature and roles of groups, the power of interest groups, and the general kinds of political techniques they use. The task of political analysis is to assess and evaluate the extent to which interest groups in specific systems do effectively and equitably perform linkage and communication functions, and thereby do contribute to democracy, and to political stability, effectiveness, and adaptation. We conclude this chapter with a discussion of the kinds of questions that should be asked in such analysis, questions relating to interest group characteristics that appear to have major consequences for effective and equitable function performance. In brief, the characteristics pertain to the size and complexity of the interest group system, the types of groups within the system, their relative autonomy, the distribution of power among and within groups, and their major targets and primary techniques for wielding influence.

TYPES OF INTEREST GROUPS

Interest groups may be classified in a variety of ways, with no classification scheme entirely satisfactory because of overlapping types and characteristics. But as explained in Chapter 3, typologies are very useful with respect to the assessment and evaluation of political institutions and processes, including interest groups.

One way to classify interest groups is by the nature of the interest or objective of specific groups. In modern industrial societies one finds numerous groups organized to protect and promote economic interests on the basis of occupation, economic role, type of economic activity, and similar bases: the United Auto Workers, the Association of Commerce and Industry, the American Farm Bureau Federation, the American Petroleum Institute. A similar variety of groups has proliferated with respect to professional, fraternal, and quasi-economic interests: the

American Medical Association, National Education Association, Citizens Committee for Postal Reform, American Legion for veterans interests, a variety of consumer organizations. Most such groups participate in politics only intermittently because they seek to promote the shared interest by internal group action or by direct negotiations with other groups. One also finds various "cause groups" in which economic factors play either no or only marginal roles, some also engaging only in intermittent political action, and others organized primarily for political action: Common Cause, National Organization for Women, Citizens for Clean Air, Women's Christian Temperance Union, Civil Liberties Union. Still other types include groups formed on the basis of interests related to perceived identities: religious, tribal, ethnic, racial, linguistic, or regional groups. These latter types are particularly prevalent in the new states of Africa and Asia. The prevalence of particular types generally tends to reflect the basic concerns of the various groups and the types of conflict patterns most prevalent in various societies (Chapter 6).

Another way to classify interest groups is by type or style of organization. Gabriel Almond has developed such a classification scheme which is particularly useful because it is related to the relative effectiveness of different types.[1] The extent to which different types prevail in specific societies seems again to be related to environmental factors prevailing within the society, as well as to the political environment in which the groups function. Almond distinguishes between four types of groups (although in the real world, the distinctions may not always be sharp and clear).

Associational groups, the more common variety in modern industrial societies, are groups deliberately and formally organized on behalf of some interest or cluster of interests. They have a formal organizational structure; formal procedures for acquiring membership, for selection of leaders, and for formulation of group policy; and usually organized means or machinery for continuing and intermittent political action such as lobbying. Examples include modern labor unions, trade, business and farmer organizations, humane societies, varied types of cause groups, formally organized caste associations in India and tribal associations in Africa. This type is generally most effective with respect to all linkage-communication functions.

In democratic and some authoritarian societies, membership in such groups is usually voluntary (although in some cases it may be required —such as membership in a union as prerequisite for a job). These voluntary organized groups develop to the extent that similar types of people

---

[1]Gabriel Almond and G. Bingham Powell, Jr., *Comparative Politics: A Developmental Approach* (Boston: Little, Brown, 1966).

recognize their common or similar interest, and associate and cooperate with others in an organized way for the promotion of such interests. In Western industrial societies this is a fairly common pattern: businesspeople recognize common interests and organize on their behalf; parents of school children organize parent associations; property owners and tax payers organize. But in some Afro-Asian and other societies, recognition of some interests—such as socio-economic—is often overshadowed by primary concern with other interests—such as tribal or religious—and by a reluctance to join formal organizations. Hence, in such societies such groups are often underdeveloped.

In some authoritarian and most totalitarian systems such groups also exist, but they are organized and controlled by the government and serve as means whereby governments can regiment people and mobilize them to pursue tasks selected by the political elites. In the Soviet Union numerous "mass organizations" exist, such as trade unions, women's groups, professional associations, and youth groups, in which membership is compulsory. Although the primary purpose of such groups is to function as "transmission belts" for "downward communication" from government to society, they do function as linkage and communication instruments to a limited extent and provide for a degree of surrogate representation in Soviet policy-making processes.

Nonassociational groups also exist and play political roles in industrial societies, but are more common and important in agrarian and developing societies. In terms of characteristics, they lack the prominent features of formal groups; they may not have a formal organizational structure, and generally are without formal procedures for acquiring membership and for such activities as the selection of leaders and the formulation of group policy. Membership in such groups is "acquired" on the basis of similar or common interest arising from such factors as birth or ethnic derivation (tribal groups in African politics, Berbers in the Middle East, Blacks and Indians in American society), religious persuasion (Muslims in India, Christians in Lebanon, Catholics in Western societies), socioeconomic or occupational status (castes in India, unskilled workers, retirees, the unemployed), or linguistic affiliation (various groups in India, Switzerland, Belgium, Canada). Even though not formally organized, these must be considered as interest groups because their members have at least some dim recognition of the interests they share with their fellow members, because such shared interests frequently form the basis for some kind of cooperation in political and other activities, because their formally or informally selected or sometimes self-appointed leaders or spokesmen do claim to work for the interests of these groups, and because they play major political roles in many systems. Tribal groups, for example, play a much more important role in African politics than do modern socio-economic associational groups. Sometimes an entire nonassociational group, or elements of such groups, may form formal organizations to promote group interests. Some castes in India have organized formal caste associations; some traditionalist Muslims throughout the Middle East have formally organized to combat the secularization of Muslim societies; some Roman Catholics formally organize on behalf of certain objectives such as governmental aid to parochial schools. Such a tendency towards formal association develops as recognition of the common interest becomes more pronounced, as members become more aware of the value of organized cooperative action, and as individuals become more willing to join and participate in formal organizations and formally organized activities. Due to such factors, in some developing societies a mixture of associational and nonassociational groups has developed. Modern labor unions have begun to develop in many African states, yet many of them are organized along tribal lines. In India separate Muslim and Hindu chambers of commerce have appeared. Although such fragmentation of group life possess some problems for these societies, the development of associational groups may in time produce a new sense of identity helpful for nation-building.

Institutional groups Institutions are also groups of individuals with common, similar, or shared interests, and they frequently engage in political action on behalf of such interests. Governmental bureaucracies, for example, although primarily decision-making institutions, also have institutional interests of their own and frequently attempt to influence other branches or elements of the governmental apparatus for the protection and promotion of their own bureaucratic interests. In many instances they act as surrogate representatives for client groups associated with the bureaucracy—such as an agricultural ministry lobbying other bureaucracies or a legislature on behalf of farm interests. Particularly in democratic and in polyarchic non-democratic systems, bureaucracies are very active in efforts to influence decision-making at parallel or higher levels of policy-making. Politics in the Soviet Union, for example, consists primarily of the push-pull of a multiplicity of diverse bureaucratic interests, with bureaucracies often acting as surrogate representatives for farm, labor, industrial, ideological, or even consumer interests. Even executive institutions lobby on behalf of executive interests. Other institutions occasionally or continually active in the political processes are military institutions (either on behalf of the military's own immediate interests or on behalf of associated clientele groups such as defense industries), and religious institutions (such as the Roman Catholic Church in some Western systems, or the Buddhist hierarchy in some Asian states). The power of religious institutions is particularly strong in those societies in which religion remains a major ingredient of the culture.

Anomic groups or outbreaks This term is used to refer to a variety of similar kinds of actions entailing some degree of potential or actual violence—protest marches, demonstrations, strikes, sit-ins, street violence, riots, even insurrections—which various kinds of groups use on occasion, sometimes spontaneously and sometimes in a well organized fashion, to advance group interests. Established associational groups sometimes resort to them, such as labor unions launching a demonstration or farmer organizations dumping surplus produce on roads to protest government agricultural policy. Sometimes they arise spontaneously among nonassociational groups as some incident which threatens group interests sparks such an outbreak—religious riots in India, student protests against university policies, or worker demonstrations against food price increases. Sometimes they are organized by leaders of associational groups, with the hope that they will attract the support of others outside the formal organization—demonstrations by caste associations in India, student-led anti-government demonstrations in France, Thailand, Germany.

Although anomic outbreaks really constitute more of a tactic used by associational, nonassociational, or sometimes even institutional groups rather than a particular type of interest group, separate classification is useful because such outbreaks frequently are truly spontaneous, because they do function in a limited way as linkage-communication instruments, and because they may be symptomatic of severe malaise in the body politic. Anomics are particularly characteristic of systems where associational groups are underdeveloped—either because of social-cultural impediments or because of government repression—and in societies characterized by complex and intense conflict patterns. They also tend to develop in more stable and peaceful societies when groups with intense demands or grievances sense that they are shut out from decision-making processes, or have few regularized channels for the articulation of their demands and for influencing governmental action.

THE POLITICAL FUNCTIONS OF INTEREST GROUPS

Interest groups are frequently viewed as malignant growths on the body politic. It is commonly charged that they subvert the public interest by their relentless pursuit of selfish private interests, that their pressure tactics and crude use of wealth and power corrupt the processes of government, and that they tend to dominate politics to the point where they in effect constitute a secret conspiratorial government. All of these charges are at least partly valid in some situations in all political systems, and in many situations in some systems. But political analysis must recognize and assess not only the existence and power of such groups, but also the linkage and communication functions they perform, and how well they perform them. The deplorable political roles of some groups in some situations and systems may be due to the inadequacies of the interest group system within the infrastructure. For without such groups for the performance of these vital functions, modern political systems simply could not govern.

The primary role of interest groups is that of interest-idea articulation: they communicate to the government, and to other groups throughout the society, the general and specific needs, problems, and opinions of the group, and the general and specific demands for governmental action to promote their interests. This function is a proper and legitimate one within the context of democratic theory or any other theory which postulates that the purpose of government is to maximize the public interest, for any such theory includes the proposition that citizens have the right to express their grievances and demands and to petition the government for what they deem to be appropriate and just action. Effective performance of this function by interest groups is also necessary for political stability and effectiveness, simply because of any government's vital need for information and expertise for effective policies, and because no other kinds of instruments seem capable of providing the timely, accurate, and specific information which specialized interest groups can provide. Business, labor, consumers, environmentalists, students, Roman Catholics, Blacks, property owners—all not only have a right to be heard, but need to be heard if a government is to function effectively. And only through organized activity can individuals be heard effectively.

Related to the articulation function is the service of "functional representation." As explained in Chapter 7, geographic representation is not adequate in large-scale complex systems. What is needed is some kind of system which can represent ideas and interests which transcend geographic frontiers. Interest groups—at least those characterized by substantial internal democracy which provides rank-and-file members with substantial influence—provide such representation. They represent the interests of individuals on the basis of their "function" in life—their occupation, socio-economic status, economic functions, or their cultural, religious, or ethnic affiliations and interests, or their ideological inclinations. They also represent such interests not only as they try to influence decision-making in legislative bodies, but also in bureaucratic decision-making processes. While the process of lobbying legislators and bureaucrats may sometimes involve deplorable tactics, in essence it involves the representation of the diverse interests of the citizenry.

Demand aggregation is another invaluable function performed by larger, umbrella-type interest groups which constitute broad coalitions of similar and yet somewhat diverse interests—federations of labor unions, business groups, farmers, some broad-based ideological or cause groups. The Association of Commerce and Industry aggregates interests of business, as the NAACP does of some Blacks, the Trade Union Congress of workers in Britain, tribal associations of their members in some African states, caste associations of theirs in India. And sometimes the conflict resolution function extends beyond individual interest federations as two or more groups engage in bargaining and compromise in the development of package proposals for governmental policy—as the UAW and auto manufacturers negotiate to develop a common program to promote the interests of the auto industry.

The political recruitment roles played by interest groups may similarly not always be compatible with the public interest, yet it would be difficult to dispense with them. They play major roles with respect to the recruitment of specialist-experts and managerial types for bureaucracies, for cabinet or ministerial positions, and for legislative committee positions, in that they train, groom, and make available for governmental positions individuals with necessary expertise and skills. They participate in nomination and election processes of politician-generalists, although again, the extent to which such activity is in the public interest may be questionable.

Interest groups may be necessary for support building and for mobilizing people behind governmental programs. In democratic systems it is essential to obtain the cooperation of affected major interest groups if a particular policy is to be successfully implemented. In non-democratic systems government-controlled groups which in some respects resemble interest groups are used for mobilization purposes. Although groups function more as propagandists than as educators, they may play socialization roles and stimulate public and governmental awareness of and concern over problems which might otherwise be neglected—the problems of racial or ethnic minorities, of small businessmen and farmers, of students or educators, or of neglected larger problems such as of a neglected environment. And although some interest groups may have a divisive impact on society, others may play an integrating role—such as chambers of commerce and labor organizations which may foster somewhat of a sense of common interests among people of different religions, racial or ethnic backgrounds, languages, or regions.

To what extent interest groups serve as instruments of public influence over government is somewhat of a controversial question. For one, the answer depends on the analyst's evaluation as to the extent the goals of specific groups are congruent with what one might deem to be in the public interest. For another, the answer depends very much on the nature and major characteristics of the entire interest group complex within a political system—a subject discussed below. It is clear that in most modern democratic political systems, interest groups are the single most important source of environmental influence over governments between elections, and that laws which finally emerge from governmental processes invariably bear the heavy imprint of group power. It is also clear that individual groups, despite their pretentions to speak for the public good, seek influence on behalf of private special interests, and the satisfaction of such interests might well have adverse consequences for the entire society. The argument normally made by interest group spokesmen—what's good for my interest is good for the country—is simply not valid in many instances. It is also clear that in those systems in which interest groups exercise substantial power, unorganized publics and interests fare poorly indeed in the governmental allocation of values. But groups do exert influence on behalf of special publics, and if the entire interest group complex within the system is adequately representative of most if not all publics of that society, then such groups can indeed constitute instruments of public control. This function may be particularly important in those systems in which political parties, elections, or other infrastructures are non-existent or poorly developed.

The extent to which interest groups perform the vital linkage-in-government function and facilitate the development of timely and effective laws similarly varies from system to system and from situation to situation. In some polyarchic and particularly democratic political systems, the influence exerted by numerous competing groups, or even the influence of a few very powerful groups, may be such as to negate governmental effectiveness: final decisions may face agonizing delays due to intense competition among groups; numerous concessions may have to be made to so many diverse groups that the final compromise law may be totally ineffective as an approach to the basic problem; or groups with sufficient power to exert a virtual veto over legislation contrary to their interests may immobilize the entire legislative or policy-making process. This kind of impact by associational groups in the United States is almost matched by the impact of institutional groups in the Soviet Union. Yet on other occasions, leaders and lobbyists of interest groups do provide some linkage-in-government by helping to produce the cooperation necessary for the enactment of decisions beneficial to their interests as well as to the general public. In sum, it would be highly unrealistic to extol interest groups as public benefactors. But it would be equally unrealistic to castigate them as blights on the body politic, for they do perform useful-to-necessary roles and functions in all kinds of political systems. What counts is the nature of the interest group system, and how adequately and equitably it performs the linkage and communication functions for most if not all of society.

THE ENVIRONMENTAL-POLITICAL CONTEXT OF INTEREST GROUPS

The nature of an interest group system is at least partly the result of the environmental-political setting in which it functions, but also has an impact on that setting. Their nature and activities have consequences for the political system as a whole and for the other components of the system—they have an impact on government and its policies, and on the society. But their nature and dynamics are also dependent on the other components of the system and are conditioned by the environmental setting and by the overall political context in which they function. This poses a problem of assessment—determining the origins and reasons for the specific characteristics of the interest group system in a particular kind of political system. It also poses significant problems of human engineering or reform: can a particular interest group system be significantly changed by some kind of direct action, or does change require changes in the environmental setting or the decision-making system?

The environmental setting impacts the interest group system in a variety of ways. In most modern democratic industrial states, for example, one invariably finds a great number and variety of groups, but the most common and powerful generally are associational groups representing varied socio-economic interests—particularly large umbrella-type groups or federations of groups. This reflects the primary concern in such societies with socio-economic interests. It also tends to reflect a willingness to associate with others and to join formal organizations to promote individual or group interests, as well as pragmatic attitudes and a willingness to bargain and compromise. It is also a product of a participatory culture, characterized by high cognitive orientations and participation and distribution demands, which prompts individuals to organize in order to influence political processes. The multiplicity and diversity of groups also reflects the distribution of power throughout the society—the condition of polyarchy and broad dispersion of the resources of power.

But other environmental factors in such societies may have different consequences for the interest group system. Intense individualism, for example, may lead to a poor associational life and an unwillingness to join organized groups and, hence, limits both the number and diversity of groups. Doctrinaire attitudes, coupled with a lack of consensus in society and the persistence of cultural, religious, or ideological cleavages, may produce splinter groups rather than coalition types, or may impede the cohesion and, hence, the power of larger umbrella-type federations. In France, for example, both labor and farm organizations represent only a fraction of workers and farmers and are split along ideological and religious lines. The power of interest groups in general, or of specific groups, may be substantially diminished because the society may view interest group political activity as illegitimate—as subversive of the public interest.

Democratic political settings also have major consequences. In such settings interest groups obviously proliferate partly because of the absence of governmental restrictions on their formation and political activity. But they further proliferate as the expanding scope of governmental tasks, and consequent potential for the allocation of values, provides incentive for organized political action. The attitudes of key decision-makers also have a significant impact. As governmental officials look on interest groups as useful or necessary instruments, respond to their demands, consult with them in the formulation of policy, or otherwise provide them with roles in decision-making, they provide incentive for organization and activity. Conversely, lack of such responsiveness may limit associational group activity, enhance the power of institutional groups representing bureaucracies, and lead to anomic outbreaks. Labor will strike for political purposes and farmers will dump their produce on highways as government officials ignore the demands of labor or farm organizations. The power of interest groups may be conditioned by the degree to which power is concentrated or dispersed within a government. Parliamentary systems in which power tends to be concentrated in the executive and bureaucracy have somewhat greater capability to resist the demands of interest groups. In systems of widely dispersed power, such as the American, such capability is reduced as interest groups have a number of points in decision-making—varied congressional committees, bureaucracies, even the judicial system—where they can exert influence.

In the new and less developed states of Africa and Asia and in some other parts of the globe, one finds substantially different interest group systems. Associational socio-economic groups have only begun to develop, nonassociational groups play more prominent roles, interest conflicts occur much more along non-economic alignments, and anomic outbreaks are much more common. This again reflects the environmental setting in these societies: primary concern with cultural, religious, ethnic, or similar interests; the persistence of such identifications which produces a fragmented group system and impedes the development of broad-based socio-economic associations; the persistence of a subject culture which limits organization for political activity; the general lack of consensus in such societies; intense and hostile cleavages along varied lines; and the greater legitimacy of violence as a political instrument. The political setting in these, as well as in totalitarian industrial societies, also impacts interest groups. Authoritarian leaders invariably attempt to inhibit the organization or political activity of autonomous groups, because they view them either as threats to power or as subversive of the public good as defined by authoritarian leaders. And the power possessed by varied institutions—religious, the bureaucracy, the military—substantially enhances the role of institutional groups.

THE POLITICAL POWER OF INTEREST GROUPS

The political power of interest groups is related to the interplay of the four components of power explained in Chapter 2: the relationship between available resources, the reciprocal need of targets for such resources, and the elements of credibility and good will. These components explain the general power of interest groups, variations in power among them, and variations in power relating to targets of influence, specific situations, and over time.

In essence, all interest groups have one or more of the resources of power. Of key importance are the linked resources of numbers and organization: organized groups of many people simply tend to be more influential than individuals. The size of the organization is important, but may be offset by other factors or resources. Organizational cohesion is equally important; when organized labor speaks with one voice, it enjoys credibility and the power that goes with organized numbers; when labor is badly divided along ideological, ethnic, religious, tribal, or other lines, its power tends to be weaker. Nonassociational groups, lacking the elements of formal organization and cohesion, tend to be weak—unless the power of numbers is reflected in the power of noise or widespread violence or other factors. The inability of associational groups to form and engage in political activity obviously limits their power in nondemocratic systems, while enhancing the power of institutional groups. Changes in cohesion over time, or from situation to situation, may produce changes in power: a chamber of commerce may be able to speak with one voice and be very powerful when it comes to tax matters affecting business; but may lose both cohesion and credibility when it comes to more peripheral issues—such as an educational policy.

Wealth or economic power is another key resource wielded by many groups, particularly by major economic groups in industrial societies.

Business or labor groups can influence by their ability to bestow or deny jobs; key labor unions by their power to disrupt the economy by means of a strike; others by their money which they can use as a bargaining resource. Also of prime importance are the resources of information, skill, and expertise. Interest groups possess the information and expertise which governments badly need to formulate effective policies, and they have the leaders, professional staffs, and lobbyists skilled in the manipulation of these resources for political influence, and who have the time and pay attention to exerting such influence. Particularly when a policy issue involves very complex and technical problems—increasingly true of most political issues—the interest groups deemed by government officials to possess the required know-how and expertise will be very influential.

But resources influence only to the extent that they are needed or valued by targets of influence. This is a key factor in explaining the power of interest groups in general, and in variations in power among them.

All governments need some degrees of support from at least some elites and varied groups in society, either simply for retention of political power, or in order to be able to carry out their policies and programs. Interest groups, by virtue of their resources, can provide or deny such support. Invariably, the more powerful groups will be those whose support is deemed most essential by governments as a whole or by individual officials. In agrarian societies, governments invariably need the support of the landed aristocracy and of such institutional groups as the religious establishment and perhaps the military. Totalitarian and authoritarian rulers generally need substantial support from their bureaucracies, perhaps again from the military institution, and perhaps from some nonassociational groups such as certain tribes or ethnic groups. The need for such interest group support, and their consequent power, may become particularly acute when the top elites within a nondemocratic system are divided over an issue. The situation differs in modern democracies only with respect to the identity of the more powerful groups, and in that the greater dispersion of power within the government may enhance the need for support. The support of key economic groups is invariably needed, although the degree of support solicited from business, financial, labor, farm, or other groups may vary with different systems and governments. And with substantial dispersion of power, the need of individual government officials for support tends to increase. Elected officials need support from some interest groups to win reelection, or to ensure passage of some pet piece of legislation. Cabinet members need some outside support to win intra-cabinet conflicts over public policy, as do bureaucrats in their conflicts with other bureaucrats, legislators, congressional committees, and even chief executives. And any government or bureaucracy needs some interest group support if it hopes to effectively implement its policies and programs.

But even more important is the need of modern governments in complex industrial societies for the resources of information, knowledge, and technical expertise possessed by associational and institutional interest groups. Governments in such societies daily face numerous extremely complex problems which require very complex approaches or solutions. Economic policies, health and welfare measures, educational programs, environmental and energy problems, housing programs, transportation needs, defense and foreign policies—these and many other modern governmental tasks require detailed information and expertise. A seemingly-simple tax bill, for example, requires detailed information not merely about the amount of revenue it will yield, but also on its precise impact on the varied sectors of a society and economy. An effective housing program requires very specific and expert information about specific housing needs in specific areas of a society, specific costs, the potential impact of various kinds of housing programs, and many other related matters. The complexity of modern industrial societies, combined with the steadily expanding scope of government, has created an explosion in the need of modern governments for technical knowledge, information, and expertise, and it is precisely the modern associational interest group as well as bureaucratic institutions which have these vitally needed resources. This need extends to governments as a whole, and to individual groups and officials within governments who cannot hope to possess the information and expertise required to deal adequately with the variety of bills, proposals, and problems they must cope with on a daily basis.

The linked elements of credibility and good will are also important with respect to the power of interest groups. To be influenced, government officials must believe that interest groups actually have the resources they are wielding, and will use them as they indicate they will. A labor union leader, for example, is likely to be influential only to the extent that he can convince a politician running for election that he actually can and will deliver a major campaign contribution, or the votes of members of the union. It is in this connection that organizational cohesion is an important resource. Even more important is credibility with respect to knowledge; expert information will persuade a legislator only to the extent that the latter believes it really is valid and expert information. An interest group which enjoys high prestige, or which has a relationship of good will with its specific governmental target, tends to enjoy such credibility with such targets: its lobbyists will tend to have a reputation for truth, honesty, and expertise. For such credibility and good will, there generally must exist some congruence of values and goals between the interest group and its targets. A labor union leader, for example, is likely to have difficulty influencing a business-oriented official who is convinced that unions have a deleterious impact on the economy; an environmentalist is likely to have similar difficulty with a legislator who is convinced that energy requirements must take precedence over environmental protection. What counts is the credibility and good will generated by similar attitudes, values, beliefs, and goals.

In a larger sense, the influence of groups varies with the extent to which there is congruence between group values and goals and those of the government as a whole, or of the society at large. For groups to be influential, they must function within a receptive environment—a political or social setting which is receptive to their political endeavors. If the prevailing culture, for example, deems interest groups in general, or specific kinds of groups, as illegitimate political instruments—as organizations prone to subvert the public interest—groups are less likely to be powerful. In some Western and many Afro-Asian systems, for example, associational economic groups have only begun to acquire the reputation of being legitimate spokesmen for varied sectors of the public, and as a consequence they are not nearly as powerful as in some other industrial states. The power of certain kinds of groups may also rise or decline as a society's values and goals change. Thus the power of environmental and consumer protection groups in the United States has increased as American values have begun to change, while the prestige and perhaps the power of older economic groups—business, labor—has somewhat declined. Congruence with the values and goals of governments as a whole, or of the key decision-makers, is equally important. In Gaullist and post-Gaullist France, for example, interest groups representing the modern sector of the French economy became much more powerful than those representing small-scale business, industry, and farming, simply because of the commitment of the French government to the modernization of the French economy.

The power of interest groups in general and of specific groups must also be assessed within the context of the general distribution of power throughout the entire political system. In oligarchic systems one or a few groups tend to dominate politics—the landed aristocracy, religious establishment, and military in feudal agricultural societies. In the early stages of industrialization groups representing business and finance may dominate political processes. A related matter is the degree to which power is concentrated or dispersed within the government. Systems of concentrated power, such as authoritarian, totalitarian, and some parliamentary democratic governments, although by no means immune to interest groups, are better able to resist their influence so long as the political elites are united. When elite conflicts erupt in such systems, or in systems of broadly dispersed power such as the American, interest groups frequently have a field day in determining the outcome of political processes.

But despite their formidable power, individual interest groups are seldom able to dominate politics in polyarchic industrial systems. For one, pluralism and polyarchy usually ensures competition and a system of countervailing power: the power of any one group, or coalition of groups, is likely to be offset by the power of competing groups and by other infrastructures—political parties, news media, constituency pressures on representatives, responsiveness to broader publics due to the need to win elections, competing bureaucracies, and similar "checks and balances" inherent in a pluralistic democratic society. The petroleum industry, for example, despite its political clout, frequently faces vigorous opposition from labor, environmental, consumer, business, and other kinds of groups. Also, pluralism of ideas and interests within individual groups frequently limits cohesion and consequently influence, as efforts to wield influence on issues not directly affecting the group's major interest tend to produce disagreement within ranks. Labor unions, for example, will tend to be cohesive and powerful on matters affecting pocketbook issues. But cohesion tends to vanish when they become involved in social, educational, or other issues peripheral to the rank-and-file's prime economic concerns. Third, interest groups seldom mobilize and use their resources on issues which do not directly affect the basic group interest: this frequently is considered a waste of organizational resources, risks group cohesion, and may raise questions about a group's credibility with regard to issues where it does not have specific expertise. And finally, most decision-makers within many governments also have a conscience: they have their own ideas as to what is truly in the public interest, are prone to listen to competing groups, and are likely to have a sense of fair play.

INTEREST GROUP TARGETS AND TECHNIQUES

The specific targets which various interest groups select for major attention, and the various tactics and techniques they use to wield influence, vary from system to system, and from situation to situation. But one general proposition can be stated with respect to both targets and techniques: interest groups seek to maximize access to centers of power and authority. Specific targets and techniques are then selected on the basis of the political and cultural context within which individual groups function.

The center of power and authority is partly determined by the political context. In essence, groups attempt to seek access to those levels, branches, agencies, or officials of the government which have the author-ity to take the actions desired by the group. If governmental authority is concentrated at national-level ministries or bureaucracies—as it is in most nondemocratic and in some democratic systems such as Britain—these ministries and bureaucracies will be the major targets. If legislative bodies wield substantial power, then the key powerholders within legisla-tures—such as key committees or senior senators and congressmen in the American congress—will be included as major targets. If authority over some matters is dispersed below the national level, these levels will be targets when interest groups are concerned over issues within the pur-view of state or local governments. When authority within a system is widely dispersed, interest groups may frequently shift targets. Thus in the American system they may first focus on a particular congressional com-mittee, then shift their attention to the second legislative house if they fail in the first, then shift to the presidency perhaps in an effort to influence a veto, then to the bureaucracy to obtain favorable administration of a law, and then sometimes even to the judicial system for a favorable interpretation or even a judicial reversal of a legislative decision. The cultural context also generally conditions the selection of specific targets, in the sense that both initial access and subsequent influence are depen-dent on "cultural congruence" between interest groups and their targets. Groups tend to concentrate their efforts on those agencies, officials, committees, or ministries which are known to share and be sympathetic with the ideas, interests, values, and goals of the resource-wielding group. They tend to avoid wasting time, effort, and other resources in seeking access to and influence over agencies or officials known to be hostile to their interests or ideas.

The choice of techniques and strategies also depends on the political and cultural context, and may involve either direct or indirect means to influence decision-making. The strategy of direct simple persuasion is the most common one in relatively stable systems in which groups have some needed or valued resources, enjoy some credibility and good will, and can anticipate some responsiveness on the part of specific branches or offi-cials selected as targets. Thus in the American, British, and many other systems, direct conventional lobbying is the more common technique: the use of a variety of resources to persuade and convince the targets that the group's interests and demands are legitimate, that its proposals are rational approaches to not just private but public needs and problems, and that at least partial accommodation of the group's demands consti-tutes simple justice and is in the public interest. But in many cases the direct strategy may include elements of inducement or even veiled or open coercion: a promise or threat with regard to voting or financial support, or to support or deny support and voluntary compliance with a public policy. In still other systems, only the more powerful groups generally favored by the government will use such direct strategies; the less-favored groups frequently denied access or favorable attention may adopt other tactics.

Depending on the specific conflict or environmental-political setting, groups may resort to a variety of indirect techniques to maximize access —to obtain at least a hearing and perhaps some responsiveness on the part of varied centers of power. They may participate in election campaigns to secure the election of candidates sympathetic to their ideas or interests, or simply to ensure some access after the election. Oil companies, for example, are prone to provide campaign funds to several political parties and to competing candidates, simply to ensure some access regardless of who wins. Public relations campaigns constitute similar indirect methods: groups seek to influence public opinion on behalf of their goals, or to enhance their image as groups who truly speak in the public and not merely private interests, to enhance their reputations with and to gain access to those decision-makers who have the authority to do what they want done. This is a favorite technique with such groups as the National Rifle Association, the American Medical Association, the American Petroleum Institute, and many others. Or groups may seek to influence agencies or officials who do not have the requisite authority to do what groups want done, but who have some influence over those who do: a sympathetic senator or bureaucrat who has influence over other senators or bureaucrats. In some settings groups frequently denied access may resort to strategies of coercion—to anomic outbreaks to express the intensity of their needs and their determination to do something about their cause. In essence, although the tactics of many groups may at times be quite deplorable, from the perspective of group efforts to promote group interests they generally tend to be quite rational given the circumstances.

THE ASSESSMENT AND EVALUATION OF INTEREST GROUP SYSTEMS

As explained in Chapter 3, the assessment and evaluation of political systems and of their component parts is a difficult yet necessary intellectual exercise. Analysis of interest group systems involves identifying the major characteristics of such systems; and assessment of the consequences of such characteristics for the performance of linkage and communication functions, as well as for the overall stability and effectiveness of the political system as an instrument of society. Evaluation entails normative considerations linked with such empirical assessment, and in relationship to interest groups entails questions relating to what specific functions we prefer to have them perform, what kinds of tactics and techniques we prefer to have them use, what values we prefer to have them maximize, or what values we are prepared to sacrifice given the inevitable necessity for some kind of a value tradeoff.

For both assessment and evaluation, certain key characteristics of interest group systems can be singled out because of their relationship to effective, equitable, and autonomous performance of the six linkage and communication functions, and their consequent bearing on overall political stability and effectiveness. Hence during the analysis of particular political systems or types of systems it is important to ask key questions about the particular characteristics of the interest group system, to determine the roots of or reasons for such characteristics (perhaps the environmental or political context), and to trace their consequences for the infrastructure and the entire political system.

The size and complexity, of the interest group system as a whole is an important characteristic. In essence, is the size and complexity of the system commensurate with the size and complexity of the society and the diversity of ideas and interests within it?

Size and complexity are most important with respect to the key function of interest groups—interest-idea articulation. While other linkage-communication instruments can be helpful—mass media, representatives in government, the bureaucratic network, election systems, political parties—only interest groups seem capable of providing the timely, clear, accurate, specific, and expert information and proposal inputs needed by governments. A large and complex interest system is needed to represent and articulate the demands of most if not all segments of society, is likely to perform the articulation function on a more equitable basis, and has greater capability for providing governments with a reliable and accurate information flow. Such an interest group universe helps to make the political system more polyarchic and perhaps even democratic, and tends to ensure substantial governmental responsiveness and relative equity of policy outputs. Conversely, a smaller and simpler interest group system tends to be less representative of the society as a whole and may provide communication channels only for selected elite groups. Unorganized interests tend to be shut out of the decision-making process; are forced to depend on not always reliable representation by bureaucracies; and may resort to anomic outbreaks with adverse consequences for political stability and effectiveness.

The performance of other functions is also enhanced by a complex interest group system. Effective and equitable political recruitment is enhanced in that political talent is made available from all walks of life. This concerns not merely the principle of equality of opportunity, but also ensures broad-based representation in the political system and equity of responsiveness. This again has consequences for effectiveness. Recruitment processes with an elitist slant—the likely outcome of a small interest group system—not only jeopardize support, but also deny the system the human talent available throughout the society, while encouraging incompetence, inefficiency, or corruption among the elites favored by the process. Political socialization, mobilization, integration and support building may also be enhanced by a large universe by providing more multiple communication channels throughout the society and between the government and society. And the potential for interest groups to function as instruments of public control is also enhanced when they provide equitable and effective functional representation for most if not all segments of society. In such instances the sum-total of special, particular interests represented within the system may approximate the more general public interest.

There are, however, some negative aspects to a large and complex interest group system. For one, interest groups still seek to influence governmental policy in the direction of private interests, and particularly when the stakes are high, are prone to use deplorable tactics, to distort information, to function as propagandists, and to ignore the public good in order to attain their goals. The more interest groups, the greater the probability of such actions. For another, a fragmented interest group complex may hinder performance of both the aggregation and integration functions. Perhaps most important, a large interest group universe may have serious adverse consequences for governmental effectiveness. Polyarchy and countervailing power have their merits in that they breed competition and more representation in decision-making and preclude domination of politics by one or a few groups. But too many groups may produce too much pluralism, countervailing power, and competition, which inhibits speedy, decisive, and effective governmental action. Two decades of attempts by the American government to develop an urgently-needed energy policy constitute but one example, as the push-pull of opposing groups has imposed numerous agonizing delays on pending bills, and has required concessions to so many special interests that final policy outputs hardly scratch the surface of the energy problem. Even the totalitarian leadership of the Soviet Union has difficulty developing needed economic policies because of the competing power of numerous Soviet bureaucracies.

The types or kinds of groups within the system is also relevant to function performance. For both democratic and effective performance, it is essential that all kinds of interests—socio-economic, ideological, cultural, ethnic, religious, tribal—be effectively represented within the group structure. Such representation not only tends to make for equity and for broad public influence, but also provides the information flow and the support that governments need. Relatively stable Western societies occasionally suffer from serious anomic outbreaks because of inadequate representation of some interests—Blacks and other minorities in American society, Roman Catholics in Northern Ireland, students in France. The effectiveness of Afro-Asian political systems is seriously impeded by the weak representation of new socio-economic interests, in contrast to the stronger representation along more traditional tribal and similar interests.

Although they have some disadvantages, broad-based coalition or umbrella-type interest groups which can function in a relatively cohesive fashion have distinct advantages with regard to demand aggregation and the resolution of conflicts among diverse interests, enjoy more power because of their cohesion, and can also promote integration in the society. A fragmented interest group system of splinter-type groups, in which several or many groups represent the same or similar socio-economic interests—such as labor or farm unions or business associations organized along separate religious, tribal, regional, or linguistic lines—tend to be less effective with respect to demand aggregation and integration. Instead of resolving conflicts, such groups tend to reinforce and intensify existing cleavages and conflicts within the society.

Associational types of groups generally perform more effectively than other types, particularly with respect to interest-idea articulation. Nonassociational groups often tend to articulate only vague, diffuse, and nonspecific moods and grievances, to suppress demands which have a divisive impact on the group rather than to resolve conflicts arising from them, and thus fail to provide accurate, clear, and specific information about group needs, problems, and demands. Their informal procedures in the selection of spokesmen or leaders also tends to make for lack of equity or participation in the formulation and articulation of group demands. Institutional groups—particularly government bureaucracies—may provide information as surrogates of varied elements of society, but they lack autonomy, tend to give priority to institutional interests; and are usually dependent on other groups or channels of information. Anomic groups communicate intense discontent, but little else.

The relative autonomy of individual interest groups is another important characteristic, particularly with respect to their articulation and recruitment roles. Autonomy from government is particularly important. Government controlled groups—such as in totalitarian and some authoritarian systems in which the government controls or dominates labor organizations, farm unions, professional associations, and similar kinds of groups—do serve to a limited extent as instruments of functional or surrogate representation, but this role is always overshadowed by their primary function as instruments of government control over the society.

With respect to communication, government control inhibits objectivity and accuracy, as those officials with roles in the communication channels may not be responsive to rank-and-file demands and grievances, and ever-fearful of losing status with their superiors, tend to report what they believe their superiors want to hear, rather than what they need to hear. The absence of autonomy may insulate governments from external pressures, but it also isolates governments with attendant consequences for stability and effectiveness. With respect to political recruitment, government-controlled institutions tend to place too great a premium on loyalty, conformity, and obedience, and too small a premium on merit and talent. For an accurate and complete information flow it is also desirable that individual groups operate autonomously of each other, and not be dominated by a few groups, or by other institutions of the infrastructure, such as by political parties.

The distribution of power among groups within the interest group system is another important characteristic. Within some systems the distribution of power among the diverse groups may generally be equitable. As a consequence, most segments and strata may have the means to levy effective demands on decision-making, the aggregation function may be performed in an equitable manner, substantial pluralism, competition, and representation may prevail during decision-making processes, and the overall role of interest groups as instruments of public influence may be enhanced—but at the price of such countervailing power that speedy and effective policy-making may be diminished (the price of democracy). Conversely, the distribution of power may be highly inequitable as a few groups representing only some sectors of society dominate governmental processes, with other groups having little effective access.

The distribution of power within individual interest groups has significant consequences for function performance. With some exceptions, interest groups are not very democratic institutions; they tend to be oligarchic in nature and to provide only limited roles in their own decision-making processes to rank-and-file members. This may be due to a variety of reasons: leadership control of internal communication channels, group funds, and of the organizational structure of the group; the limited time and attention that rank-and-file members give to group activities; or the leadership's information, skill, and expertise. A strong role for leadership is essential for any kind of organization so as to provide a sense of direction, to maintain the unity of the group, and in general to provide the dynamism needed for successful group activity. Yet functional performance is considerably impaired if the leadership dominates the group to the point that rank-and-file members have little voice in group political activity; in such instances interest groups can hardly be considered instruments of public influence. In such instances communication channels will be open only to some elites and cannot provide the complete and accurate information inputs which the political system needs; while aggregation and recruitment processes may not be equitable or effective. What appears to be most desirable is a polyarchic leadership structure within individual groups, coupled with substantial dispersion of power to rank-and-file members, so as to retain the benefits of leadership but ensure leadership responsiveness to the membership.

Major targets and techniques of political influence As previously discussed, interest group selection of targets and techniques is generally the product and symptomatic of the environmental and political setting in which groups function. Hence, their primary targets and techniques is not a characteristic directly related to effective interest group performance of linkage-communication functions. Nevertheless, such analysis is a useful exercise. It may provide clues about the nature and effectiveness of the entire infrastructure, and also about the basic nature of the political system. It may, for example, indicate where decision-making power is really located: the extent of legislative vs. executive, ministerial, or bureaucratic power; or the relative power of specific agencies, committees, or key officials or legislators. It may also provide clues as to the distribution of power among groups within the system, as the more powerful groups concentrate on direct conventional lobbying, while others may be forced to resort to indirect tactics. A frequency of anomic outbreaks on the part of associational or nonassociational groups is particularly significant, in that it may be indicative of the inadequacies of the infrastructure, of low responsiveness of the political system to certain groups or strata, of major environmental changes to which the government is not responsive, or of other factors which impede or threaten the stability and effectiveness of the system.

Political Parties and Election Systems

9

Like interest groups, political parties have their origins in the struggle for political power. The former engage in political action to influence decision-making, the latter to capture or retain control of governments. And as with interest groups, the primary concern of parties with power may have some negative consequences for the political system; they may promote conflict and have a divisive impact on a society, they may promote corruption in government, and they may promote political weakness and administrative inefficiency by placing partisan political considerations above efficiency, rationality, and the public interest. But these and other weaknesses, as Samuel Huntington has pointed out, are symptomatic of weak party systems, not of parties as such.[1] For more fundamentally, parties have developed as responses to the needs of modern political systems for performance of the varied linkage and communication functions—and particularly for the performance of those functions which no other existing institutions seem to be able to perform adequately. It is significant that parties exist not only in democratic but also in many authoritarian and totalitarian systems, primarily, of course, because political elites have found them to be useful tools to maintain

[1]Samuel P. Huntington, *Political Order in Changing Societies* (New Haven, Conn.: Yale University Press, 1968) pp. 397-433.

power, but also because the elites recognize the value of the functions they perform.

In this chapter we first explore the specific linkage and communication functions, which parties have at least the potential for performing. We then turn to the major questions that should be asked during analysis, such as: what types of parties exist within a political system? What are the major characteristics of the party system? What are the political consequences of these types and characteristics? As in the case of interest groups, these characteristics are important because they have an impact on the effectiveness and equity of linkage-communication performance, which in turn affects the nature of the overall political system, the goals of government, and political stability, effectiveness, and adaptation to change. We then briefly examine the relationship between these party characteristics and the environmental-political settings in which parties function. For as in the case of interest groups, reform of party systems may require changes in the environmental setting or in the governmental system.

The final section of this chapter discusses election systems and their relationship to party systems. Elections are of crucial importance to democracy, for free elections are a society's ultimate tool for controlling government. But such control is substantially enhanced, and may indeed require, elections in which political parties play primary roles. This again requires analysis of the particular characteristics of party systems, for these may or may not make certain types of party systems effective instruments of public control over government.

PARTIES AND LINKAGE-COMMUNICATION FUNCTIONS

Most basically, parties function as the major institutional links between the mass public, organized and unorganized groups in society, and the decision-making system. The need for such institutionalized linkage is particularly great in those societies in which participation demands are widespread, or in which demands for political participation have begun to develop. As discussed in Chapter 6, the participation challenge posed by new elites or groups demanding entry into politics poses a major challenge to the stability and effectiveness of political systems. Responding to this test requires not merely providing access to politics, but ensuring regularized and institutionalized access—means whereby groups can participate in an orderly and more-or-less predictable way. Effective political parties are the major institutions which contribute to stability and effectiveness, and provide for public influence, by mobilizing, organizing, stabilizing, and structuring mass participation. While parties may divide the body politic along party lines, an effective party structure has much more of an integrating effect, since it provides linkage and helps to bind together the variety of social forces with parochial interests. More specifically, parties function in such roles to the extent that they effectively, equitably, and autonomously perform the varied linkage and communication functions. The strongest political systems appear to be those in which the party systems most effectively perform such functions.

Political recruitment is the most visible function of parties. Through party nomination processes and their roles in elections, and even when nondemocratic elites use them for appointment and cooption, they play major roles with respect to the selection, recruitment, training, grooming, and promotion of generalist-politicians, and in some settings also of specialist-experts. In democratic systems this function is crucial not merely with respect to the recruitment of needed human resources, but also with respect to stability and orderly change. For elections regularize succession procedures, and parties as institutions capable of structuring elections and regularizing succession provide for the orderly and legitimate transfer of power and preclude the coups and mafia-style politics which are so inimical to stability and effectiveness.

Although the articulation function is generally performed in well-developed systems by interest groups, parties perform valuable supplementary roles. Parties usually consist of clusters of various kinds of social forces with which they are either directly or loosely affiliated—such as trade unions, varied occupational groups, racial minorities, certain socio-economic strata, religious groups. Although the more important function of parties is the aggregation of the ideas and interests of such diverse groups, they also serve to articulate the demands of these groups. This articulation function is particularly important in those systems with underdeveloped associational groups, or for minority groups which lack the political power to influence government directly but who constitute a latent threat to political stability.

Demand aggregation is a prime function performed by parties. Although they do generate and promote some conflict in their quest for power, effective parties serve much more to manage, structure, and moderate existing conflicts and to promote community among diverse social groups and interests. They do so to the extent that they are coalitions of diverse organized or unorganized socio-economic, cultural, and ideological forces; play effective brokerage roles among such forces; reconcile, mediate, and adjust diverse demands arising from such forces; and effectively aggregate and combine a multiplicity of demands into relatively simplified party policy and program proposals. Parties which in effect are coalitions of interest groups aggregate such groups into relatively stable coalitions which are more powerful than any single group itself, and thereby help to substitute and institutionalize a broader party and public interest for many fragmented private interests. The need for such institutions to function as intermediaries among diverse social forces, to moderate and mediate conflicts among such forces, is particularly acute in pluralistic societies.

Through such aggregation functions and effective linkage between the mass public, various groups in society, and the political system, parties can be effective instruments for socialization, mobilization, support building, and social and political integration. They may play major roles as carriers or generators of an existing or new political culture, and as such can be major vehicles for generating or maintaining support for the community and the political system. They can function as the basis of support of government, and can generate and mobilize support on behalf of governmental policies and programs. In a variety of ways they can serve as sources of legitimacy and effective authority. They can be very useful for integration, for the greater the complexity and heterogeneity of a society, the more political community depends on political institutions which can develop compatibility of interests among different social forces. As such effective institutions, parties can serve as major buckles which bind together various social forces, and thus help to create a basis for loyalty and identity transcending more parochial groupings and loyalties.

Through roles they play in elections, as well as by effective performance of articulation, aggregation, and recruitment functions, parties can serve as the most effective instruments of public influence over government. As is discussed below, elections are the major means whereby the general public can influence or control decision-making, but election systems which do not involve parties are relatively weak in this respect. At election time, parties can provide the public with meaningful choice as to who shall govern and as to what general kind of program or policy direction the government should pursue. By exerting influence over government not only via election choice but also between elections, parties bring to bear influence which is broader-based than the influence of individual interest groups or the narrower social forces which constitute parts of a party's membership—broader-based mass interests rather than narrow special interests. Even in non-democratic systems in which governments tend to control a party's recruitment, articulation, and aggregation functions, parties can serve as limited but real instruments of the public will and as checks on arbitrary and capricious authority.

Finally, effective parties serve as major institutional links among the diverse parochial, local, regional, constituency, and institutional interests which exist within any large and complex governmental system, and help to produce the harmony, cooperation, and consensus needed for the enactment of timely and effective policies. Although party loyalties divide Republicans and Democrats in the United States as they do Laborites and Conservatives in Britain and Gaullists and Socialists in France, they also provide some cohesion within their own ranks, bridge differences among constituency and other special interests which tend to divide party adherents and produce degrees of cooperation between and among legislators, executives, and bureaucrats. They thus alleviate the tensions and conflicts generated by systems of dispersed power and checks and balances, and provide the basis for the coalition-building which is essential for the formulation, enactment, and implementation of effective governmental policies.

TYPES AND CHARACTERISTICS OF PARTIES AND PARTY SYSTEMS

The major analytical questions which must be asked relate to the types and characteristics of parties and party systems. Like interest groups, parties and party systems can be classified in a variety of ways. However, analysis and classification on the basis of following major characteristics seems particularly meaningful because of the relationship between these characteristics and the performance of various linkage-communication functions. Most important is the number of parties existing within the system and the extent of real electoral competition among them. But other characteristics are also significant.

COMPETITIVE VERSUS NONCOMPETITIVE SYSTEMS

A competitive system is one in which two or more parties engage in real and meaningful competition for public offices, and in which more than one party has a real chance for election victories which provide it with either significant influence over or control of the government. Noncompetitive systems include one-party types, such as the single party system in the Soviet Union in which only the Communist Party is legally allowed to exist. Single party systems exist in most totalitarian and many authoritarian states in which the political elites find them useful for their purposes. They also exist in some quasi-democratic systems, such as the Institutional Revolutionary Party (PRI) in Mexico. Noncompetitive systems also include "One Party Dominant" types, in which several parties compete in elections, but only one party has a real chance to control the government, either because it is always assured of a majority of votes, or because the complex of opposition parties is so weak and fragmented as to give only the dominant party a real chance of significant election victory. But in such cases the minor parties do have some impact and the major party does not completely dominate politics, because the limited competition does force the major party to make some concessions in order to minimize losses and avoid the loss of power to one or more minor parties. Such is the case of the Congress Party in India, and somewhat also that of the Gaullist party in France.

Noncompetitive systems of either type have some merits with respect to some functions. To the extent that party and government power-holders permit, they can perform articulation, aggregation, recruitment, socialization, and linkage-in-government functions. In new (and some older) unintegrated societies, single party systems can and in some instances have played major socialization, integration, and support building roles to the extent that they unite in one political institution diverse socio-economic, ethnic, religious, linguistic, tribal, and similar kinds of organized or unorganized social forces. African and Asian leaders in particular have sought to use single-party systems for such objectives, as have some totalitarian leaders in East Europe. In such societies, where too rapid a mobilization of participation in government may be a threat to stability and effectiveness, they may promote stability through their capacity to restrict and control the participation of new groups, and to reduce the heat and conflict resulting from electoral competition.

Yet the empirical record suggests that competitive systems seem to be much more effective with respect to most if not all functions. For one, parties in noncompetitive systems lack autonomy from government, hence, cannot function effectively as instruments of public influence. Their lack of autonomy also inhibits effective articulation and equitable aggregation and recruitment. Single parties, or parties in one-party dominant systems, invariably are used by leaders for purposes of leadership power. Lack of autonomy, combined with absence of real competition, leads to low responsiveness on the part of such parties, both with regard to policies and recruiting candidates of real merit and public support. They have no real incentive to broaden their appeal, to encourage broader participation in politics, or even to maintain the party organization once party leaders have attained political power. And although government or party leaders sometimes attempt to use single party systems to integrate a society, they tend to emphasize unity, discipline, and party elan within the organization. This leads them to ignore or suppress divisive forces within the party, and to limit the admission of new groups which may mar unity. Instead of promoting integration by demand aggregation and mediation of conflicts, they often hinder the development of real unity by denying the existence of or covering up differences within the party and society. Finally, the absence of real choice via electoral competition obviously limits public influence over government.

COMPETITIVE TWO-PARTY VERSUS MULTIPARTY SYSTEMS

The number of parties within a system is another characteristic of major importance. A simple typology distinguishes between two-party and multiparty systems; however, this conceals many important complexities.

A two-party system is one in which most if not all of the competition involves only two parties, one of which by winning a majority is able to control the government, while the loser constitutes the opposition. Britain, where the Labor and Conservative parties alternate in control of government, is the usual classic example. A multiparty system is one in which three or more engage in meaningful competition, each one of which can anticipate winning a significant number of governmental offices (usually legislative seats), with one party only rarely winning a clearcut majority which would enable that party to control the government. France and Italy are Western examples. There are, however, a number of variations on these basic patterns.

The American system on the national level, for example, appears to be a two-party system, yet has been such in recent decades in only one respect: relative equality of opportunity to capture the Presidency. The Democratic Party has dominated the Congress for decades. Within the Congress, a virtual one-party system exists within many congressional districts. At least one-third of the seats for the House of Representatives are really uncontested at election time: they are "safe seats" for one party or the other because only one has a real chance of winning the district. The American system shares another characteristic with some apparent two-party and even some single-party systems: internal cohesion in some parties is so low that the parties are nothing more than very loose coalitions of party-like factions parading under a single label. American national parties in a very real sense are confederations of state parties, which more or less unite only once every four years to campaign for the Presidency; while some state parties are only loose confederations of local party units.

The British party system is somewhat closer to the two-party model, in that although several parties compete for many seats in the Parliament, only the Labor and Conservative parties are truly national parties, compete for all seats, and stand a real chance of capturing a majority of seats to control the government. Yet even in Britain, in the 1974 election minor parties won enough seats to deny a clear-cut majority to either of the two majors. The West German system by contrast is a multiparty system which is close to the two-party model. Several parties contest each election at both national and state levels; the two majors—Social Democrats and Christian Democratic Union—win close to 50% of the legislative seats at each election; but a very small third party—the Free Democrats —wins just enough to deny either of the majors a clear-cut majority and thus requires a coalition government (the usual price of a multiparty system).

Some of the major defects of multiparty systems are rooted in the restricted sociological composition (a characteristic discussed below) of the parties making up such systems. Instead of consisting of broad coalitions of diverse social groups as is generally the case with two-party systems, their membership and electorate are generally composed of only one or a few types of groups or strata of the society. Typically, such parties consist of specific types of religious, ideological, ethnic, racial, tribal, linguistic, or similar types of groups; or specific social strata or occupational groups; or socio-economic groups that form splinter parties because of attachment to some religious or ideological creed or for racial, ethnic, or other reasons. Consequently such parties tend to function more like interest groups. They may have high capability for the articulation function, but low capability for aggregation and conflict resolution functions. Such parties tend to be dominated by the specific social forces that form the base of their organization and they lack the institutional means necessary for bargaining, adaptation, and compromise among diverse forces. Instead of subordinating narrow special interests to broader party and public interests, they equate such interests with the public interest—what's good for my ethnic group, religion, occupational group, etc., is good for the country. The same narrow base impedes their socialization, mobilization, and integration function: they have a divisive impact on society, and tend to perpetuate and reinforce the existing social cleavages and hostilities which give rise to such parties.

Superficially, multiparty systems appear to be more "democratic" in that they provide the public with more choice, more competition, and hence greater public influence over decision-making. These appearances again are deceiving. Real competition is often absent because each party tends to be solidly rooted in some social force, each at election time mobilizes its own firm constituency, but each seldom makes any real effort to appeal to other constituencies because they are firmly wedded to other parties. They all exert specialized appeals, and only marginally compete with one another for the support of broader publics. Also, as will be explained below in connection with elections, by providing multiple choice they often provide too much and confusing choice, and lack the capability to translate the public will into effective governmental action. Finally, they function very poorly in their linkage-in-government roles, in that they have a very divisive impact on legislatures and other branches of government, and invariably require coalition governments lacking stability and effectiveness.

Two-party systems generally consist of broad-based parties which are coalitions of many diverse social forces linked together by some common interests or ideas—some compatible interests or a guiding philosophy or set of principles. Hence, although they may be weak as articulation instruments, they are much more effective at aggregation, support building, integration, linkage-in-government, and for exerting public influence. Real competition ensues, since the parties are pressured or have incentives to compete for the allegiance of a variety of social forces and to draw support from many groups. The same pressures encourage them to expand participation in politics. They also enjoy autonomy and flexibility, since they seldom are creatures of or dominated by one or a few groups affiliated with them. Their leaderships and elected officials are less concerned with the interests of such affiliated groups and much more with a broader public interest. To win elections they must hold their party coalition together, aggregate diverse interests, recruit political talent from a wide social base, and generally be responsive to a wide political community. This political necessity inherent in a two-party system forces party leaders and elected officials to relate private interests to the public good rather than to subordinate the public interest to narrow private interests, to transcend the special interests of the varied groups which make up the party coalition. A representative of the British Labor Party cannot afford to be merely a spokesman for organized labor, any more than an elected official of the American Republican Party can speak only for business, lest that official court election defeat.

Sociological Composition

Sociological composition is an important distinguishing characteristic for assessing the relative effectiveness of parties and party systems. By this term we mean the types of people and social groups which make up the respective parties—their leadership, rank-and-file membership, and in competitive systems, the party-in-the-electorate (the voters who habitually support certain parties). This characteristic is also related to the organizational complexity and depth of a party—whether it really has a membership, voter support in some depth, a real organization, and substantial linkage with unorganized or organized interest groups. The important analytical question is to determine what the sociological composition of a party and party system appears to be, and what the consequences appear to be for performance of linkage and communication functions.

Parties in some systems have virtually no real sociological base or organizational structure, and really are nothing more than political cliques or factions. In some, the party consists of nothing more than some government officials, aspirants for public office or patronage, and others who hope to benefit from politics, clustered around some political leader because of his personality, power, or ability to dispense patronage. In others, the parties consist of little more than certain members of legislative bodies who form temporary or more durable factions because of some shared interest. Such cliques and factions do not really function as parties and cannot adequately perform linkage functions.

Skeletal-type parties are similar, having at best only a thin sociological base. They may have some basic core electorate of voters who habitually support the party, but the party organization is largely devoid of any real membership—consisting primarily of the party's leadership, elected officials, bureaucrats, and perhaps a small core of rank-and-file activists. They make no real effort to develop a mass base, and serve primarily as vehicles for the interests of the party's bureaucrats and politicians. Without a larger mass membership, such parties can hardly function effectively as linkage-communication institutions.

Single-party systems tend to have two distinct types of sociological composition, as determined by the political elites who control and use these parties for their own purposes. In communist systems parties are elite-type parties: membership is considered a privilege (although a requisite for any kind of important job), is restricted to a small percentage of the population (usually 1 to 3%), requires careful screening and probation of all aspirants, and provides a means whereby the political elite of the party can control its members with positions throughout far-flung communist bureaucracies. In Afro-Asian systems comprehensive single-parties prevail. In these, the political elites make intensive efforts to include members of all sectors and strata of society in party ranks, to make the party comprehensive and representative of the entire society, and hence as vehicles not only for the retention of political power but also for socialization, mobilization, and integration functions. However, as pointed out earlier, the absence of competition severely limits function performance.

In competitive systems, although some parties may be skeletal types or nothing more than cliques and factions, parties generally tend to have some kind of real sociological base—a core of leaders, a somewhat larger core of rank-and-file members who continually or occasionally participate in party and campaign activities, and a still larger party-in-the-electorate, who are held together and support the party because of some more-or-less shared interests or ideas. Of key importance is the assessment of what kinds of ideas or interests hold the party together, what the consequent sociological base of a party is, the breadth of a party's sociological composition, and what changes appear to be taking place with respect to the party system.

In some systems the composition of parties and differences between them results from socio-economic interests and alignments: parties may be based along class lines, or appeal to different socio-economic levels or occupational groups. Left-of-center parties in Western democracies, for example, tend to consist primarily (but not exclusively) of workers, lower-to-middle socio-economic groups, and similar types of people, while right-of-center parties consist of businesspeople and middle-to-upper income groups. In other systems composition results primarily from cultural factors: parties may have some religious, ethnic, racial, or similar foundation (most common in societies where such more traditional concerns still overshadow socio-economic interests). In still others both types of factors may produce the composition of parties. Religion, for example, still plays a prominent role in party alignments in West Germany, France, and Italy, while language plays roles in Belgium, Switzerland, and Canada. In still others, ideological factors may crosscut socio-economic alignments: socialism in France, conservatism or liberalism in some American state-level parties, fascism in Italy.

The basis for and breadth of sociological composition tends to breed either narrow-based particularistic or broad-based aggregative parties. Systems in which cultural conflicts persist and in which such factors constitute a main basis for party organization tend to breed narrow-based particularistic parties—those typical of multiparty systems, in which parties tend to function more as interest groups. But with some exceptions, the trend in Western societies has been towards the development of broad-based coalition-type parties which include diverse social, economic, and cultural elements of the society. Although such modern mass parties frequently have problems of unity and cohesion and may often become overly pragmatic to the point where they sacrifice basic principles and appear to stand for nothing, the empirical record on the whole suggests that such parties are much more effective with respect to performance of most linkage and communication functions.

IDEOLOGICAL OR POLICY INCLINATIONS

Some parties have neither an ideological foundation nor a real policy inclination: parties organized by some governments to help them retain power, personality-centered cliques, some skeletal-type parties. But most bona fide parties have some kind of ideological base and some kind of policy inclination resulting from this base. The base may be some religious creed, or the values and interests of some ethnic, tribal, regional, or similar type group, which produces party policies designed to protect and promote such values and interests—some traditionalist Muslim parties, tribal-based parties in Africa. The foundation may be some fairly well-defined and explicit ideology, as some Marxist parties. Or it may be a somewhat vague, near-ambiguous, implicit, or not always consistent set of beliefs and values—Liberalism, Conservatism, Christian Democracy, Democratic Socialism. But whatever the ideological base, party leaderships tend to develop party programs and policies on such foundations.

The sociological composition of a party generally results from (and helps to produce, maintain, or change) the philosophic principles, ideology, and policy inclinations of a party. Because a party's position is in accord with their ideas or interests, certain types of people or social groups are attracted to leadership roles, rank-and-file membership, and more-or-less habitual voting support for the party. This composition in turn helps to maintain the basic party position, as groups or individuals who favor such positions tend to control the party—either through leadership positions, or as rank-and-file and voter pressures force leaders to espouse such policies. Thus liberals, lower-to-middle income groups, and labor unions are attracted to and tend to control left-of-center parties, ardent Catholics or Muslims religious-oriented parties, businesspeople, upper socio-economic groups, and conservatives right-of-center parties. This composition may also over time modify or change party positions as party leaders attempt to adapt to changing conditions in order to retain power and voter support. The existing sociological base may change its interests and preferences (a more conservative labor force); new groups may move into party ranks (minority groups into a left-of-center party); or leaders may want to attract different groups during elections (such as a more independent body of new voters). When parties within a system differ in such policy inclinations, sociological compositions also tend to differ.

Within most broad-based and some narrow-based particularistic parties, three layers of the composition of parties are also significant with respect to such policy inclinations. The leadership of a party generally tends to be more intensely attached to the party's beliefs and values, (although pressures for election victories may force the leadership to be more pragmatic). The rank-and-file membership is generally more loosely attached to party principles. And the party's core electorate—the voters who generally tend to support the party at election time due to some perception of the relationship between their own ideas and interests and the policy inclinations of the party—generally are less firmly attached to the party's basic orientation. Differences on policy questions thus tend to be more sharp between the leaderships of the various parties than among rank-and-file members and voters.

Consequently the policy inclinations of parties tend to differ. In some systems the differences may be sharp, clear-cut, and highly visible— particularly among ideologically-oriented or religious-based parties. In others the differences may appear to be minimal close to elections when parties compete for middle-of-the-road voters—the tweedledum-tweed-ledee appearance of American parties. But even in the most pragmatic systems, some differences will persist, particularly between party leader-ships who generally tend to be more firmly attached to a party's principles and policy inclinations. The existence of such differences is extremely important with respect to the parties serving as instruments of public influence, for voters ought to have a real and meaningful choice between party positions.

Among parties in Western democratic systems, but also to an increas-ing extent in non-Western systems, one common philosophic foundation which serves to divide parties from one another concerns an interrelated set of beliefs about the priority ordering of certain values, how such goals can be attained, the proper use of government for the attainment of such goals, and the desirable pace or direction of change. It is this set of beliefs which provides criteria for placement of parties along a spectrum ranging from the extreme left or radical end to the extreme right or conservative-to-reactionary pole (although caution must be used in such categoriza-tion because some parties may be quite radical with respect to some beliefs, and extremely conservative with respect to others). But normally, parties toward the left emphasize rapid change in some kind of "progres-sive" or forward-moving direction, tend to emphasize economic goals, mixed with humanitarian or social justice concerns, and tend to empha-size major use of governmental means to attain such goals. Parties toward the right tend to emphasize slow or no change, the preservation of tradi-tional principles and values, and minimal or no governmental interven-tion for the attainment of individual and social goals. Towards the center of this spectrum there have developed the "somewhat left and right of center" parties—such as those in the United States, Britain, West Ger-many—which tend to be pragmatic in their approach to public policy and hence often give a tweedledum-tweedledee no-difference appearance, but which nevertheless reflect the basic contemporary philosophic divi-sion which persists in Western societies.

Contemporary liberalism (as distinguished from somewhat different classic or 18th-19th century liberalism) is the guiding philosophy of most left-of-center parties. This stream of thought emphasizes such goals as economic prosperity and growth, but also such other values as social justice, equality, greater equity in ownership of wealth and in distribution of income, and civil rights and liberties. Contemporary liberals are prone to favor more rapid change for the attainment of such goals, and to stress the necessity for collective social rather than individual action. Hence they emphasize (but with varying degrees or intensity) the need for the interventionist state as the means for collective social action—the necessity for major governmental involvement in the economic system, for governmental programs designed to promote social justice, equality of at least opportunity, and to effect some redistribution of income by welfare and tax programs. Liberals argue that such goals can be attained via the interventionist state without jeopardy to economic prosperity, civil liberties, individualism, freedom, and human dignity—that indeed, given the nature of modern societies, use of government instrumentalities is essential for such values and ends.

Contemporary conservatism is the guiding principle of most right-of-center parties, although they, like left-of-center parties, may be prone towards a pragmatic attitude with respect to such principles or may rigidly adhere to some but neglect other principles of this creed. Conservatives generally emphasize the same goals, but some may be prone to give priority to economic growth and prosperity as the necessary pre-conditions for the attainment of other non-economic objectives, and they generally prefer a slower pace of change with helps to preserve traditional values. Instead of collective social action for goal attainment they emphasize individualism, self-help and self-reliance, voluntary cooperation, and the value of natural economic and social competitive processes. They tend to be fearful of the interventionist state not only as a threat to economic growth and prosperity, but also to human freedom, dignity, and civil rights and liberties. Some towards the right end of the spectrum charge that almost any degree of governmental involvement in economic, social, and cultural affairs paves the way for the "road to serfdom"—will invariably lead to the subordination of the individual to the state. They argue that natural competition is most conducive to economic growth, and that the benefits of economic prosperity will inevitably "trickle down" to the masses and ensure social justice.

PRAGMATIC-AGGREGATIVE VERSUS DOCTRINAIRE-PARTICULARISTIC PARTIES

While most bona fide parties have some kind of ideological foundation or policy inclination, they differ with respect to ridigity of adherence to such a foundation. Some tend to be very doctrinaire and to function as "parties of expression": they approach problems in a very dogmatic fashion, seek solutions on the basis of what their doctrines prescribe, consider compromise unacceptable because it entails sacrifice of sacro-sanct party principles, and generally function more as parties interested in expressing their principles rather than in political action. Such parties tend to be highly particularistic. Others tend to be highly pragmatic and to function as "parties of action": they tend to seek solutions to problems less on the basis of party ideology and more on the basis of what will work or what a rational approach might be. They are quite willing to at least bend some basic principles and to strive for compromise—either because criteria of rationality and efficiency outweigh party dogma, or because compromise seems essential in the interests of political action and for getting things done. Such parties tend to be aggregative types, primarily interested in aggregation of a broad spectrum of diverse interests rather than articulating a narrow range of interests.

Although it is essential that parties stand for something, have some guiding principles, and provide the public with choice among alternative principles, a doctrinaire approach inhibits effective function performance —particularly of aggregation and conflict resolution functions. It also inhibits linkage-in-government roles, because in a polyarchic system sub-stantial bargaining and compromise is essential for policy-making. Partic-ularly dangerous for stability and effectiveness is sharp and clear-cut ideological polarization between or within parties, not only because of the impact on party unity and effectiveness, but also because it may accentuate polarization in society. Carried to its extremes, polarization breeds civil wars.

DEGREES OF UNITY AND COHESION

With some exceptions, particularistic parties with a narrow social base generally enjoy greater unity and cohesion than broad-based coalitions of diverse ideas and interests. Party disunity is particularly characteristic in systems in which priority is given to local and constituency interests over party and national interests (such as in the American and French systems) and of middle-of-the-road parties which include strong and doctrinaire liberal and conservative factions. The latter is a particularly important contemporary phenomenon, for while the trend in Western societies has been towards the development of broad-based aggregative coalitions, strong extremist factionalism and some ideological polariza-tion have also developed in both American and European parties.

A degree of disunity within party ranks has its virtues. It forces party leaderships to be responsive to many publics and to function as represen-tatives of a broad party public. To win elections, leaders must strive to maintain party unity, and this requires making concessions to varied factions, constituencies, and local and regional interests. This requires careful aggregation of interests and equitable conflict resolution, and mandates drawing political recruits from a broad social base. But too much disunity can result in significant problems not only with respect to winning elections, but with respect to effective performance of linkage-communication. It may make the development of effective party policy extremely difficult because too many concessions to too many diverse elements may have to be made. It may seriously impede a party's ability to provide linkage in government, and thus impede timely and effective governmental action—a most serious problem in political systems of widely dispersed power. This in turn can reduce a party's effectiveness as an instrument of public influence because of the party's inability to translate public choice into governmental action (discussed below).

LEADERSHIP CONTROL AND PARTY DISCIPLINE

Closely related is the problem of the party leadership's role and power. Like political systems, parties can be placed somewhere along an "authoritarian-democratic" spectrum. In some, strong and almost dictatorial powers over all party organs and activities are wielded by a small central core of leaders—the extreme cases being communist and fascist parties in totalitarian systems. Strong leadership controls also exist in some democratic systems, such as the British, in which a small core of national leaders wields substantial power over constituency parties and other party organs, over funds, and over all party functions. Party discipline is also characteristic of some such systems: elected officials of the party (such as members of the British parliament) are expected to follow the party line, to give priority to party over constituency interests, and to vote as determined by the party leadership on major legislative issues. In other democratic systems (such as the American), power within parties is widely dispersed among national, state, and local leaders; national and state leaderships have little power over party funds, nomination processes, or other party activities; and few means save persuasion are available to ensure a party-line vote in legislative bodies.

As with the characteristic of the relative unity, strong centralized leadership has both advantages and disadvantages. The desirable situation would appear to be some kind of a balance between concentration and dispersion of power. Substantial concentration is desirable so that the leadership can play an effective role in party program formulation, ensure that the party's nominees and elected officials are truly representative of the party's principles and loyal to its program, develop some unity to win elections, and after election victory ensure unified party action to translate the party's program into governmental action. Yet some dispersion of power is also essential to ensure the party remains responsive to its varied elements, to enable responsiveness to new participation demands, to provide for the assimilation of new social forces, to ensure accommodation of varied demands in the aggregation and recruitment functions, and in general to force accommodation in order to maintain real, rather than facade, unity and cohesion.

THE AUTONOMY OF PARTIES FROM INTEREST GROUPS AND GOVERNMENT

In some systems, some parties are so closely linked with and dependent on certain social forces or organized interest groups (such as labor unions, business groups, religious institutions, tribal associations), that the latter dominate party leadership and policy formulation. This reduces the equity if not the effectiveness of the articulation, aggregation, and recruitment functions, and also inhibits a party's capability to function as an instrument of public control. Lacking such autonomy, the party is unable to subordinate particular parochial groups and interests to broader party interests, and cannot effectively mediate among competing social forces. Party leaders and elected representatives tend to become spokesmen for private rather than for broader party interests. Due to their dependency they cannot function as legitimate intermediaries for the moderation of group conflict, and cannot expand their loyalties to the broader political community.

Similar considerations pertain to relationships between parties and governments. Some parties (particularly single-party types) are little more than instruments of governments, and as such perform only those functions desired by governments, and serve as instruments of governmental control over people rather than the reverse. Other parties in democratic systems may be quite independent of governments as a whole, but may be so strongly controlled by those party leaders and members holding legislative or other governmental office that their real autonomy is very limited, with similar adverse consequences for function performance. This criticism, for example, is frequently made of the British and American party system.

THE ENVIRONMENTAL-POLITICAL CONTEXT OF PARTY SYSTEMS

As component parties of political systems, party systems like interest groups tend to reflect their environmental and political setting, and to have an impact on both settings.

Noncompetitive systems in nondemocratic societies basically reflect the interests and attitudes of the governing political elites who organize parties for their own purposes and suppress efforts to form opposition parties. But environmental factors also help to produce noncompetitive systems, as they do authoritarian political systems (see Chapter 6). Prevailing subject cultures and low cognitive orientations and participation demands serve to stunt party development as well as demands for a more democratic structure within existing parties. Even when competitive parties exist within such societies, they tend to be skeletal types which function more as elite factions or personality cliques.

Multiparty systems with a narrow base tend to develop in nonconsensual societies marked by numerous cross-cutting socio-economic and cultural cleavages, substantial hostility among various groups, and doctrinaire attitudes which impede accommodation, aggregation, and integration. These features even impede unity within small splinter parties. Political factors are also helpful. Political elites tend to share such environmental characteristics, and often deliberately manipulate cleavages and hostility to further their own political or other interests. Such parties of strong and doctrinaire ideological bent also tend to develop when governing elites provide no incentive for the development of broader-based aggregative parties: lack of consultation in decision-making, or lack of any meaningful legislative role, tends to generate debating societies rather than parties of action. Proportional representation election systems (see below) also tend to foster multiparty systems.

Two-party systems of pragmatic, broad-based coalition-type parties tend to develop in relatively consensual societies in which the range of conflict is relatively limited, hostilities among groups are of low intensity, class conflict is relatively moderate, ideological factors are not very prominent, and in which a large, pragmatic, and middle-of-the-road middle class plays a major moderating role. Political factors also help to produce such systems, particularly as political elites share such attitudes and seek to function within the context of a two-party or limited multiparty system rather than organize additional parties to promote their ideas and interests. A Single-Member District election system may also be helpful because the possibility of minor parties winning a significant number of legislative seats is very low, while the cost of organizing additional parties may be prohibitive.

Differences in two-party and multiparty systems may also be rooted in environmental and political factors. The American system, for example, consists of very loose coalitions of state and local parties in which unity is relatively weak, power is widely dispersed, and straight party line voting in legislatures is rare. In part this reflects American beliefs about dispersion of power, the aversion to giving too much power to any kind of political leadership, the relatively low prestige of parties, and American preferences for constituency interests. In part the American system reflects the federal system of government, which makes for decentralization of the party structure in a variety of ways. The British system, by contrast, consists of much more unified and cohesive parties over which national party leaderships exercise substantial control, in which party line voting is the rule rather than the exception, and in which constituency and regional parties are more dependent on the national organization than the reverse. In part this reflects the British unitary system of government. In part it reflects British beliefs about party government, less priority to constituency interests, the role of the Member of Parliament as a representative of his party and nation rather than primarily of his constituency, and substantial deference to leadership which ought to be given sufficient discretionary authority in order to lead.

ELECTIONS AND ELECTION SYSTEMS

Free and universal elections—characterized by unrestricted competition and campaigning, equality of votes, freedom of choice, and honest counting of ballots—are probably the most crucial instruments for performance of two major linked functions: public involvement in political recruitment processes, and public influence over government. While elections cannot provide the public with a direct voice in decision-making (save in cases of referendum when specific issues are put on ballots) they do ensure a degree of public influence by providing the public with one major and most basic decision: who shall govern and make decisions during the period between elections. In this respect they also provide degrees of public influence between elections, for parties and officials interested in re-election must be responsive to some degree to the demands of the electorate, must anticipate electorate reaction to major decisions or face defeat. Further, elections conducted within the framework of a competitive party system force the parties to function as instruments of the public will. For even parties with high degrees of leadership control and tight discipline must be responsive to maintain party unity and to have the broad appeal necessary for election success.

Elections are not, however, very effective instruments for the performance of other linkage-communication functions. And the roles they can and often do play with respect to such functions—and even the public influence function—depends on their relationship to the party system and the characteristics of that system.

Elections play only limited articulation roles. On occasion—sometimes in local elections, or in elections dominated by a single major issue, or in cases of referendums on specific issues—they do articulate the preferences of those who bother going to the polls. But more generally, elections involve and turn on many issues, and it is rarely possible for government officials to read and interpret election results as mandates for a particular kind of governmental action. More generally, elections only communicate the general mood of the public, or indicate which set of candidates the public has greater confidence in with respect to handling issues of major public concern, or articulate the general policy direction in which the public prefers to move. But even this limited articulation function is substantially enhanced when elections are conducted within the context of a democratic and effective party system. Similarly, elections involve the demand aggregation function since a coalition of many types of people and interests is required to win; but again, it is the parties which aggregate the competing interests and build winning or losing coalitions.

Elections may also be valuable means for socialization, mobilization, integration, and support building. In democratic systems they provide legal and orderly means of succession and thus legitimize governments and their actions. In nondemocratic systems, elections are regularly or occasionally held for such purposes. Merely holding elections, together with associated propaganda and indoctrination activities, may develop support for the system and mobilize the public on behalf of governmental goals. The frequent, carefully controlled and stage-managed elections in the Soviet Union, for example, serve such purposes. Given the pervasiveness of Communist ideology and its justifications for the Soviet system of rule, elections have substantial symbolic value in legitimizing Soviet authority. They give the people a psychological sense of participation, serve as safety valves by allowing some but limited measures of dissent, and psychologically help link government with the Soviet public.

NOMINATION PROCESS

Nomination processes can be as important as elections and are also either linked with and reflect characteristics of parties or have an impact on parties. Basically there are three types of nomination processes, with a variety of sub-types, and with all three in use in some political systems.

The petition system is used in some areas in the United States and elsewhere, most prominently for some local elections (such as school boards or city commissions), and in some areas for legislative seats. In this system the aspirants for public office simply circulate a petition, and if they attain the legally-required number of signatures of eligible voters, they are placed on the election ballot.

The primary election system is common throughout the United States, but less so in other democracies. There are wide variations in nature of such primaries. Generally, a candidate's name is placed on the ballot for the primary election after circulation of the preliminary petition, and the winner by plurality vote of the primary becomes an official candidate— either of a party or on a non-partisan basis—in the election. In some instances second or run-off primaries are used, with the leading vote-getters in the first primary appearing on the ballot for the second primary. Primaries have a negative impact on party strength and unity because they deny the party the vital nomination function and cannot ensure that the candidates appearing on a party's ticket are in fact loyal to a party's program.

The party nomination system is another common method, used alone or in conjunction with petition and primary systems. This system usually reflects strong party organization, and also adds strength to parties. Again, specific systems vary widely, but party rules or statutory law authorize some elements of the party organization—local committees or caucuses, state committees, state or national conventions—to nominate the party's candidates, without reference to the general electorate.

Types of Election Systems

As with nomination systems, a bewildering variety of election systems exists around the world. Most, however, are variations of two basic patterns involving two factors: the nature of the constituency, and what it takes to win.

The Single-Member District winner-take-all system (SMD), is most common in the United States and in most other democracies. In these the political unit (nation, state, province, etc.) is divided into relatively equal geographic constituencies (by size or population), to be represented in a particular legislative body by one individual (the single member). The winner-takes-all principle prevails in that the one candidate who captured the most votes (either a majority or plurality) represents the district; the losing parties, no matter how strong their voter support, win nothing. In some systems run-off elections are held, from which marginal vote-getters in the first election are eliminated; this produces victors by either a strong plurality or a majority. This system has some distinct advantages and tends to favor a two-party system. However, it discriminates against small or minority parties, and leads to underrepresentation of losing parties. The Liberal Party in Britain, for example, usually wins a far greater percentage of the total vote than the small percentage of seats it wins in the parliament. In some cases it may even give a losing party control of government: a party may win only a minority of the total national vote, yet by winning a sufficient number of legislative districts, win majority control of a legislative body. Multi-Member Proportional Representation (PR) systems are frequently (but not always) used in the context of multiparty systems. In these, several legislative seats are allocated to a particular political unit (a state, region, province, or district), and these seats are then divided among the contesting parties roughly in proportion to the percentage of the total vote each party receives in the election. Thus a party which wins 40% of the total vote within the designated political unit would receive 40% of the legislative seats representing that area. This kind of system makes for more equitable representation of minorities, and may in some systems also strengthen party organization. However, it also tends to breed multiparty systems because of the incentive it gives to the organization of minority parties which can hope to win at least a few legislative seats.

PARTISAN AND NONPARTISAN ELECTIONS

Nonpartisan elections, in which the public has a choice among candidates who are not publicly affiliated with or sponsored by political parties, do have some advantages. They tend to produce elected officials who are less subject to party influence, who may be more prone to constituency influence, and who may be more free to act and vote as their consciences dictate on the merits of a case. They may reduce the conflicts within legislatures by minimizing partisan conflict along party lines, and eliminate voting decisions made on the basis of what is good for the party rather than what is good for the public. But more frequently, nonpartisan elections reduce the effectiveness of public influence over government and may increase conflict.

For one, the party affiliation or inclination of candidates may merely be hidden from public view, with the consequence that some or many voters may elect a candidate from a party whose policy inclinations they oppose. In Michigan, for example, candidates for the State Supreme Court appear on ballots without party identification, yet are nominated by political parties. For another, (as will be more fully explained below) the absence of the party label denies the public with vital information concerning the policy inclinations of candidates, and few voters have the time, inclination, opportunity, or qualifications needed to ascertain the actual qualifications and views of the various candidates (particularly since many nonpartisan elections usually attract numerous candidates). In both respects, public influence over government is substantially reduced because the public's choice of candidates may be meaningless with respect to the subsequent course of action by the successful candidates. And finally, nonpartisan elections frequently produce more rather than less conflict within legislatures, simply because they eliminate or reduce the degree of cooperation which results from common party affiliation. And this may substantially impair the effectiveness of government.

PARTIES AND ELECTIONS

In sum, really free elections provide the public with its single most significant means for exerting influence over government. But to serve this purpose the election system must meet three important criteria. First, it must provide the public with meaningful choice. Second, it must ensure that the public's choice is ultimately translated into governmental action following the election. Third, it must provide the public with a fixed point of responsibility so that the public may hold the government accountable for its action or inaction. These criteria can best be met by a partisan election system in the context of an effective party system. And the most effective kind of party system for such purposes is a competitive two-party system, consisting of programmatic yet pragmatic broad-based coalition-type parties, capable of acting in a unified fashion, with an internal power structure which strikes a balance between concentration and dispersion of power so as to provide for both internal democracy and significant roles for leaderships.

The first criteria —meaningful choice—first entails providing the public with choice as to who shall participate in government following the election. This requires choice among various candidates for various public offices, which obviously requires a competitive system. Noncompetitive systems which limit voter options to a yes or no are simply inadequate.

But if the public is to have any real influence over policy-making, it must have choice not merely with respect to candidates, but also with respect to various alternative courses of policy or alternative programs to be pursued by the post-election government. In large-scale complex political systems, numerous, diverse, and very complex decisions must be made on almost a daily basis, and it is simply impossible to determine public preferences with regard to such specific decisions even if the public were aware of the issues and sufficiently informed as to make intelligent choices. But at the very least, for purposes of public influence over such decision-making, at election time the public ought to have the opportunity to express its preferences as to what issues merit priority attention, what general policy direction—centrist or left or right of center —it prefers, and perhaps what general kind of program it desires. Hence, when voter choice is by necessity limited to choice among candidates, it must entail informed choice—the voter must have information not merely about the qualifications, but the ideological orientations and policy inclinations if not stands on specific issues of the competing candidates. A voter who wishes the government to pursue a generally conservative policy must at the very least be able to distinguish between conservative and liberal candidates.

Campaigns for highly important and visible offices—such as for national or state chief executives—may provide many voters who follow campaigns with such information. But in democratic systems the process of government also involves numerous lower-level executives, a host of legislative seats at national, state, and local levels, and a variety of other public offices—judges, county commissioners, educational supervisors, sheriffs, prosecutors, and sometimes even dog catchers, to name but a few. In the United States it is not unusual for the voter to be faced with a ballot on which several candidates are listed as competing for each of 20 or even more public offices, from the Presidency down to township supervisor. Few if indeed any voters have either the time, background, qualifications, or inclination to gather the information needed to make informed choices about such a host of candidates. Further, even with respect to major offices, candidate policy inclinations and stands on issues are more often obscured than clarified by the sheer razzle-dazzle of campaigns, by candidate reluctance to speak out on issues lest some significant voting bloc be alienated, by limited funds which limit candidate abilities to publicize their positions, by inadequate or distorted reporting by new media, or by public boredom with the babel of voices throughout lengthy campaigns.

In most democratic systems an overwhelming majority of the voters assert their election preferences on the basis of their "party identification." That is, they tend to identify with one particular party, to establish an early and relatively durable attachment to this party, to vote for all of that party's candidates for varied offices during most elections, and to deviate from such party-line voting by splitting their tickets or bolting to opposition parties only under exceptional circumstances. Considering the extreme difficulty if not impossibility of gathering enough information about individual candidates to make informed choices, this is quite rational voting behavior—provided the party label does in fact provide reliable information about the policy inclinations and ideological orientations of individual candidates, does in fact enable a voter to predict how a candidate is likely to act and vote in policy-making processes once elected to office. If this is the case, the party label can serve as an invaluable although not foolproof guide or instrument by which a voter can make an informed, intelligent, and meaningful choice and decision.

This, first of all, requires that parties be programmatic—that they have some kind of philosophic or ideological foundation, do have some fairly distinct policy inclination, do have some kind of general program to which they are committed, and undertake campaign and other activities to at least vaguely familiarize voters with such programs. It also requires that some kinds or degrees of differences exist among parties—not necessarily diametrically opposed positions on issues, but at least differences of policy tendency so as to give voters some real choice. Party systems which can effectively aggregate diverse interests and ideas into alternative policy packages or program proposals thus serve at election time to give the public meaningful and manageable choice. Winning or losing elections thus communicates which kind of program or policy direction the public prefers from among the alternatives before it.

For the party label to serve as a reliable guide for voters it is also essential that the various candidates who appear on that label really are committed to the party's ideological foundation, policy inclination, and programs. A liberal who runs on a conservative ticket obviously cheats the voter who assumes that a conservative party fields only conservative candidates; mavericks may play useful roles in politics, but hardly function as instruments of the public will if the voters who choose them on the basis of their party label are unaware of their independent tendencies. Hence a reliable party label requires fairly unified parties in which leaderships play significant roles, and systems in which the party and its leadership have strong influence if not control over nomination processes. This is perhaps the gravest weakness of primary election systems which minimize party roles in nomination processes. Only a system which provides significant party organization leverage in nomination can ensure that the candidates running on a particular party label are indeed more-or-less attached to a party's position or program. If this is the case—if the parties do have programs, if there are differences among such programs, and if candidates are more-or-less pledged to such different programs—then the voter can make a rational and informed choice. He can then safely assume that there is a linkage between program, party, and candidate; ascertain which program he prefers in accordance with his own ideas and interests; and vote for candidates on the basis of such linkage and preference. He can then safely say: "Democrats (or Republicans) are my kind of people, are in tune with my ideas and interests, and hence, I will vote the party ticket."

At the same time, however, substantial democracy should prevail within political parties—there should be a balance between concentrated leadership power and dispersion among rank-and-file members. The latter should have substantial opportunity to control the leadership and influence policy development and candidate selection, and parties should be relatively autonomous of their elected officials and of affiliated interest groups. For even though the general public has the ultimate choice at election time, broader party publics ought to have substantial choices and opportunities to participate in the party's aggregation, program formulation, and nomination functions. The criteria of meaningful choice among alternative candidates, programs, and policy directions also indicates that two-party systems are preferable to multiparty types. Superficially, the latter type appears to be more democratic in that it provides a greater range of choice. But for one, multiparty systems sometimes produce such a complexity of choices as to confuse voters, a confusion again aggravated by the nature of election campaigns and the bedlam of propaganda from many parties and candidates. Also, parties within such systems frequently espouse a policy or program with respect to a single or only a few issues, whereas the entire range of governmental decision-making entails numerous issues, so that again the voter is denied meaningful choice—among alternative aggregated packages or policies. But most important, as will be discussed below, multiparty systems frequently nullify choices made by the electorate.

The second criteria for an election system to effectively function as an instrument of public influence pertains to the translation of the public's choice into governmental action. In essence, the candidates selected by the majority of the electorate on the basis of their party affiliation and their party's program have an obligation to attempt to enact that program into governmental decisions. Circumstances such as economic conditions may change following an election and require modification or even abandonment of certain aspects of a party program, and modifications may also be required either because of the merits of opposing programs or as the result of bargaining and aggregation processes during decision-making. But meaningful public influence requires that within such limits, concerted efforts ought to be made to translate the public's choice of program or direction into governmental policies.

This criteria again requires elections in the context of a party system, for while individual candidates can offer their individual programs, a plethora of such programs can hardly be enacted into law, and even the individual programs of candidates for top level executive positions need more than executive authority for translation into governmental policy. Parties are essential with respect to this criteria for two reasons. They provide the necessary mediating, bargaining, and conflict resolution machinery whereby the demands of varied constituencies and candidates are aggregated into party programs. And they function as linkage-in-government institutions which provide the cooperation and consensus along party lines necessary for building the coalitions essential for decision-making.

This in turn requires parties which, despite their broad-based coalition nature, can function in a relatively unified and cohesive fashion, in which the leadership has sufficient power to enhance such unity, and in which special constituency or other interests do not dominate over broader party interests. For ability to translate the public's choice into governmental action depends very much on cooperation along party lines within various governmental branches and institutions. If party cohesion is so weak and the power of leadership is so minimal that individual legislators or other officials elected on the basis of their party label are completely free to abandon their party's program, then parties can hardly hope to enact their programs into law, and the electorate in effect is cheated. Democratic voters can hardly be expected to have faith in their chosen party, the party system, and the overall political system, if the party of their choice consistently fails to implement its promises simply because Democratic legislators ignore party unity and programs and are free to defy efforts to develop a cohesive party position on major policy issues.

Some kind of judicious balance between party, constituency, and other kinds of particular interests is also essential with respect to such unity and cohesion, and again it requires effective party aggregation machinery to attain such a balance. Most Americans, for example, tend to believe that a representative's primary responsibility is to his constituency, and that if the interests of that constituency clash with party or broader interests, it is his obligation to defy his party and act as his constituency demands. This may indeed be more "democratic" if constituency influence is equated with public influence, or on those occasions when constituency opinion is loud and clear, but the principle encounters some problems in practice. For one, constituency pressures frequently turn out to be pressures exerted by special interests rather than by the general public within the constituency. For another, general constituency publics are generally not even aware of, much less informed about, the specific policy issues which representatives have to deal with. Third, most voters seldom make voting decisions on the basis of their recognition of a representative's adherence to constituency interests, but rather on the basis of the party label. And finally, it is neither conducive to effective government nor to the development of policies which are truly in the public interest to subordinate national or broader interests to special constituency, parochial, or other narrow interests. What's good for Detroit or for the auto industry may at times be good for the country, but it is not automatically so. And if constituency interests are always given priority, then party programs become meaningless, voters have no means for making intelligent choices, and the task of aggregating interests within governmental institutions becomes most difficult if not impossible.

Translation of voter choice into governmental action programs is also facilitated by broad-based, aggregative, and pragmatic parties, rather than by dogmatic splinter-types. Small minority parties are seldom able to win more than a few legislative seats, cannot hope to enact their programs on the basis of their own legislative strength, and generally are too small and particularistic to provide a strong foundation for building a larger legislative coalition. Pragmatic attitudes are also essential, even though this may require some modification and sometimes even abandonment of promises made to voters. In any democratic setting the enactment of policies requires building a winning coalition, which in turn requires substantial bargaining which cannot succeed without compromise. Hence doctrinaire parties which rigidly adhere to their ideologies or policy inclinations may keep faith with their voters by their adherence to promises; but in effect they cheat their voters by their inability to produce governmental action.

Translation of public choice into governmental action also requires either a two-party system, or a multiparty system of but a few parties. It is clearly facilitated when one party, by winning a majority or heavy plurality, is able to win enough seats in legislative bodies to dominate or control the government, and thereby enact the program selected by voters with but minimum concessions to opposition elements. Multiparty systems have very low capabilities for such action, for even the strongest parties within such systems can at best win a strong plurality of legislative seats, and, hence, no stable majority capable of governing develops. Instead, either temporary coalitions of two or more parties must be built as each controversial issue develops, or a coalition government must be formed. Such governments are inherently unstable and of low effectiveness. They are difficult to form because of the protracted negotiations and numerous concessions which must be made as the condition for the parties participation in the coalition; in some Western democracies, for example, it is not unusual for negotiations to take six to eight months. And they are inherently unstable and ineffective because coalitions are likely to disintegrate when major policy issues have to be faced. More often than not, coalition governments last only so long as they pursue a policy of status quo, a "do nothing" or "don't rock the boat" policy. When a major policy decision must be made, either because circumstances make a decision imperative or one party moves to change the status quo, one or more of the coalition partners invariably disagree, and the coalition disintegrates. A classic example is the Italian system, in which 7 major parties hold legislative seats, and which has gone through 38 governments in 32 years.

Multiparty systems which require coalition governments or ad hoc coalitions in effect deny any meaningful choice to voters, because public influence is significantly excluded when *three most fundamental decisions* are made. And although this weakness pertains particularly to parliamentary systems, it is also relevant with respect to presidential types.

1. The decision as to who shall be chief executive. This weakness is not relevant to presidential systems in which executives are chosen by direct election, but to parliamentary systems in which the executive is chosen by a legislative body. In a two-party system the legislative majority—the dominant party elected by a majority or strong plurality vote of the voters —selects the chief executive. This selection thereby reflects public choice since in most such systems voters know that if a particular party wins it will furnish the chief executive. Thus in the British system the public votes only for members of the House of Commons, but it knows that the party leader of the winning party will become Prime Minister. But in many multiparty systems, prolonged bargaining is required to form a governing coalition, and the question as to who shall be the chief executive is frequently the key issue in such bargaining. The final decision is thereby not made by the public, but by party leaders in closed-door bargaining sessions. The final choice may not even be the leader of any of the parties but some subordinate official, or a leader or member of a party which won but a small fraction of the vote.

2. The decision as to who shall be included in the government's top policy-making strata—the key decision-makers with respect to overall policy, and in respective economic, educational, and other spheres of governmental activity. Within parliamentary systems this involves the makeup of the policy-making cabinet—the key ministers of economic affairs, transportation, agriculture, and similar types. In the context of two-party systems, the selection is made by the majority party from within its own ranks, which acts in more-or-less cohesive fashion to enact the party's program. In multiparty systems the selection results again from prolonged bargaining among party chieftains over the terms of the coalition—on the basis of what spoils and honors must be awarded to individual parties as the price for their participation in the coalition, and not on the basis of the public's preference for particular parties as determined by the election outcome. Within presidential systems such a kind of cabinet may not exist (although it does in some). But even in such systems, the president who won a clear majority of votes is free to appoint members of his own party to such positions. Within a multiparty system, he must include members of other parties as the price for their support in building necessary legislative coalitions and public support.

3. Decisions as to what general policy direction shall be followed by the government, what specific issues shall be given priority, and what kinds of policies and programs shall be undertaken. This problem pertains to both parliamentary and presidential systems. Within a two-party system, effective programmatic parties with a clear-cut majority can translate the majority's choice of program into governmental action to the extent that they can maintain unity and cohesion within their own ranks. The pro-

gram the winning party promised the public need only be modified as
changing circumstances require modification, or as some modifications
may be required to maintain party unity or to more equitably and effectively aggregate diverse national, party, constituency, and other interests.
Within multiparty systems such decisions are seldom made with reference to public preferences as indicated by election results and the votes
won by individual parties. They are again made by party chieftains in
closed-door sessions, and on the basis of what price must be paid to
individual powerful politicians or to individual parties whose participation is politically essential to establish and then maintain a coalition
government. And even though the public may clamor for some major
policy or change in policy, coalitions either remain unresponsive because
the priority is maintenance of the coalition, or some parties within the
coalition attempt to respond and the coalition then disintegrates. Hence
the pattern of governmental instability combined with inaction which
prevails in most multiparty systems.

The third criterion for an election system to function as an effective
instrument of public influence requires that the public be provided with
a fixed point of responsibility so that it may hold the government accountable. If elections are to function as instruments of the public will, the
public must be able to responsibly hold someone accountable for effective or ineffective policies, or for success or failure in delivering on its
election promises. Given such a point of clear responsibility, the public
can at the subsequent election register its approval by re-electing incum-
bent candidates or parties, or its disapproval by throwing the rascals out
and taking its chances on a new set of politicians.

In any complex political system involving dispersion of power it is
exceedingly difficult to pinpoint responsibility. Decision-making invariably entails participation or individual actions by numerous branches,
agencies, committees, and individuals. Even though one individual—
such as the chief executive—may be "in charge" and, hence, ultimately
responsible, not only would it be highly unfair to pin all responsibility on
him, but voters might well do themselves a disservice by charging only
him with failure. Americans, for example, are prone to consider their
presidents as responsible; in 1928 they held Hoover responsible for
prosperity, and in 1932 for depression, whereas reality suggests that
Hoover had little to do with either. But Americans share their basic
problem of fixing responsibility with citizens of most other democratic
systems: who is really responsible, the chief executive or the national
legislature? And if responsibility can be assigned to the latter, who—what
individuals, committees, parties—within the legislature? And if responsibility can be assigned to particular legislators—such as exceptionally
powerful Senators or Congressmembers—how can the national public

take action when they are elected by individual states or congressional districts? Even with respect to individuals—executives but particularly legislators—it is exceedingly difficult for voters to assess responsibility because of the great difficulty of observing the actions and assessing the total political record of individuals. Can you, the reader, assess the role that your Senators or Representatives have played in the evolution of national or state policies and laws?

A two-party system consisting of pragmatic yet programmatic parties capable of acting in a relatively cohesive manner can be very helpful in providing such a clear point of responsibility. In such systems the individual parties legitimately can be held responsible, and voters can render their verdicts by accepting or rejecting the party's candidate at the next election. If Democrats were chosen to control government by the voters because they preferred the Democratic program, and if the Democrats either failed to deliver on their program, or their programs proved ineffective, then voters can assign responsibility and at the next election give the Republicans a chance. Assigning responsibility to the majority party is not foolproof as a guide to individual voters: circumstances may have required changes in a party's program, or individual candidates may have done their very best and not share the responsibility for failure (or success). It is also difficult, if not impossible, to assign responsibility when different parties control the executive and legislature, or control different houses of the legislature. But despite these problems, the party label can help voters to establish accountability.

In essence, effective party government—involving party programs and promises on the basis of which the electorate can make informed and intelligent choices and party efforts to implement the public's choice—can provide a better point of responsibility than any other features of democratic systems involving substantial dispersion of power. But as with respect to providing meaningful choice and the translation of such choice into governmental action, a two-party system consisting of parties capable of acting in a unified fashion is preferable if not absolutely essential. Responsibility is not clearly visible and cannot be fixed by voters when all parties within the system lack the internal cohesion or controls necessary to ensure that a party's elected officials will actively support the party program—perhaps the gravest defect of the American party system. Responsibility is even less visible within coalition governments which are the outgrowth of multiparty systems, for in such systems neither a single party nor a single individual is responsible for decisions concerning the makeup of the government or the policies to be pursued. And without such a fixed point of responsibility, public choices at the subsequent election are less meaningful, and public influence over government via the ballot box is minimal at best.

part IV

Governmental Decision-Making Systems

As explained in Chapter 1, the examination of governmental systems entails the analysis of the interrelated structures and processes which process demand inputs, resolve conflicts among them, and convert them into binding and authoritative public policies which create and allocate values. But while the immediate focus is on governmental institutions, the analysis must include consideration of effective environmental influences as relayed by linkage-communication systems.

The major empirical concern is with how decisions actually get made and why they get made the way they do. More specific questions center on the location and distribution of power. Who is involved in the process, either by direct participation or indirectly with influence over the process? What is the actual distribution of power within the system, and what structures, groups, and individuals seem to be the key power centers? What appear to be the consequences of the power structure, and of the nature of the decision-making system, for the entire political system and the society? The use of the assessment criteria discussed in Chapter 3 is again particularly relevant. What are the consequences of the decision-making system for the basic nature of the political system—does it tend to make the system more democratic, or more authoritarian or even totalitarian? What are the potential consequences of the decision-making system (as distinguished from its policy outputs) for political, social, and governmental stability? What are the system's performance characteristics as an instrument of society: what are its capabilities; to what extent can it make timely, effective, and implementable decisions; can it perform efficiently in terms of maximizing many values at relatively low cost to other values? And to what extent is the decision-making system capable of adapting to change?

Normative considerations entail evaluation as to whether the system functions in accordance with preferred values, whether power is located and distributed in the way one prefers, and whether the process tends to maximize those values which should be accorded high priority. Assessment and evaluation of what kinds of changes or reforms the system seems to require involve consideration of both facts and values: what kinds of changes are desirable and possible given the nature of the system, the location and distribution of power, and the nature of and limitations imposed by either the environmental setting or the infrastructure.

Analysis, assessment, and evaluation should view decision-making systems from two perspectives—a government's leadership role as initiator of policy, and its reactive role as it responds to environmental influences. All decision-making systems in varying degrees often merely react to varied pressures from their environmental settings, and the democratic ethos in particular emphasizes this role—the government's obligation to be responsive to the will of the sovereign people. But governments also have an obligation to play major roles with respect to defining public goals and selecting means to pursue them. As Karl Deutsch has pointed out, the image of the "ship of state" has become entrenched in political thought, and the government can be conceived of as the ship's helmsman.[1] Like the helmsman of a ship, a government needs to be responsive to its environment, to the currents and tides in society, and to the strengths and weaknesses of its overall political system, so that it may remain in control and enjoy stability and effectiveness. But the helmsman government also needs to have a sense of direction, to have some goals or some idea of the results it wishes to obtain. And all this requires not merely reaction to environmental pressures, but leadership. Hence a crucial question: what is a government's capability for exercising responsible leadership?

Chapter 10 which follows discusses the general nature of decision-making systems, and particularly similarities and significant differences among varied kinds of systems. Chapter 11 discusses the analysis of power in decision-making systems, and Chapter 12 the consequences of power structure and of other major characteristics of such systems.

---

[1]Karl W. Deutsch, *Politics and Government* (Boston: Houghton Mifflin Co. 1970), p. 5.

The General Nature of Decision-Making Processes

10

In their broadest aspects, decision-making systems in various kinds of political systems are very similar in nature. Such similarities, however, conceal differences which are extremely important from the standpoint of the nature of systems and their performance as instruments of society.

THREE COMMON FUNCTIONS AND PROCESSES

In the abstract, it is useful to distinguish among three kinds of functions and processes which are characteristic of all decision-making systems. In the real world, however, the distinctions among the three are not always clear-cut, and significant differences prevail among systems with respect to how the functions actually are performed.

The rule-making or legislative function involves processes whereby authoritative rules evolve, the processes which spawn and develop the laws which in effect constitute legal rules of behavior for individuals and groups in society. The term rule-making has come into vogue because the word legislative connotes that this function lies within the purview of the legislative branch, whereas in reality in most authoritarian systems the function is performed by the executive, and in most democratic systems it is shared by two or more branches of government. The American system, for example, is sometimes erroneously referred to as a system of divided functions; in reality it is a system of shared functions and divided power, in that all three branches share and have power with respect to the rule or law-making function.

Several stages of rule-making are also characteristic of most decision-making systems. The first stage usually involes policy-making (although the term policy is usually used rather loosely), which entails the selection of general goals and the strategy for pursuing such ends. Subsequent stages involve the making of implementing decisions, the specific rules designed to implement the strategy and to attain goals. An economic policy, for example, may have as its primary goal the reduction of unemployment to a certain level and a certain percentage increase in the economic growth rate; implementing rules entail specific tax laws, actions to create jobs, or similar measures designed to attain the primary goals. Several levels of decision-making are also characteristic of most systems. Top level policy-making is usually within the purview of the top political elites and in most modern systems involves primarily the executive branch. Lower-level executive and legislative elites may be involved in some policy-making but more usually in the development of implementing decisions. Still lower levels of government have tasks of spelling out implementing rules and the administration of such rules.

It is also useful to distinguish three phases of rule-making. The first involves initiative—the initial proposals for policies or specific rules—which in most systems has become the task of the executive branch. The second entails deliberation within either the executive or legislative branch or perhaps both, which involves discussion and perhaps modification or rejection of the initial proposal. The third entails ratification, the final action required to turn the initial or modified proposal into an authoritative rule—such as final concurrence (or veto) by the executive. Finally, rule-making seldom involves a single, simple, one-time process. More usually, and particularly in systems of dispersed power, it involves the simultaneous functioning of numerous decision-making points—as in the American system in which numerous national, state, and local agencies and officials constantly make decisions with economic impact. And it is a constant and on-going process for the "final" decision or law which emerges from the decision-making system is seldom really final. Rules are constantly being made, modified, reformulated, or unmade by a host of decision-making branches, agencies, and officials during subsequent political conflicts.

The rule-application or administrative function involves the application, administration, implementation, execution, and enforcement of rules or laws. In many political systems this entails action not merely by the executive branch and the administrative bureaucracy, but also by legislative and judicial branches. It is an extremely important aspect of policy and decision-making, for the public policy process does not end with the passage of a law. For one, laws are seldom self-executing, and require vigorous and sometimes imaginative and creative implementation if policy goals are to be attained and if the rules are to actually regulate and control human behavior. For another, rule-application invariably also entails some decision and rule-making; in the real world, the line between rule-making and application is by no means clear-cut. Sometimes the decisions made by administrators may be relatively simple and unimportant; sometimes administrative decisions border on or in fact involve policy-making. As will be discussed later in connection with modern bureaucracies, this constitutes a major problem for large-scale complex political systems.

The rule-adjudication or judicial process entails the interpretation and application of authoritative rules in the context of specific cases. More specifically, it involves the interpretation of laws and specific actions, the resolution of conflicts over and determination as to whether or not a rule has been violated, and the imposition of appropriate penalties for violations. Although primarily within the purview of judicial branches, executive and legislative branches and agencies may play major and sometimes dominant roles in this process. Again, it involves the making of sometimes relatively insignificant and sometimes crucial decisions. Depending on the power of the judicial system within a particular political system, it may involve rule or policy making. The American Supreme Court, for example, has become a major policy-maker due to its authority to interpret the Constitution, and plays a major rule-making role by its authority to nullify, modify, or ratify executive and legislative rules on constitutional grounds.

Similarities in Governmental Structures and Organization

Although they may bear different labels, very similar kinds of structures have developed over time for the performance of these three interrelated governmental functions. In all systems one finds chief executives, variously labeled presidents, prime ministers, kings, chairmen. Within executive establishments there have developed hierarchies of bureaucracies— executive departments, ministries, a variety of agencies. Within most systems some kind of legislative body exists—congresses, parliaments, the Soviets in the Soviet Union. And invariably judicial systems compose parts of a state's decision-making apparatus for the primary performance of the rule adjudication function. But what really counts is the actual power, roles, and functions performed by these structures—discussed in Chapter 11.

SIMILARITIES IN CONFLICT RESOLUTION PROCESSES

As explained in Chapter 1, governmental decision-making entails the resolution of conflicts arising from competing demands emanating either from the environment or from within the decision-making system itself. Within most systems, conflict resolution entails sometimes a pattern of indifference, some repression, and some command decision-making. But more usually some form and degree of bargaining is involved. In such bargaining situations governmental decision-makers seldom rise above the conflict among various socio-economic-cultural groups and act as impartial mediators or referees; more usually, most are active participants in the conflict, and tend to represent one way or another the groups involved in the conflict. And in all such conflicts over public policy, the competing social forces and governmental decision-makers use and apply power, and the power configuration in a particular conflict situation shapes the outcome, defines who gets what, when and how, and determines what the rules shall be. But this similarity again conceals many important differences.

DIFFERENCES AMONG DECISION-MAKING SYSTEMS

Decision-making systems differ in four very significant ways. These differences are important not merely for distinguishing among different types of systems, but also because of their consequences for the nature of political systems, their capabilities, their stability and effectiveness, and their capacity for adaptation to change. Hence, the major analytical questions that should be asked about any system relate to these differences.

THE LOCATION AND DISTRIBUTION OF POWER

This is the key distinguishing characteristic, and will be discussed in Chapter 11. Overall, this entails questions concerning where power is located within a given decision-making system, and how widely or narrowly power is distributed within it. More specific questions pertain to three aspects that need to be explored. One pertains to the power relationship between a government and its society: what is the extent of governmental power over people, and of people over government? The second pertains to power within the decision-making system itself: what is the extent to which power is concentrated at the national level, or dispersed to states and other subordinate levels? What is the extent to which power is concentrated in executive hands or dispersed among several branches? What is the extent to which power is concentrated or dispersed within individual components of the decision-making system? The third pertains to patterns of influence over governmental decision-making.

DEGREES OF PLURALISM, COMPETITION, AND REPRESENTATION

Bargaining processes differ among political systems due to different configurations of power, which in turn produce different degrees of pluralism, competition, and representation in bargaining.

Within some systems decision-making may be dominated by one or a few like-minded elites who are representative of the ideas and interests of only some segments or strata of the population. The consequence is little competition and bargaining; conflict resolution processes which resemble patterns of indifference, suppression, or command decision; and inequitable policy outputs which favor the dominant elites and the social forces they represent. This pattern is the common one in traditional feudal agrarian systems, in which bargaining is limited to competition for spoils of office among representatives of the landowning aristocracy, the military, and the upper religious elites. It is the pattern in systems dominated by some like-minded tribal or ethnic groups or by a few economic elites. But except on occasions when some vital common interest prompts diverse elites to unite on some issue—white supremacy over black masses, defense of a communist system by elites with vested interests in the system—this is a vanishing pattern in the complex contemporary world.

At the opposite end of the spectrum are most contemporary democratic systems, characterized by polyarchy and substantial dispersion of power which produces pluralism of ideas and interests among many power holders and substantial competition among them. In these settings there is also a tendency towards substantial representation of various sectors and strata of society—either in terms of elected representatives, or surrogates, or due to efforts on the part of competing elites to develop some mass support in the competitive struggle, or simply because the more are involved in decision-making the greater is the probability of representation of more ideas and interests. In such settings substantial bargaining is a necessity for the resolution of conflicts, compromise outcomes are dictated by the necessity to accommodate the diverse demands of the many with power, and the decision-making process is more likely to produce somewhat broader distribution of values. Although purists may question whether the United States or Great Britain are truly democracies, and although the accusation of inequitable allocation of values may be levied against both systems, there is little doubt that decision-making in both is highly pluralistic and competitive and involves substantial representation.

But in all complex contemporary systems—democratic, authoritarian, or totalitarian—bargaining patterns tend to be highly complex and to vary with situations and issues. A pattern of oligarchic command decision-making may prevail in some systems or in some policy spheres or situations, while in other situations the bargaining process may be highly pluralistic and competitive. In the Soviet Union, for example, the top political elite—the Politburo—generally commands with one voice when it comes to issues concerning the authority of that elite. Somewhat more but still limited bargaining occurs on issues concerning the basic nature of the Soviet system; in such situations, the varied and diverse elites coordinate their efforts in defense of the system which is inextricably linked with the vested interests of various political, economic, and technical elites. But on issues which do not directly involve such basic elite concerns substantial pluralism, competition, and even representation of some mass interests ensues during prolonged bargaining processes which tend to produce compromise outcomes. In many democratic systems the bargaining process may be highly competitive, but consistently involves competition among a few readily-identifiable groups—particularly the major socio-economic interest groups representing big business and big labor. Or the process may involve substantial competition, but one group having in effect a veto power over some issues—as for example the power wielded for many decades by the oil industry over certain tax issues. Or the process may involve amorphous competition among groups which constantly shift their alignments from issue to issue. In the United States one often finds business and labor groups locked in intense conflict, but in strong cooperative alignment on some other issues.

The analysis of the degree of pluralism, competition, and representation characteristic of a decision-making system is thus a very difficult and complex undertaking which can never be very exact. It requires careful examination not merely of the distribution of power within government, but also throughout the society. It requires assessment of the power of varied levels, branches, and agencies of government, and also of interest groups and other structures and institutions which influence decision-making. It cannot end even with such a general analysis, but must examine varied kinds of political processes as they actually function in the context of specific situations and with respect to specific issues. A rough kind of assessment can be made on the basis of empirical examination of how a particular system functions. How and by whom is the decision-making process initiated on some particular issue? How does the deliberation phase proceed? Who or what groups are directly involved in specific kinds of bargaining processes; who or what groups are indirectly involved through consultation or lobbying processes; who or what kinds of groups have an effective non-legal veto power even over mere discussion of an issue? To what extent do which authoritative decision-makers really control the three decision-making functions. This is a necessary analytical exercise because of the consequences of varying degrees of pluralism, competition, and representation, as discussed in Chapter 12.

STRUCTURAL AND FUNCTIONAL DIFFERENTIATION

As governments grow in size and as their tasks become more voluminous and specialized, a complex division of labor within government and specialized structures for the performance of varied tasks become necessary. Specialized structures for the performance of rule-making, rule-application, and rule-adjudication become essential since one institution can perform all three functions only in the simplest small-scale systems, and hence legislatures, executive institutions, administrative bureaucracies, and judicial structures developed. Even when all branches share in the performance of some functions a division of labor is necessary: separate structures for policy and legislative initiatives, for deliberation on and modification of policy proposals, and for resolution of disputes over the interpretation of rules. Separate structures also become essential for decision-making at various levels: top policy-making, intermediate rule-making within the context of policy, and rule-making as may be required for the application and administration of rules. With further expansion of governmental scope and still greater complexity of tasks inherent in modern complex systems, even more specialization is required: structures capable of making decisions with regard to tax matters, welfare problems, housing programs, the money supply and other problems connected with the economy, foreign affairs, and many other specialized spheres. Specialized division of labor is necessary not only for rule making, but also rule application and adjudication in these and other individual spheres—one structure to primarily concern itself with economic rule-making, others primarily concerned with the application and adjudication of rules pertaining to economic activity. Some structural differentiation may also be useful with respect to functions which are best performed at national, subordinate, and local levels of government.

Decision-making systems differ with respect to the extent and effectiveness of structural-functional differentiation and specialization, and such differences may be directly related to their capabilities and their effective performance of varied functions. In some, one still finds rather futile efforts to concentrate all functions in some relatively simple structure— the person of a dictator, or the cabinet or inner circle of some authoritarian leader, assisted by a highly centralized bureaucratic apparatus. In others, specialized structures have been developed for various policy spheres, but which combine all three decision-making functions: one agricultural ministry, for example, which makes, applies, and adjudicates all rules pertaining to agricultural matters. In still other systems, efforts are made to separate the rule making, application, and adjudication functions among different institutions, and within such structural-functional arrangements to provide specialization along policy lines. Even though all three branches of the American government are involved in all decision-making functions, some attempts to separate the functions persist, at least in terms of special institutions for policy initiative, deliberation and law making, and administration and adjudication. The system also provides for specialization along policy lines: special Congressional committees for special fields of rule-making, specialized bureaucracies for rule-application in varied spheres, and specialized judicial systems and courts. And the system also provides some separation of function along federal, state, and local lines.

But concomitantly with this need for specialization, structural-functional differentiation requires the development of structures capable of integrating and coordinating the specialized actions of many agencies at different levels into coherent and harmonious policies. As political systems need generalists to coordinate the activities of many experts and to ensure that narrow specialized perspectives and interests will be subordinated to broader public perspectives and interests, so systems need integrating institutions. Again, political systems differ with respect to their relative success in developing such institutions.

Hence, the analysis of decision-making systems must focus on such structural differentiation and specialization, and on coordination and integrating machinery. The analysis must ask which structures within a system actually do what, perform what roles, and with what autonomy and authority, in the entire complex of decision-making and with regard to what types of policy matters. The analysis must include assessment and evaluation of the relationship between the system's organizational structure and its apparent capabilities and effectiveness.

THE INSTITUTIONALIZATION AND FORMALIZATION OF DECISION-MAKING

We commonly make a distinction between a "government of laws" and a "government of men." Using the former term we are usually referring to a system in which both citizens and rulers are subject to law, and in which rulers make decisions by lawful processes. The latter term refers to a system in which decisions are made in an arbitrary and capricious fashion by rulers who consider themselves to be above the law.

Formalization and institutionalization entails a government of laws. By formalization of decision-making we mean that rules pertaining to their making are formalized or codified in the form of a constitution, other laws, or rules pertaining to decision-making procedures. In the absence of such formalization, government officials make decisions in any manner they wish; decision-making is arbitrary and capricious and does not follow any prescribed procedures. Rule-making, for example, is formalized when a constitution prescribes how laws shall be enacted; confers certain authority on certain branches with respect to enactment; and when a legislative body adopts formal rules and creates additional structures (such as committees) pertaining to the enactment of laws. Institutionalization is closely related to formalization, but entails the element of deep respect for and adherence to the formal rules. It involves the conferral of certain functions and authority on certain governmental structures, such as the legislature, and also respect for, and a tendency to maintain, the authority of that structure. It involves placing a high value on formal decision-making procedures and practices so that such procedures are consistently maintained and followed. Formalization entails establishing certain authority relationships among decision-making individuals, groups, structures, and organizations; institutionalization involves high respect for and maintenance and adherence to such relationships.

To institutionalize a decision-making process is to change it from a poorly organized and informal activity into a highly formalized and organized collection of habits and roles. The formalization and institutionalization of decision-making means that rules must be and most of the time are made, changed, applied, and adjudicated in certain specified ways, by specified structures, and within certain or specified kinds of limitations. But what counts is not so much the source of formalization—the existence of a constitution or law for example—but the value attached to the rules, practices, and structures by political elites and various groups in the society. If such rules and structures are highly valued and hence respected, they provide for a government of laws, for recurring patterns of behavior, for relative predictability of the behavior of decision-makers, other elites, and masses, and hence help to provide political and social stability.

Constitutions are one means for formalizing and institutionalizing decision-making and also illustrate the nature of formalization. Some systems, such as the American, have a single document which formally prescribes how the government shall conduct its affairs, with such documents formally adopted as basic law by procedures accepted at the time and subsequently as lawful. The document may subsequently have been amended, but in accordance with constitutionally-prescribed rules. Yet what it considered to be constitutional in nature—practices and institutions which are considered to be so fundamental that the political norms of the society prescribe that they must be adhered to—may include many practices and institutions not formally prescribed by the written document. Other systems, such as the British, have so-called unwritten constitutions, which consist of not a single document but several laws which are widely considered to be so basic as to be constitutional in nature, and which include some deeply rooted customs, traditions, and principles which are highly valued and again widely considered to be parts of the constitution. Still other systems have lengthy and detailed written documents, which essentially are meaningless either because their contents are so vague and ambiguous that they permit decision-makers to do anything, or because too many elites consider them as nothing more than scraps of paper, to be ignored or torn up as their interests may dictate. What counts with respect to constitutions, and with respect to other laws or customs which prescribe and allocate decision-making procedures and authority, is not mere existence but the extent to which they are widely valued and hence obeyed by both people and their governors.

But constitutions can be valuable means for institutionalization and formalization of decision-making. For one, they confer but also limit the power of government by prescribing what functions government may or may not perform. The American constitution specifies the legal authority of the federal government but also imposes limitations on such authority by various clauses, by the Bill of Rights and by various amendments which protect individuals against governmental power and minorities against majorities. Constitutions also formalize and institutionalize the structure of government by allocating, defining, and limiting the power of branches and levels of government. The American constitution divides power between the federal government and the states and among the three branches of government, while the British concentrates legal authority in the hands of the national parliament. They regularize procedures for conflict resolution and decision-making, either by specifying in general terms how the process of decision-making shall proceed, or by creating certain institutions and specifying what roles they should play in decision-making. They may also institutionalize and formalize the goals and aspirations of the society as they set forth in preambles or other content the ideals and intentions of the society. By these and other means they give the stamp of legitimacy to government, which has the effect of engendering obedience to the basic rules not only by the people but by the decision-makers themselves. The gravest crises which societies undergo tend to be so-called constitutional crises, when the most basic and valued rules seem to be threatened or questioned. For the institutionalization and formalization of decision-making rules is essential for political stability and domestic peace and tranquillity.

A substantial degree of informality is characteristic of all decision-making systems. In any kind of system informal extra-legal structures, processes, and practices invariably develop which either supplement formal processes and institutions, or have the effect of reducing the roles or powers of formal structures, or sometimes have the effect of virtually nullifying the legal authority of certain institutions. Democratic constitutions, for example, generally confer far more legal authority on legislatures than they do on executives, yet this has not halted the shift in power from legislative to executive organs. Bureaucracies are mentioned in but few constitutions, yet they have become powerful institutions with far-reaching responsibilities. Congressional committees and their chairpersons are key power-centers in the American system, but their development is the result of informal Congressional practices; while their counterparts in the British system are relatively weak because of similar informal practices. Interest groups and political parties are rarely mentioned in constitutions, yet play powerful roles in many decision-making processes. In Britain the development of informal political party practices gradually led to the institutionalization of party government, which has been a major factor in the shift away from parliamentary to executive supremacy.

Yet despite such deviations from the norm, differences in the degree of formalization and institutionalization are marked among some systems, with significant consequences for the nature of the system. In some societies constitutions, rules, or organizations may exist but be essentially meaningless. The rules may constantly be ignored, constitutions may be so vague as to be virtually meaningless, structures or organizations may not really be institutions because they are neither valued nor involve recurring and predictable patterns of behavior on the part of their members. Such a high degree of informality makes possible arbitrary, capricious, and often ruthless exercise of power by powerful people whose devotion to the public interest may be more spurious than real. As will be explained in Chapter 12, too much formalization and institutionalization has its disadvantages, but a high degree of same seems essential not only for democracy, but also for stability, effectiveness, and adaptation to change.

Hence, political analysis must include a focus on the degree of formalization and institutionalization within the system, the extent to which rules are formally laid down and adhered to, or the degree to which decisions may be based on arbitrary and capricious actions. It must focus on the impact of the rules and institutions on the actual location and distribution of power, the extent to which various structures actually wield the legal authority they possess, the roles they actually play in decision-making. And assessment must be made of the consequences of all this for the nature and performance of the political system.

Power in Decision-Making Systems

11

Since power is the currency of politics, its analysis in decision-making systems must be a key concern. But as discussed in Chapter 2, power is more than legal authority. In decision-making it entails the efforts of sometimes numerous levels, branches, agencies, and elected or appointed officials of government to influence each other in an often complex bargaining process. In most systems it also entails efforts on the part of numerous social forces and interest groups to use their resources of power and credibility to influence the thought and behavior of government officials by appealing to their needs and values.

In this chapter, we first briefly explore analytical techniques, which are useful for ascertaining the location and distribution of power within governments. We continue with a discussion of the major analytical questions that should be asked about the varied elements of power, which shape three significant power relationships: the reciprocal power between government and society, the territorial distribution of power, and intra-governmental power relationships. To further explain the varied factors that should be considered in assessing power relationships and the elements that make for decision-making power, we continue with a discussion of the nature and sources of power of the four major branches of modern government: executive, legislative, bureaucratic, and judicial structures. We conclude with a brief discussion of the patterns of influence affecting the decisions of these structures.

THE ANALYSIS OF POWER

The analysis of power in decision-making systems entails three central questions. The power relationship between the system and its environment is one aspect—the extent of governmental power over the society and the degree to which society can influence and restrain government. A second concern is the power configuration within the decision-making system itself—the extent to which power is concentrated or dispersed, and where power is located within the system. The third aspect relates to the power of some environmental groups over decision-making, the extent to which decision-making is influenced by specific groups of the society. With regard to all three concerns, the analysis ought to be a dynamic one by including consideration of what trends appear to be developing. Efforts to trace the sources of power are also very useful for locating power, understanding prevailing or developing power patterns, discerning restraints on power which otherwise might not be readily apparent, and projecting certain trends.

Four general methods of analysis are typically used as approaches to the analysis of power. However, neither one alone can provide an accurate diagnosis. The use of all methods in combination tends to produce more accurate assessments.

Constitutional analysis may be useful because of the role of constitutions in conferring, distributing, and limiting legal authority. It may help to determine the overall legal authority of a government over society, what legal authority it may have to intervene in varied economic, social, cultural, or other spheres of human activity, the range of obligations imposed on citizens, the extent to which a government may legally control and regulate the life of people. Conversely a constitution may prescribe the society's legal authority over government—the right to change governments by means of free elections, the authority to directly or indirectly participate in decision-making by means of elected representatives, the right to certain civil rights and liberties which the government may not legally transgress. Constitutional analysis also provides information about distribution of power within government to the extent that such documents allocate legal authority to specific branches and levels of government.

However, such analysis seldom provides a complete or accurate diagnosis of power relationships, and in many cases may be very misleading. As discussed earlier, some constitutions are mere facades, and the legal authority bestowed on people or certain institutions may be so ambiguous as to be meaningless—such as the authority of the Supreme Soviet and of the Russian people. A close reading of the American or West German constitutions provides important clues to the separation of powers inherent in these systems; an analysis of the French constitution reveals important data about the power of the French president as contrasted with the weak legislature; and the revised Indian constitution starkly reveals the authoritarian power of the prime minister. Beyond these generalities, however, little more can be found. A reading of the unwritten British constitution is necessary to understand the British system, but hardly locates power within it.

Institutional or structural analysis is a very common method because structures which play clearly visible roles in decision-making provide a convenient focus. Examination of the power of institutions which are most susceptible to influence from society or from special groups provide data about governmental-society power interrelationships. It also provides information about the distribution of power within the decision-making system. This approach seeks to discover which formal and informal governmental structures appear to play really powerful roles, which play intermittent or occasional roles, and which appear to be merely legitimization or ratification structures or window dressing. It seeks to determine what the actual power relationships are among varied branches, agencies, or institutions of government; to what extent power appears to be concentrated in one institution or dispersed among several; what the power configuration appears to be within the more powerful institutions; and who the real power centers appear to be within particular institutions and within the entire decision-making structure. Accuracy depends on rigorous empirical examination of the actual nature of decision-making processes to determine not only what formal but also what informal structures are involved. It also requires examination of the actual nature, internal procedures, and functioning of institutions and their actual roles in decision-making processes, based not merely on their legal authority but their overall influence and the roots of such influence. It is perhaps the most useful approach when used in conjunction with process analysis.

Process analysis focuses on how decisions actually get made: who initiates proposals for governmental action; who the active participants are during deliberation and ratification stages, who influences whom during such processes; what actually happens within formal and informal governmental structures as decisions are proposed, discussed, and ratified; what the actual flow or interchange of influence appears to be among institutions, structures, groups, and individuals during the process. The case study method is commonly used as part of process analysis, and involves efforts to actually trace a decision from beginning to end, to determine who or what had major influence over the enactment, modification, ratification, or rejection of the original proposal. But in order to be able to generalize from individual cases and processes, the approach must include analysis of decision-making with respect to various types of policies (such as tax matters, economic decisions, education policies, welfare programs); with respect to various levels of decision-making (national, local, presidential, bureaucratic); and in different situations over time. When so pursued, process analysis can provide accurate pictures of the real power of and within institutions, the actual extent of institutionalization and formalization, the actual degree of pluralism, competition, and decision-making within the system, and actual patterns of influence over decision-making by public opinions and special groups.

Elite analysis can also be very useful even though it rests on the assumption—not always valid—that elites involved in decision-making tend to represent the ideas and interests of their social origins. The focus here is not on elites in the society but the political elites—those within the decision-making system (although some analysts who use this method also may consider the influence of non-political elites). The task is to identify those elites within the overall governmental structure and process and within individual institutions, and then analyze this elite structure on the basis of certain criteria which have consequences for decision-making. The more specific tasks include:

1. Determination of the nature of the elite structure: the number of elites and the homogeneity or heterogeneity of ideas and interests among the elites involved in decision-making or among those playing crucial roles in the processes. How oligarchic or polyarchic is the structure? Are they all a like-minded group when it comes to certain fundamental issues?

2. Determination of the types of elites involved: the social, economic, and cultural origins and composition of these elites, and the extent to which social origin produces similarity or diversity of ideas and interests. Are most or all from the upper socio-economic strata, or from the business world, or from one ethnic group, and hence likely to act in concert?

3. Representation patterns: the extent to which the elite structure, and the ideas and interests represented within that structure, are generally representative of the total society. Are varied occupational groups—workers, farmers, businesspeople, technicians, others—different socio-economic strata, varied ethnic and religious groups, represented in the elite structure, either directly or by surrogates who do in fact represent such interests to some degree?

4. Elite attitudes: the norms, values, and bargaining attitudes of the elites—the extent to which they tend to be pragmatic, impartial, responsive, prone to accomodation, and concerned with narrow or broad interests.

5. Circulation patterns of various elites in decision-making: the extent to which old elites are being replaced or supplemented with new elites of different origins and interests.

SIGNIFICANT POWER RELATIONSHIPS

The reciprocal power relationship between government and society—the extent of governmental power over the society and the degree to which the society can influence and restrain government—is a key concern of power analysis. As previously discussed, legal and constitutional analysis is essential in this respect, but must be supplemented with institutional and process analysis in order to discern realities rather than merely legal possibilities or niceties. Only such methods of analysis can reveal to what extent the people in general, or individual groups, really influence decision-making. The analysis of policy outputs—discussed in Part V—is also essential to determine the power which a government is attempting to exercise over a society. Trends with respect to such reciprocal formal legal authority are also important—to what extent the balance of power may be shifting due to such factors as formal constitutional changes, interpretation of legal authority by executives, legislatures, or judicial systems, or tendencies towards greater or lesser adherence to the formal rules. Sometimes such trends are clear-cut, as in the recent shift in India from democracy towards authoritarianism. Sometimes they may be less visible, as in many Western democracies.

Significant clues to the existing or developing balance of power may be found by focusing on other than the legal component of power. Changes in its financial resources or control over the economy, or in the effectiveness of its organizational apparatus, or its prestige and credibility, may lead to substantial enhancement or diminution of the actual power of a government. These may be far more important than legal authority as a source of influence over society. Perhaps most important is the extent to which people in society perceive the need for government and expansion of its authority. Certainly such widening perceptions of need for governmental resources—its regulatory authority and capabilities, its organization, its legal authority—to manage the affairs of a complex, interdependent industrial society has been one major factor leading to the expansion of governmental power (a theme further discussed in Chapter 12). Conversely, governmental perceptions of need for mass support may enhance the influence of people over governmental decision-makers particularly in democratic systems close to election time, but also in authoritarian systems as governments strive to maintain themselves and to enact policies which people will obey.

Power resources other than legal authority may also confer substantial influence on non-governmental elites within a society. These may consequently be able to resist governmental authority, be able to induce others to question or disobey such authority, or by virtue of being powerful elites whose support is essential for governmental stability and effectiveness, be able to restrain or influence decision-makers. Thus certain traditional leaders in African and Asian countries—tribal, religious, regional and other elites who have been deprived of legal authority by new political systems—still have substantial influence because of the persistence of traditions, their prestige and credibility within their communal groups, and sometimes their wealth. In modern industrial societies similar power, based on similar or other resources, is exercised by major economic elites and by powerful interest groups. These and many other types of elites and groups may have effective "veto power" over government.

Finally, the real power of government over society may be sharply restricted by the international environment. The modern concept of "state sovereignty" holds that a country is subject to no legal authority other than its own, has no obligation to obey any command emanating from outside its own frontiers, and in general has the legal authority to make its own decisions for its own people without outside interference. This again is a legal principle but not reality. Some states are so dependent on others, need the resources of others for economic, security, or other reasons, that they must heed influences or even commands from other states. Due to modern communication technology some states may exercise substantial influence over the people in other states. And the increasing interdependence of the world has created a situation in which no state can really autonomously make its own decisions: the necessity for certain kinds of economic, political, or other decisions may be imposed by the nature of the external world.

The territorial organization of governmental power is one important aspect of the distribution of power within decision-making systems. Small and relatively homogeneous societies most often have unitary systems. In these most legal authority is vested in the national government, which in turn may at will create or do away with subordinate levels, and confer or withdraw such legal authority on subordinate units as it wishes. This is the case in Britain, France, and most African and Asian nations where the restraints on the power of national governments are primarily non-legal in nature. Federal systems generally prevail in the larger and more heterogeneous societies. In these, legal authority is constitutionally divided between the national federal government and the states. The latter are legally considered to be autonomous or sovereign, and neither their existence nor their legal authority is legally subject to change by the federal government.

While such constitutional concentration or division of legal authority remains important in systems which tend to follow constitutional directives, it still pertains only to legal authority, and sometimes even just paper authority. The extent to which power is really unified or divided, and trends with respect to this, again requires more than constitutional analysis. The Soviet Union, for example, is a federal system on paper but hardly in practice. The legal authority of states in the American, West German, and some other federal systems remains intact, yet this has not prevented a significant shift in power from subordinate to national levels of government (another topic explored further in Chapter 12). What is required is empirical examination of actual practices. Which level of government actually makes the major policy decisions? To what extent is the national level supplementing or supplanting subordinate decision-making in varied policy spheres? To what extent are the subordinate states truly autonomous or sovereign? What are the varied roots of national and state power, and what are the basic reasons for shifts of power in one direction or another?

Intra-governmental power relationships is the third key power relationship for political analysis. The major analytical problem entails the location and distribution of power within a particular government at whatever level; the extent to which power is concentrated or dispersed among and within different branches and agencies; the nature of the power relationships among the major branches; the identification of the major power centers in the decision-making system; and assessment of major trends with respect to the overall power configuration.

A key aspect is the balance of power between executive and legislative branches. Constitutional authority and arrangements may be significant with respect to this. Authoritarian constitutions invariably allocate the preponderance of legal authority to executives and sharply circumscribe the authority of legislative bodies. Democratic systems in contrast attempt either to establish legislative supremacy, or to balance power between the two branches, or to maintain strong legislative restraints on executive power. In parliamentary systems such as the British, legal authority is unified and concentrated in the parliament. Only legislators and not executives are elected by the people; the chief executive—the chief minister of the government—is selected by one or both houses of the legislature; and the executive is accountable and responsible not directly to the people but to the parliament which elected him. In presidential systems such as the American, legal authority is divided by constitutional provisions. Executives and legislatures are separately elected for separate terms of office, have separate constituencies, both are directly accountable to the electorate rather than to each other, neither has the power to oust the other, and the two branches generally have the power to check the power of each other. This is the American principle of separation of power and checks and balances. In hybrid systems such as the French, the directly-elected president is delegated substantial legal authority, but legal restraints on his power are imposed by the constitution and the conferral of power to a second executive—the premier—and to the parliament.

But such constitutional arrangements pertain to legal authority, and the realities of the power relationship may be quite different. One indicator of the real balance in parliamentary systems may be the "overthrow versus dissolution power." In such systems power is deliberately unified to facilitate unity of governmental action and to prevent deadlock in government. If and when the parliament and executive are in sharp disagreement over some fundamental policy issues, the deadlock can legally be resolved in one or two ways. The parliament may "overthrow" the executive and his cabinet, and either elect a new chief minister or call for new elections; or the executive may dissolve the parliament and call for elections for a new legislature. But the actual practices and processes of government invariably tilt the balance in one direction or another. In the French system which existed prior to 1958, for example, the premier in practice could seldom exercise his dissolution power, and the power balance was tilted in favor of parliament. In the British system the parliament has not been able to exercise its overthrow power for a variety of reasons, and the prime minister enjoys substantially more power than the parliament.

Other power relationships which are important for assessing the location and distribution of power involve the relationship of the bureaucracy and the judiciary to each other and to the other branches of government. But as with the executive-legislative relationship, legal considerations may be important, but other elements of power may outweigh the resource of legal authority derived from constitutions or other laws. The bureaucracy, for example, is legally part of the executive establishment and subject to control by the chief executive. Yet as will be discussed below, a variety of factors may make the bureaucracy a power in its own right. In some authoritarian systems the judiciary is an integral arm of the executive, yet may often be able to elude executive control. In the American system the principle is that of an independent judiciary, yet it is by no means immune to executive and even to legislative influence.

To further explain the varied factors which must be considered in assessing power relationships, we now turn to the discussion of the power of specific governmental institutions.

EXECUTIVE INSTITUTIONS AND POWER

A variety of different kinds of executive institutions exist in various kinds of political systems. The first analytical task is to determine who really functions as the system's chief executive, and who wields or shares effective executive power.

Single executives are characteristic of presidential systems. In these the president plays the dual role of chief of state (the symbol and head of the nation) and chief of government—functions separated in many systems. In democracies, presidents are selected by popular election—either directly as in Venezuela, or somewhat indirectly as in the American system of the electoral college. In either case, the president is considered to have a national constituency and to be accountable directly to the people and not to the legislature. In authoritarian systems selection usually results from a coup or from mafia-style politics among elites, with the election sometimes ratified by some kind of facade election system. But in all systems executive power tends to be shared to some degree, simply because single individuals can seldom perform all the functions and responsibilities vested in them. Presidential executive institutions generally include cabinets, "White House staffs," "kitchen cabinets," or some kind of coterie of high level officials who advise the chief executive, engage in top level policy making, and supervise the bureaucracies. Presidents may have substantial control over their cabinets or staffs by appointment, dismissal, and other legal powers, but such control is seldom absolute. Hence, some cabinet and staff members may not share executive responsibility, but in a very real sense share executive power.

Dual executives are characteristic of both democratic and authoritarian parliamentary systems. In these the chief of state may be either a monarch or a president. Some contemporary monarchs ascended their thrones on the basis of heredity, as the British Queen and the King of Thailand; others on the basis of their own or their father's military coup—the Shah of Iran. The President of the Federal Republic of Germany is indirectly elected for a fixed term of office. Most contemporary chiefs of state play only nominal and ceremonial roles; some, however, exercise real political power and in fact are the chief executives—as the Shah of Iran.

The functions of chief of government in parliamentary systems are performed by "chief ministers"—the British Prime Minister, the French Premier, the West German Chancellor. Selection methods vary widely, although they usually involve some kind of election by one house of the parliament. In the British system the leader of the majority party automatically becomes Prime Minister; his ascendancy to office is merely ratified by a formal vote in the House of Commons. In multiparty systems requiring coalition governments the selection process is more complex, but involves final ratification by parliament. The French system, being a hybrid presidential-parliamentary system, is more complex: the premier is named by the president, subject to ratification by parliament. In democratic parliamentary theory the prime minister is accountable and responsible to the parliament rather than directly to the people, and indeed is supposed to function as an agent of the legislature (although in its origins, the office functioned as an agent of the Crown). His tenure in office theoretically is subject to parliamentary control; he is required to either step down or to dissolve parliament and call for new elections when he loses the confidence of parliament or cannot get his legislative program enacted into law.

Cabinets are also integral parts of parliamentary executive establishments. In parliamentary theory the executive is a plural institution, consisting of a cabinet which includes key ministers of the government, presided over by the chief minister who is *primus inter pares*—first among equals. Policy-making theoretically is the collective task of the entire cabinet. Although the actual power of cabinets and of individual chief or other ministers varies from system to system, the general trend has been for the chief minister to function as the chief executive who loosely or closely controls and coordinates policy-making by individual ministers in their respective policy spheres. Cabinets have tended to become more advisory and coordinating organs. Nevertheless, a chief minister's appointment, dismissal, or other power over his ministers may be characteristic of a particular system. A major restraint is again that of the chief executive's need for support, which may require the inclusion in the cabinet of individuals who control powerful wings or factions of a particular party, or powerful leaders of religious, ethnic, or similar types of groups.

Plural executive institutions are characteristic of communist systems, and determining who really wields executive power often involves the difficult art of "Kremlinology." In all such systems a committee which heads the communist party—the Politburo in the Soviet Union—is vested with final executive authority. But on some occasions in some systems power is really shared among the ten to twenty individuals who make up this committee; on some occasions power is wielded by a few members; while the general tendency has been for one member—the Secretary General or Chairman of the Communist Party—to emerge as the most powerful figure. Two other executives also exist in such systems. In the Soviet Union the Chairman of the Presidium of the Supreme Soviet (the national legislature) functions as president and chief of state, but seldom exercises any real power. The chairman of the Council of Ministers functions as chief minister and chief of government, but the actual executive role he performs and power he wields varies with the political situation and may be difficult to determine—as is true of his counterparts in other communist systems.

The power of chief executives and the distribution of power within executive establishments varies widely around the world. The real extent and distribution of such power is usually a very difficult and complex assessment task which requires careful empirical examination involving constitutional, institutional, process and elite analysis. Such analysis is facilitated by considering the sources of power.

The legal authority of authoritarian executives invariably is extensive, either in terms of authority to control most or all institutions and activities of government, or control of the state's military, police, and judicial systems. The constitutions of some democratic systems also confer substantial legal authority on executives, as for example the extensive financial and legislative authority given to the French president and the West

German chancellor. Some legal authority may appear to be rather limited, yet have broader implications: the American President's authority to veto acts of Congress has substantial impact on the content of legislation because Congress, to avoid a veto, often tends to heed Presidential desires. Some constitutions contain important emergency clauses resulting in executive power. The West German constitution, for example, permits the executive to wield extensive power for a six month period; and Adolf Hitler invoked more extensive emergency clauses of the earlier German constitution to assume authoritarian rule. Legal stipulations about executive tenure may similarly add to power: as for example the fixed four year and six year terms of American and French presidents, or constitutional limitations on the power of some parliaments to overthrow their chief ministers.

The control executives have over legislative bodies is an important key to executive power, with such control emanating in some instances from legal authority, in others from practices and principles of the system. The American Congress for example, is both legally and in practice a very independent body, yet the executive establishment wields substantial influence over it for a variety of reasons. The independence of the French parliament is considerably circumscribed because of several constitutional provisions which give the executives substantial authority over legislative proceedings, yet the party and election system enables the parliament to play at least an obstructionist role. In the British system the House of Commons is theoretically the supreme policy-maker which controls the cabinet. Yet the prime minister, by virtue of his dual role as chief of government and head of the majority party, combined with the principle of party unity and discipline, dominates parliamentary proceedings to a considerable extent—he determines the House's agenda, timetable, committee system, the extent to which the House may modify executive proposals, and other crucial matters.

The power of the purse—control over the government's budget, wealth, and general economic resources—is an important key to the executive-legislative balance of power. In the American system the power to raise taxes and spend revenues is largely vested in the Congress, yet the president wields substantial power not merely because of his potential veto, but because the intricacies of national budgets have the effect of giving the presidential establishment the key role in their preparation. In other systems legal authority, or an executive's control over his political party, or simply the practices of the system may have the effect of giving the executive the real power of the purse. In the West German system, for example, the chancellor in certain specified circumstances may in effect ram his budget through the parliament. In both Britain and France the parliaments may only take actions which are politically unpalatable and hence seldom taken—increase taxes or reduce expenditures as proposed by the executive.

The degree of control an executive has over his cabinet is extremely important. Most executives have legal appointment and dismissal powers over ministers and cabinet members, yet such legal authority may be sharply circumscribed by other factors, and particularly the need to include in the top policy-making strata individuals of high prestige, with important constituency support, who control factions or wings of the political party, or whose support is needed for other reasons. The political necessity of a heterogeneous cabinet may not only reduce the power of the chief executive, but also the cohesion of the top policy-making strata and hence its overall power within the decision-making system. This is characteristic not merely of democratic but also totalitarian systems. Stalin, for example, could not rise to the top until he eliminated fellow members of his Politburo after some eight years of mafia-style politics. Khrushchev's Politburo was divided over a number of issues for many years, with the consequence that subordinate party and governmental organs wielded considerably more power during those years than they normally do.

The degree of executive control over the bureaucracy is another important factor. In general, a chief executive's role as chief administrator is a major key to executive power, giving him control over the organized bureaucracy and its resources of information, skill, and expertise. Yet in some systems (as in the American) he may have to share some of that control with cabinet members, key legislative bodies, the judiciary, or even powerful interest groups. In other systems (such as most totalitarian) the sheer size, complexity, and multiplicity of interests within the bureaucracy may limit effective executive control.

Perhaps the most important key to executive power is the need of the system (or perceived needs among decision-makers and the society) for executive leadership and for expansion of executive functions which result in the accrual of more executive power. It is apparently for this reason that policy-making and legislative initiative has been informally delegated to executives; legislatures around the world wait for executives to propose before they begin to deliberate and act. The executive power of the purse has expanded because of the sheer size and complexity of governmental budgets. The volume and complexity of modern legislation effectively limits the ability of legislatures to write complex and detailed laws; hence, a tendency has developed to write broad and general pieces of legislation which in effect delegate substantial rule-making authority to executives. The volume and complexity of modern legislation also expands the rule-application function of the executive: he now has far more laws to execute, administer, and enforce than ever before, all of which enhances his decision-making role and his power. Even more important is the need for any political system and society for leadership and a fixed point of responsibility. People, legislators, and government officials invariably look to the executive. He or she is the only generalist within the system, the only individual with a truly national constituency, usually the only official with the requisite national prestige, and apparently the only agency of government capable of swift and decisive actions. Hence, only the executive can provide such leadership, serve as the point of responsibility and accountability, and generally to function as the mainspring of the political system. It is for this reason, as explained in Chapter 2, that the American President (as most executives) combines six roles as chief politician, administrator, legislator, foreign policy maker, chief of state, and chief of the armed forces, and wields his awesome political power.

But political analysis must focus not merely on executive power, but also on effective restraints on the power that may prevail within a political system. These may be constitutional restraints which disperse governmental authority among several branches or levels of government. They may involve legislative authority or practices pertaining to the modification or rejection of executive proposals, or judicial authority and practices with similar consequences. Any executive has but limited time, information, and expertise, and, hence, becomes dependent on others— cabinet members, legislative leaders, the bureaucracy, interest group leaders, many others—and dependency means reduction in executive power and enhancement of the power of others. To govern effectively an executive needs credibility, prestige, and support, and the search for these often effectively limits what he can do. Most important is the configuration of power within which an executive functions. Polyarchy within government and the society invariably means that the executive must actively seek to maintain unity within his executive establishment, the government as a whole, the political party, and the entire society. This search for unity and for support forces him to be responsive to varied elements, to accomodate individuals and groups of different views and interests, and to modify or abandon proposals in order to maintain his power. And finally, within democratic systems, the chief executive is always subject to the most significant restraint—the need to win elections.

LEGISLATIVE INSTITUTIONS

A variety of types of legislative institutions, with wide variations in their power, also exists around the world. The prime analytical task is to ascertain the extent of legislative power in decision-making, the reasons for legislative power or lack of power, and which specific legislative bodies exercise significant governmental roles. Two main lines of analysis appear to be useful for such assessment: the roles that legislatures actually play in government, and the structures and operational procedures of legislatures which are significant with respect to their roles and power.

Participation in rule-making is a function common to all legislative bodies, but with wide variations in actual performance of this role. In most systems legislative initiative generally has passed into the hands of executives, so that most legislatures only engage in deliberation, modification, or rejection of executive proposals. Some play this role very vigorously. The American Congress, due to its independent legal authority, structure, and mode of operation is perhaps the most powerful national legislative body in the world. It is famous (or notorious) for its frequent drastic modification or rejection of presidential initiatives, and on occasion even exercises some initiative. The British parliament is substantially more restricted. It rejects major cabinet initiatives only at its peril, for members then face the prospect of dissolution and the risks of new elections, and it can seldom force major modifications on executive proposals. Yet behind the scenes it exercises substantial influence over both initiatives and during deliberation, hence, its rule-making role is still substantial. The French parliament, which enjoyed rule-making supremacy prior to 1958, today is sharply circumscribed in its role by a mixture of constitutional provisions, executive practices, and its own internal weaknesses—particularly the multi-party system. Yet parliamentary enactment of some executive proposals is still necessary, and at the very least the French parliament's capacity for obstruction remains formidable. Still other legislative bodies function variously as window-dressing or as ratification and legitimization instruments—they dutifully meet as the constitution or executive prescribes, listen to and applaud proposals, and enact such proposals into law. This is the pattern of the USSR's Supreme Soviet and in most authoritarian and totalitarian systems. In some cases, such as Kenya's National Assembly, legislators may make much noise, criticize executive proposals, and even pass legislative motions; but the executive is not bound by such actions, and more often than not turns a deaf ear.

Financial control is another function performed to some extent by some legislatures. Again in some systems—such as the American—budgets are proposed by executives, either as overall governmental budgets for the fiscal year or as recommendations for individual tax measures or expenditures, are then carefully scrutinized by legislative agencies, and legislatures are free to change either the overall package or individual items at will. In others, legislatures are required to consider only the entire budget, may not reduce but only increase taxes, and may only reduce but not increase expenditures for various purposes. In still others, legislatures hastily ratify and thereby hopefully legitimize governmental actions.

Investigations of a wide variety of matters is a function performed very vigorously by some legislative bodies, intermittently by others, and not at all by many. In the American system this function is performed on the rationale that investigation may be necessary for effective legislation— that investigations may uncover instances of poor legislation, inadequate administration, or needs for new legislation. This role can substantially enhance legislative power in that it involves the power of publicity or the power of noise. It can add to the prestige of individual legislators or legislative organs, diminish the prestige of other government officials and agencies, force executive agencies to bend to the will of legislators on particular issues, or even force presidents to resign.

The approval of executive appointments is another tool wielded by some legislative bodies. In the American system the right of the Senate to approve or reject presidential appointments to cabinet, judicial, and high bureaucratic and military positions constitutes an important restraint on presidential power and a means for the Congress to influence policy-making in varied spheres. In parliamentary systems the necessity for legislative approval of cabinet positions may be a similar restraint, although it may be somewhat weakened by the principle of party discipline.

Legal authority with respect to constitutional amendments may be another source of legislative power. In most democratic systems, proposed amendments must first be approved by parliaments, and then be referred to voters (or as in the United States, to state legislatures) for final approval. In some systems, such as the British, it takes only an Act of Parliament to amend the constitution—a difficult process despite cabinet leadership and the principle of party discipline. In others, such as India, an Act of Parliament to change the constitution is a foregone conclusion once the executive has made a decision.

Treaty ratification authority may be a source of legislative power with respect to foreign affairs. Most democratic systems require such ratification by at least one legislative house—such as the American which requires approval by a two-third's vote in the Senate. Even though the number of treaties which a nation enters into may be limited, the legal requirement for ratification, coupled with such other roles as the investigatory or financial power, may provide a legislative body with some leverage over the executive's conduct of foreign affairs.

The judicial role played by legislatures may be significant. Presidential systems usually have some procedures for the impeachment and trial of chief executives, judges, and other government officials by legislative bodies, and these may provide the latter with important restraints on executive and judicial power. Appointments of judges may be subject to legislative review, and the structure of a judicial system may require legislation, both providing legislative bodies with controls over both executive and judicial power.

As discussed earlier, the extent to which a parliament can actually exercise its power to overthrow the executive is a clue to executive-legislative relationships. In some cases, such as France, it may be sharply restricted by constitutional provisions, by legislators' fears that new elections might result in loss of their seats, or by similar factors. In other cases, such as the British, the overthrow power may be virtually nonexistent because of similar fears, as well as the principle of party unity and discipline. However, a more searching analysis of a system may reveal that the overthrow power may be less visible but nonetheless real. Several British prime ministers, for example, have been forced to resign (often on grounds of "ill health") not as the result of formal parliamentary action, but because of intense pressures from their party colleagues in parliament. In presidential systems the inability of legislatures to overthrow executives may weaken legislative power. This, however, may be offset by the president's inability to dissolve the legislature—which particularly enhances the power of those legislators with longer terms of office (the six-year tenure of United States Senators), or those who have no re-election problems (those with safe seats). In the United States the weakness of party control over nomination processes for congressional seats also tends to weaken the authority of a president over the congress.

Structure and operational procedures have an impact on the roles and power of legislatures in a variety of ways.

Some legislative bodies are unicameral; they consist of only one chamber—the Nebraska state legislature, the Knesset in Israel. Most consist of two. The bicameral legislature had its origins in the class basis of late medieval European society when one house represented the aristocracy —the House of Lords in Britain—and the other the commoners—the House of Commons (originally the uncommon commoners—the untitled but wealthy middle and upper classes). American bicameralism at the federal level grew out of the desire to represent the states in the Senate, but now more commonly is rationalized on the basis that two houses ensure more careful scrutiny of bills and provides a system of checks and balances. The power wielded and roles performed by the two houses may be equal in some systems, while in others one house wields significantly more legal authority than the other. The British parliament, for example, has in effect become almost a unicameral body since the House of Lords legally may only delay passage of legislation for a year.

The impact of bicameralism on legislative power varies partly due to such variations in the power of the two houses. Sometimes it serves to enhance legislative versus executive authority, in that executive proposals encounter two obstacle courses—as in the American system. Sometimes it serves to enhance executive power, as in the United States when one house sometimes fails to override a presidential veto, or as on occasion DeGaulle attempted to use the French Senate as a foil against the National Assembly. In the Federal Republic of Germany the Bundesrat serves as a bastion of state power in the national legislature by virtue of the fact that representatives to this house are appointed by state governments.

The kind of committee system characteristic of a legislature is an important clue to legislative power. Due to the volume and complexity of modern legislation and the size of modern legislatures, most democratic legislative institutions operate with some kind of a committee system. Bills are studied in and deliberated on in committees prior to consideration by the full body, and most of the important provisions are hammered out in committee sessions, with but few possibilities for amendments arising in full house deliberations. But the kind of committee system has substantial power implications. The American Congress operates with a system of standing specialized committees; each committee has authority over a specific sphere of policy (such as agriculture, education); each has the same members for a two-year (and usually much longer) session; committee members are those who either have some expertise or special interest in the committee's sphere of policy; and each has a paid staff of specialist-experts for necessary research, advice, bill or amendment drafting, or similar matters. All of this enables committees to bring to bear the power resources of information, skill, expertise, time, and attention; enhances the credibility of committees with respect to specific policy matters; and often produces cohesive action on the part of legislators with similar interests. In addition these specialized committees usually establish political alliances with interest groups and bureaucracies with similar interests, thereby enhancing the power not only of the latter but also of legislative committees. In some systems (such as the French), constitutional provisions limit the potential for the establishment of specialized committees. In others (the British) the practice is to consider legislation only in a few large standing committees, none of which are specialized. In both cases executive power is substantially enhanced. And it may be further enhanced when these individual legislatures—unlike their American counterparts—are denied extensive office space or funds for employment of legislative staffs.

The role and functioning of committees in legislative processes may be significant with respect to the location of power within legislative bodies. In the American system, for example, specialized committees play crucial roles, and hence are the real power centers with respect to legislation within their specific policy spheres. Congressional procedures are such that most times committees must report favorably on a bill before the full house can consider it and act; a bill may therefore in most instances be killed within a committee, or its passage may be significantly delayed. Similar kinds of procedures with respect to amendments, timetables, and other matters limit the power of the full house with respect to certain legislation, and enhance the power of the specialized committees and committees charged with determining procedures (such as the House Committee on Rules). Operational procedures vest substantial power over legislation in committee chairpersons, so that these individuals frequently are the real legislative power centers. And selection procedures with regard to committee chairpersons vest such power in the hands of a limited number of senators and congressmen, because the seniority system (now gradually being modified) automatically gives the chairmanship to the member who has served longest in the Senate or the House. Similar procedures ensure that the most important committees will be staffed with the most senior legislators.

The leadership structure within the legislature, and practices with regard to the selection of leaders, may be equally important, simply because effective leadership could produce the power resources of cohesion. Some legislatures—again the American—select their own leaders, and operational legislative procedures are determined by such leaders or by the house as a whole. In some other systems—Britain, West Germany— leaders are selected by the executive branch or by leaders of the dominant political party. This leads not merely to executive control of the leadership, but to executive determination of legislative proceedings. Also important is the composition and cohesion of the leadership. In party-dominated parliaments in which party leaders constitute or select legislative leaders, some degree of executive control invariably results; but it also generally results in a relatively cohesive leadership consisting of but a few. In the American Congress leadership is fragmented, with the net result that Congress is weakened precisely because it lacks real cohesive leadership. Party caucuses elect some leaders—majority and minority leaders and whips, the Speaker of the House—who have but little authority or real power over their party colleagues in either Senate or House; committee chairmen function as real power centers, but are selected on the basis of seniority and hence are not controlled by the party's elected leaders; while still other senators or congressmen sometimes function as leaders simply because of their prestige, or skill, or expertise.

But despite the power inherent in an effective committee system and leadership structure, the major power resource lacking in all legislative bodies is that of organizational cohesion. Legislatures are simply too large and unwieldy to function in a speedy, concerted, and cohesive fashion. Parochialism and localism inevitably dominate the attitudes of representatives elected by and responsible to small geographic constituencies; great diversity of ideas and interests makes it extremely difficult to develop the harmonious and cooperative action needed for effective legislative leadership or initiative; and the inevitable internal conflict makes it difficult to develop a majority coalition needed for positive action. In essence, a relatively cohesive executive institution often faces a fragmented legislative opposition, and the end result may be significant pressures and restraints on executive action, and modification or rejection of executive proposals, but seldom any cooperative legislative counter-initiatives or proposals. The same fragmentation of legislative interests, ideas, and power has led to the nature of modern legislation—which tends to be very broad and general in nature, and to frequently constitute broad grants of authority to the executive branch. It is not only that legislative bodies, even those with specialized committee structures, lack the necessary information and expertise needed for detailed legislation. It is also due to the fact that the more detailed a legislative proposal is, the more likely that it will encounter strong opposition by some parochial or special interests represented within the legislature. Hence to develop the majority coalition needed to pass legislation, only broad and general bills can make it, leaving decisions on the oft all-important details to the executive branch, and specifically to the executive's bureaucracy.

THE MODERN BUREAUCRACY

The primary function of the modern bureaucracy remains its traditional one: the implementation of the policies of political decision-makers. What has significantly changed, however, is the scope and significance of implementation and administration of laws, and this has led to a substantial expansion of the power of modern bureaucracies.

Modern bureaucracies play a number of roles in connection with their primary implementation function. The prime role is the administrative one, the execution and enforcement of laws and judicial decisions. This involves a bewildering variety of tasks: the administration of welfare programs, housing projects, health care benefits, social security programs, subsidy programs for farmers, and in some systems running steel mills, coal mines, farms, radio and TV stations, and many other diverse activities. Bureaucracies also provide services authorized by law: agricultural agencies conduct research to benefit varied kinds of farmers, the Small Business Administration endeavors to assist small businesses in a variety of ways. They regulate various spheres of human endeavor in the public interest as defined by law and the bureaucracies in charge: safety regulations; regulation of rates charged by truckers, power companies, bus lines; overseeing of business mergers; regulation of banks and stock exchanges. Related to regulation are their licensing activities, designed to ensure minimum standards and job qualifications for teachers, barbers, real estate and insurance agents, drivers, and thousands of others. And they function as interest articulators to the extent that they gather information as to what needs to be done, either in terms of new or improved laws or implementing regulations, in such diverse fields as environmental protection, food and drug safety, civil rights, mine safety, and thousands of other fields. This explosion of roles and functions has simply meant the explosion of the bureaucracy's impact on the daily life of a society and its individual citizens, and the gradual growth of bureaucratic decision-making power.

The power of bureaucracies varies among modern political systems, with differences due to variations in the scope and spheres of governmental endeavors, the degree of executive, legislative, and judicial controls over bureaucracies, the prestige a bureaucracy enjoys in a particular culture, the extent to which a system's bureaucracy has become a bureaucratic caste with its own vested interests and momentum, and the degree to which bureaucracies are able to establish political alliances with interest groups or other political forces (such as congressional committees). But despite these variations, they have become powerful in all systems, and several resources account for their common power: their information, skill, and expertise; the time and attention they can devote to politics; their frequent or occasional organizational cohesion in promoting bureaucratic or related client interests; and the control they may exercise of wealth or economic power—by funds subject to their disposition, decisions they can make with economic impact, or various types of direct or indirect control over sectors of the economy. Most important is again the factor of reciprocal need—the need of governments and societies for these resources. Most fundamentally, the scope of the modern positive or interventionist state, combined with these resources, has led to the expansion of the rule-application function, so that this primary bureaucratic role involves substantial and sometimes crucial rule-making and rule-adjudication.

In most political systems attempts are made to separate rule-making from rule-application. In most systems major but broad policy decisions are invariably made by a relatively small policy-making layer at the top of the political hierarchy—chief executives, members of their cabinets, perhaps key legislative leaders, perhaps a few others. Implementing policies and decisions must then be made within the context of such broad policy guidelines, either in the form of specific decisions to implement top policies, or in the form of policies within respective spheres—agricultural, educational, financial, other matters—designed to attain the general goals desired by the policy-making layer. Most such decisions and policies are made by the "political layer" of government officials—individuals elected to office and hence accountable to the public, or individuals appointed by elected officials and hence responsible to them and indirectly to the public, or individuals accountable to authoritarian leaders who have overall responsibility for government whatever their actual legitimacy. In theory, the function of the bureaucracy is then to translate the political layer's will into action—to faithfully execute the policies and decisions made by those with authority to do so. The President and Congress make top level policy, the Congress with Presidential involvement enacts implementing laws, members of the cabinet and others appointed by the President and accountable to him make important decisions within such policy and legal guidelines, and bureaucrats confine their task to the routine application of such decisions. But if such a neat and tidy division between rule-making and rule-application was ever possible, it clearly is no longer possible in a modern polity.

As previously discussed in connection with executive and legislative power, a number of factors—the expanding scope of government, the great volume, complexity, and technical nature of modern legislation, the difficulty of developing majority coalitions to pass detailed legislation—have all led to legislation which constitutes broad grants of authority to executives. Laws may spell out the objectives of governmental action, general principles to guide or direct action in pursuit of objectives, appropriate funds and specify rules with respect to their expenditure, and on occasion spell out some specific rules for the implementation of legislative policy. But invariably more specific authority must be delegated to the executive, who has no alternative but to further delegate authority to his cabinet members, who of necessity must further delegate the same to subordinate bureaucrats.

Rule-application invariably entails some decision-making, although the scope of decisions left open to an administrative official may be very restricted. In some cases the law may be very specific. In other cases fairly specific administrative rules designed to implement the law may be written or at least reviewed by top officials in the political layer. Hence certain decisions—whether a student is eligible for governmental financial aid, whether an individual is entitled to certain social security, health, or welfare benefits—these and similar types may in fact be made by those who wrote the laws rather than by rule-applying bureaucrats. But rules made at or near the top can seldom be so detailed as to precisely govern all specific cases. Intermediate layers of a bureaucracy may have the task of writing more specific implementing instructions, so that officials at this layer rather than administrators in the field decide how much of a subsidy payment a farmer is due, what kind of governmental assistance may be given to a person in business, who is eligible for food stamps, whether a particular college is entitled to government funds for certain purposes. And generally, the greater the complexity of the sphere of activity, and the greater the need for technical expertise, the broader the grants of authority to bureaucrats up and down the hierarchy tend to be. Hence, it is frequently bureaucrats who decide whether a particular merger of business firms is "in restraint of trade" and hence illegal; whether a particular bus fare or truck rate is "just and equitable and in the public interest"; what consumers will pay for eggs, milk, butter, oranges; how much money shall circulate in the economy; what environmental standards industry must conform to; what stocks may be traded on a stock exchange; which drugs may be sold over the counter, which by prescription only, and which not at all.

In all cases this entails rule-making, sometimes of major importance or sometimes less so, but in all cases it involves decision-making by appointed officials who are not always subject to control by elected officials or by those who have overall responsibility for governing. This major decision-making authority is even greater in those systems in which the government owns and operates some or all economic enterprises: the power-generating TVA in the United States; British operation of coal, steel, and other industries; the Soviet government's total control of its economy.

Discretionary bureaucratic authority is particularly inherent in so-called contingency legislation, which authorizes the executive establishment to take certain actions when certain contingencies arise—to impose wage-price controls or expand unemployment benefits or farm subsidies under certain loosely-defined economic conditions; to impose tariffs when imports threaten certain industries; to channel funds into certain areas or projects given certain conditions. Again, the rules describing such contingencies can seldom be defined with precision. Bureaucracies charged with implementing and enforcing certain laws also have de facto discretionary authority with respect to vigor of enforcement. This results partly from the fact that bureaucracies never have the personnel needed to vigorously enforce all laws, and partly because enforcement standards again are seldom precisely written into law. Hence the Department of Justice has substantial discretionary authority with regard to enforcement of anti-trust or civil rights legislation, as the Environmental Protection Agency has with enforcement of environmental standards.

Bureaucratic power also stems from the advisory roles of bureaucrats. Politicians at or near the top of the decision-making hierarchy invariably are generalists. This pertains not merely to chief executives and their inner circle of advisors, but also to top level appointed officials within cabinets or those who head the major departments and ministries. They must be generalists, for their function is to coordinate and integrate governmental activity within the framework of generalist perspectives and the broad public rather than narrow special interests. But generalists need expertise, and as such they often become captives of the specialist—experts they are supposed to control and supervise. No president, secretary of defense, minister of foreign affairs, or secretary of agriculture can function effectively without the expert information and recommendations of specialist subordinates knowledgeable about military, foreign, or agricultural matters and problems, and this need for specialized expertise extends well down the hierarchy of any government. The same resources of technical expertise have given bureaucracies a powerful role during legislative and policy-making deliberation phases. In many systems— such as the American—they function vigorously and powerfully as lobbies when policies are formulated, bills are drafted, legislatures and their committees deliberate on legislation, and presidents consider whether to ratify or veto legislation. Indeed it is quite common for policy-proposals to be spawned within bureaucracies, for bills to be drafted by them, and for amendments or counter-proposals to originate from bureaucratic offices—or from interest groups which in effect constitute the clients of certain bureaucracies.

Hence, the task of assessing bureaucratic power within a decision-making system has become an increasingly important one in both its aspects: the scope and importance of the bureaucracy's own decision-making authority, and the scope and intensity of its influence over decision-making by other structures of the system. Such analysis again entails rigorous empirical examination—both in institutional and process terms —of the roles the bureaucracy plays, the reasons for such roles, the extent to which such roles make for political power, and the controls exercised over bureaucratic activities by the chief executive, the legislature, the judiciary, or by other elements of the political system such as parties, interest groups, and press. Elite analysis can also be very fruitful with respect not only to the power of the bureaucracy but also evaluation of the extent to which it is likely to serve the public rather than merely private interests—the interests of the bureaucratic class itself, or those of the social groups or strata from which the top bureaucracy originated or is linked and affiliated with.

JUDICIAL INSTITUTIONS AND POWER

Analysis of the power of judicial institutions has two important aspects: the role of the judiciary in the power relationship between government and society, and its role within the decision-making system.

The first aspect essentially entails the extent to which the judicial system functions as a tool of government or of society. In any political system, the judiciary serves to some extent as an instrument used by government to control the entire society, as a means whereby the government can impose its will on either all people or on certain groups or strata or individuals. Yet at least within the framework of the democratic ethos, we also consider law and the judicial system as an instrument of society —as a means whereby people can protect themselves against arbitrary and capricious governmental actions, against unwarranted intrusion by governmental authority, for the protection of basic human rights and freedoms, for maintenance of some kind of balance between majority and minority rights, and as a means of ensuring equality of treatment before the law.

The independence of courts from executive and legislative branches control is one factor which tends to make the judiciary a tool of society. No judicial system is completely autonomous. Courts are dependent on other branches for financial appropriations, for laws governing their structure and procedures, for the selection of judges or for criteria governing their selection. Also, courts cannot enforce their own decisions but are dependent on executives at all levels of government and even on frequently independent-minded police agencies. Prosecutors, who in theory may be officers of the court pledged to work for justice, are members of the executive branch. Courts cannot take the initiative with respect to cases, and this task frequently falls on other branches due to the inadequate resources of individuals or groups in society. Legislatures and executives may in effect overturn judicial decisions by passing new legislation, and some do this ex post facto, as when the Indian Supreme Court held that the Prime Minister had violated the constitution, but the parliament was pressured into making her actions quite constitutional.

Yet empirical examination reveals that there are differences in judicial autonomy to the point where they are clear-cut differences in kind. In totalitarian and many authoritarian systems the courts nakedly function as instruments of government, laws are such that an individual can be punished for any action disliked by the executive, procedures give the accused no chance, and in some instances judicial decisions clearly have been dictated by executives. In such systems it is not uncommon that when a new regime or party comes to power members of the old regime are given a so-called fair trial, and then speedily hung for such offenses as treason or corruption in office.

Similar qualifications pertain to questions of judicial impartiality, objectivity, and adherence to strict norms of justice. Judges may be deeply learned in law and truly concerned with the principles of justice and equal treatment before the law. But they are also humans and as such reflect their own backgrounds, norms, values, perspectives, and prejudices. And judicial systems around the world generally reflect either the prevailing culture, or the culture of the dominant elites, and it is these and not objective norms which define justice as interpreted by judges and courts. Nonetheless, again, some judicial systems do adhere more closely to more objective standards, do strive for equality before the law. Others are quite blatantly subjective, and define justice in terms of the interests of the dominant elites.

The second aspect of the role of judicial systems entails the question whether judges merely interpret or in reality make law, or to what extent the role of the courts is limited to rule-adjudication in specific cases—the interpretation of laws in the light of specific actions, the resolution of conflicts over and determination as to whether or not a rule has been violated, and the imposition of appropriate penalties for violations. A clear-cut distinction is no more possible in this respect than it is between rule-making and application, for any interpretation may involve a modification or expansion of the text in statutes. But in most systems—in authoritarian because of executive controls, in democratic because of constitutional or other legal provisions—judicial decision-making is largely confined to the rule-adjudication function because individual decisions seldom have far-reaching implications.

By contrast, in the American system, courts play a major rule-making role—particularly but not only the Federal Supreme Court—because of the power of judicial review and the authority of courts to interpret legislation. Thus the constitutionality of legislative and executive actions upon challenge, may be reviewed by the courts, unlike in Britain where constitutionality is determined by the parliament. Actions taken by bureaucrats and executives are also subject to challenge in the courts on the basis that such actions are not in conformity with the content of specific laws, or with the intent of the lawmakers. As a consequence, policy-decisions of major magnitude have been made by the Supreme Court in such diverse spheres as civil rights, anti-trust policy, the rights of accused, representation in legislatures, and in a variety of economic, social, and religious spheres.

Both of these aspects of judicial power can be approached through a combination of legal, institutional, process, and elite analysis. Careful analysis of constitutions, basic laws, major elements of legal codes, and major judicial decisions can provide important data with regard to the primary role of courts and their roles in rule-making. However, the analysis must proceed with some care, for in many cases the rights of citizens may be so qualified that none in fact exist. Even the American Bill of Rights appears to grant people some absolute rights, but court decisions as well as executive and legislative practices have in fact modified them substantially—such as the apparent unlimited right of free speech. Combined legal and institutional analysis provides data about the structure of courts and about the rights of and possibilities for appeal through various layers of the court system. But again process analysis is essential to determine what actually happens within the judicial system, what kinds of procedures are actually in use which affect the rights, roles, and respective powers of government versus citizens. Analysis of judicial procedures and decisions are also essential to assess the rule-making role of courts —the magnitude of judicial decisions, their political impact and consequences. And elite analysis can be very useful in assessing or evaluating the probabilities for equal justice given the types of people recruited for major judicial roles.

PATTERNS OF INFLUENCE OVER DECISION-MAKING

Finally, the analysis of power in decision-making must include analysis of patterns of influence over individuals, groups, branches, and institutions within the decision-making system. For the degree of pluralism, competition, and representation which really prevails within a system depends very much on the degree which prevails within patterns of influence. Consequently, these patterns have consequences with respect to both the basic nature of systems and their capability and effectiveness. And for such analysis, process and elite analysis are much more useful than constitutional or institutional approaches.

The basic sources of influence patterns are, of course, the various factors explored in Parts II and III of this book: the ideas and interests of the society as a whole and of its various segments and strata, generated by the cultural, social, economic, and geographic setting. These in turn are relayed as demand and support inputs, of varying effectiveness depending on the extent to which they are energized by power, via the linkage-communication system. And within the decision-making system, these ideas and interests interact with those of the authoritative decision-makers, to produce policy outputs and consequent patterns of value allocation.

Specific environmentally-rooted and idea-interest based demands are transmitted and reach decision-makers in the form of three kinds of influence:

INTERNALIZED INFLUENCE

Officials with roles in decision-making (executives, legislators, bureaucrats, judges) will be influenced by their own, internalized ideas and interests, or by their "conscience." They have their own political (and sometimes other) interests to consider and the possible impact of a decision on such interests. And they have their own ideas as to what is good, rational, just, or in the public interest. Yet even their own ideas and interests are environmentally rooted. Their ideas may reflect the ideas prevailing within the society, or within the particular segment or strata from which they originated. Their perception of interests may similarly reflect common patterns of interests within the society; or the interests of the groups they originated from, are closely associated with, or represent. In essence, American policy-makers are likely to believe in American principles as Russians believe in Marxist-Leninist principles. Liberals are likely to support liberal causes, ex-business people are likely to be sympathetic to the interests of business as ex-farmers or labor leaders to agricultural and labor interests, and members of individual tribes, religious groups, or ethnic groups, are likely to reflect such interests.

But several factors combine to make decision-makers open and responsive in varying degrees, and in varying situations, to other influence sources. In specific conflict situations, they may be highly uncertain as to what might be a good and just decision in the public interest, or what the consequences of a certain kind of decision might be for their own interests. When confronted with specific problems they may be highly pragmatic, and actively seek outside information and expertise (with attendant influence) on how a specific problem is best resolved. They may recognize that their roles in conflict resolution requires accommodation and adjustment among varied competing demands. Or they may simply have a sense of fair play, and hence give many others a chance to be heard and to influence them.

INTRA-GOVERNMENTAL INFLUENCES

Specific individuals or groups of decision-makers are constantly barraged by information, views, proposals, advice, recommendations, from other individuals and groups within the government who attempt to influence the decisions of their colleagues. And individuals and groups frequently solicit such information, views, and advice on specific issues. Sources of influence include individuals and groups within the target's own branch, agency, or office; with other branches and agencies; and within branches and agencies at other levels of government. An individual legislator, for example, may be exposed to a barrage of influence from other legislators, from a variety of bureaucratic agencies, from state and local government officials, and from the chief executive. Such influences again may reflect environmentally-generated demands, or the ideas and interests of those wielding influence, or the vested institutional interests of a particular branch, agency, or level of government.

EXTRA-GOVERNMENTAL INFLUENCE

A similar barrage of influence is usually exerted by individuals and groups outside the governmental structure. Most of this usually emanates from interest groups and political parties, but may also emanate from the other sources discussed in connection with linkage-communication systems: mass media, electorate constituencies, prominent private citizens acting on their own behalf, may all have some impact, as may public opinion polls or election results.

Elite combined with institutional analysis can be helpful in determining the specific patterns of influence prevailing within a system, the configuration of power inherent in such prevailing patterns, and the degree of pluralism, competition, and representation which usually prevails. These approaches, as they focus on the social origins of the political elites within the government, as well as on other characteristics of political officials, and on similar characteristics of those with leadership roles in the linkage-communication system, can provide such general overall data. But process analysis, whereby the actual processes of decision-making with respect to varied types of policy spheres are carefully and empirically examined, tends to be more accurate and fruitful.

The Consequences of Decision-Making Systems

12

The location and distribution of power within a decision-making system is a key not only to determining the basic nature of a political system, but also to the assessment of its capabilities and effective performance. It is also a key to assessing a system's capacity to attain goals, to maintain or develop stability, and to adapt to changing conditions. This relationship between power, capability, and effectiveness poses what is perhaps the most critical problem confronting modern societies: the problem of developing some kind of "judicious balance" between concentration and dispersion of power. Concentration of power may enhance certain governmental capabilities and certain aspects of effectiveness, but it also precludes democracy and tends to impair other capabilities and other aspects of effectiveness. Dispersion of power promotes pluralism, competition, and representation in decision-making, and enhances certain governmental capabilities; however, it is often at a high cost with respect to political effectiveness.

In this chapter we elaborate on these basic themes by first exploring the political consequences of power distribution patterns for political capability and effectiveness. This is followed by a discussion of four major universal contemporary trends with respect to the power relationships discussed in Chapter 11: the expansion of governmental power over society, shifts in the direction of national rather than regional or local power, and the expansion of executive and bureaucratic power. These shifts in power appear to be related to capability; that is the perceived or actual greater capability of these levels and branches of government to effectively respond to the needs of modern societies. However, these trends pose significant challenges to the stability and effectiveness of all types of political systems, and particularly to the future of democracy. Major questions, which should be asked during political analysis, relate to these problems. To what extent does the distribution of power within the government contribute to or detract from specific governmental capabilities and aspects of effectiveness? To what extent can power within government be redistributed, considering the political culture, the socio-economic situation, and the power distribution pattern within the society? What might be the consequences for the future stability and effectiveness of the political system?

THE POLITICAL CONSEQUENCES OF POWER

Power distribution patterns affect the degree to which decision-making is pluralistic, competitive, and representative. They are also related to the two other characteristics discussed in Chapter 10: structural-functional differentiation, and institutionalization and formalization of decision-making. The dispersion of specialized functions to specialized branches and agencies of government is necessary for effective government, but it also results in dispersion of power, which may hinder effectiveness; for example, the dispersion of authority to many congressional committees and to numerous bureaucratic agencies. Power competition may also lead to the creation of more structures as government officials or interest groups scramble for the creation of special structures to promote their interests. Similar competition may produce more institutionalization and formalization in decision-making, as varied groups seek the adoption of formal legal rules in decision-making to institutionalize their power. This in turn may disperse power more widely, and reduce governmental flexibility for effectiveness. These and similar problems arise as the result of the relationship between power and capability

POWER AND CAPABILITY

Political capability requires power (among other requisites). Capability entails ability to do something, to get something done. In politics it involves influencing the thought and behavior of people—decision-makers, elites, ordinary mortals—to do what needs to be done in order to attain goals. The goals may be highly controversial since they involve value preferences, but whatever the goals, power in terms of influence over people is necessary. Even the basic domestic security function of government requires capability to maintain domestic order by influencing people. And conversely, people must have the capability to influence their government to ensure that it will function as their instrument. But just as capability is partly dependent on power, so the latter may be dependent on capability and effectiveness. When the elites or masses of a society assess their government as being capable of doing what they perceive needs to be done, the government accrues the resources of prestige, credibility, and good will. Perceived capability may enhance the government's resources of wealth and economic power as taxpayers grumble but still pay their taxes and as businesses, farmers, and workers may complain about governmental intervention but nonetheless at least tolerate a major governmental economic role. Conversely, governmental credibility and prestige will dwindle and support will erode as a government's performance is assessed as poor. The same relationship appears to exist between the power and perceived capabilities of individual levels, branches, and agencies of government. More power tends to drift into the hands of those who have a reputation for or are perceived to have greater capabilities for timely, swift, decisive, and effective action, simply because most humans are inclined to place more trust in those who seem more capable of resolving their needs and problems. But conversely, trust will decline when it is seen as having been misplaced or betrayed.

POWER AND EFFECTIVENESS

Effective performance by a system requires relative effectiveness of decision-making processes. As discussed in Chapter 3, three kinds of abilities are entailed in such effectiveness, and all three are enhanced by a judicious balance between concentration and dispersion of power.

Decision-making systems must have the ability to make timely decisions with respect to both immediate and future problems. Substantial dispersion of power, as well as formalization of decision-making and dispersion of functions among many governmental structures, inhibits this capability. In such settings prolonged and complex bargaining is necessitated by competition among plural power centers or governmental structures, and rigid formal rules often impede rather than facilitate rapid decision-making. This kind of bargaining is characteristic of the American system. Any major issue invariably arouses intense competition between and within the executive and legislative branches, among and within separate bureaucracies with institutional and other interests at stake, and among numerous and powerful interest groups. Such bargaining frequently leads to agonizing delays in decision-making even with respect to pressing problems at the moment. It also often results in situations where some powerful group or branch can effectively veto any decision likely to impair its interests. This situation is even worse in coalition governments, in which prolonged bargaining is necessary to determine the composition of the executive branch—just to decide who will make the decisions.

Timely action is enhanced when substantial influence is wielded by one branch or individual (such as the chief executive) over other institutions involved in decision-making. Concentration of power in a small decision-making group, such as a cabinet, has similar consequences. Timely decision-making is even more enhanced when power is concentrated in the hands of some authoritarian dictator or oligarchy which can function with few formal or institutional restraints. But such leaders tend to make timely policies only with respect to problems which they consider to be immediate or crucial problems—and more often than not this means problems which they consider threats to their monopoly of power. Timely policy-making requires timely and valid information about what the pressing problems of the society really are, and what kinds of lesser problems are likely to become serious in the future. Many authoritarian governments have shown even less concern than democratic ones about social injustice or religious, racial, or ethnic discrimination which tend to produce massive social unrest, or about looming energy needs, or the consequences of economic policies for the physical environment. Their usual response is to take timely action by using armed force to crush some anomic outbreak, or by jailing those who speak up about the unresolved needs of the society. In essence systems of concentrated power tend to impede the development of autonomous infrastructures whose communication function is essential for the making of timely policies, simply because such structures are viewed as threats to power.

The ability to make effective policies, which are likely to at least alleviate basic problems, is another important ingredient of effective decision-making. Over-dispersion of power again tends to have negative consequences as intense and complex competition among many power centers and governmental institutions forces accommodation of many and diverse interests during bargaining processes, and compromise outcomes which may satisfy many governmental and social groups, but fail to come to grips with basic problems. The worst cases again involve coalition governments. In these, efforts to accommodate all coalition partners—essential to maintain the coalition—produces either inaction lest one partner be displeased, or programs which satisfy all parties but merely paper over basic problems.

But the American system of checks and balances frequently has similar consequences. Attempts to develop an energy policy have required concessions to oil and coal enterprises, power companies, the automobile industry, environmentalists, varied manufacturing enterprises, truckers, commuters, Sunday drivers, and many others, with the net result that bills which do make it through the rule-making maze are hardly effective in terms of assuring future ample energy supplies at minimal costs or with minimal environmental damage. The American tax structure is a nightmare of complexity because of similar complex bargaining, and considering the numerous concessions that have to be made, it is often surprising that some economic policies sometimes do work to some degree.

Complex structural differentiation also makes it difficult to effectively coordinate and integrate varied spheres of governmental activity, as for example when the Department of the Treasury pursues easy money policies, the Federal Reserve Board a tight monetary policy, the President attempts to restrict governmental spending, and the Congress enacts bills which are certain to involve a major governmental deficit. The same kinds of ineffective policies usually result when power is dispersed among too many units of local government. Policies which effectively reduce air pollution are hardly possible when power to make them is vested in several adjacent industrial states. The principle of home rule is not only a very democratic but also very useful principle insofar as it pertains to local decisions with respect to local problems. But when it results in balkanization of local jurisdiction over an area which is one interdependent economic, social, and geographic unit—such as in 1,113 governmental units having jurisdiction over the greater Chicago area—policies which resolve local transportation, housing, education, air and water pollution, and a host of other problems, are hardly possible.

But excessive concentration of power may also have negative consequences for effective policy-making, as may informal processes which make possible arbitrary and capricious decisions by a powerful few. Authoritarian leaders may be able to eliminate bargaining, restrict participation in decision-making, and impose decisions with but minimal concessions to varied elements. However, if competition is eliminated, policy effectiveness depends solely on the wisdom, rationality, and sense of the public interest of those who monopolize power—a risky course for any society. A system may be fortunate and have wise and skillful oligarchic leaders capable of making effective policies, but there is no guarantee that goals pursued by authoritarian elites will be responses to major needs or aspirations of the society. But in any case, effective policy-making depends on a continuing inflow from society of accurate, reliable, and expert information about what needs to be done, the specifics of problems, the approaches that might work, the specifics of possible solutions—all of which require substantial competition within the kind of autonomous infrastructure which authoritarian regimes seldom tolerate.

Effective policy-making also requires some dispersion of decision-making authority to specialized governmental structures which have expertise in their respective spheres—particularly to specialized bureaucracies. Such dispersion of power poses problems in any system with respect to control by generalists at the top and with respect to coordinating and integrating multiple decisions in various individual spheres to ensure overall effective policy. Authoritarian regimes invariably have a complex and extensive bureaucratic apparatus, but one that is lacking in autonomy. This helps with respect to integration and coordination. But the emphasis is placed on centralized control, obedience to the top, loyalty and conformity rather than innovation and creativity, sharp restrictions on what those down in the hierarchy may or may not do, penalties for reporting information unpopular to those at the top, and many other factors which impede effective decision-making. In the long run, it is probably safer to count on competitive processes for rational and effective policies than on leaders who pretend to be all-knowing and all-wise.

The third ingredient of effectiveness—effective implementation—is similarly afflicted by problems of power distribution, institutionalization, and structural differentiation. Policies and programs will not be effective unless they become action programs; decisions will not be effective until they are implemented in terms of influencing human actions and behavior so that established goals are in fact attained. The concentration of power in one governmental structure inhibited by few formal rules may be conducive for execution of decisions. Authoritarian rulers may have tight control over a monolithic bureaucracy for administration of executive decrees; they may have firm control over the military establishment and police force and an army of police informants capable of extracting obedience on the basis of fear and terror; they may have a monopoly with respect to socialization processes and thus be able to wield substantial thought control over the citizenry. Yet fear and terror, and thought processes which emphasize obedience and conformity, are hardly conducive to other qualities which make for effective implementation—such as creative and innovative rule-application and decision-making at lower levels which truly ensures that policies will be implemented so as to attain goals. And in the long-run, such authoritarian systems invariably have great difficulty in attaining what is really essential for effective policy implementation—voluntary compliance, whether reluctant or enthusiastic, on the part of affected social forces, and particularly on the part of non-political elites and the otherwise politically-relevant strata of society.

Some dispersion of power is conducive also to effective policy implementation. To engender the support needed for voluntary compliance, the power structure within the decision-making system must be somewhat congruent with the power structure in the society, and this entails responsiveness to demands for participation in decision-making. The varied elites of the society who demand some participation, and who can influence people and varied social forces to support or actively or passively resist governmental decisions, must be accommodated. And if and when masses began to demand some degree of participation, and are spurned and alienated, fear and terror alone will not ensure obedience. Voluntary compliance is difficult to attain when policies are rammed down the throats of organized or unorganized interest groups and social forces. Similar considerations pertain to dispersion of power to bureaucracies charged with policy implementation. Regardless of tight and centralized controls, bureaucrats are famous for their imaginative abilities to evade, pay lip-service to, water-down, and even to sabotage and nullify policies they dislike. Hence, as bureaucrats demand some participation or autonomy in decision-making (as they invariably do), responsiveness becomes essential—not only because policy-makers need their information and expertise for making effective policies, but also because they need their information as to what kinds of policies bureaucrats and affected social forces will buy, and because they need voluntary compliance by bureaucrats to ensure implementation in an effective way.

POWER AND GOVERNMENTAL CAPABILITIES

Similar considerations pertain to the five types of political capabilities discussed in Chapter 3. Extractive, regulative, distributive, and symbolic capabilities may be enhanced by substantial concentration of power, yet these are linked with responsive capability—the ability to respond to demand inputs from various sectors and strata of the society. This is enhanced by substantial dispersion of power as well as by institutionalization-formalization and structural differentiation in decision-making. Capabilities are ultimately linked with the ingredient of support, and the latter is at least partly generated when governmental outputs roughly and in the long run match widely held expectations of benefits.

Effective extraction of material resources from the society is essential, for most policies require money and other material values. The Politburo of the Soviet Union has little difficulty in extracting taxes from its citizens: the small oligarchy can quickly make tax decisions, and has a centrally-controlled system which makes collection of onerous taxes relatively easy. In Britain as in the United States, proposals to increase taxes encounter numerous obstacles and veto points, and more often than not fail to generate the needed revenues. The military regime of Argentina, like most authoritarian regimes, has little trouble imposing a heavy tax burden, and has an army of tax collectors and policemen to extract it from the pockets of businessmen and individuals. Yet tax evasion is as widespread there as in many authoritarian states. What is lacking is responsiveness to the demands of elites and social forces whose support is essential for voluntary compliance with revenue-raising edicts; what prevails, due at least partly to low responsiveness, are attitudes which clothe tax evasion with the aura of respectability and even legitimacy. The extraction of material resources is also not merely a taxation problem. It entails the availability of material resources in the society—the state of the economy and the level and rate of economic development. And as previously discussed, over-concentration of power may have negative consequences for effective economic policies.

The same pertains to the extraction of human resources—the individuals with the requisite knowledge, skills, expertise, talent, and other qualities needed for various governmental roles. The capability of a government to attract and recruit such talent is partly dependent on the effectiveness of its recruitment machinery and on its reward system, but as discussed in Part III, autonomous and equitable infrastructures can play very valuable if not essential roles. A competetive system generally seems more likely to recruit, groom, and promote human resources of high quality, particularly since authoritarian regimes in the interest of retention of power are prone to place a higher priority on obedience, loyalty, and conformity than on skill, competence, or talent. And again the responsive capability of a system is linked to the extractive capability: individuals are more likely to be attracted to political careers if they are not alienated by the system.

Regulative and distributive capabilities are similarly linked with responsive ability. Again it appears that systems of concentrated power can make speedy decisions for the regulation of the economic, social, and cultural activities of their people and for the distribution of values to groups they select as favored beneficiaries. But both require effective policy-making so that regulation will produce material and non-material values to be distributed, and as previously discussed, over-concentration of power frequently leads to ineffective policies. Further, the ability to regulate ultimately depends on ability to influence the behavior of affected groups—businessmen, workers, ethnic or racial groups, and many others. Authoritative decisions backed by the coercive power of the state again are simply not enough; voluntary compliance, more likely to result from responsiveness, is essential. Even the symbolic capability of a government is linked with responsiveness. The Soviet system has a variety of means available for manipulating symbols and slogans to condition popular attitudes, and has tight control over socialization processes; in democracies, competition among various socialization processes inhibits the symbolic capability of governments to develop supportive attitudes. Yet the manipulation of symbols can seldom offset the disaffection and alienation which invariably develops when governments are seen as unresponsive to a people's needs and problems.

Systems of concentrated power tend to be weak in responsive capability simply because it takes power—the currency of politics—to move governments. When power is concentrated, policies tend more to be the products of the interests and ideas of decision-makers and less those of environmental forces, simply because those denied access to or participation in government lack the means to influence decision-making. Assured responsiveness requires substantial dispersion of power, substantial institutionalization and formalization to ensure access or participation, and structural differentiation to provide linkage with specialized decision-making structures and the groups affected by their decisions. Responsiveness in particular requires an effective and autonomous linkage-communication structure, which authoritarian systems invariably view as a threat to power.

Power and Adaptation to Change

Substantial concentration of power may be essential for a government to make the timely and effective policies needed for a changing society —particularly when environmental changes produce rising expectations and new or intensifying distribution demands. When the poor, or other groups and strata hitherto ignored by decision-makers—landless peasants, underpaid workers, slum dwellers, racial or religious or ethnic minorities, university students, intellectuals—begin to demand social justice and degrees of economic, social, and political equality, political systems must respond and adapt lest they face mounting instability, chaos, or revolution. The institution of reform invariably requires reform-minded regimes with the power needed to effect reforms. Yet too often, reform-minded authoritarian regimes have lost their way, have become new privileged classes out of touch with the masses whose demands for reform brought them to power, and have tended to equate reform with their own particular material or power interests. And changing environmental settings also tend to bring changes in participation demands on the part of new elites and social forces, which systems of concentrated power have a low capability to respond to.

POWER AND CAPABILITY: FOUR CONTEMPORARY TRENDS

During the past several decades four major trends with respect to power relationships have developed throughout the world—significant shifts in the direction of more governmental, national, executive, and bureaucratic power. Conventional wisdom has it that these trends have their origin in the corruptive nature of power—Lord Acton's famous dictum that power tends to corrupt and absolute power tends to corrupt absolutely. More specifically it is argued that governments, executives, and bureaucrats constantly seek to expand their power and functions, and use what power they have for such expansion—particularly more "power-hungry" presidents, legislators, and bureaucrats. There is something to this, for it is an observed natural tendency on the part of all organizations, political and nonpolitical, to seek survival and growth. But conventional wisdom overlooks the more fundamental roots of these trends—the relationship between power and capability. These power shifts have primarily developed because, rightly or wrongly, elites and masses perceive national level governments, chief executives, and bureaucrats as having the relatively greater capability and resources to cope with the needs and problems of modern, complex, interdependent industrial societies.

The Evolution of the Positive-Welfare State

Although few governments of the past have limited their functions to the basic tasks of domestic security and defense against external enemies, the scope of contemporary governments is massive when contrasted with the past. Totalitarian systems are still few in number, but governmental intervention in all spheres of human activity is today a universal phenomenon. The modern state is a positive-welfare state, which attempts to play a positive role in providing for the general welfare of the society. As such it tends to play an expanding role in managing and regulating the economic sphere, either directly by ownership and operation of some means of production, or by varied interventionist measures such as wage-price controls, direct or indirect subsidies to preferred economic enterprises, or various programs designed to have an impact on the economy. It supports or conducts a variety of programs designed to benefit either the entire society or specific elements of it—housing, health, social security, welfare, unemployment compensation, to name but a few. Its tax structure is no longer simply designed to raise revenue, but to pursue certain objectives—to indirectly subsidize certain industries or economic sectors, or to redistribute income between the rich and poor, or to promote equality. These and thousands of other governmental tasks, most of which are accepted as commonplace, were virtually unheard of a few decades ago in many systems. All of this involves a major expansion of the power of government over society, not always accompanied by a commensurate expansion of the power of a people over government. While some such expansion—particularly the total control of totalitarian systems—is due to goals and power of some governments, the fundamental root lies in the need of a modern industrial economy and society for some central point of management, control, and coordination. In an economy consisting of thousands of major and millions of minor industries, business establishments, banks, farms, labor unions, and other kinds of economic enterprises, only governments have the needed steering capability. Governments have or are perceived as having the resources—legal authority, economic power inherent in its legal authority, organizational resources, information, skill, expertise, and sometimes credibility and good will—to perform such needed functions. The law of supply and demand and the operation of the market place may at one time have been adequate for running simpler economies, but it alone appears to be no longer adequate for today's economic settings. And although the idea of free enterprise is still an integral part of many cultures, in the real world the controversy swirls not around the principle of governmental intervention, but about the degree of such intervention and the allocation of benefits resulting from it.

In Chapter 6 it was explained that there seem to be four conditions in which people stop seeking goals through self-help and voluntary cooperation and convert their demands into political demands. All four are present today, and are leading to demand patterns which result in expanding governmental action. The revolution of rising expectations among both the poor and the affluent has caused people to define more wants as needs which must be met—a higher standard of living, better housing and health care, security of income and in old age, more educational opportunities, and many other things. The complexity of modern society has made it difficult if not impossible to meet these culturally-defined needs by self-help or voluntary cooperation, hence governmental programs are demanded, and varied socio-economic forces call for governmental action to meet either general needs or those of specific groups —wage-price controls, programs to balance business-energy-environmental protection goals, programs to promote the interests of big business, small business, workers, farmers, consumers, the indigent, the elderly, students, and educators. Conceptions of scope have steadily expanded as the consequence of both demands and governmental action, so that governmental intervention in varied spheres is legitimized. And demands for governmental action multiply as varied groups acquire some resources of power, and either because of their own past experience or the experience of other groups, anticipate some degree of success in their efforts to pressure governments. The net result is the expansion of the functions of government, of its legal authority to perform them, and of its power over the society.

THE EROSION OF FEDERALISM AND LOCAL POWER

The same relationship between power and capability to respond to needs appears to be the major root of this universal trend. Although significant differences continue to prevail among political systems with respect to the territorial organization of authority, the general tendency has been a shift in political power away from subordinate levels and in direction of central national governments. The United States, Canada, Brazil, and some others continue to function as viable federal systems, in which substantial authority continues to be wielded by state and local units of government. Indeed the functions and the bureaucracies of these units have substantially expanded during the past few decades, and the degree to which state and local units of government have jealously guarded their prerogatives has created significant problems for the solution of problems which transcend the frontiers of these units. But despite these reservations, the universal trend has been in the direction of more authority and the performance of more functions by central national governments. Subordinate units are relegated more and more to positions of administrators of national policies, recipients of federal funds for their own programs, and decision-makers within the confines of nationally-directed policies and directives.

This trend is most basically due to the complexity of modern society and the development of the positive-welfare state. Modern societies are no longer decentralized ones which in an earlier age were relatively self-sufficient at local, provincial, or state level. An urbanized, mass, industrial society is an interdependent national society (and indeed is becoming more and more an interdependent international society, which raises questions even about the viability of the modern nation-state). Industrial economies are national economies, while state economies are simply inextricable parts of the whole. Major economic problems—of unemployment, recession, inflation, energy supplies—require national approaches, as do problems of pollution resulting from national economic growth. Other needs—transportation, welfare, education, social security, health care—similarly are interrelated national needs which defy independent local or state approaches. In the United States the expanding interpretation of certain constitutional clauses by the executive, legislative, and judicial branches—the interstate commerce, general welfare, and other clauses—has merely facilitated this shift of power. The real root lies in the simple reality that the political frontiers of states today are archaic; they are products of history and no longer constitute viable or rational social, economic, or cultural frontiers. Only larger units of government are capable of meeting needs and resolving problems which transcend such frontiers.

THE EXPANSION OF EXECUTIVE POWER

The shift in power away from legislative bodies in the direction of executive power is frequently exaggerated. Even in the days of more limited government, policy-making and legislative initiative was usually in the hands of the executive, while the legislature performed the function of restraining the executive and modifying, ratifying, or rejecting executive proposals. Also, some legislatures continue to function as vital and powerful elements of government. The American Congress continues to be the most powerful legislative body in the world and substantially restrains the Presidency; while the British House of Commons, which often gives the superficial appearance of functioning as a rubber stamp, plays a significant role in rule-making. But nonetheless the contemporary tendency is clear-cut and manifested by two trends. One is the demise of democracy—and consequent legislative authority—in many societies. The second is prevalent in those systems in which democracy continues to survive, manifested either by the continued growth of executive power without a concomitant growth in legislative power, or the declining role of legislatures as restrainers, modifiers and nullifiers of executive initiatives. And this tendency is apparent also at state and local levels of government.

Again, in some instances this trend may partly be due to the deliberate expansion of the powers of the office by some ambitious incumbents. But again the more fundamental root appears to be the objective or perceived greater capability of executive institution to meet the needs of modern governments and societies.

The development of the positive-welfare state has involved major changes in the nature of laws and other governmental actions. While the basic traditional function of law has been and continues to be the maintenance of social stability by defining the rights and obligations of citizens, modern law now involves all-embracing rules in a variety of economic, social, and cultural spheres. Further, modern legislation is marked by great technical complexity. Detailed and complex rules are required in a great variety of technical economic matters, and in social spheres such as housing, health and welfare, education, environmental protection, and race relations. This has led to the decline of legislative and the rise of executive power in several ways. First, due to the greater pluralism and diversity of interests and ideas present in mass complex societies, the organizational cohesion of legislatures and their capabilites to exercise leadership and power has further declined. Second, the volume and complexity of modern rule-making has led legislatures to concern themselves primarily with laws of an all-embracing broad-principle type, which define goals and the general nature of actions to be taken to pursue them, and then delegate to the executive broad discretionary and contingency authority with respect to the specifics of action. Third, the sheer volume of modern legislation has required great expansion of the implementation or administration role of the executive branch, which has involved expansion of executive decision-making authority, of the organizational resource of his bureaucracy, of economic resources and patronage which the executive can manipulate. Fourth, in such a large-scale complex political system the need for a top-level generalist who can effectively organize, plan, direct, supervise, coordinate, and provide a single point of leadership is accentuated. The overall consequence has also been a substantial increase in the prestige of the executive office, in the public tendency to focus on the executive as the point of leadership and responsibility, and even in the credibility of executives (with attendant consequences not merely for the executive office but the entire political system when public credibility and trust in the office declines).

THE EVOLUTION OF THE BUREAUCRATIC STATE

The development of the positive-welfare state and the expansion of executive power has in turn led to the evolution of the bureaucratic state. This has entailed not merely the expansion of the size but much more significantly of the functions and decision-making roles of the bureaucracy. As discussed earlier, bureaucrats are no longer merely administrators; modern rule application involves substantial rule-making and adjudication. Bureaucrats the world over are heavily involved in top-level policy development and in rule making at all levels due to their roles as advisors, lobbyists, and consultants in executive and legislative processes, and because the implementation of laws and executive decisions simply entails sometimes relatively unimportant but often highly important bureaucratic decision-making. As the positive-welfare state has entailed a tremendous growth in the volume and complexity of governmental tasks and legislation, and as such legislation has produced broad grants of discretionary authority to chief executives, so the sheer volume and complexity of decisions to be made has of necessity forced chief executives to further delegate such authority to their administrative arms—the bureaucracy.

This expansion of bureaucratic functions and power is another manifestation of this relationship between perceived or objective capabilities and power. Again, organizational dynamics has played a role: once established, bureaucracies—because of institutional needs and goals, their drive for self-preservation, and the extent to which bureaucratic job security, possibilities for increased pay and for promotion are linked with expansion of bureaucratic functions—seek to expand their roles and power. But much more significant is the capability of bureaucracies, inherent in their resources of information, skill, and expertise. Only government can meet the needs of a highly complex society, and the complex tasks of government require an army of specialists, experts, and managers.

IMPLICATIONS OF CONTEMPORARY TRENDS

The relationship between power and perceived or actual capability to meet the needs of modern society thus appears to be the most fundamental root of these universal trends. But these developments confront political systems with major problems relating to structural-functional arrangements, institutionalization of decision-making, and reordering of power relationships. In essence, what is involved are major problems of political adaptation to ensure stability, effectiveness, and efficiency in value creation and allocation.

The inadequacies of all types of modern governments are clearly visible and need not be spelled out at great length. If modern economic systems are incapable of running themselves, governmental economic intervention has not brought desired degrees of economic stability and growth. If self-help and voluntary cooperation are inadequate means for protecting the environment, enhancing security and improving standards of living, relieving the plight of the poor and underprivileged, meeting the health, housing, transportation, and other needs of urban societies, promoting equality, or generally improving the quality of life, governmental actions in these and many other spheres have also fallen far short of expectations. Governmental inadequacies are certainly the result of many factors—pressures from various powerful social forces, inadequate material resources to match rising expectations, vices and weaknesses of interest groups and political parties, and even incompetence among some governmental leaders and officials. But they can also be partly traced to institutionalized structural arrangements and power relationships.

Effectiveness requires a rational division of functions among and within branches of government and a rational complex of specialized structures to perform specialized tasks. It requires institutionalization so that explicit roles and functions with respect to decision-making are established and followed, and so that those with requisite information and expertise have access. And it requires power and authority commensurate with responsibility—the capability to do what is expected and needed. But to restructure a government so that all these requirements are met is a terribly complex and elusive task which involves many frustrating dilemmas and agonizing choices. For the establishment of the many specialized structures and institutions required for so many political tasks invariably entails substantial dispersion of power, with all the many negative consequences for effectiveness.

The universal response to the need for concentrated power and for a central point of leadership, coordination, and control has been the institutionalization of the power and roles of the chief executive and the subordination or elimination of the roles of legislatures. But in some instances this has led to an excessive concentration of power, in most systems to dispersion of power throughout a vast bureaucratic apparatus, and in many cases to a very ambiguous executive-legislative relationship. The United States is a case in point of the latter: we look to the Presidency for leadership and action, are fearful of giving the office the power commensurate with its responsibility, recognize congressional weaknesses, and tend to be quite ambivalent about the proper roles of the President and the Congress with respect to various policy spheres. Legislative institutions need restructuring so that they may function as responsible restraints on executive power and play effective decision-making roles. The dilemmas inherent in this are again exemplified by the American Congress. Effectiveness is enhanced by the dispersion of power to specialized and expert committees; responsiveness is enhanced by the principle of accountability to constituencies; but both effectiveness and responsiveness are significantly weakened by this dispersion of power to committees and individuals, by the inability of the Congress to function as a cohesive and coherent unit, by suspicions about political parties serving as unifying links, and by the fears and rivalries which preclude a unified leadership within the Congress.

Power relationships between national and lower levels of government also need restructuring, and the American system is another case in point. Despite its greater capability to deal with problems which transcend the frontiers of state and local governments, the growth of power of the federal government (and also of some state and city governments) has entailed the Curse of Bigness: in politics as in business, greater size often means greater effectiveness and efficiency, up to a certain point;

beyond that point it results in an enterprise which is so massive and top-heavy, overloaded, and ensnarled in its own red tape that ineffectiveness and inefficiency become its hallmarks. Restructuring is essential, involving the assignment of tasks and requisite power to those territorial units best qualified to handle varied kinds of responsibilities, but also involving requisite power to higher units to ensure capability for coordination. It probably also entails either the re-drawing of many state and local frontiers, or the development of new regional units of government with the power to deal with the problems which are regional in scope. And at each level of government the same dilemmas concerning executive-legislative relationships need resolution.

Acute as these power-capability dilemmas are for effectiveness, they are even more frustrating with respect to political efficiency. In some systems a society's needs may be so basic that concentrated power for capability to attain a single goal may be the overriding consideration—such as economic development in a society in which population growth is rapidly exceeding the food supply. But in most societies human goals are multiple and diverse, so that political efficiency is also necessary—the ability to maximize several values at minimum cost to others. Freedom from want is an important value, but so are freedom in other aspects, human dignity, justice, and security. Concentration of power may help to create the value of wealth for the society, and by so doing may in the long run advance social justice and real freedom of choice for those groups now too poor to enjoy real freedom. But at least in the short run, authoritarian systems invariably impose onerous costs in terms of the values of freedom, human dignity, and justice. Such systems may also provide substantial security by imposing strict law and order, but real security can hardly exist when a government rules through fear and terror and any person is subject to arbitrary arrest. Yet over-dispersion of power may have similar adverse consequences for efficiency. It may, by making systems overly responsive, lead to a situation in which the satisfaction of insatiable and self-indulgent human appetites becomes the principle goal of government.

Democracies have generally displayed greater capability for efficiency than authoritarian systems, but the four power trends confront democracies with major challenges. The positive-welfare state and the expansion of executive power represent a significant expansion of governmental and executive power over people. This poses the problem of structuring and dispersing power to ensure substantial pluralism, competition, and representation in decision-making, so as to ensure responsiveness and public influence over government but without substantial sacrifice of effectiveness. Within most democratic systems significant restraints persist with regard to governmental and executive power—dispersion of legal authority among several branches, the polyarchic configuration of power, the government's and executive's need for support, the final sanction of the ballot box. But history has amply supported the validity of the dictum that power tends to corrupt, and the "judicious balance" between concentration and dispersion of power continues to elude most democratic systems. The same holds with respect to the territorial organization of power. Reality suggests that in a modern large-scale society "grass roots control" is simply not feasible. Also, the conventional wisdom that local and state governments are closer to the people and hence more subject to popular control is somewhat questionable, for geographic proximity does not ensure responsiveness. In many smaller units of government substantially less pluralism prevails, decision-making tends to be dominated by a few powerful interests, and governments respond primarily to certain favored groups. In the American system, the less powerful groups of society have generally obtained more satisfaction at the national rather than at state or local levels of government. Nonetheless, the shift in the direction of national power does pose problems of responsiveness, and particularly responsiveness to special local, state, or regional needs.

The expansion of bureaucratic functions and power poses perhaps the most formidable problem for the effectiveness and efficiency of all political systems, and particularly for democracies. Governments need bureaucracies of size and complexity commensurate with the volume and complexity of governmental tasks. Rational efficiency and effectiveness requires division of labor and functional specialization and organization for the performance of specialized tasks. As the functions of government expand, ever-larger bureaucratic organizations, consisting of myriads of specialized agencies, become necessary. Specialized bureaus must be created for a vast complex of specialized economic functions—in agriculture, business, finance, commerce, labor; specialized service functions—in health, education, welfare, housing, transportation; and thousands of other tasks in varied social and cultural spheres. Such delegation of decision-making functions invariably entails substantial dispersion of power to the nooks and crannies of huge bureaucratic organizations.

Such dispersion of power poses problems with respect to both timely and effective decision-making. Timely decisions may be precluded by the time required to clear and coordinate decisions through a vast and complex bureaucratic maze—through sometimes dozens of agencies which have some interest in or function related to a particular decision or policy. Complex bargaining over what the policy or decision should be, with many concessions to bureaucratic interests, is invariably required, with frequent negative consequences for effective policies. Coordination and integration of the far-flung decisions and activities of numerous bureaus, to ensure that overall agricultural, financial, transportation, health, and other policies in individual spheres form a harmonious whole, or are coordinated and integral parts of a government's economic, social, or cultural policies, become more and more difficult to achieve as the bureaucracy grows larger. The principle of hierarchy for integration and coordination is helpful but not a simple or perfect solution. Related activities are grouped together into a single hierarchy—a Ministry of Health or Department of Commerce. The hierarchy is subdivided into a number of pyramids of related activities under the apex at the top. Someone at the top has complete authority over the entire hierarchy, as do various subordinate officials at each level of the authority structure, so that authority flows downward and accountability upward. And the entire hierarchy under the control of some minister and his subordinate officials, who in turn are under the control of the chief executive, should function as an effective, efficient, and coordinated decision-making apparatus. Unfortunately no political system, democratic or authoritarian, has yet devised an organizational structure or dynamic to transform this ideal into reality.

Related to this problem of specialization and dispersion of power is the problem of political or generalist control for effectiveness. Bureaucrats are and must be specialists. Some may be very narrow specialists—the expert in some particular health or financial field; some may have relatively broad perspectives and responsibilities, but still are primarily attuned to some specialized sphere of activity—a minister of health, or economic affairs, a secretary of defense or agriculture. As such, in theory they are supposed to be subject to control by generalists at the top of the bureaucratic hierarchy—the chief executive and his immediate assistants, those who have broader perspectives, who have the ultimate responsibility for government, and who in democratic systems are ultimately accountable to the public. As such, bureaucrats are supposed to be politically neutral and objective, to make decisions within the context of policies formulated at the top, and to function within the context of a command-obedience relationship.

Unfortunately, reality does not always reflect theory. Specialists tend to be devoted to their special interests, bureaucrats have their vested bureaucratic interests, and bureaucracies are always affiliated with and sometimes even controlled by powerful client groups—farmers, workers, businesspeople, teachers, doctors, housing interests. And those in charge at various levels of the various bureaucratic pyramids—bureau chiefs, department heads, ministers, chief executives—have but little time at their disposal, often lack the information or expertise needed for effective control of subordinates, and the sheer size and complexity of modern bureaucracies simply defies close control and supervision. Hence, a command-obedience relationship seldom exists even in totalitarian systems; commands from the top often must compete with other and sometimes stronger influences at work within bureaucratic hierarchies; and bureaucrats are often left to follow their own interests and momentum. The frequent net result is poorly coordinated decision-making in various nooks and crannies of the bureaucratic jungle; and on occasion or in some systems it may be decision-making in direct or disguised defiance of policies from the top.

These problems of structuring the bureaucratic state for effectiveness afflict all types of modern political systems. But they again pose some special problems for democracies—problems of ensuring responsiveness to the public will. Theoretically, policies are made by "political layer" of the government—by elected officials directly accountable to the public, or by top-level bureaucrats appointed and subject to dismissal by such elected officials and hence indirectly accountable to the public through these superiors. In theory, lower level officials are public servants who merely implement and administer the decisions made at or near the top. In theory they are accountable to their superiors, and not to other influences. Merit-based civil service systems which exist in all democracies reflect such theory. Designed to ensure competence, expertise, objectivity, and political neutrality, they base selection and promotion of civil servants on merit and qualifications for office, demand political neutrality and obedience to demands from the top, the administration of laws as demanded by the chief executive regardless of which party is in power, and in return are granted tenure. They may not be removed from office on political grounds (to preclude the incompetence which invariably results from spoils systems which enable politicians to staff public offices with their political adherents); and removal from office invariably entails complex and time-consuming procedures. Such arrangements are absolutely essential for effectiveness and efficiency, and many if not most civil service systems tend to produce the kind of public servant who functions as the theory demands.

But the basic problems remain. Civil servants are not mere administrators; more and more major decision-making is shifting out of the hands of elected representatives of the public and into the hands of appointed bureaucrats. More and more public policies tend to be spawned by appointed officials, and then sold to those accountable to the electorate. Regardless of their dedication as servants of the public, bureaucrats are also dedicated to their sphere of expertise and tend to define the public interest in terms of their special interests. Bureaucrats tend to be responsive to vested bureaucratic interests, and to the interests of their client interest groups, and the combination of these two frequently constitutes a formidable power bloc in politics. In modern complex systems a command-obedience relationship between chief executive and bureaucrat cannot exist. These problems cannot be resolved by eliminating or reducing the size or functions of the bureaucracy; neither can be done because modern political systems cannot function without them. The problem must be solved in realistic terms—how to structure the bureaucracy and establish power and function relationships which provide for effective democratic government.

The Policy Outputs of Political Systems

part V

So far we have been primarily concerned with the sources of and procedures relating to public policies, by which governments create and allocate values. Parts II and III discussed how environmental forces and linkage-communication structures generate policy initiatives and affect governmental decision-making with respect to such initiatives. Part IV discussed the characteristics of decision-making structures and processes and the role of power in such processes. Political analysis along these lines can tell us much about the nature, effectiveness, and efficiency of systems, and their prospects for stability and adaptation to change. But we must also include substantive analysis, such as the examination of the substance of public policies and their actual and potential consequences. A system's policy outputs constitute the final test of the extent to which the system functions as an effective and efficient instrument of society.

In Chapter 13 we turn to the subject of public policy analysis. We discuss first what such analysis involves, and what aspects of policies must be examined. We continue with a discussion of problems inherent in the assessment and evaluation of public policies, and particularly the problems relating to the relationship between means and ends. The chapter concludes with a discussion of the analysis of policy consequences: their impact on society's needs and problems, and their patterns of value creation and allocation inherent in policies.

Chapter 14 deals with a much broader theme, and to an extent summarizes the book by discussing policy outputs and their relationship to political change. We review the individual components of political systems (environmental settings and linkage-communication and decision-making systems), and we discuss questions which should be asked about changes possibly occurring within such components, their relationship to the policies of a system, and the potential consequences of such changes. This kind of analysis is of crucial importance, for it can tell us much about the prospects of future stability and effectiveness of any system, and about what needs to be done to either maintain or develop effective democracy.

The Analysis
of Patterns
# of Public Policy

13

Public policies constitute the expression of a political system's goals
and the means with which it pursues them. The purposes and objectives
of policies are to promote the professed values and goals of the society
or government, and the content of policies are the political action programs designed to pursue such values and goals. Public policy analysis
consequently is a most important sphere of political analysis, for it concerns itself with the system's ends and means. Yet it is also perhaps the
most difficult and complex aspect of political inquiry. It involves first of
all empirical examination of the policies themselves—the scope of public
policy, the apparent objectives of government in varied spheres, and the
general and specific content of policies. Considering the broad range of
contemporary governmental activity, this in itself is a challenging task.
But the primary purpose of such empirical inquiry relates to an even more
difficult task—empirical assessment and normative evaluation of the actual or potential consequences of policies, and their immediate and long-
range impact on the system and society.

To further complicate the problem, policy analysis cannot focus exclusively on the policies themselves. Once a decision is made to do something in some sphere, then subsequent decisions have to be made as to
how it shall be done, and processes or patterns of activity related to such
decisions have to be set in motion. Policy entails the selection of goals

and priority ordering among several goals. It also involves extracting and mobilizing resources so that goals may be pursued and the distribution of costs and benefits of policies and programs throughout the society. Finally, it entails implementation measures and controls for all of these processes, and subsequent modifications or changes of policy as governments recognize the need for alterations. In essence, policy analysis must consider the overall action programs of a government in general and in specific spheres, and not merely paper programs.

Considering these complexities, it obviously would take many volumes to adequately treat the subject of policy analysis. In the pages which follow, we confine ourselves to some broad generalizations about the nature and importance of such analysis.

THE SCOPE, OBJECTIVES, AND CONTENT OF POLICIES

One aspect of policy analysis entails the empirical examination of policy patterns to determine their general content and scope and the objectives they are designed to attain.

TYPES OF POLICY OUTPUTS

It is useful to distinguish among four types of policies which either singly or more typically in combination are involved in the pursuit of selected goals.

Extractive policies are designed to extract human and material resources from the society for public purposes. They include tax laws designed to extract needed revenues, sometimes the takeover of economic enterprises, the conscription of humans for civil or military services, or varied measures designed to recruit human talent and services needed for the performance of functions to attain varied goals.

Regulative policies are intended to regulate or influence the behavior of either the entire society, or of specific groups, for goal attainment. Wage-price controls may be imposed to combat inflation, interest rates or taxes may be manipulated to influence the behavior of investors, safety standards may be imposed to regulate the outputs of industry, equal rights legislation may be enacted in efforts to regulate the behavior of property owners, employers, or the society as a whole. Regulative policies may also be intended to enhance extractive policies.

Distributive policies directly or indirectly allocate various material and non-material values throughout the society. Social security and welfare programs distribute money to the elderly and the poor; civil rights measures are designed to distribute equality of opportunity; graduated income or other tax measures may have as their objective the redistribution of income from the more affluent to the poor. Procedural policies directly or indirectly establish structures and prescribe procedures with respect to the government and political system. Measures which attempt to control lobbying, prescribe nomination or election procedures, specify authority relationships between various levels and branches of government, establish new bureaucracies or reorganize the bureaucracy, fall into this category.

POLICY OBJECTIVES

Policies are formulated on the basis of certain objectives or goals which policy-makers strive to attain. One analytical task involves determining these apparent intentions of regimes, the values they apparently hope to create. But for this purpose the analyst must probe beneath the publicized statements of top-level policy-makers. For one, a rhetoric-reality gap frequently exists in most systems. Regimes may publicly proclaim certain goals, but actually strive to attain others; or some policy-makers may wish to steer in one direction, while others actually steer on a different course. Conservative regimes which pursue policies slanted in favor of certain elites frequently proclaim goals of reform and social justice strictly as window-dressing. Or top policy-makers in some systems may be truly committed to proclaimed goals of socialism, while others within that same system actually pursue economic and social policies of an entirely different sort.

For these and other purposes it is useful to distinguish between two levels of policy objectives. Most regimes subscribe to certain long-range aspirations formulated on the basis of the ideological framework which is used to legitimize the system. They may strive for rapid economic growth and industrialization, or for the elimination of economic dependence on other states. They may aspire to the goals of greater social justice and equality, land reform and the reduction of the gap between the rich and the poor, or the elimination of racial or religious discrimination. Or they may aspire to the maintenance or development of a new social order: democracy, democratic socialism, socialism, communism. In some instances such proclaimed aspirations may be sincere, in others they may be publicized only to enlist support. In either case, the extent to which shorter-range policies seem to match or seem likely to attain such longer-range objectives must be probed.

Intermediate or shorter-range objectives, ostensibly formulated within the context of long-range aspirations, are the goals which regimes strive to attain within a shorter time-frame. Policies to reduce inflation and unemployment may be designed to attain economic stability; top policies may be intended to stimulate business activity and to attain economic growth; anti-trust policies may be designed to maximize democracy and competition by curbing the economic and political power of giant economic enterprises. Nationalization of some industries, or the regulation of the economy, or land reform programs may be intended to pave the way for eventual social democracy or socialism. Or long-range social goals may involve specific policies intended to reduce inequality and discrimination. The analysis of such intermediate objectives should include not merely examination of the objectives themselves, but also the extent to which they appear to fit into the broader framework of long-range goals, and whether the probable consequences of short-term policies are such that long-range goals are likely to be attained—the means-ends problem to be discussed later. A regime may, for example, proclaim an objective of economic self-sufficiency, yet pursue specific energy policies which increase dependence on imported oil. Or a totalitarian elite may proclaim the aspiration of developing a truly classless egalitarian society, yet structure its socio-economic system so that it produces a new privileged class.

THE SCOPE OF POLICY OUTPUT PATTERNS

This analytical task involves assessment of the extent to which governmental actions and policies seem to be replacing individual efforts and voluntary cooperation among groups in society for the attainment of certain goals. More specifically, it entails assessment of which spheres of human activity—economic, social, cultural, political—seem to be of prime concern to governmental authorities; which spheres they appear to emphasize or neglect; the extent to which the sum total of public policy involves governmental intervention in all or specific spheres; and what trends seem to be developing with respect to patterns of governmental intervention.

Despite the universal trend in the direction of the positive-welfare state, significant differences continue to prevail with respect to degrees of intervention. In the economic sphere, some regimes practice the policy of public ownership of all or most means of production; others try to merge capitalism with state control in some form of state capitalism; still others opt for substantial economic planning by the state and strong direct controls over private enterprise; still others limit their economic roles to a variety of direct but more often indirect controls. Similar differences prevail with respect to social and cultural spheres: minimal to massive government policies and programs in varied housing, health care, education, social security, athletic, visual and performing arts field. The general scope of governmental action can be determined in a variety of ways. Examination of the volume and apparent importance of rule-making and application in varied spheres provides substantial data. Varied statistical indices may be available as rough measurements of governmental intervention: the percentage of the gross national product (the total of all goods and services produced by a society) purchased by government; the number and types of industrial or business enterprises owned and operated by government; the proportion of land owned by government; the share of all medical expenses paid by a government; the percentage of the labor force employed by government. Budgetary analysis may also provide similar data.

GOVERNMENT BUDGETS

A government's budget is its primary tool for planning and control of varied activities. Budgetary analysis can be a fruitful way of determining a government's priority goals, its extractive and distributive policies, and the scope of governmental action in varied spheres. Examination of the revenue side of budgets, combined with analysis of the tax structure, can reveal how much revenue a government extracts from its citizens, the proportion of national income so extracted, and which socio-economic strata or sectors of society tend to be favored or more heavily burdened. Some taxes, such as direct and indirect sales and flat rate income taxes, tend to be regressive in that they require lower income groups to pay a greater share of their income to governments than upper income groups; progressive types such as graduated income taxes shift more of the burden to middle and upper income groups. Special exemptions or deductions, such as oil depletion allowances, or for capital investment purposes, or for interest on home mortgages, favor some business groups or home owners by providing them with an indirect subsidy. Deliberate deficit financing, involving continuing expenditure levels above anticipated tax receipts, may also be indicative of a government's social policy. It may be deliberately resorted to in an effort to provide subsidies and services to varied elements of the population. But it may also be used to stimulate or may result in inflation, which invariably places a heavy burden on certain people—such as those on fixed income, creditors, and small businessmen.

The expenditure side of the budget, which indicates how a government plans to spend its tax and other revenues, provides important data about the nature, scope, and objectives of policies. It provides clues as to goal priorities and trends: what proportion of total expenditures is planned for defense spending, for varied economic purposes, for varied domestic purposes such as health care, education, manpower training, housing. It indicates what spheres and problems are being neglected by government either by omission or only minimal expenditures for certain purposes. Most important, expenditures involve the allocation of scarce resources for varied goals and spheres—the government's decisions as to who shall get what—how much for unemployment compensation, for food stamp or other welfare programs, for subsidies or other forms of governmental assistance to businessmen and farmers. And governmental spending plans, combined with its tax policies, may indicate sometimes fairly clearly whether the government is giving priority to stimulation of the economy by benefiting business, industry, and commerce; or to effect some redistribution of wealth by providing tax benefits and subsidized services to the poor.

The Nature and Content of Specific Policies

This involves analysis of major specific laws and governmental action programs and of the cumulative content of such actions over time, to determine the objectives of governments and the major characteristics of its policies in various spheres. It involves analysis of what a government is doing or attempting to do—the characteristics of the methods employed and the actions undertaken—to meet certain kinds of needs and problems or to resolve certain kinds of conflicts. Considering the scope of modern governments the field is obviously a vast one. It involves questions as to what the government is doing in the economic sphere to promote economic stability or growth, to control inflation, to deal with unemployment, to ensure adequate energy supplies, to ensure a sound agricultural sector. It involves examination of governmental actions in a variety of social matters: its programs in housing, education, consumer protection, and many other fields. It involves analysis of actions and policies in the political sphere, to reform or change the decision-making system and related political processes and institutions. And it involves analysis of governmental policies with regard to human rights and freedoms, both in the narrow sense of civil liberties, and in the broader sense of promoting real freedom by providing more people with real economic and political choices. It also entails analysis of non-decisions—deliberate decisions to do nothing in certain spheres, or simple neglect of some significant needs and problems of the society. The examination of policies themselves is also not sufficient. The analysis must include consideration of the implementation of programs, for some policies may be

vigorously enforced, while others—equal opportunity or anti-trust policies—may be virtually neglected by a particular administration.

PROBLEMS OF POLICY ASSESSMENT AND EVALUATION

Policy-making should entail the "rational" selection of goals and of
actions designed to attain them. Policy-analysis entails objective assessment of such "rationality" in the selection of means and ends. The
primary purpose of examining the scope, objectives, and content of policies is to assess and evaluate them in terms of their consequences. Policy
analysis should entail an empirical, rational, and objective assessment of
the extent to which the selected means do in fact contribute to goal
attainment, and what the other consequences of policies appear to be.
However, complete objectivity and rationality in both policy-making and
analysis is hindered by several constraints and impediments.

CONSTRAINTS AND COMPLEXITIES   P 258   BCP

Rationality is one of the qualities we expect of policy-makers. We give
them or accept their authority with the expectation that they will make
decisions on the basis of rational consideration of what is likely to resolve
problems and promote the public interest. But even though it may be
quite proper to hold decision-makers formally responsible for success or
failure, or for good and wise versus bad and foolish decisions, the real
responsibility may not be exclusively theirs. For a number of complexities
and constraints plague decision-making processes.

For one, policy outputs are products of the entire political system, not
merely the decision-making apparatus. In any setting, politics entails
some degree of interaction between governments and their environmental settings. Influences emanating from such settings—the domestic and
international environment, the physical or human setting—as relayed by
the linkage-communication system frequently are such that they give
policy-makers little choice with respect to their policies. This is frequently
the case with economic policies: governments are often virtually forced
to adopt policies which may be economically unsound, but politically wise
because only such policies will generate the degree of support essential
for stability, for voluntary compliance, or for re-election. In essence,
policy-making always entails questions as to what other elites, or the
public, will accept.

Second, policy-making invariably involves making sometimes agonizing choices among several goals, and the allocation of scarce resources

to varied goals. Value tradeoffs and cost-benefit complexities are inherent in questions relating to priority ordering among several values and of resource allocation to favored over less-favored goals. How much unemployment can be tolerated to deal with inflation? To what extent can we tolerate pollution and damage to the physical environment in the interests of economic growth and an ample energy supply? How much capital shall be invested in solar energy as contrasted with atomic energy or in housing programs as opposed to education? To what extent shall the government vigorously promote equality of opportunity at the expense of freedom of individuals to discriminate? These and similar questions involve extremely difficult choices which sometimes defy so-called rational approaches.

Third, major constraints may limit the real alternatives and choices available to decision-makers. The constraints may result from the scarcity of resources—a low state of economic development which forces priority on economic growth in order to cope with rising expectations; a dwindling supply of petroleum which requires priority to the development of energy resources; a major need for technicians which requires the rapid expansion of technical education. It may be constraints imposed by overriding pressures from society—the inability to adapt an economic policy of austerity because of intense demands for lower taxes and more governmental services. Or it may be constraints imposed by the international environment—economic conditions which require unpopular economic policies, or political conditions which require the allocation of more funds to defense spending.

Fourth, policy-making entails substantial uncertainty because policy makers seldom have absolutely complete and accurate information about needs and problems, and because policy-making entails the hazardous art of prediction. Effective decision-making requires fairly accurate and precise data about such varied things as the reasons for and extent of economic problems, the distribution of unemployment and poverty in the society, the country's housing, health, or educational needs, or the degree of social instability or crime which can be traced to various sources. Some of these things cannot be measured; others can, but complete and precise data is seldom available. The impediment of incomplete information is compounded by the problem of prediction, for policy-making entails predicting that policies will have certain consequences. Economic policy-making entails not only incomplete data about the nature and scope of economic problems, but also uncertainties about whether certain tax cuts, spending programs, monetary policies, and other actions will produce the intended effects. Policy decisions are also made at certain points in time, and unforeseen developments—an economic downturn in a particular industry, an increase in the price of oil, international developments—may quickly date an otherwise rational policy.

Finally, policy-making involves problems of implementation and control. In a system of dispersed power, initial policy proposals may be changed so that the final product is hardly recognizable. Policy entails action programs, which require the cooperation of the bureaucracy; and even totalitarian systems have found it impossible to totally control their bureaucratic empires. And at least in democratic societies, action requires voluntary compliance on the part of affected groups, which again is frequently difficult to predict with any degree of assurance.

PROBLEMS OF IMPACT ANALYSIS

Some special problems also complicate the rational empirical assessment of the consequences of policies and their impact on society. Even though such assessment is of great importance, until recently it has been a neglected field of inquiry—possibly because of inherent difficulties and complexities. Governments around the world are notorious for enacting all kinds of economic, social, educational, and other kinds of policies and programs, without ever reviewing them to determine whether they are really accomplishing their purposes. Consequently few very effective techniques for assessment of consequences and effectiveness have to date been developed. Considering the complexity of forces at work in modern societies, how does one go about assessing the effectiveness of a government's policy with respect to economic stability, housing needs, racial discrimination, and a multitude of other problems?

Part of the problem is due to the difficulty of predicting and establishing a cause-effect relationship between policies and subsequent events or developments. In a world in which many complex forces are at work, how can policy-makers predict with any degree of assurance that a policy will have a certain effect? The economic condition of a society will be affected not merely by government policies, but also by the dynamics of the economic system, by international developments, and by changes in the cultural and social setting which have economic consequences (such as rising expectations or a waning of the work ethic). And for post-decision assessment, how can analysis accurately attribute certain developments to certain governmental policies? The fact that an economic policy was followed by a period of economic prosperity does not establish a cause-effect relationship because the effect may have been generated by non-governmental causes, or by unrelated governmental policies—such as a poverty or social security program which had the side effect of increasing the society's purchasing power. Tracing political, social, or economic developments back to the unintended effects of policies is even more hazardous. The deterioration of American cities can in part be traced back to the impact of the federal highway construction program, but other forces were also at work. And when a cause-effect relationship does in fact exist, it may be as difficult for the analyst as for the decision-maker to perceive.

VALUES AND MEANS-ENDS PROBLEMS

Complete "rationality" in both policy-making and analysis is particularly hindered by problems of objectivity, simply because both processes entail value considerations relating to both means and ends. Policies are means to ends—their purpose is to promote preferred values and attain the desired goals of society or government. The purpose of analysis is to assess the extent to which the means do in fact promote such ends, and what the actual results of policies appear to be.

The crucial means-ends relationship entails two basic questions: do the ends justify the means, and what appears to be the ends, the actual outcomes or consequences, of choosing certain means? The second question entails two aspects of means or policies. First, are the means selected —political action and the specific policies themselves—likely to attain the selected ends? Second, are the selected means likely to result in ends which are congruent with desired goals, or are they likely to result in ends which may not be desired by government or society? All these questions involve both facts and values, which to some extent are separable and which ought to be separately considered during both policy-making and analysis. Yet they all entail some normative evaluations which preclude complete objectivity by both policy-makers and analysts.

The first question—whether the ends justify the means—is basically a normative question. The answer depends on the value placed by policy-makers and analysts on goals as contrasted with values being sacrificed to attain them. Whether or not rapid economic growth justifies mass regimentation of people and denial of freedom of economic choice, or an ample energy supply warrants extensive damage to the environment, depends on values assigned to economic growth. But facts are not irrelevant—about the criticality of energy supplies or the need for crash economic programs, about the potential consequences of mass regimentation. Similar normative questions as to whether population control in India justifies the forced sterilization of parents, domestic peace the denial of civil liberties, welfare programs the heavy taxation of citizens, warrant consideration of facts about the impact of less coercive birth control measures on a critical population explosion, whether or not crime rates or social strife are so acute as to warrant draconian remedies, and about the extent and depth of poverty and its potential consequences for social instability.

The second basic question concerning the consequences of selected means is basically an empirical question, yet normative considerations are bound to intrude and influence the assessments of both policy-makers and analysts. The decision to do something by the enactment of public policy entails a decision to do something by political means, to use the instrumentality of the government to attain some economic, social, or cultural goal. Hence, inherent in this second question are problems related to the fundamental permanent issues of politics discussed in Chapter 3: the legitimate scope and functions of government, what values a government should maximize, what preferred ends should be incorporated into governmental goals. Specific issues and policies invariably entail normative questions about the extent to which and under what conditions the government may encroach on certain individual rights, where the line might be between individual rights and the collective needs of society, and what constitutes an equitable allocation of values.

From the standpoint of both policy-making and analysis, the question entails, first of all, consideration of what specific needs and problems appear to be critical and of such a nature so that governmental intervention appears to be necessary. In addition, it is the task of both policy-makers and analysts to determine what critical human problems appear to be neglected by government, either in terms of inaction or inadequate action. This requires analysis of facts—about the criticality of economic and energy needs, the intensity of social conflict, the extent and nature of housing and health needs, the disparities between rich and poor. Value preferences will inevitably intrude. Some policy-makers and analysts will be inclined to favor public action, others will favor voluntary action and cooperation on the part of groups of the society or non-political approaches based on natural social or economic competition. But facts are essential not merely to determine how critical the problems are, but also about the likely outcome of non-political action: about the actual extent and results of economic competition, about the ability of the poor to pull themselves up by the bootstraps, or the ability of low income people to obtain adequate medical care and housing. Facts are also necessary to assess the potential consequences inherent in the neglect of problems: of an inadequate energy supply, of intense social strife, of alienation developing because of social injustice or the lack of equal opportunity.

Once assessment is made as to whether a particular problem requires governmental action, the policy-maker faces more specific means-ends questions: to what extent government should intervene in various spheres, and what specific policies ought to be to stimulate economic growth, to assure ample energy supplies, to stabilize the population, to alleviate poverty. The task of the policy analyst is to assess the extent to which governmental actions are attaining the desired goals. In such analysis values are bound to intrude and preclude completely objective assessment. Incomplete data and different theories about human, social, and economic behavior invite different and subjective interpretations of facts, different assessment of the consequences of policies, different perceptions of cause-effect relationships, and different determinations as to whether a policy has been a success or failure. A policy analyst committed to free enterprise economic theories is more prone to assess governmental economic intervention in negative terms than an interventionist. An individual who believes that poverty is best alleviated by individual action on the part of the poor, or by the creation of jobs through economic growth, is likely to draw different conclusions about the impact of governmental welfare policies than one who firmly believes in the inherent merits of such programs. Different value priorities will similarly affect assessment: one analyst may assess law enforcement policies a failure because he places a high value on civil liberties; another may judge welfare policy a failure because he places a high priority on economic growth and calculates that economic costs of welfare programs are too high.

Similar value judgments will invariably impede completely objective assessment of the value creation activities of government—to what extent policies are actually creating values which ought to be maximized in the public interest. And they impede objective assessment of value allocation patterns—the extent to which government distributes values on an equitable basis, or serves the general welfare rather than merely the welfare of a few. Again an analyst (and policy-maker) who firmly believes that governmental benefits tilted in favor of business or upper income groups ultimately redound to the entire society will assess such value distribution as relatively equitable. One who firmly believes that social justice can only be attained by governmental policies designed to reduce disparities of wealth is likely to draw different conclusions.

But despite these difficulties and complexities, empirical assessment of policy consequences is a highly important task of both policy-making and analysis. If a society is to use its political system to attain certain goals, then it obviously becomes imperative to formulate policies on the basis of rational calculations about the consequences of various policy alternatives, and to constantly assess and evaluate adopted policies to determine whether actual outcomes warrant their modification or abandonment. Too often political systems grind out policies and allocate scarce resources to resolve certain problems, without concerted efforts to determine whether policies are having effects as intended, whether certain side-effects or unforeseen consequences are consonant with desired goals, or whether the taxpayer in fact is getting his money's worth. Through careful analysis of empirical data, and an approach of at least disciplined subjectivity, such assessment is possible.

THE CONSEQUENCES OF POLICIES

As discussed earlier, the means-ends problem requires assessment and evaluation of the apparent, probable, and possible consequences of policies in two respects: the extent to which the consequences indicate that policies are effective in resolving the needs and problems they are aimed at, and the broader impact of policies on the system and society.

THE EFFECTIVENESS OF POLICIES

Despite the previously discussed difficulties, empirical analysis can establish somewhat of a cause-effect relationship between policies and subsequent developments and to assess the degree to which policies are actually accomplishing what they are intended to accomplish. Although due consideration must be given to other political or non-political forces which may be at work, it is possible to assess whether economic policies are producing a desired rate of economic growth or reducing the degree of inflation or unemployment as intended. It is possible to make some determinations as to whether poverty programs are alleviating the lot of the poor, anti-discrimination measures do result in greater equality of opportunity, environmental actions are helping to clean up air and water, or political reforms are cleansing the political system of corruption. Effectiveness assessment is also possible and necessary with respect to efficiency or the cost-benefit ratios of policies—what material or value costs seem to be involved in effective or ineffective policies. Some kinds of at least crude assessments can be made as to the extent social security or welfare programs entail high monetary costs or may be impeding economic growth, or the environmental damage costs entailed in energy and economic policies.

Effectiveness assessment should also include efforts to trace the causes of policy inadequacies or failures, for only such causal analysis can provide a rational foundation for changes of policy. Inadequacies may be clearly due to the nature and content of the policies themselves, yet changes may be difficult because the pluralistic nature of decision-making processes precludes truly effective policies. Or policies may be foredoomed because required resources are not available or cannot be extracted—capital and resource shortages or international economic recessions may preclude effective economic policies, or a taxpayers' rebellion may doom efforts to improve education. It may be that sound policies fail because of inadequate funding: the allocation of only token funds may in effect scuttle housing or urban renewal programs. Or it may be that rational policies prove inadequate because of inadequate implementation: law enforcement officials may ignore anti-trust legislation; an inadequate corps of meat inspectors may be unable to police slaughter houses; abuses in welfare and health programs may be widespread because of quantitative or qualitative weaknesses of administrative personnel.

THE BROADER CONSEQUENCES OF POLICIES

Major policies or even individual decisions of lesser importance frequently have an impact which extends well beyond the individual problem or sphere of activity they are intended to deal with. Hence, policy analysis must include consideration of what Samuel Beer calls the "spectrum of hidden policies"—hidden either because all their consequences were not foreseen, or because their foreseen consequences were not explicitly considered or pronounced at the time of policy decision.[1]

Policies may have certain foreseen or unforeseen side effects, consequences unrelated to intended objectives. A tax policy intended to stimulate economic recovery by giving tax cuts to business or middle-income taxpayers so that they will have more money to spend may have the effect of shifting more of the tax burden to low-income groups, and thereby aggravate poverty and discontent. A minimum wage policy designed to raise wage levels may impose a heavy burden on small businesses and reduce their ability to compete with big business. A decision to expand the educational system may arouse intense conflict over allocation of educational facilities and teaching posts among different tribes or religious groups.

Closely related are the unforeseen or unintended consequences of policies. The American federal interstate highway program is fairly effective with respect to its intended objective—improved highway transportation. However, it has had major unintended consequences on the decay of cities, the growth of suburbs, changes in the geographic distribution of population and jobs, and the aggravation of race relations. American agricultural policies have not been very effective with respect to their intended objectives—to reduce farm output and raise farm income. But

[1]Samuel H. Beer, *Modern Political Development* (New York: Random House, 1974) pp. 52–55.

they have effectively helped to increase farm production, raise farm efficiency, lower food costs for consumers, and make available great reserves of grain.

Of particular importance is the assessment and evaluation of the broad implications of particular major policies and of the overall pattern of public policy outputs, over a period of time, on the society and the political system. Such analysis takes us back to the most basic question: who gets what? More specifically: what kinds of values is the system creating, how is it allocating values, and with what efficiency?

PATTERNS OF VALUE MAXIMIZATION

It is probably impossible for any political system to maximize all the values demanded by various groups of the society. Hence, analysis must focus on what values, either by intent or not, are actually being maximized, at what cost to other values, and which values are being neglected.

Some systems, for example, may be concentrating on the immediate present, with little thought to future needs and problems. They may emphasize rapid economic growth but take no action with respect to the possible depletion of scarce land, mineral, or energy resources. Some may be allocating so many resources to immediate external and domestic security needs—to the development of major military arsenals and police forces—that resources available for impending or future other domestic needs may be totally inadequate. Some, deluded by temporary social stability, may be neglecting policies to deal with simmering social, ethnic, racial, or religious unrest and tension, and act only when the society explodes.

Neglected spheres of policy is another appropriate focus for analysis, particularly with regard to spheres in which facts indicate that individual action or voluntary cooperation will not suffice to resolve basic human needs and problems. The facts suggest that balancing environmental protection with economic prosperity requires some governmental intervention, yet the former sphere is sadly neglected by many governments. Health and housing needs may require some governmental policies, yet be ignored or subordinated by policy-makers. While economic growth may be necessary to maximize social justice, the record again suggests that socio-economic forces alone cannot be relied on to reduce disparities of wealth and income, to ensure equality of opportunity, and to relieve the misery of the poor. Some systems are at least making efforts with respect to such problems. Others, perhaps blissfully unaware of the explosiveness of gross social injustice, are neglecting such spheres of human needs.

Policies may also have the effect of accentuating existing or creating new problems which may be neglected by policy makers. The American federal highway program aggravated or created major problems with respect to mass transportation, urban blight, air pollution, and intensification of racial segregation. Agricultural policies created problems relating to a huge agricultural surplus, rural poverty, and the flight to the cities of much of the rural population. Tax cuts designed to stimulate an economy may accomplish that purpose, but result in inflation. Unemployment, social security, and welfare benefits may have the side effect of reducing incentives to work, or may impose heavy financial burdens on employed persons and the youthful sector of the work force. Land reform programs involving the break up of large estates and their distribution to numerous peasants may achieve the intended objectives of breaking the political power of the landed aristocracy and of creating a class of small landholders who contribute to social stability. But they may entail high costs in agricultural productivity, and in the long run provoke instability because of consequent economic decline. Even political reforms may entail some high costs and create new problems. Enhancement of home rule in the interests of grass roots democracy may make it extremely difficult to attain the kind of cooperative or authoritative action needed to resolve regional problems. Primary nomination systems may enhance popular participation, but at high cost to party unity and effectiveness.

The value-creation consequences of policies should be assessed and evaluated from the perspective of the apparent efficiency of policies—the ratio of benefits for some values to costs in terms of other values, and the judicious use of scarce resources. The benefits accruing to the present generation by the economic and other policies must be assessed against costs to future generations, as must the benefits inherent in national security and space programs against the costs to domestic programs and earth-bound transportation needs. Efficiency is a prime consideration when assessing policies which strive to attain a balance: economic growth and environmental protection, social justice and economic prosperity, equality and individual freedom of association. Efficiency generally requires some kind of judicious balance among varied material and other tangible and less tangible values. Some regimes attempt to maximize economic growth by mass regimentation of people, at high cost to the values of human freedom and dignity. Some attempt to ensure domestic order and security by means which deny humans any fundamental rights and freedoms. Even the basic law and order function of government requires a judicious balance: the need and right of security for domestic peace and order, and the right of the accused to due process of law.

Questions such as these involve a combination of empirical assessment and normative evaluation. Any approach ought first to focus on the basic empirical question—what are governments doing and not doing by way of formulating and implementing policies to deal with major needs and problems. Value preferences inevitably will intrude as one attempts to determine whether a need or problem is indeed significant or critical, and the extent to which one assesses that governmental action rather than private endeavor is preferable. But facts also must be considered in assessing the criticality of needs, the need for political action, and the probable consequences of inaction in a particular sphere.

PATTERNS OF VALUE ALLOCATION

The analysis of the distribution of values and costs also entails both empirical data and normative judgments, but fact-value separation is again possible and necessary, as is consideration of facts when making value judgments.

Budgetary analysis is a major tool for such assessment and evaluation. The revenue side of the budget, or a government's overall tax structure, provides data for determining which elements of a society bear what proportion of the tax burden. Questions need to be asked about the proportion of revenue derived from business establishments as contrasted with individual tax payers, and which kinds of business ventures receive preferential treatment by way of special tax rates, exemptions, or "loopholes." Questions have to be asked about the share of the tax burden imposed on various socio-economic groups: which income groups seem to be required to pay a larger proportion of their income as the result of the combination of income, sales, social security, property, and other taxes; which kinds of taxpayers—the wealthy, the middle-income groups, the poor, the elderly, city dwellers—are given special exemptions or other forms of special treatment which reduce their share of the burden and increases the share of other groups.

The revenue side of a government's budget also provides some data about the distribution of governmental benefits. Special tax benefits or deductions are in effect "welfare" measures in that they indirectly subsidize certain business enterprises, occupational groups, or income groups. By being required to pay less taxes than other business, occupations, or income groups, such groups are in effect given money by government. Home owners are in effect subsidized at the expense of others when a government permits deduction of property taxes and mortgage interest payments from income tax; the petroleum industry is allocated special benefits when it is accorded special tax treatment; farmers are favored when tax laws give them certain deductions not available to other occupational groups; college education is subsidized when parents of college students are permitted to deduct college tuition. The expenditure side of a budget, and various specific expenditure actions, provide data about the distribution of government benefits. Certain welfare measures may visibly identify recipients: direct payments or food stamps to certain low income groups; subsidized below-cost health and housing programs; compensation for the unemployed. Other kinds of welfare programs may also clearly identify the beneficiaries: direct subsidies to certain industries; low-cost loans to small businesses; educational grants to certain types of students, educators, or educational establishments. Some benefits to certain groups may be less visible but nonetheless real: highway programs tend to benefit the trucking and bus industries, but not other forms of mass transportation; financing of airport construction aids the aviation industry and certain communities; below-cost postal service helps publishers and mail order firms; conservation programs are sometimes primarily geared to benefit hunters and fishermen. The actual impact of government programs must also be analyzed to determine the primary beneficiaries. Housing and urban renewal programs, intended to benefit low-income groups, often confer primary benefits to the construction industry, real estate interests, and middle-to-upper income groups. Or a government's direct and indirect expenditures may favor certain geographic regions, or urban, suburban, or rural areas.

Benefits may also be distributed by policies and actions which do not directly involve the expenditure of money. Civil rights legislation may allocate values to minority groups; consumer protection actions may or may not protect consumers; tariff policies may enhance the profit of some industries; labor-management policies may enhance the bargaining position of one side or the other in labor-management negotiations; public utility regulation policies may enhance the profit of power companies or favor individual or industrial consumers of electricity; anti-trust policies may or may not enhance the competitive position of small business.

Value judgments will invariably intrude in the assessment of the consequences of such value allocation patterns and in evaluation of whether they are fair, just, in the public interest, and tend to promote the general welfare rather than just the welfare of some special interests. But the initial task is an empirical one—determination of what the allocation patterns really are. Facts have to be considered in assessing consequences —whether certain welfare programs really help to reduce disparities of income, tax exemptions or subsidies to business really create jobs or otherwise redound to the benefit of the entire society, tax cuts to upper income groups really create the buying power necessary to stimulate the economy. And facts have to be considered in assessing the possible broader consequences of value allocation patterns: the eventual impact of tax and subsidy programs on the economy, or the eventual impact of gross inequalities on social stability.

Factual assessment is also necessary to determine what hidden costs may be involved in governmental policies. Efforts to exclude imports from abroad may benefit certain industries and protect some jobs, but involve higher prices for consumers and harm industries and jobs related to foreign trade or exports. Failure to support certain industries or farmers may initially reduce costs to taxpayers, but ultimately entail high costs in unemployment and welfare benefits. The cost of occupational training or job programs at governmental expense may ultimately be more than offset by reduced unemployment and welfare costs and by increased tax payments by the newly-employed. Value allocation patterns which are tilted away from cities, the poor, and various minority groups may or may not be deemed equitable, but assessment of their potential consequences for domestic tranquillity requires an empirical and not just a normative approach.

Political Systems, Policy Outputs, and Change

14

The preceding chapter treated public policies as outputs of governments, and discussed assessment of policy consequences primarily in short-range terms—their immediate impact on society. But policies are products of political systems, of governments functioning as component parts of such systems and interacting with environmental forces as transmitted by linkage and communication systems. To complete the chain of interaction, policy outputs may have long-term consequences for the entire political system or the individual environmental, infrastructure, and decision-making components. The policies themselves, or their interaction with non-political forces in the society, may be generating significant changes with respect to the nature, dynamics, performance characteristics, stability, and effectiveness of the political system which generated them in the first place. It is these relationships between political systems, policy outputs, and change with which this chapter is concerned.

THE PROBLEM OF CHANGE

The problem of change is one of the major frontiers of social science, which is another way of saying that we know far too little about this complex phenomenon. Changes of any kind are often difficult to recognize, even though they may be occurring right before out eyes. The sources of change in many instances appear to be a riddle wrapped up inside a mystery inside an enigma. To predict the continuity, direction, or pace of change is hazardous, and it is even riskier to predict the consequences of change. Yet change is something the human race must live and cope with, particularly in the sphere of politics. For political action invariably entails either efforts to change things, or efforts to maintain things in the face of pressures for change. Hence it is essential for political analysis to focus not merely on static situations, on things as they are, but also on change.

THE UNCERTAIN ROOTS AND NATURE OF CHANGE

The world of the past has gone through many major upheavals, and despite the valiant efforts of historians, the basic origins of past gradual or sudden changes cannot be definitely pinpointed. The same uncertainty prevails with respect to the contemporary world, in which the only certainty is that, with the exception of a few relatively static corners, change in all spheres of human organization and activity is rapid and widespread.

One major riddle is the cause-effect relationship between environmental and political change. Is political action a prime agent of change, or are major changes primarily the result of non-political or self-generating environmental forces? If the former, what kinds of political action, and what produces them? If the latter, what kinds of environmental forces—cultural, social, economic, technological—and to what extent can political action be used to stimulate or impact environmental change?

A review of the historic record initially suggests the primacy of environmental forces. Wrenching political upheavals of the past—the French, Russian, Chinese, other revolutions—and the more gradual changes which occurred in such nations as Britain and the United States, seem to have been the result of gradually accelerating socio-economic and cultural forces and changes. In the contemporary world technology has been a prime agent of change. It clearly has been the source of major economic, communication, and military changes with far-reaching social, cultural, and political consequences. It is a prime root of the modern, affluent, complex industrial economy, which makes modern political frontiers increasingly archaic. New industrial, communications, and military technology has created a host of new and acute problems, and has set in motion dizzying cultural, social, and economic changes all of which have major political implications.

But the record also suggests a causal role for political forces. The French, Russian, and Chinese revolutions occurred as old and new social forces organized to overthrow unsatisfactory political systems. Socio-economic and cultural changes produced these new social forces and their alliance with older forces, but such environmental changes had at least been impacted by the policies of the old regimes. Political factors —notably the weakness of the old regimes and their failure to adapt to change—made the revolutions seem necessary to old and new forces, and also led to revolutionary success. The successful revolutionary forces then used their political power to shape new environmental settings. A similar interplay between enironmental and political factors occurred in Britain, the United States, and other societies in which political change came about more gradually; except that in these systems the political elites sometimes reluctantly but nonetheless gradually adapted to changing conditions. In today's world the positive-welfare state is the major feature of the political landscape, and its constant expansion of functions indicates the extent to which government has become a major engine of change in all spheres of human activity.

In essence, change like political dynamics appears to entail constant governmental-environmental interaction. Changes in environmental settings—in a society's political culture, socio-economic system, configuration of political power, and conflict and cooperation patterns—result from the interaction between political action and relatively uncontrolled environmental forces. These changes produce changes in the nature, content, intensity, and sources of effective demand and support inputs from varied groups in the society. Changes in such inputs in turn generate changes in the nature, structure, dynamics, and policy outputs of decision-making systems, which in turn impact the environmental setting and generate still further changes in demand and support inputs. In essence, at least in the contemporary world, the pattern seems to be a complex and ongoing circular process.

Normative Problems of Change

Any kind of effort to shape, steer, or control changes which affect human beings involves fundamental value questions, and such normative considerations apply particularly to the use of political action to affect change. One question is related to the fundamental question about the legitimate scope of government: to what extent should the political system be used to generate or shape change? A second question pertains to goals: in what direction should change be steered, what changes may be desirable in value creation and allocation patterns, what is the nature of a good society towards which the government should steer? A third question pertains to the pace of change and involves political means: under what conditions might a very rapid pace of change be desirable;

is evolutionary preferable to revolutionary change; when is revolution justified? A fourth question also pertains to means to pursue ends: what specific kinds of structural and procedural changes, particularly those affecting the location and distribution of power, seem desirable so as to ensure that all preferred values are maximized and that desired ends will in fact be attained?

Since these are normative questions, answers will vary with the value preferences of human beings. But a few empirically-based propositions relate to such value questions. First, the potential for steering or controlling change through individual action or voluntary cooperation seems low. Such action may produce change in one sphere of human activity—the economic, for example—but often in an uncontrolled way, and often out of harmony with changes in other spheres. So long as the political system does perform as an instrument of society, it would appear to be a major tool whereby the human race can attempt to control its own destiny rather than progress or regress by mindless drifting. Second, there may indeed be instances in which extremely rapid change in some sphere—political, economic, cultural, social—may be necessary, or in which revolutions seem desirable. But the human and economic costs of revolutions or other sudden upheavals are usually extremely high. Third, human society needs its political instruments for the pursuit of at least some goals, and whatever functions the political system is to be charged with, it must have the necessary stability and effectiveness to function as an instrument of society. Fourth, political systems must adapt to changing conditions, for failure to adapt invariably results in the loss of stability and effectiveness, and in the long run can lead to disaster. A system which stubbornly adheres to the status quo, or an outdated system which is no longer capable of performing essential functions, may temporarily be able to survive either because of its coercive force or because of residual support provided by the political culture. But attempts to preserve such systems are in the long run self-defeating: ineffectiveness invariably produces instability, disintegration, decay, or collapse. Finally, adaptation entails changing either the goals and policies of the system, or transformation of political structures and processes, or both.

SYSTEM CAPABILITIES FOR ADAPTATION

The assessment of the capability of a political system to adapt to change is another analytical exercise fraught with uncertainties. One clue may be provided by the past record of the system, how well it adapted to previous changes. This, however, poses the risk of projecting past trends and developments into the future. That the British have in the past somehow

always managed to "muddle through" their crises is no guarantee that
they will continue to do so. A somewhat safer approach would be to focus
on the absence or presence within the system of constraints on change:
the power of elites firmly attached to the status quo versus those committed to change; the vested interests that elites, political leaders, and bureaucrats have in the existing system and policies; the potential for
intense social instability should major pressures for change develop. But
there are no real short cuts to such complex assessment. The surest road
would seem to be to examine changes occurring throughout the four
components of a political system. We need to discern which changes pose
major problems of political adaptation, analyze the responses of the
system to change, and assess the possible consequences of both uncontrolled changes and policy outputs for the nature, goals, and performance
characteristics of the political system.

CHANGE: STABILITY, EFFECTIVENESS, AND DEMOCRACY

From the foregoing, it follows that a key analytical concern is with the
probable consequences of policies and political-environmental change
for political stability and effectiveness. A related normative concern, at
least in western societies, is with consequences for the maintenance or
development of democracy. These two aspects of change are separate yet
related. Rising participation demands, pressures for greater individual
freedom, or dispersion of power resources may require a shift in the
direction of more democratic processes for authoritarian systems to retain stability and effectiveness. In democracies, rising distribution demands, or persisting economic and other problems which tax existing
capabilities, may necessitate a shift in the direction of more concentrated
power. Indeed, there is little doubt that the major challenge which confronts Western civilization is the development of more effective democratic institutions.

During the past several decades a substantial theoretical effort has
focused on the question of whether there are certain fundamental requisites for democracy and for political stability and effectiveness—whether
certain conditions must exist for democracies to develop and thrive, and
what conditions seem essential for the stability and effectiveness of any
type of system. Substantial disagreement persists as to whether there are
any common requisites and what precisely they might be. However it is
apparent that certain conditions, if not absolutely essential in all cases,
seem to favor democracy and stability and effectiveness, and that changes
in these conditions tend to have major consequences for the nature and
performance of systems. Despite persisting uncertainties, these apparent

requisites—which pertain to all components of a political system—provide a useful way of approaching the problem of change and adaptation. Analysis can focus on what trends appear to be developing within the various components of a system, and what the apparent or potential consequences of such trends may be in terms of such requisites. The analysis should particularly consider the magnitude of the challenge these trends pose to adaptation, the impact of public policies on such significant trends, and what kinds of policies or policy changes seem essential to maintain or develop these requisites. We shall first briefly list those requisites on which there is substantial agreement and then discuss changes within political systems which pertain to them.

REQUISITES FOR DEMOCRACY

Five conditions seem to be either essential for or conducive to the development and maintenance of democratic systems, and three of these relate to environmental factors discussed in Part II.

A participatory culture prevailing among elites and the politically-relevant strata seems to be essential either for the establishment of democratic systems or for such systems to survive.

Tension-moderating conditions must exist, for democracy seems to require a balance between cleavage and consensus. Such conditions seem to entail a fair degree of economic abundance to minimize conflict over material values, prevailing attitudes which help to facilitate conflict resolution, and perhaps a fairly large middle class which plays a moderating role in class and other conflicts.

The power configuration must be pluralistic—a configuration of polyarchy with substantially broad dispersion of power resources throughout a large politically-relevant strata.

A relatively effective, equitable, and autonomous linkage-communication system must exist for reasons discussed in Part III.

The decision-making system must be characterized by substantial dispersion of power and formalization-institutionalization of decision-making processes, and must be staffed by individuals who respect democratic norms and values.

REQUISITES FOR STABILITY AND EFFECTIVENESS

Seven conditions seem to be either essential for or conducive to the stability and effectiveness of any type of political system, with five of these relating to environmental factors. It might be noted that these conditions overlap substantially with requisites for democracy, and that democracies consequently may have at least a greater potential for effectiveness.

Legitimacy and substantial support seem to be most essential, which in turn requires substantial congruence between prevailing conceptions of authority and scope and the realities of the system. It also requires a long-term pattern of policy outputs which more-or-less match the expectations of elites and the politically-relevant strata.

Tension-moderating conditions are at least conducive if not essential, and include conflict patterns of minimal range, complexity, and intensity, as well as attitudes which help to moderate conflict.

Attitudes—particularly among elites—which are conducive to change are essential if a system is to remain effective by adaptation.

Human and material resources, to the extent needed by the system to meet value expectations and to resolve both immediate and future critical problems, also seem essential. This entails both availability and extractability of such resources.

Substantial congruence between the power configuration in the society and the government must exist if the system is to enjoy support and legitimacy.

A relatively effective linkage-communication system, capable at least of input or articulation functions, seems at least highly desirable for long-term effectiveness, and this requisite also makes a relatively autonomous and equitable linkage system highly desirable (Part III).

The decision-making system should be characterized by a degree of structural differentiation and institutionalization to the extent required by the scope and complexity of governmental functions. Also necessary are effective integrating structures to ensure coordination and generalist control. Essential appears to be such concentration of power as to enhance capability and effectiveness (Part IV).

POLICIES, CHANGE, AND ENVIRONMENTAL SETTINGS

Environmental changes may result from either uncontrolled forces or governmental policies or both, and really significant trends and their roots may be difficult to identify. But assessment of the nature, pace, and direction of change is essential to determine probable long-term political consequences, the role of government in shaping or adapting to change, and what apparently needs to be done for adaptation. Analysis is facilitated by focusing on individual environmental factors: the political culture, socio-economic setting, patterns of power distribution, and conflict patterns. However, a narrow analytical focus should not ignore the constant interaction among these factors.

THE POLITICAL CULTURE

Most important is the analysis of changes which may be taking place with respect to elite and mass perceptions of a system's legitimacy; the degree of support it has; the extent to which prevailing attitudes moderate tensions and conflicts in the society; and whether or not elite and mass attitudes are conducive to change. Legitimacy and support are partly dependent on congruence between prevailing conceptions of authority and the realities of a system—the degree to which the actual system of rule matches ideas prevailing among elites and the politically-relevant strata as to how rule should be exercised. In the contemporary world, shifts in the direction of a more participatory conception of authority are undermining the stability and effectiveness of many authoritarian systems. Exposure to the outside world and other cultures, domestic socialization agents, rising standards of living and other factors are breeding ideas about rights of man, human equality, and the right to participate in political processes at least to the extent that citizens have a right to express their demands and grievances. Government policies frequently generate or help to disseminate such ideas: education policies and the spread of literacy and higher levels of education; economic policies which generate new elites and breed new distribution and eventually participation demands; even official ideologies such as Marxism-Leninism or African Socialism which emphasize that the system's ultimate aspiration is to create "true egalitarian democracy." Governmental responsiveness to participation demands from some elements of society, such as to a new professional-technical-managerial elite whose support is essential, may generate similar demands from other social forces. Authoritarian regimes which attempt to reform themselves—Spain, Czechoslovakia, Argentina—invariably go through a dangerous period: once heavy-handed authoritarian controls are loosened, participation demands invariably spread and intensify. Whatever their source, rising participation demands confront authoritarian systems with a major adaptation dilemma. Failure to respond and accommodate such demands will undermine support for the system and eventually its legitimacy. But even partial accommodation threatens the power of elites unwilling to yield power, or may result in a dispersion of power which impedes effectiveness.

Democratic systems may also be troubled by changing conceptions of authority. The legitimacy of elitist or representative democracy is being undermined by spreading ideas of egalitarianism and participatory democracy. British culture has been aptly labeled a "fading deferential culture"—the idea of deference to upper classes and to leadership and of yielding substantial discretionary authority to government is rapidly fading and undermining support for traditional political institutions and processes. The notion that people ought to directly participate in the making of major decisions and that representation in government is not adequate for expression of the public will, has substantially eroded support for the American as well as other systems. But in some systems the cultural shift seems to be in another direction. In France the participatory culture still prevails, but a tendency to accept a stronger executive and a weaker parliament has strengthened the effectiveness of the current system. Whatever the case, changes in conceptions of authority confront systems with problems of adaptation, and actions taken to adapt may provide significant clues about the future of both authoritarian and democratic systems.

A system's support and consequent effectiveness may also be affected by prevailing or changing conceptions of scope. The distribution challenge discussed in Chapter 6 may be generated by environmental forces, or by a government's initiatives in various policy spheres, or its responses to demands from some elements which tend to generate demands from more elements of society. In some instances governmental effectiveness may be inhibited by cultural lag, by lingering attachment of elites and masses to limited conceptions of scope. A characteristic of many contemporary systems is that more groups continue to demand more of government, yet are unwilling to provide government with the authority and resources it needs to respond to multiplying demands. In other settings prevailing conceptions of scope may be matching demand inputs, but to the point where a society may be heading in a collectivist direction, posing problems not only with respect to the power of government over its citizenry, but also with respect to the capability of government to do what is expected of it. As Samuel Beer has pointed out, a modern polity like a modern economy depends on a massive and continuous process of demand creation. Governmental policies which stimulate the multiplication of demands may have the net effect of undermining a government's capability to respond to the demands it helps to generate.[1]

Legitimacy and support are also dependent on the extent to which policy outputs and the general performance of governments match expectations among elites and the politically-relevant strata. What counts is not objective performance but how performance is perceived by elites and masses. Hence, it is important not merely to assess how effective and equitable the system's value creation and allocation in fact appears to be, but how various groups and strata of the society evaluate policy outputs. Support for a regime or system may erode significantly when it is widely perceived as being incapable of ensuring economic stability, or domestic tranquillity, or security against external threats. Racial, religious, ethnic,

[1]Samuel H. Beer, *Modern Political Development* (New York: Random House, 1974), pp. 64–66.

tribal, regional, or various minority groups may become alienated when governments fail to respond to their demands, or evaluate policies as slanted in favor of other groups or unduly for the benefit of the majority. Middle class discontent is becoming quite common in many democracies as governmental policies are seen as slanted in favor of either big business, big labor, or the poor. Elite or mass evaluations of a system's efficiency may similarly affect its support and effectiveness. Many modern democratic and authoritarian systems are troubled by wide-spread feelings that governmental policies entail too many costs—either direct monetary costs, or costs in terms of human freedom, dignity, equality, or majority or minority rights.

Tension-moderating attitudes among elites and masses are very helpful for stability and effectiveness and essential for democracy. Again such attitudes may be generated by environmental forces, by governmental policies, or by both. But whatever their origins, governmental policies must cope with factors which affect attitudinal changes and must promote such attitudes. Particularly important are the attitudes described in Chapter 4: a procedural if not substantive consensus, a respect for law among both rulers and ruled, a sense of mutual trust among groups in society, and elite attitudes which emphasize the peaceful and pragmatic adjustments of conflicts. Even attitudes pertaining to the relationship between individual rights and the collective needs of society may be significant and can be impacted by governmental action. Unrestrained individualism which emphasizes relentless egoistic pursuit of material values or pleasure can quickly undermine the solidarity and cohesion of any society.

Nation-building or horizontal integration is a major problem which confronts many democratic and authoritarian societies. As discussed in Chapter 6, nationality conflicts persist in many older states such as the Soviet Union, Belgium, Spain, and seem to be re-awakening in others such as Britain, France, Canada. Most of the new states of Africa and Asia are not nations but conglomerations of different racial, tribal, ethnic, religious, and regional groups with no sense of common identity or interest. The United States, Britain, and some other societies face problems of racial, religious, or regional integration which may be smaller in scale, but nonetheless extremely significant. Some of these horizontal cleavages and hostilities are simply the inheritance from the past. But hostilities and conflicts are often generated by governmental policies— the expanding scope of government, governmental responses to the demands of some groups but not others, or policies which arouse expectations. Policy outputs can have a major impact on such attitudes. Some governments resort to policies of repression or forced assimilation of minorities, which generally results only in greater hostility. Others attempt to make concessions, either by favoring some nationalities or minorities with material benefits, or by granting them some degree of political or cultural autonomy. Such policies may reduce hostilities, but may also reinforce and perpetuate social cleavages, or arouse hostility on the part of groups not so favored.

Policies which promote vertical integration, or which at least decrease the sense of distance and levels of hostility among socio-economic classes, are also essential. Class cleavages and attitudes again may be the products of the historic past or of the economic system or the culture, but governmental allocation of values can do much to decrease, reinforce, or intensify existing cleavages and hostilities. This again may pose major dilemmas for some systems: policy patterns may stimulate egalitarianism and arouse hostility against upper classes; attempts to pursue social justice and to effect some redistribution of wealth and income by tax and welfare measures may arouse upper or middle class antagonisms or impede economic growth; or an economic recession may re-activate old class conflicts, but require governmental austerity measures which have the net effect of intensifying class antagonisms.

Finally, attitudes conducive to change are necessary for systems to adapt to change. Evolutionary political change is facilitated to the extent that political and other elites recognize the need to at least modify existing political and other institutions in the light of changing needs; that they value innovation and creativity rather than stubborn adherence to established traditions; and that they recognize that stability and effectiveness, and perhaps even their vested interests, are dependent on adaptation. A respect for law and constitutional constraints is important for democracies, but may be dangerous if it is coupled with stubborn adherence to law designed to protect the status quo. In democracies mass attitudes may also be important. A society which continues to venerate over-dispersion of power, low tax rates, and a minimal role for government may face serious problems when at the same time it demands more governmental services and more effective governmental action in a variety of spheres.

THE SOCIO-ECONOMIC SETTING

Socio-economic changes may be significant for stability and effectiveness insofar as they affect the availability of material and human resources needed to match material and other expectations, and insofar as they impact conflict patterns and tension-moderating conditions.

Of prime importance is the economic setting and the impact of governmental policies on economic stability and growth. Material resources are needed by any system, and while the capability to extract them may be a matter of supportive attitudes, availability depends on the economic setting. Availability depends on the society's resource base—land, minerals, energy supply, population—and on the efficiency of its economic system. But in the contemporary world of political economies, public policies are an important and sometimes crucial factor. The availability of material resources may be promoted or retarded as policies have an effect on the resource base, economic organization and growth, population growth rates, the food supply, and the training of skilled personnel. Non-economic policies may also have consequences in terms of needed material resources: the system may be stimulating rising expectations, and perhaps in some states to the point where the society lives beyond its means—beyond the standard of living which can be provided by the economic base. Or welfare policies may have the side-effect of reducing incentives to work. In such instances future stability and effectiveness is related to the system's capability to either expand the economic base or to reduce mass expectations.

Governmental policies with respect to the use made of the fruits of the economic system may also be significant. Consumer-oriented political economies in which the production and distribution of material goods is determined by consumers with effective buying power, may have advantages in that they may maximize immediate production and freedom of choice. But governmental policies may be required with respect to the future availability of material resources: future energy or food needs and resources, capital investment to ensure continuing economic growth, action to deal with the possible depletion of mineral and other basic resources. Governmental policies may also be needed, and may or may not be effective, to ensure that material resources are used not merely to gratify immediate human appetites, but to improve the quality of life of the society—to provide decent health care, housing, education, transportation facilities, security in old age or during economic down-turns, urban centers, cultural and recreational facilities, and peace among the society's conflicting groups and strata. Neglect of these aspects of material resources may be as dangerous for future stability and effectiveness as economic decline.

Human resources are also needed for political effectiveness. Political systems need individuals of requisite knowledge, skills, talents, and competence not only for political and governmental positions but throughout the society for the performance of varied economic, social, and cultural functions. The continued availability of such human resources again may depend on forces operating more-or-less independently of the government—such as the growth and direction of the economic system or the extent to which the norms of society provide equality of opportunity. But governments can have a significant impact by way of educational policies which promote literacy and the kinds and levels of education needed by the present and future society; economic policies which may enable expansion of education; and social policies which may ensure equality of educational and vocational opportunity.

A fairly prosperous economic setting which enables the system to create and allocate material and other values seems even more essential for democracy. Economic development by itself does not ensure democracy, but helps to establish conditions which make possible its development. Economic growth and abundance makes it easier to distribute wealth and income on a more equitable basis: as the size of the overall economic pie becomes large or continues to increase, the size of the individual slices received by various socio-economic strata will also tend to increase, and groups tend to be less prone to increase the size of their slice at the expense of some other group. Hence, abundance helps to blunt the edge of conflict, to create tension-reducing attitudes, to moderate hostilities along class, racial, religious, or other lines. Economic abundance makes possible the expansion of education, the growth of literacy, and the development of an informed public—all of which seem essential for democracy. It makes possible a wider distribution of wealth—and hence greater dispersion of one resource of power. And it makes possible real human freedom, for political rights and freedoms are meaningless to people who have no economic and social freedom because they are locked into poverty.

Finally, the analysis of socio-economic changes and public policies affecting them must focus on changes in class stratification patterns and their consequences for conflict patterns and participation and distribution demands. Governmental policies or economic development may be producing new elites and classes. Industrialization in any kind of political setting invariably produces a more complex class structure: an industrial working class, a variegated middle class, new technical-managerial-professional elites, and various kinds of economic elites. Of particular importance may be the size and nature of the middle class, whose emergence may result in changing a pyramid-like social structure into a diamond-like pattern, and which may play a balancing and moderating role between extremist groups in political conflict. Such stratification changes tend to produce attitudinal changes, with consequences for a rise in participation and distribution demands, and the growth of a politically-relevant strata. Such socio-economic changes, and governmental efforts to adapt to them, may be significant in terms of both social and political stability and future effectiveness.

THE POWER CONFIGURATION IN SOCIETY

Democracy requires social pluralism: polyarchy and substantial dispersion of power resources to ensure competition in influence and equitable governmental responsiveness to demands. For stability and effectiveness power is related to support: systems need the support of those with power. This mandates a degree of congruence between the power configuration in society and the distribution of power in the decision-making system, for elites not represented in decision-making are not likely to support the system. Yet as discussed in Chapter 12, effectiveness also requires a judicious balance between power concentration and dispersion. But whatever the case, significant trends with respect to the power configuration will tend to have major consequences for systems and pose problems of adaptation.

A focus on changes in the elite structure is consequently important. Socio-economic changes may bring about a shift in the direction of polyarchy, while some elites (such as big business) may be rising in power and others (small business, traditional elites) may be declining in influence. Governmental policies may also enhance the influence of some elites by giving them privileged access to decision-making, or by policies which enhance their economic power. Changes in elite attitudes may also be significant—the extent to which old or new elites are receptive to democratic norms and to mass participation in politics.

Significant changes with respect to the politically-relevant strata may also be taking place. Economic development may be dispersing the resources of money, and knowledge to the masses, or otherwise giving them the incentive and means to influence political processes. Or governmental actions may have a similar effect: the expansion of the suffrage to new groups; the right to organize labor unions or other kinds of interest groups; primary systems which may enhance public influence in nomination processes.

CONFLICT PATTERNS

Changes in conflict patterns result from the interaction of the three primary environmental factors, but warrant a special focus. Democracies need a balance between conflict and cooperation, prevailing attitudes, and other factors which tend to facilitate peaceful adjustment and accommodation. The requisite for stability and effectiveness is similar: complex patterns of intense conflicts tend to produce such social instability as to defy the efforts of the most efficient governments, invite coercion which eventually will lose support, and also have negative consequences for both the availability and extractability of needed material and human resources.

In some societies traditional conflicts among tribal, religious, racial, or other kinds of sub-cultural groups may persist, with the addition of new conflicts along socio-economic, occupational, or ideological lines. Or conflict patterns may be changing along geographic lines: between different regions of a society, or between rural, urban, and suburban areas. Such complex patterns may be producing a degree of chaos which taxes the capability of any government. Conversely, such patterns may help to integrate the society by producing cross-cutting cleavages which facilitate conflict resolution. Labor unions, for example, while they promote conflict along occupational and socio-economic lines, may produce a new sense of identity and common interest among workers of different ethnic, tribal, religious, or regional origins. The reawakening or development of a sense of regional identity may have similar consequences. Changes in the intensity of conflicts may also be important. Particularly significant is the extent to which conflicting groups and their leaders tend to be more doctrinaire or pragmatic, or are prone to relentlessly pursue narrow group interests or are committed to finding solutions on the basis of broader interests.

Although conflict patterns may be rooted in environmental factors, governmental actions may play significant roles with respect to both conflict activation and resolution. Expansion of governmental functions may activate conflicts among various groups as prizes—government jobs, educational facilities, economic rewards—can be won through political action—a common phenomenon in Africa and Asia where until independence numerous tribal, religious, and linguistic groups managed to live together in relative peace. Governmental allocation of material or nonmaterial values to some groups may provoke other groups into levying competing demands for governmental benefits. Perceptions of inequitable rewards may decrease tension-moderating attitudes and increase hostilities in the society. Or governmental machinery may provide effective means for resolution of conflicts between labor and management, or among regional or cultural groups. Most crucial in this respect is the system's performance of its most basic function: the peaceful resolution of conflicts.

Of special importance may be the degree to which a society is becoming polarized along ideological or other lines, or to which various groups are becoming radicalized. In such diverse places as Chile, Argentina, Southeast Asia, Lebanon, and white-ruled Africa such radicalization and polarization has produced social chaos and eventually more heavy-handed authoritarian rule. When a government controlled by arch-conservative elements, or by status-quo oriented majorities, centrist groups, powerful economic interests, or even minorities, refuses to make concessions to opposing camps, it tends to increase the militancy of the opposition and to radicalize such groups in both their objectives and methods. Liberal reformers become radicals, and eventually revolutionaries, which in turn tends to radicalize right-wing and sometimes even centrist forces in the system. Dangerous polarization—the division of society into two hostile camps—of the type that produces revolutions may be the eventual outcome. As mentioned earlier, the development of a large middle class tends to enhance the potential for democracy by changing the social structure from a pyramid to a diamond-shaped pattern—but provided the middle class does play a moderating role in class conflict. When the middle class stubbornly insists on the status quo and refuses to make concessions to minorities on either the left or the right, or becomes linked in its interests and ideas with conservative forces and makes no concessions to underprivileged socio-economic, racial, or religious groups, it contributes to radicalization and polarization. This may be the root of the current political troubles of France and Italy, and of the milder form of polarization which appears to be developing in American, British, and West German political parties.

POLICIES, CHANGE, AND INFRASTRUCTURES

Democracies need effective, equitable, and autonomous linkage-communication systems to provide means for effective demand inputs, to ensure equitable governmental responsiveness, and to enhance public influence over decision-making. The stability and effectiveness of all types of political systems is enhanced to the extent that a similar kind of infrastructure provides for the effective performance of the seven linkage-communication functions discussed in Chapter 7. Although changes in the linkage system may have their primary roots in environmental changes, governmental policies can have significant consequences and should aim to develop the kind of system needed for either democracy or effectiveness.

THE GENERAL NATURE OF THE INFRASTRUCTURE

In general terms, the analysis should focus on the extent to which a well organized and differentiated linkage system, commensurate with the needs of the political system for effective performance of linkage functions, appears to be developing, and what actions appear to be necessary in this respect. As systems become more complex, they need more elaborate and specialized infrastructures for specific demand and information inputs from the more varied sectors of society, for more complex conflict resolution, and more specialized political recruitment. In most systems this analysis should probably focus on interest groups and political parties, but other means may also be important. Changes in representation patterns, such as reapportionment of legislative districts, may provide more equitable representation and means for citizen communication. Changes in decision-making patterns—open meetings of governmental bodies, greater formalization and institutionalization of procedures— may somewhat enhance opportunities for direct citizen participation. The bureaucracy may tend to become more (or less) of an institution for citizen inputs. Changes in the control, practices, or policies of new media, in governmental controls over the media, or in polling techniques and the use made of polls, may all have some consequences.

INTEREST GROUPS

A major concern is the impact of policies and environmental developments on the key characteristics of interest groups discussed in Chapter 8, and what kinds of policies seem to be required to enhance their autonomous, effective, and equitable performance as linkage-communication instruments.

Key questions pertain to the size and complexity of the "interest group universe"—what types of groups appear to be developing, the extent to which associational are replacing or supplementing non-associational and anomic groups, what new interests or ideas are being organized for political action. The proliferation of associational groups to include new and more varied occupational, professional, regional, or other types of interests may be leading to a more equitable pattern of functional representation. This may enhance effectiveness by more effective performance of the articulation function, but may have negative consequences by increasing pluralism and the number of veto points over policy-making. Governments may enhance or inhibit such proliferation in a variety of ways. They may grant or deny the right to organize to specific kinds of groups or to all types of groups, or use repressive measures against certain groups. They may consult only with associational groups, and hence provide incentive for the organization of such groups. They may provide access to decision-making to some groups, and hence encourage other interests to organize. The establishment of new government agencies may stimulate the formation of new groups—as environmental or consumer protection agencies may provide incentive for the organization of conservation and consumer interests. Equally important may be shifts with respect to the autonomy of groups: communist regimes may be relaxing controls over mass organizations so that these can function somewhat as objective communication instruments for their members; or labor parties may have less of an inhibitive impact on associated labor unions. Governmental practices—such as consultation only with leaders of large organizations—may provide incentive for the formation of coalition-type groups capable of demand aggregation and conflict resolution.

Interest group power, and the relative power among groups, may be impacted by governmental policies. A shift in the direction of more concentrated power within government, or vigorously-enforced laws to control lobbying, financial activities, or other tactics, may reduce interest group influence. Favored access and established consultation with certain groups—Big Business, Big Labor—may enhance the power of the favored few, while governmental controls, suppression, or indifference may reduce the influence of others or lead to more anomic outbreaks. Governmental benefits to certain sectors of the economy—big farmers, the defense industry, the maritime industry—may enhance the financial, economic, and other resources of power of some groups. Certain power centers within the government—specific bureaucracies, congressional committees—may establish close clientele relationships with some groups and thus enhance their power. Power within groups may similarly be affected: governments, for example, may attempt to control the internal affairs of labor unions, to provide some degree of internal group democracy.

POLITICAL PARTIES AND ELECTION SYSTEMS

Similar questions need to be asked pertaining to changes related to the major characteristics of party and election systems discussed in Chapter 9. The key questions relate to the major functions: demand aggregation, political recruitment, public influence, and linkage within government. The focus of analysis ought to be related to trends with respect to what appears to be the better type of party system: a competitive two-party system, consisting of programmatic yet pragmatic coalition-type parties, possessing substantial degrees of unity, and providing for both internal party democracy and significant roles for leadership. Although environmental forces may play major roles with respect to party development, governmental policies can also have a significant impact.

The attitudes and practices of those government officials with significant power can be extremely important. Political leaders who refuse to develop a base of party support, who deny party leaders any consultative role in decision-making, or who deny legislative bodies any significant role as decision-makers, do not provide the incentive needed for the development of vigorous and effective parties. Instead, such practices tend to produce ideologically-oriented splinter parties or debating societies. Governmental leaders may deliberately manipulate existing cleavages and hostilities for their own purposes, with similar consequences. Government officials in their roles as party elites may have a similar impact on parties: by using parties merely as vehicles for power, by denying the party-outside-government any real autonomy, or by ignoring party platforms or the demands of the party rank-and-file, they can have an inhibiting impact on the development of an effective party system. A dangerous radicalization and polarization of parties may also result from such attitudes and practices, as government officials ignore the party or governmental aggregation function and turn a deaf ear to (or become captives of) liberal or conservative wings of parties or to minority parties substantially left or right of center.

Policies to effect political reforms should also be assessed in terms of their impact on the party system and the possible costs entailed in reform benefits. Decentralization of authority to state or local units of government may have the consequences of decentralization of power within parties, which entails some benefits but also costs in terms of party unity and leadership roles. Expansion of primary systems may enhance popular participation in nomination processes, but with significant costs in terms of party roles in elections and government. Scrapping the American system of the electoral college in favor of direct election of the President has many advantages, but also may entail significant costs in terms of further weakening of the party system. And substitution of a proportional representation system of election for the single-member district system may provide for more equitable representation, but may also provide the incentive needed for the organization of many splinter parties. In essence, for democracy, public policies need to be geared to the development of parties which provides the public with meaningful choice, which can translate election choice into governmental action, and which can give the public a fixed and clearly-visible point of responsibility. And for effectiveness, policies ought to produce parties capable of demand aggregation, socialization and mobilization, political recruitment, and integration of decision-making functions.

DECISION-MAKING SYSTEMS: DEMOCRACY AND EFFECTIVENESS

Democracies seem to require decision-making systems with substantial dispersion of power and formalization-institutionalization to ensure pluralism, competition, and representation; equitable and effective access to decision-making; equitable governmental responsiveness; restraints on governmental power; and substantial public influence over government. Stability and effectiveness requires structural differentiation and institutionalization to the extent required by the scope and complexity of governmental tasks; effective integrating structures to ensure coordination and generalist control; such concentration of power as may be needed to enhance capability and effectiveness; and requisite human resources.

As discussed in earlier chapters, the nature and dynamics of government are significantly affected by environmental factors and infrastructures. But in the final analysis, the policies and practices which change the structure and processes of government emanate from the decision-making system itself—either in the form of expressed laws or decisions, or in actual if not formally expressed practices.

Trends in the distribution of power within the system, and in influence patterns over decision-making, are of key concern. Shifts of power among the branches and levels of government as discussed in Chapter 12, and in the nature and location of rule making, application, and adjudication functions, may have major consequences for the nature and effectiveness of systems. Greater concentration of power in the executive and bureaucracy may enhance the system's extractive, regulative, and distributive capabilities, but perhaps at the expense of responsive and symbolic capabilities and equitable patterns of value allocation. More pluralism in influence resulting from a proliferation of powerful interest groups may enhance democracy, but at the cost of party influence and of timely and effective decision-making. Contemplated or ongoing reform programs to make systems more democratic and responsive must be carefully examined to determine what the costs might be in terms of stability and effectiveness. Reformist regimes which undertake crash social reforms may alienate middle classes and radicalize the political right, to the point where they undermine their stability and invite reactions which ultimately scuttle reform programs. The devolution of power to state and local levels of government may provide more grass roots control, but lead to loss of political effectiveness when such levels of government lack financial resources or the ability to resolve problems which transcend their political boundaries. Legislative reforms may similarly have adverse consequences. Greater restraints on legislative leaders and broader dispersion of power within legislative bodies may make such bodies more democratic, but perhaps at the expense of legislative effectiveness and the consequent enhancement of executive power.

Decisions (or inaction) with respect to the structure of government, and practices within governmental institutions, need to be examined from two perspectives: the need for greater openness and accessibility as participation demands increase, and the need for greater effectiveness as governmental tasks become more numerous and complex. Decision-makers in all branches may need greater autonomy from public influence if they are to make effective decisions, but inadequate consultation with external forces may jeopardize public influence, support, and effective policies. Structural reorganization may be imperative for continuing or enhanced effectiveness and public influence, but pose some major dilemmas. In general, specialized structures must be organized for the performance of specialized tasks. Related tasks must be grouped together, either within single or closely related structures. Effective coordinating machinery must be established at various levels to ensure harmony and coordination in policy-making, generalist control over specialists and experts, and political control by top-level generalists who directly or indirectly are accountable to the public or who have overall responsibility for policy-making. In addition, decision-making systems need substantial institutionalization and formalization to ensure respect for established procedures and prevailing forms of decision-making, and for ensured and effective access by representatives of the public. But structural reorganization to meet all these criteria is not a simple matter.

The committee structure of a legislative body must provide for specialized legislative roles—rule-making, financial functions, investigations, controls over the bureaucracy, and also for specialized spheres of policy-making. But the consequence may be a proliferation of committees and a dispersion of power which inhibits coordinated and effective legislative action. Effective performance mandates the delegation and dispersion of functions and power to specialized bureaucratic agencies, the grouping together of agencies with similar or related tasks, effective coordinating machinery at various levels of the bureaucracy, and effective control by the chief executive. Coordinated and effective economic policy, for example, is not likely when functions and powers are scattered among a plethora of agencies—Ministries or Departments of the Treasury, Labor, Commerce, Agriculture, Energy, a Federal Reserve Board, and many others—without an effective and authoritative central control point. Effective energy policies are hardly possible when functions related to energy matters are scattered among numerous agencies. Yet the grouping together of agencies with related tasks may be extremely difficult due to the complexity of governmental tasks. It may also result in huge bureaucratic structures which lack effectiveness because of their unwieldy size, and which elude political-generalist control because of their great power and their low responsive capabilities. And while institutionalization and formalization of bureaucratic procedures may provide respect for established norms and procedures and access to decision-making, it may also substitute red tape, inertia, and slavish conformity for initiative, innovation, and creativity.

The quality of human resources within the decision-making system becomes of even greater concern as the tasks of government multiply. For effectiveness, governments obviously need individuals of requisite competence, talent, expertise, and skill, who conform to the rules of the system and are loyal to top-level generalists, but who also are capable of innovation and creativity. For democracy, the system requires humans who adhere to democratic norms of decision-making, who are responsive to the public will, who consider themselves ultimately accountable to the public, but who also are aware of leadership roles and responsibilities. The extent to which a government enjoys such human resources depends partly on the environmental setting and the infrastructure. A society which holds politics in disrepute is not likely to attract individuals of talent for tasks of government, and political recruitment processes which require costly and prolonged campaigning and deny candidates any private life also do not provide much incentive. But government recruitment processes play crucial roles, particularly insofar as policies affect infrastructure recruitment processes, and governments which emphasize loyalty to the regime, conformity, and obedience, or which do not seek talent from all walks of life, deny themselves the vital resources they need. Finally, the system must be able to attract humans with attitudes conducive to political change. Systems which are staffed by officials who respect the rule of law enjoy many advantages, but not if either the respect or the law emphasizes stubborn adherence to the status quo, to archaic customs and traditions, to some rigid ideology, or to certain sacrosanct vested interests.

In essence, given the reality of a changing world, the human race must accept the necessity of changing and adapting political systems to changing conditions. This does not imply change for the sake of change, change just to try something new, or a realistic pragmatism devoid of principles and values. It does imply efforts to engineer and control change to the extent that is humanly possible, so that people will have a political system which governs and pursues goals in accordance with carefully-considered human values. It further implies that contemplated changes and reforms ought to be carefully considered from two perspectives: given realities, it is possible to translate proposed changes into action; and what are the potential consequences of proposals for the system's performance as an instrument of society.

This in turn requires consideration of a theme repeatedly emphasized throughout this book: every change, like every policy, involves some value tradeoffs and some cost-benefit assessment and evaluation. Reforms to promote more democracy, or a more open system, may entail significant costs in political effectiveness, while steps taken to enhance effectiveness may entail costs in democratic values. There is a grave danger of pushing popular rule to the point where the costs in effectiveness may be so high that they may undermine or ultimately destroy democracy; just as there is a danger that concentrated power to maximize effectiveness may produce an authoritarian system incapable of functioning as an instrument of society. Political reform invariably entails agonizing choices, and yet decisions must be made. This is the dilemma which confronts modern democratic societies, for the contemporary challenge to democracy may be the most fundamental crisis of our time.

Bibliography

ALMOND, GABRIEL, and G. BINGHAM POWELL, JR., *Comparative Politics, A Developmental Approach.* Boston: Little, Brown and Company, 1966.

_____, and SIDNEY VERBA, *The Civic Culture.* Princeton, N.J.: Princeton University Press, 1963.

APTER, DAVID, *The Politics of Modernization.* Chicago: University of Chicago Press, 1965.

BEER, SAMUEL H., "Part One, The Analysis of Political Systems," in *Patterns of Government* (2d ed.), eds. Samuel H. Beer and Adam Ulam. New York: Random House, 1962.

_____, *British Politics in the Collectivist Age.* New York: Alfred A. Knopf, 1966.

_____, *Modern Political Development.* New York: Random House, 1974.

BLAU, PETER, *The Dynamics of Bureaucracy.* Chicago: University of Chicago Press, 1955.

DAHL, ROBERT A., *A Preface to Democratic Theory.* Chicago: University of Chicago Press, 1956.

_____, *Modern Political Analysis* (3d ed.), Englewood Cliffs, N.J.: Prentice-Hall, Inc., 1976.

_____, *Who Governs? Democracy and Power in an American City.* New Haven, Conn.: Yale University Press, 1961.

_____, and CHARLES E. LINDBLOM, *Politics, Economics, and Welfare.* New York: Harper and Row, 1953.

DEUTSCH, KARL W., *The Nerves of Government.* New York: The Free Press, 1963.

_____, *Politics and Government.* Boston: Houghton Mifflin Company, 1970.

DOWNS, ANTHONY, *An Economic Theory of Democracy.* New York: Harper and Row, 1956.

DUVERGER, MAURICE, *Political Parties,* trans. Barbara and Robert North. New York: Wiley Science Editions, 1963.

EASTON, DAVID, *A Framework for Political Analysis.* Englewood Cliffs, N.J.: Prentice-Hall, Inc. 1965.

_____, *The Political System* (2d ed.), New York: Alfred A. Knopf, 1971.

_____, *A Systems Analysis of Political Life,* New York: John Wiley and Sons, 1968.

FRIEDRICH, CARL J., *Man and His Government.* New York: McGraw-Hill Book Company, Inc., 1963.

HUNTINGTON, SAMUEL P., *Political Order in Changing Societies.* New Haven, Conn.: Yale University Press, 1968.

KAUTSKY, JOHN H., *The Political Consequences of Modernization.* New York: John Wiley and Sons, Inc., 1972.

KEY, V. O., JR., *Politics, Parties, and Pressure Groups.* New York: Crowell-Collier and Macmillan, 1967.

————, and MILTON C. CUMMINGS. *The Responsible Electorate.* Cambridge, Mass.: Harvard University Press, 1966.

KORNHAUSER, WILLIAM, *The Politics of Mass Society.* New York: The Free Press, 1959.

LANE, ROBERT E., *Political Thinking and Consciousness.* Chicago: Markham, 1969.

LAPALOMBARA, JOSEPH, and MYRON WEINER, eds., *Political Parties and Political Development.* Princeton, N.J.: Princeton University Press, 1966.

LASSWELL, HAROLD, *Politics, Who Gets What, When, How.* New York: Meridian, 1958.

————, and ABRAHAM KAPLAN, *Power and Society.* New Haven, Conn.: Yale University Press, 1963.

LATHAM, EARL, *The Group Basis of Politics.* New York: Octagon, 1965.

LEVY, MARION, *The Structure of Society.* Princeton, N.J.: Princeton University Press, 1952.

LINDBLOM, CHARLES E., *The Policy-Making Process.* Englewood Cliffs, N.J.: Prentice-Hall, Inc., 1968.

LIPSET, SEYMOUR MARTIN, *Political Man.* Garden City, N.Y.: Doubleday and Company, Inc., 1960.

MERTON, ROBERT K., *Social Theory and Social Structure* (rev. ed.), New York: The Free Press, 1957.

MICHELS, ROBERT, *Political Parties.* New York: Collier Books, 1962.

MOSCA, GAETANO, *The Ruling Class.* New York: McGraw-Hill, 1939.

NEUSTADT, RICHARD E., *Presidential Power.* New York: John Wiley and Sons, Inc., 1960.

PYE, LUCIAN W., *Aspects of Political Development.* Boston: Little, Brown and Company, 1966.

————, and SIDNEY VERBA, eds., *Political Culture and Political Development.* Princeton, N.J.: Princeton University Press, 1969.

RANNEY, AUSTIN, *The Doctrine of Responsible Party Government.* Urbana, Ill.: University of Illinois Press, 1962.

————, *The Governing of Men* (rev. ed.), New York: Holt, Rinehart and Winston, Inc., 1966.

RIKER, WILLIAM H., *The Theory of Political Coalitions.* New Haven, Conn.: Yale University Press, 1962.

ROKKAN, STEIN, *Citizens, Elections, Parties.* New York: David McKay, 1970.

SCHATTSCHNEIDER, E. E., *The Semisovereign People.* New York: Holt, Rinehart and Winston, Inc., 1961.

SCHUMPETER, JOSEPH, *Capitalism, Socialism, Democracy,* (3d ed.), New York: Harper and Row, 1950.

SIMON, HERBERT A., *Administrative Behavior* (2d ed.). New York: Macmillan and Company, 1957.

TRUMAN, DAVID, *The Governmental Process.* New York: Alfred A. Knopf, 1964.

WEBER, MAX, *Theory of Social and Economic Organization,* trans. A. M. Henderson and Talcott Parsons. Glencoe, Ill.: The Free Press, 1958.

Institutional conflict, 10–11, 160
Institutional interest groups, 169–70, 175, 185
Institutional power analysis, 235, 255, 257
Institutionalization-Formalization:
  and democracy, effectiveness, 275–76, 322–24
  linkage by political parties, 189–90
  meaning and importance, 229–32
  relationship to power, 262, 320
Instructed representatives, 163
Integration (*see* Community; Governmental; Identity; Nation-building)
Interdependence (*see* Community)
Interest groups:
  assessment of, 182–87, 320–25
  environmental-political context of, 114–16, 174–76
  functions of, 170–74
  nature of, 18, 165–66
  power of, 176–80
  and public interest, 170–71, 173, 184
  tactics of, 25, 170, 181–84, 187
  targets of, 180–81, 187
  types of, 166–70
Interest-idea articulation, 154–56, 171, 252
Interests:
  bureaucratic, 280
  common and cooperation, 18–20, 123
  and interest groups, 165, 168–69
  and parties, 197–98, 199–201
  and demand inputs, 13–15
  overlapping, and cooperation, 122–25
  of politicians, 59–63
  socio-economic roots of, 109–17
Internalized influences, 259
International factors:
  and demand inputs, 12–13
  and environments, 30, 84, 111, 113, 147
  and interdependence, 125, 238, 272, 292
  power, 33–34
Interventionist systems, 76–77
Intra-Governmental influences, 259–60
Issues of politics, 67–70, 93

Judicial (*see also* Rule Adjudication):
  access to system, 5
  functions, 223, 257
  impartiality, 256–57
  power, 240, 245, 247–48
  review, 257
  role in system, 256
Justice:
  as governmental objective, 4–6, 25
  and policies, 295–96, 300, 303

and power, 145
variant definitions of, 6, 14–15, 67

Knowledge as power, 46–47, 177, 178

Law, 2–4, 7
  legitimacy of, 9, 40–41
  nature of modern, 244, 251, 253–54, 273
Leadership:
  executive, 250, 274, 276
  governmental, 26–27, 220, 325
  of interest groups, 186–87
  legislative, 250–51
  of political parties, 203–4, 206
  by politicians, 43, 60–63
Legislative function (*see* Rule-making)
Legislatures:
  cohesion problem of, 250–51, 273, 276
  committees of, 249–50, 324
  declining roles and power of, 273–74
  functions of, 221–23, 245–51, 256
  leadership in, 250
  power of, 231, 241, 243, 245–51
  in presidential, parliamentary systems, 239–40
  problems of, 276–78, 322–26.
  types of, 23, 245, 248
Legitimacy (*see also* Support):
  challenges to, 131–36
  and constitutions, 231
  and environmental change, 311–14
  environmental roots of, 95, 127–31
  and government authority, 8–10, 27, 35
  and government power, 36, 40–41
  and scope of government, 144
Legitimization role of cultures, 95
Liberalism, 94, 199–201
Limited governmental systems, 76–77
Linkage-Communication:
  analysis of, 152–53, 319–20
  definition of, 151–52
  functions, 154–61
  and political effectiveness, 264–67
  and responsive capability, 269
  structures and processes, 161–64
Lobbying, 258–60, 287
  by bureaucracy, 169, 255, 274
  by interest groups, 167, 169, 181–82
  and the public interest, 173
  as representation, 171–72, 320
  skill and tactics, 47, 54–57

Managerial roles in government, 157–58
Marxism-Leninism, 90, 94, 95, 97, 111, 124
Mass movements and cooperation, 18
Mass organizations, 74, 168